INDUSTRIAL RELATIONS RESEARCH
ASSOCIATION SERIES

Employee Representation:
Alternatives and
Future Directions

EDITED BY

Bruce E. Kaufman and Morris M. Kleiner

9-11

#29143939

First edition

Library of Congress Catalog Card Number: 50-13564

ISBN 0-913447-56-0

PRICE $28.00

INDUSTRIAL RELATIONS RESEARCH ASSOCIATION SERIES
    Proceedings of the Annual Meeting (Summer publication)
    Proceedings of the Spring Meeting (Fall publication)
    Annual Research Volume
    Membership Directory (every fourth year)
IRRA Newsletter (published quarterly) and IRRA Dialogues (published semiannually)

Inquiries and other communications regarding membership, meetings, publications, and general affairs of the Association, copyright requests, as well as notice of address changes should be addressed to the IRRA national office.

INDUSTRIAL RELATIONS RESEARCH ASSOCIATION
7226 Social Science Building, University of Wisconsin, 1180 Observatory Drive, Madison, WI 53706 U.S.A. Telephone 608/262-2762

CONTENTS

PREFACE

The publication of this research volume would not have been possible without the contributions of many individuals. First and foremost are the twenty-one authors and co-authors of the chapters in this publication. Working under relatively short time deadlines, they produced chapters that we think will be widely recognized as significant scholarly contributions to the subject of employee representation. We thank them for their willingness to undertake this project and for their unflagging cooperation and good nature. Second, an acknowledgment of appreciation is also due the members of the Editorial Committee of the IRRA and particularly to the Editor-in-Chief, John Burton, Jr., who gave us the opportunity to develop and produce this volume. We appreciate their vote of confidence and hope that we have delivered a high-quality product for them.

We received valuable help from several individuals who read early drafts of the chapters and provided the authors with comments and suggestions. This is generally an unappreciated activity, but one that is nevertheless crucial to an interdisciplinary volume like this book. We would like to thank Marick Masters, University of Pittsburgh; Robert Wolff, University of Minnesota; and Victor Devinatz, Illinois State University, for their comments and reviews.

Last, but not least, we would also like to express our sincere appreciation to Kay Hutchison, IRRA National Office Administrator, who helped keep us organized, on track, and the staff of the IRRA who helped produce and edit the volume.

BRUCE E. KAUFMAN
MORRIS M. KLEINER

Employee Representation: Alternatives and Future Directions

Bruce E. Kaufman
Georgia State University

Morris M. Kleiner
University of Minnesota

Arguably the concept most central to the field of industrial relations is *employee representation*. The field was founded in the early 1920s by progressives in both academe and the business world who were repelled by the inefficiency, inequity, and authoritarianism that permeated the workplace of that era. Their desire was to use scientific investigation to discover new methods, institutions, and principles that could resolve these problems and thus create a "win-win" outcome of higher productivity, profits and wages, and more harmonious relations between employers and employees.

How was this goal to be accomplished? Whatever their other differences, these progressives were united in one fundamental belief—that a prerequisite for improved industrial relations is some form of employee representation or "industrial democracy." By industrial democracy, the founders of industrial relations had several ideas in mind: that workers should have an explicit voice in the governance and operation of the workplace, that this voice should take a collective form in which the employees designate certain of their colleagues to act as their representatives to management, and that the rights and interests of employees be protected from arbitrary or opportunistic management actions by a workplace system of due process.

While a consensus existed among the founders of industrial relations as to the basic principles of employee representation and

1

the salutary effects of employee representation on workplace efficiency and equity, a great difference of opinion emerged among them as to the best institutional form for employee representation. One group favored independent trade unions, while a second favored some type of employer-sponsored organization, such as a works council, shop committee, or "company union."

From the perspective of the proponents of trade unions, the employer-sponsored "company unions" were fatally flawed as an instrument of workplace democracy because they were created and controlled by management, the leaders served at the discretion of management, and they had little or no independent power to protect workers' rights. As these people saw it, trade unions were a far superior form of employee representation on all three counts— unions were independent of management, the leaders were chosen by the rank and file, and the union could use the strike and other forms of concerted activity to put muscle behind its collective voice.

Proponents of nonunion employee representation plans, on the other hand, saw the traditional labor union as most often part of the problem, not the solution. As they saw it, unions hindered efficiency through restrictive work rules and strikes, fostered adversarialism between the employer and employees, and union leaders were prone to engage in undemocratic and corrupt practices. The company union was, in their view, a superior means to achieve industrial democracy because it provided workers with formal channels for voice while at the same time it avoided the adversarialism and strikes associated with representation by an outside "third party."

From the earliest days of industrial relations in the 1920s, therefore, the field has been united on the need for some form of employee representation but also deeply split over the appropriate institutional form that employee representation should take. This split in viewpoints has, in turn, been manifest over the years in shifts in public policy and public sentiment towards unions.

The 1920s, for example, were the heyday of "welfare capitalism." During this period public opinion and policy were favorable toward employer-sponsored labor organizations and relatively hostile toward trade unions and collective bargaining. With the coming of the Great Depression in late 1929, however, the pendulum swung the other way and company representation plans not only fell out of favor but were made illegal when the Wagner

Act was enacted into law in 1935, while the growth of trade unions and collective bargaining skyrocketed. The New Deal system of employee representation reached its zenith of power, coverage, and popular approval in the 1950s, only to then suffer a gradual erosion over the next twenty years. The pendulum of public policy and public sentiment then swung markedly away from the trade union/ collective bargaining form of workplace governance in the 1980s, leading to dramatic declines in union membership and power. Simultaneous with the decline of the union sector was the emergence of a new nonunion "high ɔvolvement" form of work organization that featured various employer-initiated institutional devices for promoting voice and due process, such as self-directed work teams, quality circles, and formal grievance systems utilizing arbitration, mediation, and peer review.

It is evident from this brief review of historical trends that the American industrial relations system appears to be in the throes of a profound transformation. It is also evident that the role of employee representation in the workplace, and its appropriate institutional form, lies at the center of this transformation, much as it did when the field of industrial relations was born in the 1920s. Thus academics, employers, unionists, and policymakers are con- fronted with some momentous issues. For example:

* Does the United States currently have the optimal level of employee representation to promote maximum efficiency and equity? If not, what level and form of representation could better accomplish these goals?

* Are trade unions and collective bargaining the most effective form of employee representation? What structural changes in the industrial relations system could improve the performance of collective bargaining?

* Has union membership declined because workers no longer demand this type of representation, or is there still a large demand for union services but it is frustrated by employer resistance? What are the implications for labor law?

* Is there a significant demand among American workers for some other type of employee representation? What form would this representation take? Would it be a substitute for, or complement to, trade unions?

* Should the involvement of employees in the operation and governance of the firm be limited to plant-level human resource

issues or should employees also have a voice in strategic business decisions?

* Are European-style works councils an alternative system of employee representation that the United States should consider? What about enterprise-based unions? Codetermination?

* Does the current corpus of American labor law promote the optimal level of labor-management cooperation? If not, how should the law be changed? Given the current legal system, what can firms and unions do to initiate and sustain cooperative efforts?

* To what degree can employees achieve representation through the political process, rather than through a workplace-based institution? Can the political process effectively represent workers without a strong organized labor movement?

We think these types of questions will be at the forefront of debate among policymakers and at the leading edge of research by industrial relations scholars in the 1990s. To help push the process forward, the 1993 annual research volume is dedicated to the subject of employee representation and, in particular, a consideration of alternative forms of employee representation and future directions for public policy. Toward that end, the volume contains eleven chapters on various dimensions of employee representation written by leading experts in the field. Provided below is a brief summary of the chapters (listed by authors).

Chapter Summaries

Freeman and Rogers—"Who Speaks for Us? Employee Representation in a Nonunion Labor Market." Freeman and Rogers provide a thorough and provocative analysis of the demand for and supply of employee representation in the U.S. They begin their chapter with a review of empirical studies on the economic impact of employee representation and conclude that this impact is often positive. In the next section Freeman and Rogers document that the traditional form of representation in the workplace—collective bargaining—now covers only about 15 percent of the work force, yet nationwide surveys indicate that a large majority of workers desire some form of representation. They conclude, therefore, that a large "representation gap" exists in the U.S. They then turn to a consideration of alternative forms of representation, with particular attention paid to the European system of plant-level works councils.

They find that works councils seem to perform reasonably well and attribute this success to the fact that the councils perform primarily a "voice" function in the plant with regard to operational and human resource matters while the more adversarial process of bargaining over wages and benefits is done by unions at the industry and national level. The authors conclude that the United States would benefit from providing employees with greater channels for representation and that the labor law should be changed to promote more plant-level councils.

Weiler—"Governing the Workplace: Employee Representation in the Eyes of the Law." Weiler begins [1] is chapter with an examination of the factors behind the decline in union density in the American economy. Although he finds that collective bargaining is a net "plus" for the economy, he nevertheless concludes that it faces a bleak future under current conditions due to the hostile attitude of employers and the weak legal protection given to unions and their supporters by the law. He argues, therefore, that we need to consider alternative forms of employee representation. One that he considers is government regulation of the workplace, a second is employer-sponsored employee involvement programs. Weiler argues, however, that neither can effectively protect workers' interests. Is there an alternative? Weiler says there is and outlines a two-part solution. The first part is to level the playing field for workers and unions by reforming the Wagner Act, both to simplify and expedite the union representation process and to increase the penalties upon employers for unfair labor practices. He concludes that these steps are not enough to provide the desired level of employee representation and that a new form of plant-based representation is required. He calls this new model an "employee involvement committee" and discusses how the committees would operate and the changes in the law necessary to establish them.

Farber and Krueger—"Union Membership in the United States: The Decline Continues." Farber and Krueger examine the factors behind the decline in union membership in the United States. Using a demand/supply framework and several new data sets, they find that most of the decline in union membership is due to a decline in worker demand for union representation. They provide evidence that a significant cause of this decline in demand for union membership is that nonunion workers are more satisfied with their jobs than had been true in earlier years. They also consider whether structural shifts in the demographic composition of the work force and industrial composition of employment have been contributing factors, but find that these factors have played only a modest role. Farber and Krueger then turn their attention to why union membership has declined so much more sharply in the U.S. than Canada. They conclude that about one-half of the difference in union density between the two countries is due to a lower demand for union membership in the U.S. and that the other one-half is attributable to a smaller supply of union jobs in the U.S.

Mahoney and Edwards—"Evolving Models of Work Force Governance: An Evaluation." The chapter by Mahoney and Edwards is devoted to an exploration of alternative models of work force governance and the pros and cons of each. They note that the subject of employee representation is generally considered a part of industrial relations (narrowly defined to mean labor-management relations) and, for that reason, is seldom explicitly discussed in the more management-oriented field of organization theory. Mahoney and Edwards claim, however, that this neglect is unwarranted for work force governance is an integral part of the structure of every organization. The authors then proceed to analyze the implications of economic theory and social psychological theory for the optimal design of governance systems. They find that the economics' perspective emphasizes short-term contracting, distributive (win-lose) bargaining, and divergent interests—a combination of behaviors that imparts a distinct adversarial and litigious character to the employment relationship. The approach followed in social psychology, on the other hand, emphasizes long-term relationships, mutual obligations and expectations, and the importance of procedural justice—perspectives that emphasize the elements of trust, equity, and mutuality to the functioning of the employment relationship. Mahoney and Edwards then use this conceptual schema to examine the pros and cons of what they claim are the three major types of governance systems: the authoritarian, collective bargaining, and direct participation models. While all three perform well in certain contexts, the authors conclude that in most cases the direct participation model has the best "fit" with the environment and is thus most likely to yield the highest level of efficiency and equity.

Greenfield and Pleasure—"Representatives of Their Own Choosing: Finding Workers' Voice in the Legitimacy and Power of Their Unions." Greenfield and Pleasure argue that much of the theorizing done about unions is misguided because the focus is on the efficiency effects of unions when the more appropriate criteria are the legitimacy and power that unions have as an instrument of employee voice. The true test of legitimacy, they claim, is whether the mechanism provided to workers for voice permits them to exercise basic democratic rights in the workplace. The most fundamental of these rights, in turn, is the ability to choose representatives of their own choosing—a right found in trade unions but not in employer-sponsored company unions or quality circles. Greenfield and Pleasure go on to say that, in addition to legitimacy, a system of workplace voice must also possess independent power to protect and promote workers' interests, otherwise the exercise of voice is rendered futile. On this point unions also score well, while employer-sponsored forms of voice again have significant shortcomings. While they claim that the appropriate grounds upon which to judge unions is legitimacy and power, the authors go on to argue that the case for unions as the preferred form of employee representation is strengthened further when the positive effect on economic efficiency is taken into account.

Verma and Cutcher-Gershenfeld—"Joint Governance in the Workplace: Beyond Union-Management Cooperation and Worker Participation." The subject of this chapter is a relatively new form of employee representation that the authors label "joint governance." The unique aspect of joint governance, they claim, is that it combines aspects of both traditional-style collective bargaining and newer forms of employee participation and involvement—the workers are represented by a union but the arms-length, adversarial approach to bargaining and work force governance is replaced by a system that emphasizes power sharing, problem solving, and joint decision making. In the next part of the chapter the authors summarize nine case studies of joint governance in the United States and Canada. They develop a number of hypotheses and conclusions from these cases concerning the antecedents of joint governance, the internal dynamics of joint governance, and the consequences of joint governance. They conclude that joint governance has considerable promise as an alternative form of work force governance, but that its growth and development is hindered by both legal and institutional obstacles.

Lewin and Sherer—"Does Strategic Choice Explain Senior Executives' Preferences on Employee Voice and Representation?" In this chapter Lewin and Sherer explore the conceptual and empirical role of employee representation in firms' business strategies. They note that to date most discussions of the strategic role of employee representation has been narrowly framed in terms of the impact of unionization/deunionization upon firm performance. They argue, however, that the sharp decline in union density, the development and diffusion of a wide range of employee voice mechanisms in the nonunion sector (e.g., employee involvement programs and formalized dispute resolution systems), and the shift from traditional command and control forms of business organization to flatter, "high involvement" structures all suggest that a broader conceptualization of employee voice and representation (EVR) is required and that EVR systems need to be explicitly considered as a strategic choice variable. Lewin and Sherer then develop a conceptual model in which EVR strategic choices are portrayed as a function of environmental forces and employer and employee preferences. In the second half of the chapter they use survey data collected from American and Japanese business executives in the U.S. to determine to what degree differences in employer preferences shape strategic choices about EVR systems. They find that Japanese executives rank employees as a more important stakeholder in the firm than do American executives. Japanese executives also have more favorable attitudes regarding the use of EVR systems in the formulation of business strategy, while American executives favor EVR systems in the implementation of strategic business decisions. These results, they conclude, provide concrete evidence that attitudes and values of top-level executives influence strategic choices regarding EVR systems.

Delaney and Schwochau—"Employee Representation Through the Political Process." Delaney and Schwochau consider the extent to which the political process provides individual employees with effective voice over workplace issues. Using three different data sets, they examine respectively the extent to which individual

Americans engage in political action and their views on major issues; the extent of political activity by labor unions and their position on major issues; and the extent to which other interest groups in society pursue political action regarding workplace issues and the degree to which their positions match those of unions and individual employees. They conclude that most Americans are relatively inert in the political process; that interest groups play a crucial role in the political arena; and although no interest group fully represents the average employee's political preferences on workplace issues, the organized labor movement probably comes closest. The authors conclude, therefore, that the decline of the union movement in the United States is a source of concern since it reduces the availability of employee representation both in the workplace through collective bargaining and in the legislative arena through political action.

Addison, Kraft, and Wagner—"German Works Councils and Firm Performance." This chapter provides an in-depth analysis of the German system of codetermination through works councils and the impact of works councils on firm performance. The authors begin with a review of the legal and institutional background surrounding German works councils. They then move to a discussion of the predicted impact of works councils on firm performance. Viewed from a neoclassical "monopoly model" perspective, works councils are predicted to cause a misallocation of resources and redistribution of firm revenues from profit to labor cost; from the perspective of an "exit-voice" model, however, works councils are predicted to have a positive impact on productivity through better information sharing, reduced employee quits, and greater labor-management cooperation. These hypotheses are then econometrically tested using data on profit, productivity, capital investment, and wages for approximately 50 establishments in Germany, some of which had a works council and some of which did not. The empirical analysis failed to find much evidence that works councils had either a net positive or negative effect on firm performance.

Rubinstein, Bennett, and Kochan—"The Saturn Partnership: Co-Management and the Reinvention of the Local Union." This chapter examines one of the most innovative systems of work force governance in the United States—the "partnership" between the

Saturn Corporation and the United Automobile Workers' Local Union 1853. The authors describe the key organizational features of the Saturn partnership and the system of joint governance or "co-management" that the system attempts to foster. They then examine in considerable detail the roles and function of the local union in the partnership and the conflicts and organizational dynamics that result as it endeavors to simultaneously promote efficiency of the enterprise and protect the contractual interests of the membership. The final section of the chapter considers whether the union adds value to the enterprise. The authors conclude that it does by improving the decision-making process and its substantive outcomes.

Nelson—"Employee Representation in Historical Perspective." Nelson provides a thorough account of the origins and evolution of the company union movement in the United States from the turn of the twentieth century to the passage of the Wagner Act in the mid-1930s. Nonunion employee representation plans or "company unions" emerged shortly before World War I, attained a zenith of influence and popularity in the 1920s, and then fell into disrepute during the depression years of the early 1930s, finally to be outlawed by the Wagner Act. The author claims that companies were guided by diverse motives in establishing employee representation plans. Some were formed as a reaction to government pressure, others were developed as an antiunion stratagem, while others were established out of the conviction that they improved profits by fostering employee loyalty, cooperation, and morale. Nelson claims that it is the employee representation plans in the latter group of companies that have the most historical interest and relevance for today. He documents that operating a successful employee representation plan was a time-consuming, expensive undertaking for the company, but that the resulting improvement in the labor relations climate and productivity was generally regarded as worth the cost. He also concludes that employees derived tangible benefits from a well-run company union, such as improved fringe benefits and handling of grievances. The company unions were, on the other hand, largely ineffectual in dealing with economic issues such as wages and layoffs. Nelson concludes that the company union movement made some significant contributions to the development of progressive personnel practices in American industry, but that these contributions were largely discredited by the events of the Great Depression and the actions of those employers who used them to thwart union organization.

Conclusions

Although employee representation has been central to the field of industrial relations for many years, much of the academic literature on this subject has focused more narrowly on issues related to trade unions and collective bargaining. The long-term decline in union density to 10 percent of the private-sector work force, the growth and development of new forms of worker representation in both the United States and other countries, and the interest of the Clinton administration in labor law reform, all suggest that the time may be ripe for a fundamental, broad-ranging reconsideration of the role of employee representation in the workplace and economy. Our hope and expectation is that the chapters in this volume will prove to be a significant contribution toward that end and a considerable stimulus to further research.

Chapter 1

Who Speaks for Us?
Employee Representation in a
Nonunion Labor Market

Richard B. Freeman
Harvard University and NBER

Joel Rogers
University of Wisconsin-Madison

Private-sector labor markets in the United States now approximate the "union-free" ideal of professional antiunionists. After a 40-year decline, private-sector union density has fallen to a pre-Wagner Act level of 11.5 percent (BLS 1993, 239). At current rates of new organizing, density will drop to 5 percent by the turn of the century.[1] Given the absence of formal modes of collective voice in nonunion firms and U.S. labor law restrictions on company unions, only a few workers will have any form of worker representation within private enterprises.

The U.S. is hardly the only advanced industrial economy in which union membership fell in the 1980s; decline occurred in most OECD countries. But the U.S. is a leader in deunionization, and it lacks any structure of worker representation, inside or outside the firm, to compensate for declining union coverage. In Europe, falling union membership in the 1980s followed a decade of increased unionization, with the result that rates of organization were still relatively high at the outset of the 1990s and comparable to their level in the early 1970s. Moreover, mechanisms to extend collectively bargained wages to nonunion workers, while weaker than in the past, remain operative. And legally mandated works councils provide workers with collective voice in nonunion firms. In Japan, where union declines over the past 20 years have been pronounced, the *shunto* economy-wide wage adjustment system remains robust. And company unions and other means of consensual decision making, including joint consultation committees, provide some mechanism for worker voice within large enterprises.

What is the effect of the loss of worker representation in the U.S. on workers, firms, and the economy? Has falling unionization created a "representation gap" for labor? How do works councils and related modes of representation function in other advanced industrial economies? What does foreign experience and the U.S.'s historical experiments with nonunion forms of worker representation tell us about possible future modes of collective representation in the country?

This chapter explores these questions, concentrating on institutions of intrafirm worker representation. We begin with a general assessment of the place of formal channels of worker representation in a market economy. We then present evidence that the decline of American unions has indeed created a substantial representation gap in the United States. Putting the U.S. in context, we move on to a description of mandated works councils in Europe and, more briefly, company unions and plant committees in Japan. We then consider American experience with nonunion forms of workplace-based worker representation, including "company unions" and current "employee involvement" (EI) programs. We conclude our review of these different forms of intrafirm worker representation with some design lessons for an improved worker representation system in the U.S.

Our major claim is that the decline of private-sector unionism in the U.S. and lack of an alternative formal mechanism for collective voice has created a representation gap inside firms that is harmful to the nation's economic progress and social well-being. We show that most American workers, and some leading business analysts and managers, favor new forms of intrafirm representation and that other countries provide such with no discernible damage to their economic health. While many factors—from legal precedent to imbalances in political power and fears of the unknown—make reform of intrafirm worker representation in the U.S. a difficult business, reform is clearly needed. We offer this essay as a contribution to discussion on how it might proceed.

FIGURE 1

Comparative Union Density, Selected OECD Countries

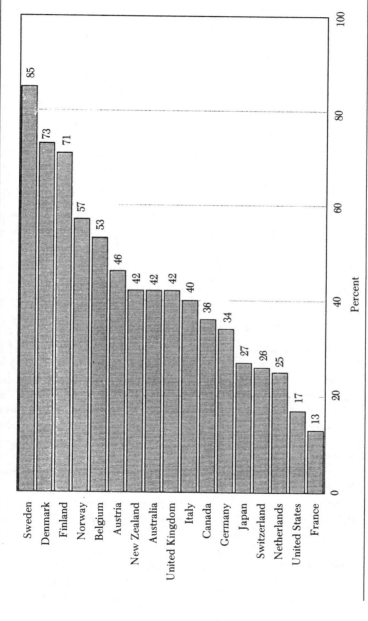

Percent

Source: Visser, Jelle. "Trends in Trade Union Membership," in OECD Employment Outlook July 1991.

TABLE 1

Comparative Changes in Union Density, 1970-88

	1970	1980	1988	Absolute change			Percent change 1970-88
				1970-80	1980-88	1970-88	
Australia	50	49	42	−1	−7	−8	−16
Austria	60	54	46	−6	−8	−14	−24
Belgium	46	57	53	11	−4	7	15
Canada	31	35	35	4	0	4	11
Denmark	60	77	73	17	−4	13	22
Finland	51	70	71	19	1	20	39
France	22	19	12	−3	−7	−10	−46
Germany	33	37	34	4	−3	1	2
Italy	37	49	40	12	−9	3	8
Japan	35	31	27	−4	−4	−8	−24
Netherlands	37	35	25	−2	−10	−12	−32
New Zealand	46	55	42	9	−13	−4	−9
Norway	51	57	57	6	0	6	13
Sweden	68	80	85	12	5	17	26
Switzerland	31	31	26	0	−5	−5	−15
United Kingdom	45	51	42	6	−9	−3	−7
United States	30	23	16	−7	−7	−14	−45

Source: OECD Employment Outlook, July 1991, "Trends in Trade Union Membership," pp. 97-134.

Note: Percentages may not appear exact due to rounding.

Benefits and Costs of Worker Representation

A point of consensus in discussion of labor relations in the U.S. is that the system of industrial relations codified in the Wagner Act, while perhaps appropriate to the 1930s, does not work well in the 1990s. There is a mismatch between old institutions and "new realities" of intensified international competition, rapid technological change, new forms of work organization, changed work-force demographics and career patterns, and altered employee expectations of work.

In face of this mismatch, many argue that the U.S. no longer needs a formal system of collective worker representation—that labor markets, facilitated by advanced personnel management techniques, will adequately perform the tasks of representing worker interests. We argue to the contrary. Modern economic analysis shows that a well-designed system of worker representation can produce benefits to workers, firms, and the markets in which they operate and can usefully supplement state efforts to regulate labor market outcomes. Such a system helps satisfy basic democratic

FIGURE 2

Trends in Unionization, 1970-1990:
Europe, Japan, and the U.S.

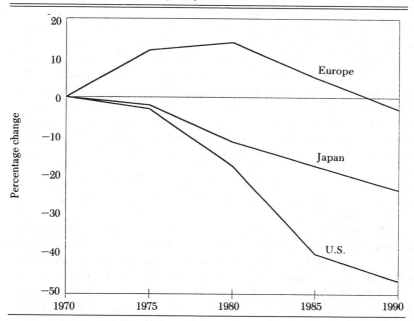

Source: OECD, *Employment Outlook,* July 1991; OECD, *National Accounts,* 1992; U.S. Bureau of Labor Statistics, union membership data gathered from various sources, 1992; The Economist, *Book of Vital World Statistics,* 1990.

Note: "Europe" includes Austria, Belgium, Denmark, Finland, France, Germany, Italy, Netherlands, Norway, Sweden, Switzerland, and the U.K. Union density figures for Europe were weighted using the 1988 size of labor force of each country. For 1990, union density rates for Europe and Japan are 1988 figures.

norms. Under plausible conditions, moreover, there is no viable alternative to collective worker representation as a means of achieving these ends.

Enterprise-Efficiency

Modern analyses of firms recognize that management faces information, coordination, and motivation problems in devising competitive strategies that go beyond the simple calculus-based black box models of optimizing behavior of the neoclassical firm. These analyses stress the crucial role of information held by diverse employees in firm performance, strategic behavior by people in using their information, the need to motivate optimal effort, and the value of firm-specific human capital.

Recognition that information exists at various levels of organizations implies that in many situations it is inefficient for management to make key decisions. Just as the center cannot efficiently run a centrally planned economy, neither can the center in general efficiently run a large modern enterprise. Aoki's (1990, 1988) models of Japanese firms capture this point nicely. He shows that hierarchies work best when there is very low or very high uncertainty at workplaces (so that workplace-specific information provides little guidance on optimal decisions) but that at intermediate levels of uncertainty, giving workers the authority to make some workplace decisions is efficient, as they can react better (more quickly with a response informed by appropriate local knowledge) than centralized management to workplace-specific shocks or unusual circumstances.

The potential for divergent interest groups within firm hierarchies to use information for their own benefit at the expense of the firm implies that there may be payoffs from devising information and incentive structures that link top management to workers outside the standard hierarchy. Diverse principal-agent models make this point in various ways. For instance, Tirole (1986) develops it in the context of a three-level firm hierarchy: top management, supervisors, and workers, where a major issue is the possibility for coalitions among the players. While economists have long recognized the need to motivate labor (see Marx's distinction between labor and labor power), not until recently have formal models made effort a key element in the production process. Some of this literature has focused on incentive pay systems, such as rank-order tournaments (Lazear and Rosen 1981; Lazear 1991), profit sharing (Estrin, Grout, and Wadhwani 1987; Weitzman and Kruse 1990), "gainsharing" schemes such as the Scanlon, Rucker, and Improshare plans (Eaton and Voos 1992; Kaufman 1992), or employee ownership through employee stock ownership plans (ESOPs) and other mechanisms (Bloom 1986; Blasi 1988). A second strand stresses worker participation in management (Levine and Tyson 1990; Eaton and Voos 1992). The major finding is that productivity does increase if employees are given substantial decision-making authority—"strategic participation"—and a share of resulting gains. Weitzman and Kruse report favorably on profit sharing. The GAO (1986, 1988) and Conte and Svejnar (1990) find that the productivity effects of ESOPs are substantial and positive when the ESOP links worker stock ownership to substantial participation in daily firm management but not when worker participation is weak or ambiguous. The importance of such linkage finds general support, over a wide range of incentive schemes, in the reviews of Levine and Tyson (1990) and Eaton and Voos (1992).[2]

The success of Japanese firms that rely on worker loyalty and tenure, as opposed to mobility, provides further evidence of the economic advantages of labor relations practices based on voice instead of exit. Human capital analyses of investment in firm-specific skills point to the advantages of job rotation and consultation (Koike 1984, 1989; Cole 1979, 1989; Morishima 1991a, 1991b) and highlight the incentive to make investments in training specific to enterprises when workers and firms expect low turnover.[3] This contrasts with studies documenting the limited firm training efforts directed to "front-line" production workers in the U.S. (CSAW 1990; OTA 1990; Osterman 1990).

The routes by which employee representation can improve enterprise efficiency have been formally modeled by Freeman and Lazear (1992). They stress the virtue of (a) increasing information flows from management to labor that can lead to worker concessions in difficult economic times, saving troubled enterprises; (b) increasing information flows from workers to management outside the hierarchical chain; (c) providing a forum for both sides to devise new solutions to problems; and (d) motivating workers to make longer-term commitments to the firm. In this analysis, collective voice in the workplace has benefits to the enterprise beyond discouraging strikes due to unmet grievances (a major goal of the Wagner Act) or saving the costs of turnover by reducing quits or giving workers the compensation package they desire (stressed by Freeman and Medoff 1984). It alters the way management and labor operate, creating a more cooperative and informative decision process.

The way it does so, it bears emphasis, is by changing the power relations between workers and management. On the side of workers, it is their greater control over the use of information they provide to management that leads them to provide it in the first place. Without such control, workers are reluctant to provide the information useful to improving enterprise efficiency for fear that gains in efficiency will come at the expense of their security or compensation. On the side of management, the same increase in the ability of workers to constrain management explains the most commonly observed efficiency effects on management. First, knowing that workers will interrogate decisions that affect their jobs, management must consider more fully the costs and benefits of actions it proposes to take. This limits costly mistakes arising from simple lack of reflection. Second, a management that must discuss its labor decisions with employee representatives will invest more in knowing how workers currently fare and the likely consequences to them of a change in action than a management concerned solely with stockholders. Imagine two interlocutors, A and B, at point X. A wishes to move to point Y; B, with blocking power, must be persuaded of the wisdom of doing so. In seeking to persuade B that a move to Y is in B's interest, A has incentives to familiarize itself intimately with B's present circumstance, if only better to show B that (perhaps contrary to B's initial perception of things) this move is in fact in B's interest and to learn of the least costly means (to B) of making it. Along the way, A will gain knowledge of how B works and of alternative ways of getting from X to Y. It will in general become more skilled in making X-to-Y changes in incremental steps and in more routinely spotting opportunities for incremental improvement. In this way, the change in power relations helps underwrite continuous improvement in the organization of production and work—the alleged *sine qua non* of contemporary business success.

The change in power relations that can thus help the firm, however, carries obvious risks to managers. In principle, a redistribution of property rights within the firm should have no *per se* effect on efficiency (Coase 1960); such follows only if the rights are "muddied" as a result of the redistribution. But since the redistribution of rights inevitably also redistributes "profits" toward workers, it may harm management and thus be resisted by them. The danger that effective systems of worker representation reduce the firms' share of the pie proportionately more than they increase the size of the pie explains why management rarely voluntarily cedes much power to worker representatives (Freeman and Lazear 1992).[4]

Collective worker representation does not come free of cost. There are the direct administrative costs of supporting organizations of representation or processes of negotiation. There is lost production time as some workers become "professional" representatives and move out of the work force or as workers and managers gather in meetings. There are the costs of training worker representatives to assume greater responsibilities. While no one has assembled adequate data for a formal benefit-cost analysis,[5] most analysts familiar with the works councils in Western Europe believe that they have a positive net effect (Rogers and Streeck, forthcoming). And while conservative critics sometimes gainsay this positive contribution (Giersch 1990), virtually no one argues that they are a drag on firm or economic performance.

Market Efficiency

Worker representation schemes invariably require management to provide information to employees about the situation of the enterprise that would otherwise be kept secret. Such provision can improve the efficiency of the labor market even when it does little for the firm. It can do this by eliminating the deleterious effect of information asymmetries on some market outcomes. If managers know they will close the plant but do not tell workers, the workers will be unable to plan for this event and are likely to suffer substantial dislocation losses. Whether the profitability of the firm would increase or decrease is less clear due to the firm's loss of its monopoly on information. Most of the empirical literature on advance notice of plant closing supports the notion that workers gain from early notice (see, e.g., Ehrenberg and Jakubson 1988), with the most negative studies claiming only that notices are neutral (Addison and Portugal 1987, 1992).

A second area in which worker representation can improve market, though not necessarily enterprise, efficiency is in job training. Firms that cannot fully pass on the costs of general training to workers will provide only narrow firm-specific training. Recent evidence for this in the U.S. is provided by Lynch (1992). Because workers are anxious to preserve employability on the external labor market, provision of worker voice in the training area tends to broaden the nature of training (Ferman et al. 1991). The immediate benefit redounds to workers and society, not to firms, but extension of such a training practice to an entire market means that no firm need suffer: it will be able to replace workers it trained with workers trained in other enterprises, as Soskice (1991) notes in his discussions of German apprenticeships.

State Regulation

Every society regulates some market outcomes, either to remedy market imperfections or externalities or for reasons of income redistribution. In the U.S., government inspectorates usually enforce regulations, often joined by private attorneys pursuing statutory rights through civil actions. In many areas of public concern, however, including the labor market, neither of these means of regulatory enforcement is adequate. Sites of regulated activity are too numerous (6 million worksites) for any plausibly sized state inspectorate to monitor, and activity within them is too heterogeneous for a distant state agency to decide the best means of achieving desired outcomes. Private litigation, on the other hand, is a very costly and brittle way to settle disputes about standards of behavior, and its cost makes it least amply supplied to the less skilled who typically are most in need of standard enforcement. The result is often regulatory failure—inadequate performance standards, cumbersome reporting requirements on matters of uncertain relevance to desired ends, inflexibility in adjusting standards to varied or changed circumstance, and weak enforcement.[6] The prominence of regulatory agents and lawyers in the compliance process is widely perceived as a barrier to the intrafirm understandings and practices needed to get desired results.

The example of worker safety and health suffices to carry the general point. U.S. workers rate safe working conditions at the top of their expectations of company performance (NSWI 1992, 10), and the 1970 Occupational Safety and Health Act (OSHA) commits the government to "assure safe and healthful working conditions for working men and women" (Public Law 91-596). But OSHA enforcement, which relies chiefly on 2,000 federal and state inspectors, falls short of these expectations. Since OSHA's enactment, some 200,000 workers have been killed on the job; 1.4 million have been permanently disabled; and another 2 million have died from occupationally related diseases (about 300 per day). As of the early 1990s, about 9 million workers sustained workplace injuries each year, of which 2.5 million were "serious," 70,000 resulted in permanent disablement, and 10-11,000 were fatal. Along with nearly

incalculable suffering, this carnage carries costs in the form of sur-
vivor benefits, insurance for hospitalization and other treatment,
and days lost in production estimated to run to some $200 billion an-
nually (NSWI 1992).[7]

Disturbing as these numbers are, more troubling still is the fact
that, on some critical dimensions, U.S. health and safety performance shows no improvement since the first enactment of
OSHA. The rate of workdays lost due to job-related injury or illness,
for example, has climbed 75 percent above the rate in 1972 when
the Act became fully enforceable (NSWI 1992, 1).[8] Moreover, the
U.S. effort appears to fall short in comparative terms. Health and
safety data are difficult to compare cross-nationally due to different
reporting methods, incomplete reporting, and underreporting
(particularly in the U.S. itself). These difficulties acknowledged, a
comparison of countries that use the same reporting measures on
occupational fatalities, fatalities per 100,000 hours worked—the
U.S., Sweden, and Japan—shows the lag in U.S. performance.
Death rates in the U.S. are 3.5 times those in Japan and 5.8 times
those in Sweden (ILO 1988).[9] Both Sweden and Japan also show
greater improvements in performance over time. In the 1980s, for
example, the percentage reduction in Japan's rate of workplace
fatalities was better than twice that of the United States.[10]

While many factors contribute to the U.S.'s poor occupational
health and safety record, experts view the U.S.'s regulatory mechanism as a key factor (Bardach and Kagan 1981; Noble 1986). U.S. reliance on state inspectors to enforce health and safety standards
contrasts to Japanese and European (and, increasingly, Canadian)
reliance on mandated worker health and safety committees within
plants to supplement direct state regulatory efforts. These committees operate with delegated legal powers; they monitor, and in some
measure enforce, compliance with regulations while enjoying more
or less broad discretion in bargaining with management (usually
also represented on the committee) in choosing the most appropriate local means to achieve regulatory goals.[11] In principle, a system
that lodges responsibility for monitoring compliance with health
and safety committees, who should be better informed about problems than government inspectors, and that gives those committees
some authority to address problems, should enlist the knowledge of
regulated actors in finding ways in particular settings of satisfying

publicly determined standards. That it does so in a context of declared representation rights, moreover, mitigates use of costly litigation. Deputizing workers as local co-administrators of health and safety regulation, of course, carries costs of its own. Worker deputies must be trained and given time off from work to carry out committee responsibilities. Still, most observers believe that the committees provide a more efficient regulatory regime for safety and health than inspectorate or civil liability schemes (Bryce and Manga 1985; Deutsch 1988; US DOL 1988; GAO 1992).

Observing that efficiency gains may follow from allowing recruiting local agents with local knowledge to make key decisions is not novel. A traditional justification of U.S. collective bargaining was that it let labor and management make the relevant trade-offs on working conditions, based on their specific situation and preferences rather than relying on the heavy hand of government (Bok and Dunlop 1970). Now that unionism has dramatically declined and government workplace regulation concomitantly increased, however, the point has heightened force. A variety of regulatory cases are similar to occupational health and safety in that public goals for workplace behavior may be best met by giving intended beneficiaries some collective power to supplement state enforcement efforts and to bargain with management about how those goals are best achieved.[12]

Democracy and Collective Voice

Democracy is rooted in respect for the moral equality of persons, each of whom should have the same opportunity to influence the actions of the state: one person, one vote. Commitment to the ideal implies limiting inequalities in public life due to ethically irrelevant differences among citizens and guaranteeing equal treatment under law, equal access to public goods, and so on, for all citizens. Does the democratic ideal also call for a commitment to workplace democracy? We believe that it does.

The case for workplace democracy can be made on both instrumental and noninstrumental grounds.[13] The instrumental argument is that workplace democracy strengthens democracy in the broader society. Democracy requires some equality in the distribution of material resources, and this is unlikely without some measure of worker representation inside firms (Cohen and Rogers 1983). Also, democracy requires citizens capable and confident in their exercise of deliberative political judgment, and these citizen attributes are unlikely to arise in a society that shows no respect for such attributes at work (Pateman 1970). To take an extreme case, there may be no logical inconsistency between individuals being slaves in the economic sphere but voting citizens in the political sphere, however, such a society is utterly implausible.

The noninstrumental argument proceeds by extension of democratic principles beyond formal politics. One way of putting the idea of democracy is that those involved in a socially cooperative activity and bound by its rules ought to have a right to determine those rules. This principle has applicability beyond the state to other sorts of rule-governed cooperative activity, including the cooperative activity of the firm (Dahl 1985, 1989). And this may be particularly so when, as in the case of corporations, the democratic state itself charters and protects the institutions governing such activity.

If these sorts of arguments for workplace democracy are familiar, the arguments for qualifying commitments to workplace democracy are equally so. Two objections might be distinguished. The first is that people can more easily avoid autocratic bosses than they can autocratic governments. In a market economy, they can quit their jobs and find a different employer or set up their own business. But it is easy to exaggerate the power of exit. Quitting unsatisfactory conditions is an attractive, even exhilarating prospect if you can rapidly find a job paying comparable compensation elsewhere. But in practice substantial unemployment, large wage differences across firms and sectors, and many firm-specific, nonportable social benefits, makes exit nonviable for many workers and potentially least useful to those most in need of protection from autocratic management—the less skilled. Moreover, even where exit options from undemocratic conditions exist, they are not recognized in formal politics as compelling arguments against remediation. That it is possible to move from a town that denies its citizens the right to vote, for example, is never seriously offered as a reason not to reform that town's government. Employing the obverse of the extension argument used above, there is no reason such an argument *not* respected outside the workplace should be respected within it.

A second objection goes to the different functions of formal government and firms. Firms, the argument goes, are designed to produce economic value, not to govern social life, and this implies different criteria of performance. Governments are at least in part judged by representativeness. What firms are judged by is the "market test" of profitability. This objection, which denies any force to the extension argument, might be answered in two ways. First, the distinction between firms and governments is overdrawn. Governments are routinely judged by their success in producing economic value. As a vast literature in comparative politics attests, economic performance is the single best predictor of stability in government (Eulau and Lewis-Beck 1985; Lewis-Beck and Lafay 1991). And firms are routinely judged by standards of conduct more encompassing than profitability. While firms must meet the market test, along the way to doing so they must typically meet other tests, including the recruitment and nondiscriminatory treatment of an adequate labor force. Second and more directly, however, the argument has little practical force. If workplace democracy extracted immense losses in production, we might decide that it was not worth the cost. But while we could undoubtedly devise forms of workplace democracy that are economically costly, the analysis just offered and the practical experience of successful capitalist economies with high levels of worker representation suggests that the opposite is more likely to be true in the real world; a well-designed system of workplace democracy can raise social production.

Finally, the sheer novelty (in the U.S.) of workplace democracy raises fears of its noneconomic effects. Any scheme of worker representation means giving representatives real powers, which carries dangers. The representatives may not act as perfect agents of their principal. Or they may act too perfectly, on behalf of a principal that is shortsighted and narrow in its perspective, distinguishing too sharply between insiders and outsiders, harming workers who are not members of the group or lobbying to capture socially wasteful rents from the state. There is the danger that the interests of the collective will be asserted in ways that violate individual rights. White employees may vote to limit promotions to whites. Individuals may be forced to rely on elected representatives they opposed to carry a grievance to management or to decide the grievance. And so on.

But these are the dangers of any democracy—neither unique to nor uniquely pointed in the workplace. Majority rule does not always produce morally valid outcomes. There is need in any collective decision-making system for protection of minority rights. In the U.S. the "duty of fair representation" provision of the Labor Management Relations Act (LMRA) is an effort to deal with this problem in union settings, requiring unions to represent fairly all workers at a worksite. Just as commitment to democratic ideals should impel society to favor workplace democracy, so too should it impel society to limit the authority of workplace institutions and guarantee rights for minorities. With such protections, however, the argument for workplace democracy remains robust.

What about other, less collectivist ways to advance the "moral equality of persons" at workplaces? The three most widely cited alternatives to collective voice (excluding exit with which we have dealt) are: individual communication to managers, detailed specification of the terms of individual employment contracts, and government regulation of personnel practices. Might any of these advance worker voice enough that there would be no need for collective representation?

We think not. A voice regime limited to individual communications to management has benefits. It avoids principal-agent problems between the collectivity and the representative of collective voice and the danger of collective suppression of dissenting individual expression. But individual voice does not promote deliberation among employees about shared preferences, leaving management with conflicting signals from disagreeing workers. The inequalities in power that define an employment relation make individual voice an uncertain channel of communication, inducing many employees to keep silent. The "chilling effect" of unequal power on employee expression is not a relic of the bad old days before advanced personnel policies. A 1988 Gallup poll showed that only 56 percent of workers thought that their boss "typically reacts positively to concerns raised by individual employees"; that 45 percent reported that "there are concerns I'd like to raise with my employer but I've held back"; and that 54 percent stated that "I'd feel more comfortable raising workplace problems through an employee association, rather than as an individual."[14] Even of those who report their employers respond positively to worker concerns, 43 percent say they've held back raising issues, and 51 percent say they'd be more comfortable with an employee association. The reality is that for a large percentage of the work force, voice is extremely unlikely absent collective representation.

While more complete contracts or detailed government regulations may solve some problems, they too are insufficient. Almost no relationship, the employment relationship hardly excepted, can be fully specified in advance. Even the most laborious attempts to do so inevitably leave room for disputes over contract interpretation. And the very attempt to specify contracts fully can undermine flexibility. As to government regulation, the previous discussion showed that in principle and in fact government regulators are no substitute for "on the ground" monitoring and enforcement and a local capacity to develop appropriate compliance strategies.

In sum, if one is a democrat, facilitating collective representation is "the right thing to do." Along with private markets and public hierarchies, workplace associations should be recognized as important complements to social self-governance.

A "Representation Gap" in the United States?

Even if readers agree that formal worker representation in the U.S. is inadequate, they may still be tempted to dismiss the preceding discussion as interesting but irrelevant to real world concerns. Intellectual cases can be made for eating spinach, exercising daily, or watching less TV, but it would be foolish to try to foist these activities onto a public that may have other preferences. Do American workers, management, and unions see a need for additional representation, or is ours simply an academics' case?

Worker Demand for Representation

To see if workers perceive a gap between their representation in the firm and the representation they would like, we use two public opinion polls: a 1988 Gallup poll commissioned by the AFL-CIO and a 1991 poll conducted by Fingerhut/Powers, commissioned by the Labor Research Association and Local 1199, National Union of Hospital and Health Care Workers.[15] Both polls have the virtue of going beyond the "Would you vote for a union?" questions analyzed by Farber and Krueger (1992), Riddell (1992), and others to probe the sources of support and disapproval of unions and the representation issues of most concern to workers. The Gallup poll, in particular, asked about potential worker support for institutions of worker representation beyond unions. While asking about hypothetical institutional forms risks the "Perot Poll Phenomenon" of people saying something sounds good without knowing its content, the answers provide a valuable addition to those based solely on current institutions and suggest possible desirable ways to modify current institutions.

To begin with existing institutions, the polls show considerable approval of unions (see Tables 2 and 3). Among Gallup respondents, 61 percent "approved" of unions and only 25 percent disapproved. Sixty-nine percent of the overall sample and 31 percent of those who "disapproved" of unions agreed with the statement, "Labor unions are good for the nation as a whole." Among Fingerhut/ Powers respondents, 60 percent thought that unions have been "basically" good for "American working people," with 23 percent disagreeing. That so many workers approve of unionism is striking given that both polls show considerable skepticism about the efficacy of U.S. unions and discontent among union members about union performance. Among Gallup respondents, while 68 percent (80 percent of those approving of unions; 49 percent of those not) agreed that "without union efforts, most laws which benefit employees would be seriously weakened or repealed," 52 percent (67 percent among those approving; 48 percent among those disapproving) also thought that "unions have become too weak to protect their members." Among Fingerhut respondents who were members of unions, 43 percent rated union performance "only fair" or "poor," and only 23 percent rated it as "excellent."[16]

Both polls also show that most of the public believes managers actively discourage unionization, judges management action to be unfair, and wants it corrected. In the Gallup poll, 69 percent (67 percent of those disapproving of unions) agreed that "corporations sometimes harass, intimidate or fire employees who openly speak out for a union"; 73 percent (68 percent of those disapproving) agreed that in recent years corporations had effectively weakened worker rights and capacities to organize unions; 78 percent (62 percent of disapprovers) thought employer resistance to worker organization was "unfair"; and 66 percent (47 percent of disapprovers) favored tougher protections for workers seeking representation. In the Fingerhut/Powers poll, 79 percent thought it "very" or "somewhat" likely that nonunion workers "will get fired if they try to organize a union" at their workplace and 83 percent thought it likely that they would be fired for striking. Among employed nonunion respondents, 41 percent thought that they

TABLE 2

Gallup Survey of Attitudes Toward Representation

	Total sample	Approve of labor unions	Disapprove of labor unions
Total sample	100	61	25
Percent who agree that:			
Labor unions are good for the nation as a whole	69	87	31
Unions can solve workers' problems on the job even when all other approaches have failed	55	67	32
Without union efforts, most laws which benefit workers would be seriously weakened or repealed	68	80	49
Corporations sometimes harass or fire employees who support unions	69	71	67
Employees should have an organization to discuss and resolve concerns with their employer	90	94	82
Existing American laws should be strengthened to prevent corporations from denying workers rights to organize	66	76	47
It's not fair for employers to resist employees' union organizing efforts	78	86	62
Workers' rights and abilities to organize unions have faced a strong challenge from corporations in the past few years	73	81	68

	Total sample	Approve of labor unions	Disapprove of labor unions
Percent who agree that:			
Labor unions have become too weak to protect their members	52	56	48
Most unions are not concerned about the welfare of the company with which they are bargaining	46	38	70
A union establishment is much more likely to go out of business than a nonunion establishment is	35	33	45
Unions are responsible for much of the decline in U.S. industry[a]	43	37	80
The presence of a union increases tension between employees and employers	61	55	78
Most people who form unions are looking for a way to be less productive without suffering any consequences[a]	31	29	52
Most strikes by union employees are justified[a]	45	62	27
If employees attempted to form a union in my workplace, serious conflict among employees would be inevitable[a]	44	46	63

Source: Synopsis of the 1988 Gallup Study of Public Knowledge and Opinion Concerning the Labor Movement.

Note: Results based on sample size of 1029 respondents.

[a] Total sample percentage is for total approve and disapprove responses, and does not include "can't say" responses.

TABLE 3

Fingerhut/Powers Survey of Attitudes Toward Representation

	Agree (percent)	Disagree (percent)
Total respondents:		
Unions have been "basically good" for "American working people"	60	23
From what I understand, American workers do have the legal right to form a union	94	3
From what I understand, American workers do have the legal right to strike	88	7
There should be laws to protect workers who support a union from being fired or punished	68	19
Strikers should permanently lose their jobs when companies hire replacement workers	17	73
It is "very" or "somewhat" likely that:		
• union members will get fired if they strike	53	43
• non-union workers will get fired if they try to strike	83	11
• non-union workers will get fired if they try to organize a union	79	16
Labor unions in the U.S. are very or fairly strong	56	42

	Agree (percent)	Disagree (percent)
Employed non-union respondents:		
It is likely that I will lose my job if I tried to form a union	41	50
There should be tougher laws protecting workers who support unions	79	16
If a union did try to organize my workplace, I would be inclined to support it	47	36
It is likely that I would lose favor with my employer if I supported an organizing drive	59	34
If I knew there were laws protecting workers supporting unions, I would be more likely to join	15	80
Having a union at my workplace would help	28	72
Union members:		
I am proud to be a union member	76	20
My union is doing an excellent or good job of representing me	54	43
Labor unions should be more aggressive in actions to force politicians into meeting workers' needs	74	20

Source: 1991 Fingerhut/Powers National Labor Poll.

Note: Results based on sample size of 778 respondents.

would lose their own job if they tried to form a union and 59 percent thought that they would "lose favor" with their employer ("not get future promotions and things like that") if they supported an organizing drive. Among the same group, 79 percent favored tougher laws protecting workers seeking representation. Overall, 73 percent disapproved of the employer practice of hiring permanent strike replacements.

These numbers suggest that most American employees are acutely aware of the personal costs of seeking union organization against management wishes. This awareness is likely to depress affirmative responses to questions about the willingness to vote for a union in an NLRB election and contaminate efforts to infer an intrinsic "demand for unionism" from questions about voting intentions, as sophisticated analysts of those questions are aware (Farber and Krueger 1992). Still, we note that the four surveys asking this question since 1977[17] have shown at least a third of the nonunion work force (roughly 30 million workers in 1991) desire unionization.[18] The Fingerhut/Powers poll asked a variant of this question that tells a similar story: "If a union did try to organize the place where you work, would you be inclined to support the effort or oppose it?" Nearly half (47 percent) of employed nonunion respondents answered affirmatively—which translates into approximately 40 million workers—a larger number than indicated by the other surveys. On the other hand, only 28 percent of nonunion workers in Fingerhut/Powers thought a union at their workplace would help, which suggests less substantive support for unions. The specific wording and framing of "do you want unions?" questions affects responses substantially.[19]

Support for unionism in general, belief that unions are relatively weak and troubled, and fear of management responses to organizing drives suggest that an even larger number of workers might desire some alternative form of representation to traditional U.S. union-management conflictual relations. In fact, this is what the survey data show. A vast majority—even of those disapproving of unions—favor some form of institutionalized representation of workers within firms. In the Gallup poll, 82 percent of those disapproving of unions (and 90 percent of all respondents) agreed with the statement that "employees should have an organization of co-workers to discuss and resolve legitimate concerns with their employers." Accepted at face value, this suggests an unmet demand for representation of some 80 million employed wage and salary workers—or two to two-and-a-half times the number who would like to be unionized. Moreover, variation across occupational class in attitudes toward employee associations is much smaller than variation in attitudes toward unions. Employee associations enjoy overwhelming support across all occupational groups.

TABLE 4

Approval of Unions and Employee Associations by Occupation

Occupation	Percent who approve of unions	Percent who disapprove of unions	Percent who approve of employee associations	Percent of those disapproving of unions who approve of employee associations
Professional workers	60.9	23.1	92.3	86.1
Skilled trade workers	68.7	24.4	89.3	78.2
Semi-skilled	56.1	28.0	89.1	87.0
Manager, executive or official	45.5	41.8	90.9	82.6
Runs own business with two or more employees	47.6	42.9	95.2	95.2
Clerical	62.5	20.2	92.5	75.0
Manufacturer's representative	42.9	42.9	85.7	83.3
All occupations	60.1	25.3	89.7	82.6

Source: Synopsis of the 1988 Gallup Study of Public Knowledge and Opinion Concerning the Labor Movement.

The Gallup poll is also instructive on what such an organization might look like. Again, taking the views of those disapproving of unions as our bounding case, the key factors leading to disapproval are the negative effects unions supposedly have on economic performance and career advancement: 80 percent of disapprovers thought unions were "responsible for much of the decline of American industry," and 70 percent doubted union concern about "the welfare of the company with which they are bargaining." Asked to compare union and nonunion workplaces, disapprovers rated unionized workplaces as better in wage compensation, security, and benefits, but worried about "advancement or promotion opportunities" and "recognition for work well done." And 63 percent thought that "serious conflict among employees would be inevitable" if a union attempted to organize their workplace. Finally, the desire among disapprovers for some "organization of co-workers" appears to derive from a perceived need for collective voice: 41 percent reported that there were "concerns I'd like to raise with my employer, but I've held back." An equal number reported that "I'd feel more comfortable raising workplace problems through an employees' association, rather than as an individual."

Assuming that an alternative workplace institution ought to address seriously the concerns of union disapprovers, the Gallup figures suggest that such an organization would have to advance employee interests in nonadversarial ways that contribute to economic performance and that accommodate individual ambition. It is not, we believe, a demand that organizations be weak. Recall the concern about current union weakness. Rather, the responses point to concerns about how goals are advanced: Americans want workplace institutions that will advance their interests in a manner compatible with the goals of the firm.

Management Views on Worker Representation

How does management see alternative forms of worker representation? The poll data just reviewed indicate that most managers approve, in principle, of some sort of organized employee voice. A large part of the reason for that is that managers increasingly recognize that greater employee involvement in firm decision making can improve the operation of enterprises. Current management discussion of human resources and production increasingly revolve around employee involvement and "worker empowerment."

The background for this discussion is familiar enough. American firms operate in a competitive environment far more exacting than 20 years ago, to which they have reacted with a mix of strategies aimed at cutting costs and improving performance on such product attributes as quality, variety, customization, timeliness, and service. Responding to the challenge of the Japanese in particular, many firms recognize that flattening management hierarchies and assigning workers an increased role in production decisions in the name of "lean production" (Womack, Jones, and Roos 1990) or "high-performance work organization" can save costs and improve quality. The ideal is a production chain in which all employees are responsible for performing at a high standard and motivated to do so.[20] In the limiting case, this involves continuous reordering of the firm into flexible, self-directed and self-monitoring work teams, with highly capitalized groups of individuals coming together to solve a given problem, then disbanding and forming new teams as new and different problems arise. Such a reorganization of work is meant to combine the best aspects of craft production (attention to quality and detail, responsibility for the total product, full use of intelligence in solving new problems) with the scale, distribution, and capitalization capacities of traditional mass production. A manager we recently interviewed put the corporate goal succinctly: "Empowerment means letting workers use their brains to help the corporation."

But if such reorganization is to work, employees must agree on the legitimacy of firm goals. Otherwise employees will be unwilling to work closely with others in self-monitored pursuit of those goals, to communicate freely with management about problems in achieving them or will continually demand a redistribution of the pie in their favor.[21] The goal of "empowerment" is to offer employees sufficient autonomy to enlist their energies and intelligence while ensuring that they try to achieve corporate ends. This is, not surprisingly, a difficult trick to turn, as many managements have learned, for it requires that management give up some powers in fact as well as in name.

A large and growing number of U.S. firms embrace some form of employee "participation" and "empowerment," involving either reorganization of work (e.g., team production; job enlargement and rotation; and increased worker responsibility for scheduling, material ordering, and the like) or building consensus and openness in communicating to management through incentive schemes aimed at promoting self-monitoring, quality circles, ad hoc task forces or problem-solving committees on particular issues. In 1990, some 30,000 U.S. firms, including 80 percent of the top 1,000 firms, now report having some worker involvement program—an increase of 50 percent in the incidence of programs over 1987 (Katz 1992).

But two recent surveys suggest that often these schemes are largely talk: trivial routinization of management access to employee opinion rather than substantive changes. Delaney, Lewin, and Ichniowski's (1989) 1986-87 survey of human resource practices among some 500 large firms found efforts at deep participation to be modest. The best gauge of the seriousness of employers in their survey was the amount of authority firms vested in workers active in participatory schemes. On a scale of 1 to 5 (1 = no authority, 5 = complete authority), the mean score of authority assigned workers was between 2 and 2.5. In the entire survey, moreover, no example of "full" (level 5) worker empowerment was reported. A Hay Group survey (Bernstein 1991) also found "advanced worker participation" practiced in only 10 percent of American firms. Only 18 percent of hourly employees, for example, reported having a chance to put their ideas into use. Such data indicate the difficulty of turning the "trick" of empowerment—eliciting greater effort without surrendering control—noted above.

The source of the difficulty is clear enough. Analyses of participation programs have found that success requires concrete payoffs to participants, including the front-line workers whose "empowerment" defines a full-scale transformation of work. But giving workers cash compensation or guarantees of job security is not attractive to management that focuses on short-run profitability. While giving workers greater autonomy might induce greater effort absent increased compensation, such autonomy can eventually be used to bargain for compensation. Moreover, from management's perspective there are real differences between schemes of individual worker payoff that include mechanisms of collective voice and those that do not. The former threaten managerial power more directly. Within the workplace, however, especially within a workplace characterized by high degrees of flexibility and continuous job reassignment, plans that do not allow for collective voice always threaten to create voice. Managers see a real danger that aggressive "worker involvement" programs may follow the path that early "meet and confer" laws had in the U.S. public sector: acquainting workers with the virtues of representation and opening the door to unions and collective bargaining (Freeman and Ichniowski 1988; Ichniowski and Zax 1990). Once again, real and hard concerns about power relations between collectively organized workers and managers—not merely concerns about how best to persuade individual workers to assume greater "responsibility" on the job—affect the choice of a participation scheme.

In brief, many American managers would like active, involved workers, but on management's own terms. The interest of at least some management in experimenting with different sorts of "involvement" programs and work reorganization is real. But so too is the desire to preserve management control over those programs and fear that such programs risk old-style unionization or some new and equally threatening form of collective empowerment. And this invariably limits the effectiveness of most participation programs.

Union Views of Representation

Unions distinguish between alternative modes of representation in unionized firms and provision of nonunion modes of collective representation in other firms. They generally take a positive view of the former but are as uneasy as management about the latter. Most unions recognize that to survive as institutions and serve their membership they must play a positive role in the economic restructuring of firms. In addition to scattered efforts to assume ownership positions in troubled firms, unions are active in worker training, where they are *de facto* leaders in efforts at industrial upgrading (Ferman et al. 1991) and seek points of entry in decisions over advanced technology use. They have institutionalized cooperation with management outside the collective bargaining relation. The proliferation of labor-management cooperation committees, now present in about 50 percent of the private unionized sector, is evidence of such (Cooke 1990). Finally, union involvement in new forms of worker participation tends to be a net plus for such programs and for firm productivity overall (Mishel and Voos 1992).[22]

Union views on independent nonunion worker representation schemes, such as works councils, are more complicated. Many union leaders fear that even if such organizations are not dominated by management, they threaten to substitute for unions. Historically, unions in the U.S., U.K., and Germany have opposed works councils or shop committees on precisely this ground (see discussion below). In theory, the state could assign such bodies the powers needed to avoid this fate. But the enormous political effort needed to do that, most unionists argue, is probably as great as that needed for substantive strengthening of protections for unions themselves. Given this, and given that unions are a proven form of representation, efforts should be directed to them, not councils. Thus, unions generally oppose management-led employee participation programs in nonunion settings and certainly oppose permitting such programs to operate as an alternative to unions in the collective determination of wages and other benefits.

Traditional union concerns notwithstanding, some prominent labor leaders have come to believe that mandated works councils are worth exploring. In the late 1980s they succeeded in getting the AFL-CIO's Committee on the Evolution of Work to consider councils. The AFL-CIO Committee discussion ended without consensus and therefore without any positive recommendation for action. But in the years since, the AFL-CIO has supported one version of the idea: limited purpose, statutory committees to assist in public regulation. Proposed OSHA reform, backed by the AFL-CIO, is distinguished by its mandate of such committees in the health and safety area. And the AFL-CIO conditioned its support for a massive new training measure on a like mandate of joint labor-management committees in all firms involved in federal education and training programs. Where unions already exist, the functions of these committees would be assumed by unions; where they did not, secret ballot elections among employees would determine their representatives. These gestures of support for nonunion independent committees, albeit statutorily limited ones, suggest considerable movement in organized labor's views toward representation institutions for nonunion workers.

Conclusion

We conclude that the United States does indeed have a substantial representation gap—a level of worker representation in nonunion settings below that which workers desire. As many as 30 to 40 million workers without unions say they want unions, and some 80 million workers without unions, including many who disapprove of unions, want some form of collective voice. To a limited degree, the latter interests are coincident with management interests in worker "empowerment." Some unions, while suspicious of management manipulation of employees in ersatz participation schemes, now support at least some forms of independent nonunion representation. Thus it seems useful to examine the operation of nonunion representation schemes in other countries and the U.S.'s past experience with such schemes.

Worker Representation in Advanced OECD Countries

How are workers represented within firms in other advanced democracies? What are the lessons for the U.S. from their experiences? To answer these questions, we examine the institutions of worker representation in Western Europe and Japan. Although our primary concern is with institutions that represent workers within firms, notably works counci¹⸍ councils cannot be assessed in isolation. Their character and operation within firms depends in part on the external labor relations environment in which they are lodged and thus on institutions that represent workers in politics, labor parties, and in negotiating wages with employers or employer federations, often in settings where governments extend collective contracts to nonunion workers. In both of these areas the U.S. diverges greatly from other advanced countries.

The External Setting

In comparative terms, the U.S. is anomalous in its lack of institutions linking workers in the political system or in wage setting beyond direct collective bargaining. There is no labor nor labor-dominated party, and American politicians rarely articulate or explicitly direct issues to achieving the aims of workers qua workers. Since the New Deal, unions have been allied with the Democratic Party, occasionally dominating local party machines. But labor was a junior partner in the New Deal coalition and by the late 1970s had become an unfavored one (Ferguson and Rogers 1986). In the 1980s it faced "an indifference bordering on contempt" from party leaders (Trumka 1992, 57). More broadly, unions have had a largely clientelistic relation to the Democrats, looking to the party for patronage, favors, and select program supports, not as a "second arm" to achieve its vision of a good society.

The U.S. situation contrasts with Western Europe, where social democratic or labor parties govern countries regularly; with Canada, where unions affiliate with the New Democratic Party; and with Japan, where socialist parties are represented in national and regional government and where the new Rengo union federation has run candidates for political office. In the U.S., by contrast, labor's main route of influence in the political system is through special interest lobbying rather than through direct electoral power. Table 5 shows the relative weakness of labor in government, itself substantially a function of low union density, as Figure 3 indicates.

The relative political weakness of American labor helps explain why the U.S. provides fewer benefits to citizens in the form of universal "social wages" than European countries. On a rank ordering of OECD states by social funding of pensions, health care,

TABLE 5

Cumulative Index of Left Presence in Government

Country	Index
Sweden (1979)	111.84
Denmark (1980)	90.24
Norway (1979)	83.08
New Zealand (1979)	60.00
Finland (1980)	59.33
Austria (1977)	48.67
United Kingdom (1976)	43.67
Belgium (1977)	43.25
Germany (1979)	35.33
Australia (1979)	33.75
Netherlands (1979)	31.50
Switzerland (1979)	11.87
France (1979)	8.67
Japan (1979)	1.92
Italy (1978)	0.00
Canada (1980)	0.00
United States (1978)	0.00

Source: Wallerstein, "Union Organization in Advanced Industrial Democracies," *American Political Science Review*, 1989, from Wilensky's (1981) index of cumulative left governments from 1919 to given year.

Party dominance is measured by the amount and continuity of participation in government from 1919 (or the closest date to the beginning of competitive party politics in an independent nation) through the year given. A score of "1" is assigned for each year that the left party has substantial, but not major or dominant power in the government. A score of "2" is assigned for each year that the left party is the major party in the government without being dominant. A score of "3" is given to a left party for each year that it is either the sole member of a majority government or the dominant partner in a coalition government. A score of "0" is given for each year in which left parties did not meet the minimum criterion for left party power. The scoring system was modified for countries with strong presidencies (France, Finland and the U.S.). The index was created for the whole period combining left party power and number of interruptions in left power. Center parties are coded as non-left. Fascist parties are excluded, as well as periods of nondemocratic rule.

unemployment insurance, and the like, the U.S. is second to last (Esping-Andersen 1990). As a consequence, the well-being of workers depends on market earnings and employer-provided benefits more in the U.S. than in most other countries. Moreover, taxes and cash transfers are less redistributive than in other countries. Comparing the effect of tax and transfer programs on poverty among a group of OECD countries, for example, shows an average 79 percent reduction in poverty abroad and only a 33 percent reduction in the United States (Mishel and Bernstein 1992).

The greater universalism of nonwage benefits overseas, which takes these benefits "out of competition," has an important

FIGURE 3
Union Density and Left Government

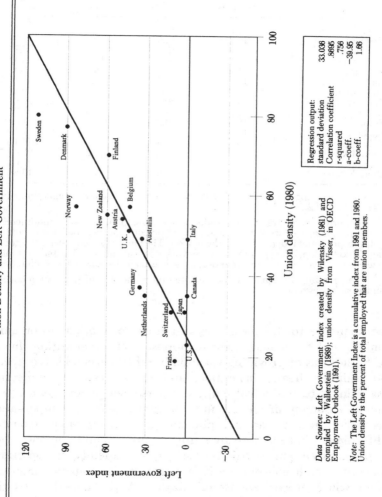

Union density (1980)

Left government index

Regression output:	
standard deviation	33.036
Correlation coefficient	.8695
r-squared	.756
a-coeff.	−39.95
b-coeff.	1.66

Data Source: Left Government Index created by Wilensky (1981) and compiled by Wallerstein (1989); union density from Visser, in OECD Employment Outlook (1991).

Note: The Left Government Index is a cumulative index from 1991 and 1980. Union density is the percent of total employed that are union members.

TABLE 6

The Strength of the Welfare State
in Selected OECD Countries[a]

	Pensions	Sickness	Unemploy-ment	Combined score[b]
Sweden	17.0	15.0	7.1	39.1
Norway	14.9	14.0	9.4	38.3
Denmark	15.0	15.0	8.1	38.1
Netherlands	10.8	10.5	11.1	32.4
Belgium	15.0	8.8	8.6	32.4
Austria	11.9	12.5	6.7	31.1
Switzerland	9.0	12.0	8.8	29.8
Finland	14.0	10.0	5.2	29.2
Germany	8.5	11.3	7.9	27.7
France	12.0	9.2	6.3	27.5
Japan	10.5	6.8	5.0	27.1
Italy	9.6	9.4	5.1	24.1
United Kingdom	8.5	7.7	7.2	23.4
Canada	7.7	6.3	8.0	22.0
United States	7.0	0.0	7.2	13.8

Source: Esping-Andersen, *The Three Worlds of Welfare Capitalism*, 1990, Tables 2.1 and 2.2.

[a] Reported here are Esping-Andersen's cross-national "de-commodification" scores for major welfare state programs. The "de-commodification" of a benefit denotes its provision independent of the market. The higher the score here, the greater the market-independence of the average worker in that country. The scores summarize ease of access to benefit programs, as well as their size and potential duration.

[b] The combined score has been weighted by proportion of population covered under each program.

consequence for the incentives and ability of workers to organize unions and for management to oppose such organization. In the U.S. the onus of providing vacation benefits, parental leave, access to training, health insurance, and so on, falls on collective bargaining or individual employer personnel policy. As a result, union-nonunion differences in these components of compensation as well as in wages are exceptionally great. Large union-nonunion differentials in turn motivate employer opposition to unions: when a union is certain to bargain for greater expenditures on fringe benefits which will put the firm at a cost disadvantage, management will fight hard against unionization. At the same time, the dependence of important benefits on nonunion personnel policies reduces worker willingness to oppose management: if your health insurance comes via your job, you will be more circumspect in opposing management than when insurance is universal.

FIGURE 4

Left Government and Social Spending

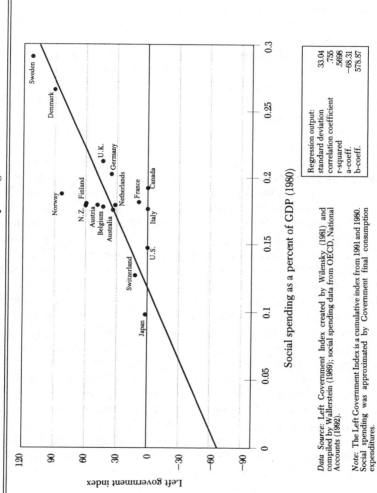

Social spending as a percent of GDP (1980)

Regression output:	
standard deviation	33.04
correlation coefficient	.755
r-squared	.5698
a-coeff.	−68.31
b-coeff.	578.87

Data Source: Left Government Index created by Wilensky (1981) and compiled by Wallerstein (1989); social spending data from OECD, National Accounts (1992).

Note: The Left Government Index is a cumulative index from 1991 and 1980. Social spending was approximated by Government final consumption expenditures.

Another potential effect of labor's political weakness in the U.S. is the relatively unfavorable terms for workers to organize. In part, organizing labor overseas is easier because of the mandated works councils that we examine below. In equal part, however, it reflects the failure of American labor law to establish effective penalties for management unfair labor practices and the consequent inability of the law to protect workers from possible job loss when they seek to unionize. That labor law is less favorable to unionization in the U.S. than in Canada, which has a highly similar labor relations system, is universally accepted (Weiler 1990). Labor's lack of independent political power is also evinced in its inability to get Congress to enact even mild revisions of labor law, as in the abortive 1977 labor law reform bill.

In terms of wage setting, the U.S. is the prime decentralized system in the developed world. Most collective bargaining and firm wage setting is done on a firm-by-firm, even plant-by-plant, basis. Moreover, except for "prevailing wage" statutes in government construction (and some procurement), the U.S. has few mechanisms, particularly in the private sector, for extending the results of union-employer bargaining to nonunion employees.[23] The government plays little role in wage-determination (itself a consequence of the political weakness of labor) and sets the minimum wage at levels that do not affect general wage patterns. Lack of extension of collective bargaining settlements means that coverage by collective contracts is essentially synonymous with union membership. In 1992, only 1.2 percent of private-sector wage and salary workers were both nonunion and covered by some union agreement (BLS, 1993, 239). This contrasts with Europe, where many governments extend the terms of collective contracts to nonunion workers in a sector or region, and Japan, where the *shunto* offensive establishes economy-wide wage patterns. The U.S.'s decentralized wage setting, with rent sharing between prosperous firms and their workers, and limited provision of "social wages" puts the country at the top of the developed world in wage inequality.[24]

Implications for Intrafirm Representation

The absence of a labor party and of encompassing wage-setting mechanisms has important implications for the character of representation within firms. In the U.S., unions bargain for fringe benefits that are guaranteed by the state elsewhere and bargain for wages that are set outside the firm in other countries. Because higher fringes and wages can put firms at a competitive disadvantage compared to others, confrontation at the bargaining table lies at the heart of labor relations. In Europe—and to some extent even Japan—by contrast, where general welfare benefits and wages are determined outside the firm, there is greater space for the expression of cooperative employee voice and bargaining within the firm. In effect, both sides can "afford" to cooperate because their positions are secured or restrained outside the firm. Workers know that their basic social benefits will remain intact and that their wages will keep pace with those of other workers whatever trade-offs they make within the firm. Management knows that the works council will not place it at a competitive disadvantage through within-firm bargaining. External guarantees—be they social benefit guarantees, centrally determined wages, or rights-based sanctions on job loss—in some measure render moot much intrafirm disagreement about the division of the surplus. By taking many intrafirm disputes over the surplus "off the table," these guarantees underwrite internal cooperation and flexibility toward the joint goal of increasing firm performance. Standard principles of rational behavior imply that when the share of the pie is exogenous, self-interested parties will cooperate to make a bigger pie, as this is the only way they can benefit themselves. When the share of the pie is "up for grabs," by contrast, there is danger of noncooperative, low-output solutions to prisoners' dilemma problems, including strikes, withholding information that might raise output, and the like.

The implication of this analysis is that all labor relations systems face a fundamental trade-off between external flexibility on one side and internal cooperation and the flexibility that depends on cooperative arrangements on the other. More flexibility in the external market implies less cooperativeness in the internal market. European labor relations systems resolve the tension by a dual channel of labor representation. They provide external guarantees through encompassing collective bargaining and state provision of certain benefits, and seek internal cooperative relations through within-firm worker councils, to which we turn next.

Works Councils in Western Europe[25]

As Table 7 indicates, except for Ireland and the United Kingdom, the advanced countries in Western Europe have legislatively mandated works councils or, in the case of Denmark and Italy, permit labor or management to establish such institutions at their discretion. Some countries supplement this with mandatory health and safety councils. Typically, national law requires elected works councils in establishments above certain sizes. It specifies the size and structure of the councils, rules for council elections, and other elements of procedure. It specifies enforcement mechanisms for agreements; conditions for works councilors to obtain paid time-off for council activity; and sanctions on violations of specified rights, including fines, imprisonment, and punitive damages. All councils have mandated rights to information from the firm and must be consulted on decisions relating to labor. With the exception of Spain, councils are not permitted to strike.

Consistent with our hypothesized trade-off between internal and external flexibility, the formal scope of issues addressed by councils varies inversely with the degree of extra-firm wage setting. In Northern Europe, where unions are strong or extension of collective contracts highly elaborated, the scope for council activity is narrowly defined. The German Works Constitution Act (Betriebsverfassungsgesetz) forbids councils to strike or bargain over the basic wage contract. In France, where the Ministry of Labor extends collective contracts and where minimum wages are important, councils have power to determine the firm's social expenditures, but not in other areas. Belgian law explicitly declares that "works councils exist to promote collaboration between employer and employee." (See Appendix 1 for typical provisions, Belgian Works Councils.)

By contrast, where the external institutional structure is less elaborated, as in Spain, Greece, or Italy, council powers more closely resemble those of a local union. The Spanish Workers Status Law (Ley Estatuto de los Trabajadores), in fact, permits councils to bargain over all matters, including wages, and allows them to strike. In Italy, the Workplace Union Representatives (Rappresentanze sindacaliaziendali) are often simply the chosen representatives of the union. Still, even in the strongly "dual-channel" systems, union members typically dominate councils (approximately 80 percent of German councilors are unionists), while the "union/council" formations in Southern Europe have a much smaller role in wage determination than "local unions" in the United States.

More important than the formal scope of permitted council activities is the depth of their power. The critical distinction is

TABLE 7
Works Councils in Europe

	Germany	Belgium	Denmark	Spain	France	Great Britain	Greece	Ireland	Italy	Luxembourg	Netherlands	Portugal
Works Councils												
Conditions of existence	5 workers	>100	>35 if firm or majority of workers want	>50	>50	none	Private sector: >20 if union; >50 if nonunion	none	>15	150	35	no size
Composition	elected	6-22 elected employer chairs	equal worker management	5+	3-15 elected employer chairs		3-7 workers	—	union delegates	6-16	no	3-11
Role												
information	yes	yes		yes	yes		yes				yes	yes
consultation	yes	yes			yes		yes				yes	yes
codetermination	yes			yes	yes				yes	yes		
social funds	yes			yes								
other												
negotiations									yes			
cooperation		yes	yes									
Meeting/Facilities	paid time	paid time/ month	paid time	15-40 hours			2 hours/ week		8 hours/ month	none	60 hrs/ year	40 hrs/ month
Health and Safety Committees												
Conditions of Existence	>50 workers (single rep if 20-50)	>50	>10 group >20 committee	>100	>50		>50 workers (single rep if 20-50)	20 workers	none	none	none	none

Source: Belgian Socialist Trade Union summary document.

between the council's information and consultation rights and its right to co-determination over select management decisions. Information and consultation rights are universal and effectively define what is meant by having a mandated "council." Works councils laws invariably obligate employers to disclose to the council information about major new investment plans, acquisition and product market strategies, planned reorganization of production, use of technology, and so on. And council laws invariably require employers to consult with the council on workplace and personnel issues, such as work reorganization, new technology acquisition, reductions or accretions to force, transfers of work, overtime, and health and safety.

Typical of the information and consultation requirements are the provisions of the 1971 Dutch Works Council Act (Wet op de Ondernemingsraden):

> Information: The employer must provide the council with all information which it may reasonably demand for accomplishing its tasks, more in particular, and at least once every year, with respect to the legal status of the firm, its financial and economic position, its long-term plans, and its social and personnel policies;
>
> Consultation: The employer must seek the council's advice with respect to decisions concerning a transfer of ownership of (parts of) the firm, merger, takeovers, plant or shop closure, major reduction, change or extension of activities, major changes in work organization, change in the location of production, the employment or lease of temporary staff, major investment, major capital loans, and assignments given to outside consultants or experts on any of the above issues. The council's advice is also needed on proposals concerning the dismissal and appointment of members of the executive board. The right of advice in matters of merger, takeovers and consultants does not apply when one of the firms involved is located outside the Netherlands.

Deeper rights of joint decision making are typically assigned councils in countries that limit the range of council powers. In Germany, the council enjoys information rights on financial matters and substantial changes in overall firm operation and information and consultation rights in matters of personnel planning and work reorganization. In addition, however, it has:

Co-determination Rights on Social Matters: For example, principles of remuneration and introduction of new payment methods, fixing of job and bonus rates and performance-related pay, allocation of working hours, regulation of overtime and short-time working, leave arrangements and vacation plans; the introduction and use of technical devices to monitor employees' performance.

Moreover, the council has "veto rights" on individual staff movements, including hiring, evaluation, transfer, and dismissal in many cases.

Finally, the rights accorded councils in different areas vary inversely with the importance of those areas to the firm. Even in co-determination systems like Germany's, the strength of councils lies in enforcement of state regulation and social agreements (the general contract of the "social partners" on wage regulation) and in personnel planning and assignment. Councils have little power near "the core of entrepreneurial control." German managers run German firms; works councils do not. Still, strong co-determination rights on personnel decisions provide workers with a tool to leverage employer acquiescence in other areas. An aggressive works council can use its right to veto the scheduling of vacations or overtime, for example, to gain additional compensation. And worker representation on the supervisory boards of companies effectively establishes the council as a power with which to contend throughout the enterprise.

Worker, Union, and Management Views of European Councils

What do workers and managers think of councils? To judge by participation in council elections and the scattered poll data that exist, workers strongly support mandated councils. Indeed, after several decades of experience, mandated representation within the workplace has become part of European political and business culture. Asking workers whether they dislike having councils in the workplace is akin to asking people if they'd like to give up their right to vote.[26] Indeed, there is some evidence that workers regard their councils more favorably than they do their unions. One survey of West German workers showed a larger proportion regarded works councils as "representing worker interests" and having "done a lot to help workers" than so viewed unions. Workers were more favorable to increasing the power of worker councils than the power of unions (Hobson and Dworkin 1986).

Union views of councils are more complicated. Councils endanger unions in at least two ways: councils may be "excessively" cooperative with management and may gain worker loyalty at the expense of unions. Having independent powers, councils can undermine global union projects through "wildcat cooperation." A union attempting to achieve employer consent to a solidaristic wage policy, for example, may be frustrated by employer-council alliances in firms wishing to opt out of that policy. And just as U.S. unions fear that worker involvement programs substitute for unions, European unions worry that councils may displace them as European labor relations decentralizes. At the same time, however, councils provide unions with a *de facto* reach into the enterprise otherwise lacking in most European systems. This, in turn, permits unions greater flexibility in responding to decentralization. The German case is exemplary. One reason German unions have maintained their density, encompassing wage policies and political power, is that councils densely occupied by union members give unions an institutional base with which to address issues that arise in decentralized settings. Similarly, although union membership fell sharply in the Netherlands in the 1980s, unions remained a potent force, since members dominate works councils. Sweden presents a contrasting case. A high degree of union centralization and weak nonunion worker voice inside the firm has meant that pressures for decentralization threaten the stability of encompassing arrangements. The absence of an effective second channel now compromises the integrity of the first.

The story in less determinately dual systems suggests at first blush greater problems for unions. In France, Spain, and other systems with weak unions, councils appear to substitute for unions. Still it is difficult to believe that union power in France would be significantly greater absent councils than with them, simply because the existing union structures were never robust enough to sustain themselves in face of decentralization pressures. And Spanish unions invariably win most council seats, so that the substitution of councils for unions may be one of form rather than substance. In France, Spain, and Italy, council presence within firms maintains a political presence for unions belied by their declining numbers. Falling membership is less harmful to unions in these countries than, say, in the U.S. As long as workers elect union representatives or slates to works councils, unions maintain a legitimate claim to speak for workers, despite declining numbers.

What about managers? To obtain management's perspective on European works councils, we interviewed top personnel managers at several U.S. and European multinationals in 1991-92. Though our sample is small and not statistically representative, the interviews were sufficiently one-sided on several points, which we have not seen disputed elsewhere, to give some confidence in the typicality of what we heard.[27] What we heard, overwhelmingly, was that while councils have costs (slowing management decision making, taking employee and manager time away from other work, etc.) and can malfunction, they have important positive effects which in general make them a net benefit to firms. More specifically, many of the pressures that lead U.S. managers to favor some tractable form of "employee involvement" also lead European managers to favor councils whether as an alternative or supplement to unions. Managers used to working in highly centralized systems applaud the flexibility that councils give the firm relative to centralized bodies or regulations. Managers widely report that councils facilitate communication with employees, increase employee commitment and force advanced planning in areas that require council consultation that improve management's own initiatives. Virtually all managers we interviewed saw councils as basically good and only one, with a badly functioning council, viewed its council as a drag on the firm.

Representative of the general view, the manager of a major automobile production facility for a U.S. multinational in Germany reported:

> There are three major advantages of councils. First, you're forced to consider in your decision-making process the effect on the employees in advance . . . This avoids costly mistakes. Second, works councils will in the final run support the company. They will take into account the pressing needs of the company more than a trade union can, on the outside. And third, works councils explain and defend certain decisions of the company toward the employees. Once decisions are made, they are easier to implement.

As this and other managers attest, works councils force industrial upgrading:

> They even pressure us to improve the training of the apprentices . . . For instance, we have been trying from

TABLE 8

Select Management Views of Works Councils

	Yes	No	Not reported or no opinion
Economic Effects			
Benefits			
Improve management by correcting errors or avoiding errors	9	0	2
Increase employee commitment to firm	7	0	4
Improve employee communication to management	7	0	4
Improve management communication to employees	7	0	4
Improve reliability/speed of implementation	5	1	5
Improves firm training efforts	2	1	8
Provide check on quality of middle management	3	0	8
Costs			
Slows management decision-making	7	0	4
Leverage assigned powers to gain in other areas	5	0	6
Misrepresent true preferences of employees	3	0	8
Take employees away from work	5	0	6
Net Costs/Benefits			
Overall, councils benefit the firm economically	7	0	4
Design Lessons			
Councils should be mandated/have secure legal basis	8	1	2
Should be supplemented by codetermination	2	2	7
Should have legally specified obligations as well as rights	3	0	8
Effects on Unions			
Councils substitute for unions	1	1	9
Council reduce union-management conflict	0	0	11

my area to improve the machinery in our apprentice shop.
And knowing the present situation [at our parent
company], these investments always got low priority and
were put aside, and then, on a certain occasion the works
council made a big fuss . . . We then decided "let's look at
that project again . . ." Then we released means to
improve the machinery in the apprentice shop. Without
the works council having made such a big fuss we
probably still would not do it.

They make suggestions for productivity improvements:

> In the press shop, the works council, having talked to the people there . . . made many concrete proposals . . . but they were always refused [by management]. And then, all of the sudden, three weeks ago [November], a working group by management came to the identical conclusions and we would not have been in this situation if we had followed their advice. The proposals are usually very simple. Making sure there are sufficient racks to put parts on as they come off the line; ensuring that a foreman is available to train new workers; movement of personnel to other press lines in order to compensate for a faster-moving press line whose parts are in higher demand. Things like that.

Along the way, they provide additional channels for management communication with employees:

> There was a quality problem discovered by an individual worker three-quarters of a years ago, put before foreman, presented to superintendent, mentioned to someone else, but nothing happened. Then, one day a council member mentioned it, top management went down to the floor, looked at it and it was immediately changed. There was a case some years ago where a manager had a problem that he could not change; he was so frustrated that he called the council and said, "Why don't you bring this up at the next meeting with top management." This is not uncommon.

And, of great interest to management, councils tend to be more enterprise-oriented than unions:

> [The parent company made] an agreement with the works council to introduce a flexible work-time system, around-the-clock operation through Saturday, starting again Sunday night. They were under tremendous pressure from the union not to do this, but let us go ahead. We couldn't have gotten that out of the union. Only in Japan I have seen an even more . . . definite identification with the company. Our works council people are not hostile to rationalization or automation. On the contrary, they ask us to automate, to modernize our machinery so that our operations can be competitive. They say, "We know that we lose jobs by this, but we agree that this is a good thing."

Finally, councils can, like unions, combine these functions to manage employee discontent during periods of punishing downsizing and other work force restructuring. Here is the role one council played, to the great satisfaction of management, in working through a major downsizing that involved closing one of two neighboring plants, while sharply increasing utilization rates at the plant that remained. As a result of council action, the company adopted an innovative shift schedule, involving three teams staffing two shifts (with longer hours per shift but fewer days per week and long breaks between work periods), rather than the more traditional three-team/three-shift approach to round-the-clock production that it is now recommending elsewhere.

> The works council was told of the closing plans, and a working committee was set up consisting of the three union representatives to the council, plus the two salaried councilors along with several managers. The work group developed various alternative solutions. Then meetings were held in small groups of twenty-five to inform every employee in the plant about the problem, to describe potential solutions including a three-shift proposal, and to request input for other alternatives. A video of the company president was shown and a works council member was on hand to answer questions. The company hired 25 extras so it could make different groups available. These meetings resulted in stacks and stacks of alternatives which the working group narrowed down to 20. These were brought to the negotiating group—local union delegates, provincial officials, and company industrial relations and personnel managers—two were selected to put to the employees for a vote: a three-shift system and the three-team/two-shift proposal that was suggested by an hourly worker in the hard body trim section. The company felt that the two systems were equal in terms of cost and productivity. Initially a number of the council delegates felt that ten-hour shifts were too long. So a group of 30, including 12 works council members, visited [workers in a plant in another country that had engaged in a similar experiment] and talked to people on the floor about whether they were able to work [the longer shift]. Then the two were put to an employee vote, and 50 percent voted for the three-team/two-shift system, with 26 percent

against. In a recent referendum on this decision, 65 percent of the workers voted to continue with the current system. None of this would have been possible without the council. It could have all been much much worse than it was.

What these and other examples indicate is widely accepted as obvious in European managerial circles. Whether management favors or disfavors the formation of councils (it generally did not initially want councils and resists them today on a European-wide basis), managements are quite able to work within, and in some measure come to value, the constraints on managerial autonomy that they impose.

Japanese Experience

While Japan does not have mandated works councils, it does have company unions and "joint consultation committees" that the Ministry of Labor recommends companies institute. At one stage western observers viewed Japanese company unions as tools of the enterprise rather than legitimate representative of workers, but this appears to have been an erroneous reading. Koike (1988) provides considerable evidence that Japanese unions operate much like German works councils, and consultation committees fit in the same mold. Shirai (1983, 120) also regards the Japanese company unions as functionally comparable to works councils.

While union density has declined in Japan in recent years (see Table 1 and Figure 2), consultation committees have become, if anything, more prevalent. In 1984, 72 percent of establishments with over 100 employees had committees; 88 percent of unionized establishments had them and 40 percent of nonunion establishments (Morishima 1991a; 1991b). Even in unionized establishments, joint consultation is more common than U.S.-style grievance procedures (Hashimoto 1990).

Japanese consultation committees differ from European works councils in two ways: they are not legally mandated, and in union settings, "the distinction between collective bargaining and workers' consultation has never been very clear" (Hanami 1987, 205-6). The committees deal with the spectrum of issues that councils deal with in Europe: personnel policies, social welfare spending by firms, new technologies, plant closing, health and safety. They do not negotiate over wages, and issues under discussion by the committees are viewed as "nonstrike" issues (though disagreement could produce a strike). Over 80 percent of unions give "expediting communication" and "promotion of cooperative relations" as the prime purpose of the committees. Many receive confidential business and financial information as part of joint consultation, and only 3 percent of unions complain about the nature of information sharing (Morishima 1991a, 1991b).

Studies by Morishima (1991a, 1991b) on the effect of joint consultation and resultant information sharing on collective bargaining and enterprise performance indicate that at least in union settings joint consultation has the type of efficiency gains we would expect from well-functioning works councils. In enterprises where consultation is stronger, labor costs increase less rapidly and productivity and profitability is better than in enterprises where consultation is weaker. In addition, wage settlements appear to be moderated by consultation—in marked contrast to the situation Kleiner and Bouillon (1988) find for information sharing in union and nonunion U.S. firms. The apparently different effects of information sharing through Japan's joint consultation committees and in U.S. enterprises highlights the importance of external labor relations systems on how institutions operate within the firm—a point we stress throughout this essay. Unfortunately, Morishima's evidence does not relate to the operation of joint consultation in nonunion firms, which is especially germane to our analysis.

Conclusion

Many OECD countries legally mandate or institute with informal government support/union power within-firm institutions for employee representation. The general consensus is that while these systems are imperfect, they work reasonably well in the European or Japanese labor relations systems. The 1984 report of the Belgian tripartite National Labor Council gives a reasonable summary of European thinking: "Both sides of industry admit that after 30 years' experience, works councils have a positive track record" (Monat and Sarfati 1986, 191).

U.S. Experience with Councils, Shop Committees, and Company Unions

The U.S. has never mandated nonunion collective worker representation, but American firms have "experimented" at various times with institutions that give elected nonunion employee committees a role in firm governance. Called "employee representation plans," "shop committees," or "company unions" (depending largely on the sympathy of the observer), these organizations grew in periods when employers worried about finding tractable forms of employee voice to forestall unionization or to reduce labor market strife that threatened war time production or, most recently, when employers sought to involve workers in responding to international competition. The U.S. experience is valuable because it shows how representation institutions function in a decentralized labor market absent legal or other external mandating.

Early U.S. Experience

U.S. shop committees date back to 1833, and the giant cigar-maker Straiton & Storm developed an elaborate employee representation scheme, including independent arbitration for the resolution of employee-manager disputes in the late 1870s (Montgomery 1987, 350; Hogler and Grenier 1992). The first great wave of employer representation plans in the U.S., however, came during World War I. Introduced to curb wartime strikes (they typically involved explicit renunciation of the strike weapon), and with an eye to inoculating the public against communist agitation, "works councils" or "shop committees" were promoted by various wartime authorities. From virtually zero in 1917, their number grew spectacularly. By 1919 the National Industrial Conference Board (NICB) reported 225 plans covering half a million employees, and by 1922, 725 plans operated throughout the country. Employers reported decreased threats of unionization, lower turnout, and reduced grievances, as obvious benefits of the plans. With the exception of a small number of plans that provided more or less extensive participation rights, including representation in plant committees, representation on boards of directors, and participation in profits and stock ownership or collective bargaining,[28] however, most of these plans gave workers no real power in decision making.[29]

After the war, some large firms continued their company unions and welfare programs. Many of those who introduced shop committees under pressure from the NLB, however, dropped them (NICB 1919, 1922). In the mid-1920s, popularization of the "American Plan" open-shop drive to prevent unionization led many smaller firms to introduce representation plans. Over 1919-1928, total membership in employer-initiated representation schemes grew from 0.4 to 1.5 million. Along with declining union membership during the 1920s, this dramatically shifted the relative strength of the two representation forms. In 1919, plan membership equalled only 10 percent of union membership; by 1928, the ratio was 45 percent (Millis and Montgomery 1945, 837).

With the coming of the Great Depression, representation plans ebbed again: membership fell to 1.3 million over 1928-1932. But the National Industrial Recovery Act (NIRA) of 1933, which brought about a marked growth in trade union activity and organization, also led to a resurgence in company unions. The NIRA forbid employers from forcing employees to join company unions, but not from encouraging the formation of such bodies (an encouragement that was often tantamount to force). With increased threats of union organizing, the company union movement again grew sharply. NICB and BLS data indicate that, by 1935, over 3100 companies with 2.6 million employees had some significant percentage of their employees covered by representation plans, of which two-thirds had been established since 1933 (Wilcock 1957). The ratio of representation plan membership to trade union membership surged to 60 percent (Millis and Montgomery 1945, 841). In some sectors coverage was even more widespread. For example, after passage of the NRA, most basic steel companies established employee representation plans, which spread to cover from 90 to 95 percent of the industry work force (Bernstein 1970). This, however, was the highpoint for representation plans. In the late 1930s the massive organizing drives of the CIO, aided by prohibition on employer "encouragement" of worker representation in Section 8(2) of the National Labor Relations Act, effectively killed most of them.

During World War II, the government again promoted cooperative workplace relations, this time the form of joint labor-management committees, chiefly in union shops. These flared during the war, growing to cover some 7,000,000 workers, but faded immediately thereafter (de Schweinitz 1949). In the early postwar period, again chiefly in the organized portion of the work force, scattered efforts were made to formalize labor-management cooperation. The best known of these were the Scanlon, Rucker, and other schemes aimed at increasing employee productivity through profit sharing and bonuses. Outside a few specific sites, however, these efforts never caught on the union sector; economy-wide, their appeal was also limited (Derber 1970, 478-482).[30] One survey found that no company with more than 1,000 employees and no establishment with more than 5,000 employees enjoyed an actively cooperative relationship with its union. With very rare exceptions, the "cooperative" strategy was limited to medium-sized, closely held firms, or to marginal companies; even here, it essentially disappeared in the late 1950s (Harris 1982, 195).[31]

As the prime historic case of employer-initiated works councils operating in a largely nonunion decentralized labor market, the U.S. experience in the 1920s to 1950s provides valuable insight into the potential for councils in such a setting. It shows, first, that employer-initiated councils were neither a long-lived stable institution nor one that was extended to the majority of the work force. Even at its peak the council movement covered only a minority of workers, largely in big firms, and the peak came under threat of outside unionization. Still, this minority was at times above the modest private-sector unionization rates of the early 1990s. Second, the NICB reports (1919, 1922) and historical investigation (Jacoby 1989; Jacoby and Verma 1992; Nelson 1993) of the operation of councils shows considerable diversity. In many cases, company unions were the sham they have come to be widely viewed, but in some cases they offered significant and meaningful means of worker representation. Taking the NICB studies as valid, absent a guarantee of hard worker rights to such things, or unionism or its immediate threat, "successful" worker representation depended on management commitment—as evidenced in regular meetings, education, and, ideally, concrete payoffs to workers through, for example, profit-sharing (collective dividend) systems (NICB 1922, Report 50). Not contemplating an actual extension of hard worker rights within the firm, the NICB concluded that "where management is not thoroughly sold to the idea . . . a Works Council should not be formed" (NICB 1922, Report 50, 10).

Recent U.S. Experience

Renewed interest in employee participation began building in the early 1970s. Focused on "Quality of Worklife" (QWL) programs, it was initially motivated by concerns about worker alienation (the "blue-collar blues"), which many viewed as responsible for increased militance by assembly line workers. The

National Commission on Productivity and Quality of Working Life and the Ford Foundation sponsored a number of QWL experiments in the early 1970s in both union and nonunion plants. The most widely known included the Rushton Mining Company, General Motors (GM) Tarrytown plant, which prior to the QWL program had one of the poorest labor relations and production records of all GM plants but within a few years of QWL adoption became one of the company's best performing assembly plants. But implementation of QWL programs was never widespread, and most of the most visible experiments faded by the late 1970s—when government funding stopped (Kochan, Katz, and Mower 1984, 6-7).

In the 1980s driven by competitive pressures and management recognition of the need to enlist employee energies to meet them, QWL programs enjoyed a resurgence. As noted, some 80 percent of the top 1,000 firms in the U.S. reported having employee participation or employee involvement programs, and many smaller firms experimented with one or another form of employee involvement. The 1980s programs come under various names[32]—QWL committees, quality circles, autonomous work teams, gainsharing and employee stock ownership plans (ESOPs)—and varied considerably in structure, representativeness, scope of issues, substantive decision-making power, and links to other changes in work organization. Cutcher-Gershenfeld (1987) estimates that 10 to 15 percent of all American organizations had worker participation programs in the 1980s, covering about 20 percent of the work force. Cooke (1990) estimates that 40 to 50 percent of the unionized sector is involved with quality circles, quality of worklife programs, or some other form of employee involvement; of these, between one-third and two-thirds are jointly administered. About one-third of the unionized sector has committee-based participation with health and safety being the most common focus.

Studies of these experiments confirm the 1920s experience. The economic effects of worker involvement are most likely to be positive when workers are empowered in decision making and receive concrete payoffs to cooperation (Blinder 1990). In unionized settings, where worker power exists independent of management, the evidence shows the greatest gains from cooperation (Eaton and Voos 1992; Kelley and Harrison 1992). In nonunionized settings, where workers have no reserved rights, the performance and stability of the programs depends on management attitudes, which vary widely across firms and over time and which are subject to an important core ambivalence: even where managers recognize "empowerment" as necessary to productivity gains, they are reluctant to relinquish discretion and control. Much more is needed to guarantee effective empowerment than management will provide on its own.

Conclusion: Toward a New Worker Representation System

That European works council and Japanese company unionism and consultation committees "work" does not imply that the United States could resolve its representation gap by importing these institutions. European councils are part of a labor relations system with industry or national collective bargaining that takes wages out of the purview of councils, where workers receive extensive mandatory benefits, and where there is little union presence/threat of strikes at local workplaces. Japanese joint consultation committees and discussion are part of the distinct operation of Japanese enterprises. In the U.S. environment, these institutions would operate differently. Similarly, management-initiated council-type institutions or company unions that have worked on occasion in the U.S. environment provides only crude guidance to what might work in general. The management attitudes and commitment to worker representation needed for success are not readily transportable from the few successes to other firms. Still, this foreign experience, joined with the economic analysis with which we began, offers some important design lessons for improving intrafirm representation in the U.S.

Elements of Design

At the outset, it is critical to recognize that different representation functions can be performed by different sorts of institutions. Our comparative review showed that foreign systems offer workers an avenue for political advancement and wage compensation through institutions external to the firm and separate mechanisms of voice within firms on concerns best addressed on a local level. The latter, in addition to performing important "voice" functions, supplement state regulatory efforts and private bargains on wages that are an outcome of the first channel. The implication is that a comprehensive redesign of the U.S. system should say something about the role of labor in the political system and market or institutional modes of wage setting across firms as well as of intrafirm representation issues. Although we recognize the problem of trying to assess the effects of reforms in one area of labor relations by itself, we nonetheless confine ourselves to considering what a successful new intrafirm representation system might look like in the U.S.

We draw three general lessons from our comparative analysis. First, council-like institutions of intrafirm representation work best when their powers are "real"—capable of enforcement and enjoying a presumption of permanence—and guaranteed by the state. That councils need real powers follows from all that we have said and seen about the role that power plays in producing efficiency effects. If councils have no bite, they have no salutary effect. That powers should be guaranteed by the state follows from any realistic analysis of incentives facing competing sources of council authorization, namely employers or unions. Employers rarely unilaterally give more worker power than is useful to the firm in a given time period, with the result that few establish councils and those that do keep them on short tether; unions are reluctant to grant a potentially competing institution of workplace representation. Councils need an independent legal basis.

Second, the powers of councils need to be clear and definite— "limited" in the constitution sense. Clarity and limits avoid unnecessary competition and confusion with other institutional sources of workplace power, which facilitates interaction with those other sources. More generally, clarity is needed for efficiency. Rights to information, consultation, action in specific worker protection areas, joint decision making on training, or anything else, are property rights. And the most efficient regime of property rights is one which is clear (Coase 1960).

Third, whatever powers are assigned to councils, they should not include powers to engage in wage bargaining. We regard decentralized wage bargaining by councils as undesirable because it would augment tendencies in the U.S. job market toward wage segmentation achieved through "monopoly union" sharing in firm- or industry-specific rents. As in Western Europe, councils should be a device to enable labor and management to increase enterprise surplus, not to fight over their respective shares, and this requires a separation of these two activities.[33] The gains to workers should come through profit sharing or related mechanisms, through greater job security and promotions as the firm does better and so on, and not through wage bargaining.

Elements of Reform

Within these broad principles of design, would it be feasible[34] and desirable to graft council-type institutions onto our present labor relations scheme? Yes, we think it would. U.S. councils might be called "Employee Participation Committees" (EPCs).[35] They could be granted general information and consultation rights on a par with those enjoyed by councils throughout Europe and be used to help with certain regulatory tasks, for example occupational safety and health or training.[36] Membership in these committees should be determined by workers, and the committees themselves should be terminable only at worker discretion. Combined with their independent legal basis, this last provision would remove, in nonunion settings, the most obvious difficulties of reconciling their operation with the "company union" bar of Section 8(a)(2) of the LMRA.[37] In unionized settings, the functions and powers of councils would simply be assumed by the certified bargaining representative.

Should such councils be mandated? A good case can be made that they should, as in Western Europe. But a case can also be made on efficiency grounds for national encouragement of their voluntary formation. On net we believe that, outside specific regulatory programs with clearly defined aims (e.g., the OSHA or training cases), EPCs should not be generally mandated until they prove their worth in the American context. This said, government encouragement of EPC diffusion during a trial period should be vigorous. The government should consider making EPCs a condition for firms receiving special benefits, such as continued tax breaks on ESOPs (Freeman 1991), new tax breaks on training (Kochan and Osterman 1991), or relief from regulatory reporting or inspection burdens. Through such actions, government would send employers the message that it favors independent forms of worker voice and will smooth employer adoption of them.

Moreover, while business should be encouraged to form EPCs, workers should also be able to trigger their formation. In mandatory council systems, this trigger is set extremely low; essentially any demonstration of worker interest in forming a council suffices.

During the trial period we recommend here, however, we favor a more demanding trigger mechanism: "card check" certification (i.e., the use of authorization cards signed by employees) by a substantial proportion of employees in a unit defined broadly to include white-collar as well as blue-collar workers. Depending on the way the card check procedure operated, the definition of the unit, the length of time that cards were valid and other details, we could envisage a plurality of 40 percent or so of workers desiring a council serving as the legal trigger.[38]

We believe that EPCs can be justified on their own terms for all the reasons already given for justifying councils—greater efficiency within firms, greater worker representation, greater regulatory effectiveness. Inevitably, however, their introduction to the American system will be disruptive to both management and unions and resisted for that reason. Moreover, European experience shows that councils work best when they draw support from other worker organizations, preeminently unions, in exercising their legal rights. Finally, from our review of the "representation gap" in the U.S. and managerial innovations with management-supported worker participation committees, we doubt that councils per se will meet the diversity of forms of representation desired by American workers and managers. These considerations lead us to recommend a simple package of reform in existing labor law to accompany the introduction of councils.

Broadly described, this package would trade enhanced organization rights under Section 7 of the LMRA for modification of Section 8(a)(2)'s restriction on company unions. The former would permit workers, again, to join or form unions when they want to. The latter would permit managers seriously interested in employee "empowerment" to pursue advanced participation schemes.

For workers and unions, specifically, we favor strengthening penalties for employer unfair labor practices; the reinstitution of card check certification for choosing bargaining representatives;[39] clarification of existing law to permit "minority union" membership and activity (Summers 1990; Rogers and Wooton, 1992), in contexts where no majority union bargaining representative has been chosen;[40] and an extension of rights to union membership to supervisory employees. For managers, we favor a modification of 8(a)(2) to permit employer involvement in supporting nonunion forms of worker participation. The "company union" bar—the core and legitimate purpose of which is to prohibit management from choosing those workers who will represent others[41]—has the unhappy consequence of also barring entirely legitimate nonunion employer attempts to promote advanced schemes of worker participation and "empowerment."[42] This overbreadth should be corrected. Even with a strengthening of worker rights to form unions, the vast majority of American employees are not going to join AFL-CIO unions anytime in the foreseeable future. If their employers feel that providing them with greater representation or participation rights is good for the enterprise, they should be allowed to do so.

The result of these reforms would be to open up a genuine market in appropriate form of worker representation, while effectively shifting national policy toward a presumption of some form of employee voice. Competitors in this market would include plans provided by employers and plans devised by workers (sometimes joined by a majority of their colleagues and sometimes not). With the possibility of exit from oppressive or otherwise unsatisfactory schemes assured, workers would be sovereign "consumers" of representation services. The schemes judged by the market to be best—councils, minority unions, traditional unions, employer-sponsored participation plans—would dominate. Respectful of the design lessons of comparative experience, this package would effectively close the intrafirm representation gap in the United States.[43]

Summary

The arguments in this paper can be summarized briefly.

● Modern economic analysis and empirical evidence suggest that employee representation in firms can be socially beneficial in terms of productivity and regulation. Moreover, even if employee representation was neutral, or (contrary to extant evidence) modestly costly, democratic principles argue for their establishment as part of democratic life.

● Survey evidence shows that American workers would like greater collective voice at their workplace. Some managements and business experts also perceive the need for greater representation, while unions are increasingly willing to support nonunion forms of collective voice.

● Most European countries and Japan have systems of collective intrafirm worker representation that work reasonably well.

● To close the intrafirm representation gap in the U.S., the nation should design a new system of intrafirm worker representation informed by this foreign experience and America's historical experience with employer-initiated councils. Strong encouragement of works council-like structures, with information and consultation rights and some regulatory responsibilities, is recommended. So too is a strengthening of the right to organize or join a union and correlate relaxation of restrictions on management support for nonunion forms of worker participation.

Acknowledgments

Our thanks to Barbara Wootton, Stephanie Luce, and Stephen Hinds for research assistance and to Sarah Fox, Wolfgang Streeck, and the editors for comments on a previous draft. This work was supported in part by grants from the Ford Foundation and the Graduate School of the University of Wisconsin-Madison.

Endnotes

[1] At current rates of new organizing this would describe a new equilibrium for private-sector density. There is, however, no reason to assume current organizing efforts will be sustained by a substantially reduced membership. In 1992 the AFL-CIO estimated that it would lose an additional 500,000 members (DLR 1992), or approximately 5 percent of its dues-paying base. A continuation of that trend suggests a roughly 40 percent reduction in membership by the end of the decade. The costs of recruiting new members through NLRB elections has also increased. Chaison and Dhavale (1990) estimate that maintenance of current density levels will require unions to make, over and above current organizing budgets, an expenditure of $300 million annually. With rising new-member costs, a shrinking base, and essentially fixed costs for servicing existing members, the 5 percent figure could be simply another point on the line of continuing decline. On the other hand, innovative techniques of organizing, particularly outside NLRB elections, and the shrinkage of unionization to its most supportive core groups, could produce a new equilibrium above the 5 percent forecast. In either case, however, we see no signs of a "burst" of unionization to an equilibrium above current rates of density.

[2] Firm experiments with Quality of Work Life (QWL) and Total Quality Management (TQM) programs, discussed later, suggest that managers recognize this link but still have problems developing successful participation schemes. Despite the widespread finding that worker participation is key to the success of ESOPs, for example, the GAO (1986) estimates that only one in four ESOP programs includes greater employee input into decision making.

[3] In Germany, to take a prominent example, the effect of intrafirm representation is to force management to train more broadly than would otherwise be the case. Since pervasive council representation effectively diffuses this effect across firms, however, no firm is uniquely disadvantaged with regard German competitors by training more workers or more broadly than it would otherwise choose. And the economy as a whole benefits from the resulting effort.

[4] Alternatively, of course, management might be indulging a "taste" for domination or making a political calculation that it needs to resist such cooperation in order to preserve its superordinate position. But we abstract from such matters here.

[5] Indeed, given that European countries mandate works councils, it is difficult to "prove" with econometric evidence that they have their claimed positive effects. The problem is that there is no valid natural experiment allowing researchers to compare firms with councils and those without. Firms and workers who choose not to have mandated councils are a very selective group rather than a random sample whose performance could be compared to those of others. The result is that comparisons of such firms with those having councils yields inconclusive statistically uncertain results. The evidence that firms with more participatory structures or with profit sharing in the U.S. and those with stronger joint consultation committees in Japan have positive productivity effects is, at the minimum, consistent with the notion that forms corporate governance that give workers council-like powers or incentives have positive effects on economic outcomes.

[6] The resulting regulatory failure is evident in low and uneven compliance with a range of statutory protections—from child labor laws to occupational safety and health (GAO 1990, 1991).

[7] This estimate includes the costs of deaths, injuries, and occupationally related disease. Deaths alone (calculated on a 7,000/yr. basis) are estimated to cost about $40 billion (Moore and Vicusi 1990) and workplace injuries more than $80 billion (Hensler et al. 1991).

[8] While this could be explained by more complete reporting, there is no evidence of such.

[9] This comparison reflects adjustments for underreporting, applicable both to the U.S. and Japan by the National Safety and Work Institute.

[10] This comparison uses the same ILO series, but without adjustment for underreporting. It shows a 67 percent decline in the rate of workplace fatalities in Japan over 1981-89, as compared to a 29 percent decline in the United States (ILO 1991).

[11] For overviews of Europe, see Bagnara et al. (1985) and Gustavsen and Hunnius (1981); for a review of Japan, see Wokutch (1992); for a report on Ontario, the most developed of the Canadian cases, see ACOHOS (1986).

[12] Note that we recommend this as "supplementary" to state inspection efforts. An independent state presence needs to be maintained to guard against labor-management collusion on regulatory enforcement harmful to society (e.g., a worker agreement to ignore employer pollution, that might increase job security or permit higher wages).

[13] This is a generalization. Elster's (1986) argument for workplace democracy on "self-realization" grounds, for example, falls into neither category. See Cohen (1989) for a useful inventory of existing arguments.

[14] This poll is reviewed extensively below, in our discussion of the U.S. representation gap.

[15] The Gallup survey was a national home survey of 1029 persons; the Fingerhut/Powers poll a national phone survey of 778.

[16] The data also confirm familiar criticisms of national unions as relatively distant organizations to which members feel little attachment. Only 3 percent of Fingerhut respondents could name the current president of the AFL-CIO, for example; only 38 percent of union members could name their own national president. Still, 76 percent in the Fingerhut poll reported that they were "proud to be a union member."

[17] These are the 1977 Quality of Employment Survey (Quinn and Staines 1979), a Louis Harris survey done for the AFL-CIO in 1984 (Louis Harris and Associates

1984), the 1991 General Social Survey (Davis and Smith 1991), and Farber and Krueger's own survey, reported in Farber and Krueger (1992).

[18] We take the employed wage and salary work force to be 103 million (its 1991 level) and union membership to be about 16 million (16.5 in 1991, but falling fast), yielding an employed nonunion work force of 87 million. In what follows, we will round this last number up to 90 million.

[19] Given the chilling effect of anticipated employer reprisal on responses, it is difficult to determine what the demand for unionization might be in a system that reduced worker fears. One way surveys might be able to determine the "true" demand for unionism would be to ask the question "If your employer was neutral on unionization, would you support a union/vote for a union at your workplace?" Or, surveys could ask "Given the possible response of your employer, would you support a union/vote for a union at your workplace?" and list a set of possible employer responses.

[20] Note, however, that this "ideal" is not universally shared even among those firms reasonably classed as "lean" producers. Some (approximating the ideal referenced in the text) combine high wages, high capitalization, and extensive training with "advanced" efforts in work organization, quality assurance, and inventory and logistics. Others, typically operating as niche suppliers to cost-pressed original equipment manufacturers, exhibit only the latter. And still others combine reasonable wages with severe limitations on worker autonomy. An important problem in American industry at present is that the second sort of lean producer (in particularly, the low-wage one) is far more common than the first. Arguments for the potential utility of workplace representation need explicitly to recognize this; they will carry more weight with the former class of firms than the latter.

[21] This might be compared to Burawoy's (1979) characterization of the work process under more traditional mass production. Burawoy emphasizes the local autonomy and choice workers enjoy and commonly use to preserve their identity through acts of opposition, within very severe restraints. Under the scheme described in the text, the effective price of loosened constraints is the end of such "games."

[22] Given this experience, the consensus view of unions is that management enthusiasm for management-led employee-participation programs cannot be explained on productivity grounds or on the grounds that unions are impossible to work with, but rather is explained by management interest in capturing a disproportionate share of productivity gains, retaining disproportionate discretion in the workplace, or deceiving employees into thinking that independent worker representation is unnecessary.

[23] Pattern bargaining (the copying of a limited set of key bargains such as steel or autos in many other parts of unionized manufacturing) and spillovers of union wage and benefit gains to nonunion workers due to the threat of unionization produced some implicit institutional coordination in U.S. wage setting. While even at its peak pattern bargaining dominated only a few unionized sectors, some experts believed that patterns spread informally to white-collar workers in unionized firms and as nonunion firms raised blue-collar pay to forestall unionization to dominate the overall labor market (Bok and Dunlop 1970).

[24] Freeman (1991) and Card (1991) find that declining unionization accounts for one-fifth of the increased variance in male wages over 1973-87. Lemieux (forthcoming) attributes 40 percent of the greater inequality in wages in the U.S. than in Canada to the difference in the rate of unionization.

[25] This section draws on the Works Councils Project, directed by Joel Rogers and Wolfgang Streeck for the National Bureau of Economic Research. The project considered the operation of councils or other mandated forms of plant-based worker representation alternative to unions in France, Germany, Hungary, Italy, the Netherlands, Poland, Spain, Sweden, the EC, and the U.S. and Canada.

[26] This does not mean that workers in countries with councils will report themselves as being more satisfied with their jobs. U.S. evidence suggests that "voice" makes workers more likely to express criticism of their situation than those without voice, so that the effect of councils on satisfaction would depend on whether they improved working life more than they increased democratic criticism.

[27] For instance, Kirsten Wever's (1991) interviews with German managers, conducted at roughly the same time as ours, give a picture of German management's view of councils that is similar to ours.

[28] Brandes (1976, 131-132) notes that company unions had some success in wage and hour negotiations at both Kimberly Clarke and the Colorado Fueland Iron Company and developed wage scales at Standard Oil of New Jersey.

[29] These included Filene's, Dutchess Bleacheries, Boston Consolidated Gas, Louisville Railroads, Columbia Conserve Company, Philadelphia Rapid Transit, Dennison, and Nash (see Derber 1970, 267-268).

[30] Harris (1982, 138-139) also describes efforts at "progressive" firms, notably U.S. Rubber and General Electric, that were allied with the Committee for Economic Development and the National Planning Association, two industry associations that encouraged labor-management cooperation to raise productivity through labor-management cooperation.

[31] See Nelson (1989) for an analysis of the historic roots of divergent managerial strategies in the rubber industry.

[32] See Eaton and Voos (1992, 208-210) for a comprehensive glossary of terms used to describe contemporary innovations in employee participation and work organization.

[33] The contrast with traditional collective bargaining may be controversial in relying too much on a characterization of the latter as concerned only with dividing the economic pie rather than expanding it. We recognize that such division is not the only function of collective bargaining, much of which is concerned with non-material benefits (e.g., rules on notice and fair treatment), with transfers among workers (e.g., "solidarity" bargaining), and with the appropriate form material gains should take (e.g., wages versus benefits). Still, determining the worker share of the production surplus is the key function of collective bargaining and the one which conditions performance of most others.

[34] We abstract here from questions about political feasibility; our question only goes to the institutional logic and workings of a system including councils. In effect we are asking, "Given all that is different about the U.S., and given the context of existing institutions, could councils even work here?"

[35] This is the perfectly sensible name suggested by Weiler (1990), whose suggestions track our own.

[36] On occupational safety and health, see Rees (1988) and GAO (1992). For a proposal on training, see Kochan and Osterman (1991).

[37] Section 8(a)(2) of the LMRA makes it unlawful for an employer to "dominate or interfere with the formation or administration of any labor organization or contribute financial or other support to it." Deliberately, "labor organization" is elsewhere defined broadly to include not only labor unions, but "any organization of any kind or any agency or employee representation committee or plan" that features (a) employee participation, (b) the representation of some employees by others, in (c) dealings with the employer regarding (d) one or more of six traditional subjects of collective bargaining: grievances, labor disputes, wages, rates of pay, hours of employment, or conditions of work.

[38] The requirement that the substantial support also represent a plurality opinion (i.e., one that is numerically dominant over alternatives, if not an absolute majority) is meant simply to avoid a situation in which a council is formed over the objection

of a majority of the workers. Satisfying this condition, while keeping the trigger below an absolute majority threshold, would clearly require some way of determining the views (neutral, opposed) of those not actively supporting council formation. Just how to make this determination is one of many important institutional details we abstract from here.

[39] In some provinces of Canada, 55 percent is required for a card check to certify a bargaining representative. Whether a simple majority or this (or some other) supermajority rule is desirable depends on the specific rules governing card checks: whether people have opportunity to change their minds, the length of time the cards are valid, and so on. The basic design point is that (abstracting from the opportunity costs associated with the decision) the costs to workers of expressing and realizing a preference for unionization should be sharply reduced; if a majority of workers in fact want unionization, they should be allowed to have it.

[40] A requirement of "meet and confer" might be triggered by minority union membership reaching say 20 to 30 percent of a bargaining unit.

[41] This was the issue in the very first case decided by the National Labor Relations Board, *Pennsylvania Greyhound Lines*, 1 NLRB 1 (1935), enfd. denied in part 91 F.2d 178 (3d Cir. 1937), revd. 303 U.S. 261 (1938). As the Greyhound manager in charge of the company union challenged there summarized management's goals:

> [I]t is to our interest to pick our employees to serve on the committee who will work for the interest of the company and will not be radical. This plan of representation should work out very well providing the proper men are selected, and considerable thought should be given to the men placed on this responsible Committee.

Cited in *Electromation Inc.*, 309 NLRB 163 (1992).

[42] For example, an employer that sets out the purposes and powers of a committee making decisions concerning the terms and conditions of employment (e.g., on health and safety), subsidizes that committee, appoints some of its managers to it, and then permits workers free choice in selecting their representatives to it would likely be in violation of 8(a)(2), even though what we regard as the core offense 8(a)(2) seeks to remedy—preventing managers from telling workers which other workers would represent them—would not have been committed.

[43] A more complete argument for the proposed system is provided in Freeman and Rogers (1993).

References

ACOHOS (Advisory Council on Occupational Health and Occupational Safety). 1986. *Eighth Annual Report, April 1, 1985 to March 31, 1986*. Vol. 2. Toronto: ACOHOS.

Addison, John T., and Pedro Portugal. 1987. "The Effect of Advance Notification of Plant Closings on Unemployment." *Industrial and Labor Relations Review* 41, no. 1, pp. 3-16.

————. 1992. "Advance Notice of Unemployment: New Evidence from the 1988 Displaced Worker Survey." *Industrial and Labor Relations Review* 45, no. 4, pp. 645-664.

AFL-CIO (American Federation of Labor-Congress of Industrial Organizations), 1984. Louis Harris and Associates survey.

Aoki, Masahiko. 1988. *Information, Incentives, and Bargaining in the Japanese Economy*. New York: Cambridge University Press.

————. 1990. "Toward an Economic Model of the Japanese Firm." *Journal of Economic Literature* 28, no. 1, pp. 1-27.

Bagnara, Sabastiano, Raffaello Misiti, and Helmut Wintersberger, eds. 1985. *Work and Health in the 1980s: Experiences of Direct Workers' Participation in Occupational Health*. Berlin: Edition Sigma.

Bardach, Eugene, and Rogert Kagan. 1982. *Going By The Book*. Philadelphia: Temple University Press.
Bernstein, Harry. 1991. "Southern California Job Market; Worker Participation Survives Early Woes." *Los Angeles Times*, September 16, p. 15.
Bernstein, Irving. 1960. *The Lean Years: A History of the American Worker, 1920-1933*. Boston: Houghton Mifflin Company.
————. 1970. *The Turbulent Years: A History of the American Worker, 1933-1945*. Boston: Houghton Mifflin Company.
Blasi, Joseph R. 1988. *Employee Ownership: Revolution or Ripoff?* Cambridge, MA: Ballinger.
Blinder, Alan S., ed. 1990. *Paying for Productivity: A Look at the Evidence*. Washington, DC: Brookings Institution.
Bloom, Steven. 1986. "Employee Ownership and Firm Performance." Department of Economics, Harvard University. Unpublished Ph.D. dissertation.
BLS (Bureau of Labor Statistics). 1992. "Employed Wage and Salary Workers by Occupation, Industry, and Union Affiliation." *Employment and Earnings* 40, no. 1, p. 239.
Bok, Derek C., and John T. Dunlop. 1970. *Labor and the American Community*. New York: Simon & Schuster.
Brandes, Stuart. 1976. *American Welfare Capitalism*. Chicago: University of Chicago Press.
Brown, Bernard E. 1989. "Worker Democracy in Socialist France." City University of New York: Center for Labor-Management Policy Studies. Occasional Paper No. 7.
Bryce, George K., and Pran Manga. 1985. "The Effectiveness of Health and Safety Committees." *Relations Industrielles* 40, no. 2, pp. 257-282.
Burawoy, Michael. 1979. *Manufacturing Consent: Changes in the Labor Process Under Monopoly Capitalism*. Chicago: University of Chicago Press.
Card, David. 1991. "The Effect of Unions on the Distribution of Wages: Redistribution or Relabelling?" Princeton University: Department of Economics. Mimeo.
Chaison, Gary N., and Dileep G. Dhavale. 1990. "A Note on the Severity of the Decline in Union Organizing Activity." *Industrial and Labor Relations Review* 43, no. 4, pp. 366-373.
Coase, Ronald J. 1960. "The Problem of Social Cost." *The Journal of Law and Economics* 3, pp. 1-44.
Cohen, Joshua. 1989. "The Economic Basis of Deliberative Democracy." *Social Philosophy and Policy* 6, no. 2, pp. 25-50.
Cohen, Joshua, and Joel Rogers. 1992. "Secondary Associations and Democratic Governance." *Politics and Society* 20, no. 4, pp. 393-472.
————. 1983. *On Democracy*. New York: Penguin.
Cole, Robert E. 1979. *Work, Mobility, and Participation: A Comparative Study of American and Japanese Industry*. Berkeley: University of California Press.
————. 1989. *Strategies for Learning: Small Group Activities in American, Japanese, and Swedish Industry*. Berkeley: University of California Press.
Commission on the Skills of the American Workforce. 1990. *America's Choice: High Skills or Low Wages!* Rochester, NY: National Center for Education and the Economy.
Conte, Michael A., and Jan Svejnar. 1990. "The Performance Effects of Employee Ownership Plans." In Alan S. Blinder, ed., *Paying for Productivity: A Look at the Evidence*. Washington, DC: Brookings Institution.
Cooke, William N. 1990. *Labor-Management Cooperation: New Partnerships or Going in Circles?* Kalamazoo, MI: W. E. Upjohn Institute for Employment Research.
Cutcher-Gershenfeld, Joel. 1987. "Collective Governance of Industrial Relations." In *Proceedings of the 40th Annual Meeting, Industrial Relations Research Assn.* Madison, WI: IRRA.
Dahl, Robert. 1985. *A Preface to Economic Democracy*. Berkeley: University of California Press.
————. 1989. *Democracy and Its Critics*. New Haven: Yale University Press.

Daily Labor Report. 1992. "Bush Announces NAFTA Accord: Labor Calls it a Disaster." *Daily Labor Report* 157, August 13, p. A-A.

Davis, James Allan, and Tom W. Smith. 1991. *General Social Surveys, 1972-1991 (machine readable data file).* Chicago: National Opinion Research Center.

de Schweinitz, Dorothea. 1949. *Labor and Management in Common Enterprise.* Cambridge: Harvard University Press.

Delaney, John Thomas, David Lewin, and Casey Ichniowski. 1989. *Human Resource Policies and Practices of American Firms.* U.S. Department of Labor, Bureau of Labor-Management Relations and Cooperative Programs, BLMR 137.

Derber, Milton. 1970. *The American Idea of Industrial Democracy, 1865-1965.* Urbana: University of Illinois Press.

Deutsch, Steven. 1988. "Workplace Democracy and Worker Health: Strategies for Implementation." *International Journal of Health Services* 18, no. 4, pp. 647-658.

Docksey, Christopher. 1985. "Employee Information and Consultation Rights in the Member States of the European Communities." *Comparative Labor Law* 7, pp. 32-69.

Drucker, Peter F. 1949. *The New Society: The Anatomy of Industrial Order.* New York: Harper & Row.

Eaton, Adrienne E., and Paula B. Voos. 1992. "Unions and Contemporary Innovations in Work Organization, Compensation, and Employee Participation." In Lawrence Mishel and Paula B. Voos, eds., *Unions and Economic Competitiveness.* Armonk, NY: M. E. Sharpe, pp. 173-215.

Ehrenberg, Ronald G., and George H. Jakubson. 1988. "Advance Notice Provisions in Plant Closing Legislation: Do they Matter? Working Paper No. 2611. Cambridge: National Bureau of Economic Research.

Elster, Jon. 1986. "Self-Realisation in Work and Politics: The Marxist Conception of the Good Life." *Social Philosophy and Policy* 3, no. 2, pp. 97-126.

Esping-Andersen, Gosta. 1990. *The Three Worlds of Welfare Capitalism.* Princeton, NJ: Princeton University Press.

Estrin, Saul, Paul Grout, and Sushil Wadhwani. 1987. "Profit-Sharing and Employee Share Ownership." *Economic Policy* 2, no. 1, pp. 13-62.

Eulau, Heinz, and Michael Lewis-Beck, eds. 1985. *Economic Conditions and Electoral Outcomes.* New York: Agathon Press.

Farber, Henry, and Alan B. Krueger. 1992. "Union Membership in the United States: The Decline Continues." In Morris Kleiner and Bruce Kaufman, eds., *Employee Representation: Alternatives and Future Directions.* Madison, WI: IRRA.

Ferguson, Thomas, and Joel Rogers. 1986. *Right Turn: The Decline of the Democrats and the Future of American Politics.* New York: Hill & Wang.

Ferman, Louis A., Michele Hoyman, Joel Cutcher-Gershenfeld, and Ernest Savoie, eds. 1991. *Joint Training Programs: A Union-Management Approach to Preparing Workers for the Future.* Ithaca, NY: ILR Press.

Fingerhut/Powers. 1991. "National Labor Poll." Washington, DC: Fingerhut/Granados.

Freeman, Richard B. 1991. "Employee Councils, Worker Participation, and Other Squishy Stuff." *Proceedings of the 43rd Annual Meeting of the Industrial Relations Research Association,* pp. 328-337.

Freeman, Richard B., and James L. Medoff. 1984. *What Do Unions Do?* New York: Basic Books.

Freeman, Richard B., and Casey Ichniowski, eds. 1988. *When Public Sector Workers Unionize.* Chicago: University of Chicago Press.

Freeman, Richard B., and Edward P. Lazear. Forthcoming. "An Economic Analysis of Works Councils." In Joel Rogers and Wolfgang Streeck, eds., *Works Councils,* Chicago: University of Chicago Press.

Freeman, Richard B., and Joel Rogers. 1993. "Reforming U.S. Labor Relations." Unpublished.

Gallup (Gallup Organization). 1988. "Public Knowledge and Opinion Concerning the Labor Movement. Princeton: Gallup Organization.

GAO (General Accounting Office). 1986. *Employee Stock Ownership Plans: Benefits and Costs of ESOP Tax Incentives for Broadening Stock Ownership. GAO/PEMD-87-8.*

_____. 1988. *Employee Stock Ownership Plans: Little Evidence of Effects on Corporate Performance.* GAO/PEMD-88-1.

_____.1990. *Child Labor: Increases in Detected Child Labor Violations Throughout the United States.* GAO/HRD-90-116.

_____. 1991. *Occupational Safety and Health: OSHA Action Needed to Improve Compliance with Hazard Communication Standard.* GAO/HRD-92-8.

_____. 1992. *Occupational Safety and Health: Worksite Safety and Health Programs Show Promise.* GAO/T-HRD-92-15.

Giersch, H. 1990. "Lessons from West Germany." Paper presented to OECD Conference on the Transition to a Market Economy in Central and Eastern Europe.

Gustavsen, Bjorn, and Gerry Hunnius. 1981. *New Patterns of Work Reform: The Case of Norway.* Oslo: Universitetsforlaget.

Hanami, T. 1987. "Conflict Resolution in Industrial Relations." In T. Hanami and R. Blanpain *Industrial Conflict Resolution in Market Economies.* Deventer: Kluwer, pp. 203-215.

Harris, Howell John. 1982. *The Right to Manage: Industrial Relations Policies of American Business in the 1940s.* Madison, WI: The University of Wisconsin Press.

Hashimoto, Masanori. 1990. *The Japanese Lr ' or Market in a Comparative Perspectis with the United States.* Kalamazoo, MI: ʏ. E. Upjohn Institute for Employment Research.

Hensler, Deborah R., et al. 1991. *Compensation for Accidental Injuries in the United States.* Santa Monica, CA: Rand Corporation.

Hobson, C., and J. Dworkin. 1986. "West German Labor Unrest: Are Unions Losing Ground to Worker Councils?" *Monthly Labor Review* 109, no. 2, pp. 46-48.

Hogler, Raymond L., and Guillermo J. Grenier. 1992. *Employee Participation and Labor Law in'the American Workplace.* Westport, CT: Quorum Books.

Ichniowski, Casey, and Jeffrey S. Zax. 1990. "Today's Associations, Tomorrow's Unions." *Industrial and Labor Relations Review* 43, no. 2, pp. 191-208.

ILO (International Labour Organization). 1988. *Yearbook of Labour Statistics.* Geneva: ILO.

_____. 1991. *Yearbook of Labour Statistics, 1990.* Geneva: ILO.

Jacoby, Sanford M. 1983. "Union-Management Cooperation in the U.S.: Lessons from the 1920s." *Industrial and Labor Relations Review* 37, no. 1, pp. 18-33.

_____. 1989. "Reckoning with Company Unions: The Case of Thornton Products, 1934-1964." *Industrial and Labor Relations Review* 43, no. 1, pp. 19-40.

Jacoby, Sanford M., and Anil Verma. 1992. "Enterprise Unions in the U.S." *Industrial Relations* 31, no. 1, pp. 137-158.

Kandel, E., and Edward P. Lazear. 1992. "Peer Pressure and Partnerships." *Journal of Political Economy* 100, no. 4, pp. 801-817.

Katz, Diane. 1992. "Unions, Employers Watch Case on Labor Management Teams." *Detroit News*, September 1.

Kaufman, Roger T. 1992. "The Effects of Improshare on Productivity." *Industrial and Labor Relations Review* 45, no. 2, pp. 311-322.

Kelley, Maryellen R., and Bennett Harrison. 1992. "Unions, Technology, and Labor Management Cooperation." In Lawrence Mishel and Paula B. Voos, eds., *Unions and Economic Competitiveness.* Armonk, NY: M. E. Sharpe.

Kleiner, Morris, and M. Bouillon. 1988. "Providing Business Information to Production Workers: Correlates of Compensation and Productivity." *Industrial and Labor Relations Review* 44, no. 4, pp. 605-17.

Kochan, Thomas A., Harry C. Katz, and Nancy R. Mower. 1984. *Worker Participation and American Unions: Threat or Opportunity?* Kalamazoo, MI: W. E. Upjohn Institute for Employment Research.

Kochan, Thomas A., and Paul Osterman. 1991. "Human Resource Development and Utilization: Is There Too Little in the U.S.?" Working Paper, Sloan School of Management, MIT.

Koike, Kazuo. 1984. "Skill Formation Systems in the U.S. and Japan: A Comparative Study." In Masahiko Aoki, ed., *The Economic Analysis of the Japanese Firm.* Amsterdam: North-Holland, pp. 44-75.

_____. 1988. Understanding Industrial Relations in Modern Japan. London: Macmillan Press.

_____. 1989. "Intellectual Skill and the Role of Employees as Constituent Members of Large Firms in Contemporary Japan." In Masahiko Aoki, Bo Gustafsson, and Oliver Williams, eds., The Firm as a Nexus of Contracts. London: Sage Publications, pp. 1°5-208.

Lazear, Edward P. 1991. "Labor Eco. .mics and the Psychology of Organizations." Journal of Economic Perspectives 5, no. 2, pp. 89-110.

Lazear, Edward P., and S. Rosen. 1981. "Rank Order Tournament as Optimum Labor Contracts." Journal of Political Economy 89, no. 5, pp. 841-864.

Lemieux, Thomas. Forthcoming. "Union and Wage Inequality in Canada and in the United States." In David Card and Richard Freeman, eds., Small Differences That Matter: Labor Markets and Income Maintenance in Canada and the United States. Chicago: University of Chicago Press.

Levine, David I., and Laura D'Andrea Tyson. 1990. "Participation, Productivity, and the Firm's Environment." In Alan S. Blinder, ed., Paying for Productivity: A Look at the Evidence. Washington, DC: Brookings Institution, pp. 183-243.

Lewis-Beck, Michael, and Jean-Dominque Lafay. 1991. Economics and Politics: The Calculus of Support. Ann Arbor: University of Michigan Press.

Louis Harris and Associates. 1984. A Study on the Outlook for Trade Union Organizing. New York: Louis Harris and Associates.

Lynch, Lisa. 1992. "Private Sector Training and the Earnings of Young Workers." American Economic Review 82, no. 1, pp. 299-312.

Millis, Harry, and Royal Montgomery. 1945. Organized Labor. New York: McGraw Hill.

Mishel, Lawrence, and Jared Bernstein. 1992. The State of Working America, 1992-93. Armonk, NY: M. E. Sharpe.

Mishel, Lawrence, and Paula E. Voos, eds. 1992. Unions and Economic Competitiveness. Armonk, NY: M. E. Sharpe, Inc.

Monat, J., and H. Sarfati, eds. 1986. Workers Participation: A Voice in Decisions, 1981-85. Geneva: International Labor Office.

Montgomery, David. 1987. The Fall of the House of Labor. Cambridge: Cambridge University Press.

Moore, Michael J., and W. Kip Viscusi. 1990. Compensation Mechanisms for Job Risks—Wages, Workers' Compensation and Product Liability. Princeton, NJ: Princeton University Press.

Morishima, Motohiro. 1991a. "Information Sharing and Firm Performance in Japan." Industrial Relations 30, no. 1, pp. 37-61.

_____. 1991b. "Information Sharing and Collective Bargaining in Japan: Effects on Wage Negotiation." Industrial and Labor Relations Review 44, no. 3, pp. 469-475.

NICB (National Industrial Conference Board). 1919. Works Councils in the United States. Boston: NICB.

_____. 1922. Experience with Works Councils in the United States. New York: Century.

Nelson, Daniel. 1993. "Employee Representation in Historical Perspective." In Morris Kleiner and Bruce Kaufman, eds., Employee Representation: Alternatives and Future Directions. Madison, WI: IRRA.

_____. 1989. "Managers and Unions in the Rubber Industry: Union Avoidance Strategies in the 1930s." Industrial Relations Research Review 43, no. 1, pp. 41-52.

Noble, Charles. 1986. Liberalism at Work: The Rise and Fall of OSHA. Philadelphia: Temple University Press.

NSWI (National Safe Workplace Institute). 1992. Basic Information on Workplace Safety & Health in the United States, 1992 Edition. Chicago: NSWI.

Osterman, Paul. 1990. "Elements of a National Training Policy." In Ferman, Louis A., Michele Hoyman, Joel Cutcher-Gershenfeld, and Ernest Savoie, eds., New Developments in Worker Training: A Legacy for the 1990s. Madison, WI: Industrial Relations Research Association, pp. 257-281.

OTA (Office of Technology Assessment, U.S. Congress). 1990. *Worker Training: Competing in the International Economy.* OTA ITE-457. Washington, DC: GPO.

Pateman, Carole. 1970. *Participation and Democratic Theory.* Cambridge University Press.

Quinn, Robert P., and Graham L. Staines. 1979. *The 1977 Quality of Employment Survey: Descriptive Statistics with Comparison Data from the 1969-70 and 1972-73 Surveys.* Ann Arbor, MI: Institute for Social Research.

Rees, Joseph. 1988. *Reforming the Workplace: A Study of Self-Regulation in Occupational Safety.* Philadelphia: Temple University Press.

Riddell, W. Craig. 1992. "Unionization in Canada and the United States: A Tale of Two Countries." Mimeo. Victoria: University of British Columbia, Department of Economics.

Rogers, Joel, and Barbara Wooton. 1992. "Works Councils in the United States: Could We Get There From Here?" Prepared for Works Councils Project conference, Geneva.

Rogers, Joel, and Wolfgang Streeck, eds. Forthcoming. *Works Councils,* Chicago: University of Chicago Press.

de Schweinitz, Dorothea. 1949. *Labor and Management in a Common Enterprise.* Cambridge: Harvard University Press.

Shirai, Taishiro. 1983. "A Theory of Enterprise Unionism." In Taishiro Shirai, ed., *Contemporary Industrial Relations in Japan.* Madison, WI: University of Wisconsin Press, pp. 117-143.

Soskice, David. 1991. "German Apprenticeship." Paper delivered at NBER Conference on Private Sector Training, London, December.

Summers, Clyde W. 1990. "Unions Without Majority: A Black Hole?" *Chicago Kent Law Review* 66, pp. 531-548.

Tirole, Jacques. 1986. "Hierarchies and Bureaucracies: On the Role of Collusion in Organizations." *Journal of Law, Economics, and Organization* 2, no. 2, pp. 181-214.

Trumka, Richard L. 1992. "On Becoming a Movement: Rethinking Labor's Strategy." *Dissent* 39, no. 1, pp. 57-60.

United States Department of Labor. 1988. *The Role of Labor-Management Committees in Safeguarding Worker Safety and Health.* Washington, DC: Government Printing Office.

Visser, Jelle. 1991. "Trends in Trade Union Membership," *OECD Employment Outlook* (July): 97-134.

Wallerstein, Michael. 1987. "Union Centralization and Trade Dependence: The Origins of Democratic Corporatism." Working Paper Series 126, University of California at Los Angeles.

_____. 1989. "Union Organization in Advanced Industrial Democracies." *American Political Science Review* 83, no. 2, pp. 481-501.

Weiler, Paul C. 1990. *Governing the Workplace: The Future of Labor and Employment Law.* Cambridge: Harvard University Press.

Weitzman, Martin L., and Douglas L. Kruse. 1990. "Profit Sharing and Productivity." In Alan S. Blinder, ed., *Paying for Productivity: A Look at the Evidence.* Washington, DC: Brookings Institution.

Wever, Kirstin R. 1991. "Labor's Leverage in a Post-Fordist World: Cases from Germany, Lessons for the U.S." Working Paper, Northeastern University.

Wilcock, Richard C. 1957. "Industrial Management's Policies Toward Unionism," in Milton Derber and Edwin Young, eds., *Labor and the New Deal.* Madison, WI: University of Wisconsin Press, pp. 275-315.

Wilensky, Harold L. 1981. "Leftism, Catholicism, and Democratic Corporatism: The Role of Political Parties in Recent Welfare State Development." In Peter Flora and Arnold J. Heidenheimer, eds., *The Development of Welfare States in Europe and America.* New Brunswick, NJ: Transaction Books, Inc., pp. 345-382.

Wokutch, Richard E. 1992. *Worker Protection, Japanese Style: Occupational Safety and Health in the Auto Industry.* Ithaca, NY: ILR Press.

Womack, James P., Daniel T. Jones, and Daniel Roos. 1990. *The Machine that Changed the World.* New York: Rawson Associates.

APPENDIX 1

Typical Provisions: Belgian Works Councils

Relevant provisions	Undertakings covered	Representative bodies	Subject matter of consultation	Scope of consultation
Act of 20.9.1948, amended 1975, extended to non-profit sector by Royal Decree of 24.1.84 (definitions, establishments of Works Councils).	Undertakings ('technical operating unit' equals plant/ establishment' may include legal entity) which employ at least 100 employees.	Works Council (exists to promote collaboration between employer and employees).	—works rules —criteria for dismissal, re-engagement —holidays —social services —working language	Codecision.
Collective Agreement No. 9 of 9.3.1972, extended by Royal Decree of 12.9.1972, amended/ extended 1974. Royal Decree of 27.11.1973 (competence and functions)		Established at technical operating unit level. No obligatory worker representation at group level.	—labor standards —vocational training —criteria for dismissals and recruitment —job classification —handicapped workers	Works Council has right to advise and consult, i.e., formulate suggestions, objections, opinions; employer must indicate response.
Collective Agreement No. 24 of 2.10.75, extended by Royal Decree of 21.1.1976.	Undertakings which employ at least 20 employees.	Works Council or Union Delegation or (in default) the work force or its representatives.	—changes in the structure of the undertaking (see 'information') —measures to avoid or limit collective dismissals or transfers —program of collective dismissals, transfers and alterations —social measures to be taken	Inform on: —economic, financial and technical reasons which cause or justify change. —economic, financial and social consequences thereof.
Collective Agreement No. 5 of 24.5.1971.	Undertakings covered by collective agreements concluded at Joint Committee or undertaking level.	Union Delegation	Application of social legislation, collective agreements and work rules.	Right to exercise certain rights of Works Councils or Safety Committee where less than 50 employees.

APPENDIX 1—*(Continued)*

Typical Provisions: Belgian Works Councils

Relevant provisions	Undertakings covered	Representative bodies	Subject matter of consultation	Scope of consultation
Collective Agreement No. 39 of 13.12.1983 extended by Royal Decree of 25.1.1984.	Undertakings which employ at least 50 employees.	—Information: to Works Council or, if none, to Union Delegation. —Consultation: with Works Council, Safety Committee, Union Delegation, as appropriate.	Social consequences of introduction of new technology, i.e.: —employment prospects, re staff, structure, planned social measures —organization of work, working conditions —health and safety of employees —skills required and possible training measures	At least 3 months before employer introduces new technology with significant collective effects on employment, work organization or working conditions must: 1. provide written information: —nature of new technology —economic/financial/technical factors justifying its introduction —periods for putting it into operation —social consequences brought about. 2. Concert on social consequences (attempt to reach common approach).
Royal Decrees of 11.2.1946 and 3.12.1946. Act of 10.6.1952. General Regulation for Protection of Labor.	Undertakings which employ at least 50 employees.	Committee on Safety, Health and Improvement of the Workplace.	—policy of preventing work accidents and occupational diseases —employer's annual plan of action, together with changes, implementation and results, thereof —all proposals and measures affecting safety and health (advice only).	Formulate advice and proposals (employer must draw up annual plan of preventive action to protect safety and health, provide it before each November 1 to Committee).

Source: Docksey (1985).

APPENDIX 1—(*Continued*)

Typical Provisions: Belgian Works Councils

Scope of information disclosure requirements	Timing of Information	Information to be communicated	Enforcement
Works Council has right to discuss information, ask questions, receive explanations.	1. After each Works Council election (every four years) in writing.	1. 'Basic information' legal status, competitive position, production and productivity, financial structure, budgets and cost, personnel costs, research, public aid, future plans, organization chart.	—Criminal fine and imprisonment (for between 8 days and 1 month) —In default of above administrative fine may be imposed (Act 30.6.1971) —Fine may be multiplied by number of employees employed in contravention of law up to statutory maximum. —Penalties doubled in the case of a second offense.
The Works Council must be given a clear and accurate view of the overall situation and development of the legal entity, the undertaking or any economic or financial group to which it belongs.	2. Annually, within 3 months of end of financial year, in writing. Where undertaking is part of group with consolidated yearly accounts, appropriate details must be given to Works Council.	2. Written, report up-dating Basic Information. Balance sheet, profit and loss accounts, wages. Staffing situation, structure + evolution of, and prospects for employment. Evaluation of economic and social impact of introduction of new technology.	Secrecy Certain information may be withheld where disclosure is liable to cause problems for company, which must obtain prior approval of official of Department of Economic Affairs.

APPENDIX 1—(Continued)
Typical Provisions: Belgian Works Councils

Scope of information disclosure requirements	Timing of Information	Information to be communicated	Enforcement
The term group covers multi-establishment undertakings, multinationals and groups of undertakings constituting an economic entity. The information supplied must be placed in its economic, national and sectoral context, with guidance as to particular features of the regional/group situation. If the undertaking (or group) is a company:	3. At least quarterly. Orally, backed by written summaries. 4. Occasional: whenever decisions are taken or events occur which can have 'important consequences' for the undertaking, especially where manning levels are likely to be affected, eg: structural changes (see 'consultation').	3. Business situation, management strategy and changes, update of employment prospects. 4. Comments on expected consequences of event or decision on development of company's activities and situation of employees.	Confidentiality —Members of Works Council must use information with proper discretion in order to protect company's interests. Penal sanctions for breach —Employer may specify confidential aspects of information which, if diffused, might cause problems for company. Department of Economic Affairs official may settle disputes on nature of information. New technology Where employer is in breach of obligations and employee is dismissed as result of introduction of new technology, dismissed employee is entitled to special compensatory payment equal to 3 months gross pay.
—Works Council must discuss information before annual general meeting (minutes given to shareholders).	In good time before transfer.	Information on economic/financial/technical factors which justify change in undertaking, and effects of transfer on employment prospects, organization work, and general employment policy.	
—Any document given to shareholders must also be given to Works Councils.	Before collective redundancies.	—reasons for redundancies. —number of employees to be dismissed. —number of employees normally employed. —period over which dismissals to be effected.	

Source: Docksey (1985).

CHAPTER 2

Governing the Workplace: Employee Representation in the Eyes of the Law

PAUL C. WEILER
Harvard University

One weekend in the fall of 1991, the nation sat transfixed in front of its television screens watching the dramatic confrontation between Clarence Thomas and Anita Hill. Apparently riding on the outcome of the struggle was our future constitutional policy towards such vital issues as abortion and affirmative action. The immediate question, though, was which of the protagonists was telling the truth about an episode of on-the-job sexual harassment that allegedly had occurred a decade earlier. An insistent challenge put by Thomas's supporters was how could one believe that Hill, a lawyer trained in Title VII jurisprudence, would not have lodged a complaint at the time this violation of her legal right against a sexually hostile work environment was supposedly taking place. The public response of many women supporters of Hill was that they too had experienced the compulsion to keep quiet about incidents of sexual maltreatment by their bosses for fear that an even worse fate would befall them—either in their immediate workplace or in their future careers. Whatever the broader political and constitutional dimensions of this imbroglio, Thomas vs. Hill did bring vividly home the reality of the representation gap experienced by employees in the American workplace.

Just a few weeks earlier, oral argument had taken place in a case called *Electromation*, the major National Labor Relations Board (NLRB) case of the 1991-92 term. The issue was whether a committee structure the employer had established in its plant to tap employee views about a number of workplace issues was a "company union" prohibited by the National Labor Relations Act (NLRA). In the hearing, the business community asked the Bush Board—and presumably will eventually ask Clarence Thomas and his colleagues on the Supreme Court—to reinterpret our labor law away from the adversarial model envisaged by Congress in the 1930s and give American enterprise the flexibility it needs to devise more cooperative personnel policies for the 1990s.

Sexual harassment and employee involvement are only two of the host of workplace issues that have been debated in one legal forum or another over the last decade. Among other questions that have risen to and fallen from public attention are:

1. Do women in female-dominated jobs suffer from discriminatory pay inequities? (Weiler 1991a).

2. Should we lament or applaud the rising numbers of suits about wrongful dismissal (many brought under the orbit of anti-discrimination law)? (Dertouzos, Holland, and Ebener 1988; Donohue and Siegelman 1991).

3. Is randomized drug testing necessary for firm safety and productivity, or is it an unacceptable invasion of employee privacy? (Symposium 1991).

4. How can one best accommodate work and family responsibilities; e.g., through unpaid or even paid leaves? (Dowd 1989).

5. Should employers be permitted to hire permanant replacements of its employees who exercise their right to strike? (United States Congress 1991).

Each of these topics, taken by itself, poses difficult substantive issues about *what* should be done—issues whose resolution depends principally on arguments drawn from the disciplines of economics, sociology, and industrial relations. But as De Tocqueville observed about the America of the 1830s, and as is even truer of the America of the 1990s, ultimately every important issue of public policy in this country becomes a question of law and for lawyers. And in designing a law of the workplace, we must confront a crucial institutional theme that runs through every one of the issues just mentioned— *who* is going to represent the interest of employees in settling these and other workplace dilemmas? The standard assumption of present day lawyers is that we should rely on federal or state legislators, on judges in the court rooms, and/or on government officials running administrative programs. This reaction in my profession is unsurprising, given that the bulk of these actors are lawyers themselves. From a broader perspective, though, legal actors are only one candidate for that employee representation role. Among the other possibilities are, interestingly, *other* employers exerting the pressures of an impersonal but competitive labor market, personnel managers devising human resource policies in the executive suite, and union leaders sitting at the bargaining table in negotiations with management. The candidate I would add to this list are employees representing themselves through guaranteed participation in a committee structure designed to give workers some meaningful voice in the affairs of the firm.

The Decline of Private-Sector Unionism

Sixty years ago this crucial issue at the center of the workplace was the subject of a national debate in both the political and the constitutional arenas (Jacoby 1985). For the previous half century, a combination of property, contract, corporate, and antitrust law had nurtured the virtues of an unfettered labor market within which more benevolent employers had developed some forms of employee representation plans within their "open shops." While this American Plan, as it was called, attracted widespread support in the 1920s, unsurprisingly it looked much less attractive in the Great Depression of the 1930s with unemployment rates running at 25 percent. Thus one found the United States Congress taking a formal position on the central jurisprudential question being debated in law schools at that time:

> Under prevailing economic conditions, developed with the aid of governmental authority for owners of property to organize in the corporate and other forms of ownership association, the individual but unorganized worker is commonly helpless to exercise actual liberty of contract and to protect his freedom of labor, and thereby to obtain acceptable terms and conditions of employment . . .

Through the combination of the Norris-LaGuardia Act (from which I quoted) and the Wagner Act enacted three years later, the Congress adopted as our national legal policy the promotion of worker organization into independent unions of their own choosing. Under this institutional arrangement employee interests would be actively represented by elected leaders who sat down with management to arrive at collectively negotiated solutions to workplace conflicts.

That New Deal labor law policy narrowly won the go ahead from the Supreme Court (*Jones and Laughlin* 1937), thereby ushering in a revolution in constitutional thought under which it was liberals who applauded and conservatives who deplored judicial restraint in the face of such legislative initiatives. For the next two decades, the labor law policy of fostering and encouraging collective bargaining was remarkably successful in its own terms. In the early 1930s, shortly before Senator Robert Wagner introduced the NLRA, roughly 15 percent of private-sector employees in the United States were covered by collective agreements. Under the auspices of the new legal policy, private-sector union representation soared to around 40 percent by the mid-1950s. But then began a period of steady, and eventually steep, decline to the present point where once again less than 15 percent of the employees of American business are members of labor unions (Chaison and Rose 1991).

Bare statistics cannot, however, answer the more interesting question about what is the true underlying explanation for these trends. Is it a lack of *demand* for collective bargaining on the part of American workers, or is it a lack of available *supply* of this institution, due especially to obstacles placed in the way by employers? Most popular, and some scholarly, views assume that collective bargaining was and is primarily suited for male, blue-collar, production workers in goods-producing industries—the bastion of unionism in its heyday in the 1950s. The institution is felt to be of little interest or appeal to female, white-collar, knowledge workers in the service industries—the prototype of the new labor force in the post-industrial economy of the 1990s. The attractiveness of the union movement—with its image of Big Labor—is further lessened by the fact that over the last thirty years many American managers have learned a good deal about how to substitute themselves as the vehicles for responding to the needs of their employees. To the extent, then, that this demand-side story is an accurate account of what lies behind the statistics, there is little that labor *law* can legitimately do about such lack of interest on the part of the new breed of American worker in the old brand of American unionism.

There is a good deal of truth to that account. But this benign explanation for the decline of American unionism is by no means the whole story. For example, a purely demographic explanation is belied by the fact that in the last thirty years the American school teacher—predominantly female, white-collar, knowledge worker, in the (public) service sector—has become the most highly unionized occupational group in the country. And in trying to understand the extremely sharp decline, both absolutely and comparatively, in American *private*-sector unionism, one cannot ignore the fact of a coincident and dramatic increase in intense, often illegal, resistance by American business to union representation for its employees. This is one crude statistical index of this phenomenon of employer suppression of prounion sentiments: whereas back in the mid-1950s the NLRB annually secured a right of reinstatement for roughly 1,000 workers illegally fired for supporting a union, by the 1980s that rate had soared to as high as 7,000 or so illegal firings a year, and among a sharply lower number of potential victims who had supported unions in representation campaigns (Lalonde and Meltzer 1991; Weiler 1991b).

One should emphasize that the impact of such activity is by no means confined to work sites run by what still is a *minority* of employers who engage in such crude retaliation. A large majority of American businesses do make it a basic aim of their corporate strategy to remain (or to become) as union-free as possible in their domestic (if not their foreign) operations. This strategy influences the firms' patterns of investment, their location decisions, the design of their compensation packages, and the types of employees they interview and hire. The success of *all* employers in union avoidance is greatly enhanced by the illegal activities of the "bare knuckles" minority. Thus one finds widespread awareness of such illegal antiunion activities among the American work force. A 1988 Gallup Poll found that 70 percent of employees believe that "corporations sometimes harass, intimidate, or fire employees who openly speak up for a union"; while Lou Harris discovered that 40 percent of employees believe that their *own* employer would use such tactics on *them* if they ventured to support a union (Weiler 1990).

The cumulative result of these trends is a bleak prospect for the American union movement. Recall that every union faces a process of natural attrition, through which the union loses members from existing units whose firms go out of business, whose plants are relocated, or whose markets shrink in the face of nonunion competition and changing consumer tastes. Simply to stay even in absolute size of membership, let alone to grow in tandem with a rising labor force, a union must establish footholds in a significant number of additional units every year. NLRB statistics for the last three decades demonstrate that American private-sector unions have not been able to make successful use of the national labor laws for that purpose. The net result of that annual union deficit has been a steady, and now steep, loss of ground in the American economy, to a point where it is estimated that private-sector union density will eventually "stabilize" at well under 10 percent early in the next century.

Is Collective Bargaining Worth Saving?

Much of my own scholarly work, both in Canada and in the United States, has been devoted to figuring out how to reform the historic labor law model to save collective bargaining from that fate. But empirical facts cannot by themselves justify major policy changes. Indeed, one might read a very different message into the fierce resistance mounted against unionization by so many employers, as also into the apparent disinterest exhibited by so many employees. Perhaps this aging institution just doesn't fit with the new marketplace and the new work force of the 1990s.

To its proponents, the collective bargaining model of employee representation has always served two vital social functions. It provides workers with *protection* against substandard wages and benefits and against arbitrary and unfair treatment on the job— protections that can be tailored to the special features and needs of particular firms, and that can be revised or discarded as the situation changes. Collective bargaining also affords workers a considerable measure of workplace *participation* throughout the representation cycle—from the initial decision to have a union, through the election of union officers, formulation of a bargaining agenda, deciding whether to accept a contract proposal or to go on strike, and in settlement or arbitration of grievances during the life of the contract.

But to contemporary critics, this glowing image of collective bargaining faded long ago. American unions are now typically portrayed as large, remote, bureaucratic organizations. When one thinks of "union," the image that comes to mind is not an *activity* engaged in by members, but rather an external *entity* run by distant officials. The prevailing collective bargaining model draws only to a small extent on direct participation by employees, and it tends to restrict the bargaining agenda to a limited range of employee concerns. Union contracts have always concentrated on protecting employees from harmful things that a firm might do to them rather than enlisting employees in a positive contribution to the success of their enterprise. This orientation no longer fits the aspirations and self-conception of many employees today, especially the growing corps of professional or knowledge workers (Heckscher 1988).

It would be a mistake to paint an unduly "yuppified" picture of the labor market. There are large numbers of fast food service workers or back-office machine operators (to take two fast-growing occupations) whose principal need on the job is basic protection from arbitrary management action. They would be happy to accept some reduction in their personal voice and contact in exchange for the ability to draw on the power and resources deployed by a large organization to win them decent guarantees in a labor contract. The problem is that for many of these workers, unions have also lost much of their ability to deliver tangible economic benefits and security. And where unions still do wield considerable power for the protection of employees, that fact is viewed by management as precisely its problem. As the American economy has undergone profound changes in its labor force, technology, and capital and product markets, firms find they need to make continual adjustments to survive. In this new climate, business executives regularly lament that too many union leaders stick rigidly to contracts sometimes running 500 pages long, contracts that contain provisions as outmoded as the production technology in use when the terms were first negotiated. Even those executives who accept a union presence now regularly adopt hard-nosed strategies to force contract concessions (e.g., about increasingly costly health insurance premiums). And more and more executives unscrupulously use bargaining disputes to rid themselves of a union entirely.

To my mind there is some truth, but considerable myth, to that line of criticism of collective bargaining. Careful scholarly examination of the facts demonstrates that, far from being the reason for a loss of competitiveness of American industry, collective bargaining generally tends to enhance rather than detract from employee productivity (Freeman 1992). And in those particular trouble spots that do exist, too often the pet prescriptions of outside pundits are contradictory. Union leaders are exhorted both to extend more direct democratic participation to rank-and-file members and also to cease stubborn resistance to accommodating the needs of the immediate employer; critics rarely appreciate that the feelings of local employees usually are the major obstacle to contract givebacks.

But whatever one's ultimate verdict about the merits of this institution, it is undeniable that as unions have declined in the outside world, so also has the Wagner Act model of collective bargaining lost favor in the world of legal opinion. The question that must be addressed, though, is what institution will take the place of supposedly outmoded union representation?

Notwithstanding the brief flirtation by both the Reagan administration and the law and economics professoriate with the attractions of an unfettered labor market (Freed and Polsby 1989), that institutional option does not seem politically acceptable. At the "gut" moral level Americans simply are not prepared to expose to the full vicissitudes of a competitive marketplace the basic human needs of workers and their families—dependent as we all are upon what happens to us on the job. As well, contemporary labor economists have rediscovered the truth first explored by their intellectual forebears, people such as John Dunlop and Clark Kerr, that labor markets are idiosyncratic, imperfectly competitive processes (Kaufman 1988). The employment relationship inevitably permits the exercise of authority within a broad leeway left by the workers' option of exiting to another employer. With the decline of collective bargaining as the legally favored means by which workers can try to shape and civilize the exercise of authority by their own management, two other instruments have emerged to fill the gap. One is government regulation (for example, against sexual harassment), the other, management-sponsored employee involvement programs (such as the one at *Electromation*) which afford workers some measure of participation in the enterprise. While American unions have been in marked decline, these other forms of representation have been on the rise.

Government Regulation

For the last twenty-five years this country has experienced a sharp expansion in the reach and intensity of direct government regulation of the employment relationship. This trend began with civil rights and fair employment laws, followed by occupational safety and health programs, efforts to protect the security and value of retirement pensions, and so on. For much of that period the major developments took place in the legislative and administrative spheres, with government bureaucrats taking the lead in representing the interests of workers. Admittedly in the early Reagan years, there was a considerable drop in the intensity of the administration's efforts on behalf of employees. But by that time, the focus of attention was shifting to the courts, partly through judicial fashioning of new rights through "interpretation" of old statutes (for example, reading freedom from sexual harassment into Title VII), partly through major inroads upon common law employment-at-will, via wrongful dismissal litigation in which a lawyer representing an individual employee asks a judge and jury to scrutinize some aspect of an employer's personnel practices (such as programs for mandatory, random drug-testing).

This regulatory model does have evident initial advantages in comparison with collective bargaining. The law addresses each specific issue—such as use of lie detectors on the job—on its intrinsic merits, rather than letting the matter be buried beneath more pressing "bread and butter" issues that tend to dominate the final agenda at the bargaining table. Once an issue is addressed, the right is defined in terms of the moral and legal principles that should apply to *every* employment relationship. Duties and entitlements do not depend on the accident of the relative bargaining power enjoyed by parties in the wide variety of employment settings across the economy. Government regulation gives each individual worker whose needs are being protected a personal *right* to (at least hire a lawyer to) enforce the employer's obligation in front of the appropriate tribunal, rather than leave him or her dependent on the good will and resources of a union bargaining agent—constrained only by a vague duty of fair representation owed to unit members.

In spite of all these virtues, particularly attractive to the legal mind, in practice government regulation also displays characteristic failings. The most vociferous critic of government intervention is, of course, the business community, which regularly complains about erratic and expensive jury verdicts and the inflexibility and cost of regulatory directives (Dertouzos and Karoly 1992). Of course, that business laments legal restraints on its own prerogatives is hardly a decisive argument. Regulatory programs are adopted in the first place because of popular sentiment that an imperfect labor market simply is not providing sufficient safety, security, or fair treatment to employees. The more telling critique of the regulatory model, then, is that too frequently the burdens imposed on employers are *not* matched by corresponding benefits for employees.

Research on occupational safety and health enforcement, for example, finds only marginal reductions in workplace injuries (Viscusi 1986), while capital expenditures needed for compliance with the legal rules are often quite substantial (Bartel and Thomas 1985). Even when new labor protections do produce appreciable gains for employees, too often these gains are distributed primarily to the more educated, highly paid workers. The reason is that those workers who are most likely to sue for a violation of their legal rights are those who were fired or forced out of their jobs and, of these potential candidates, the ones who are most likely to be able to induce a lawyer to take their cases, are employees whose personal traits and circumstances promise the highest damage award from a sympathetic jury. And where the aim of the law is to protect ordinary plant and office workers in their daily lives on the job, under laws such as OSHA and ERISA, for example, the actual benefit of these laws is much more likely to be enjoyed by employees who can call upon a union representative to help them (Ippolito 1986; Weil 1991; Rabin 1991).

In sum, the object of progressive employment legislation was to extend the protective umbrella of government to those workers who lacked the personal, market, or human resources to look after themselves. A quarter century of experience demonstrates how far we are from success in that endeavor. There is no better index than the theme noted earlier in the drama of Anita Hill vs. Clarence Thomas, in which the nation's consciousness was "raised" about the severe practical difficulty faced by a woman who would like both to remain in her job and to enforce her legal right against sexual harassment on that job. And the ultimate irony of this *contretemps* is that shortly after Thomas was confirmed for the Supreme Court, political concern about irate women's groups forced the President and the Congress to agree on passage of yet another civil rights *law*, supposedly making it easier for women (and minorities) to sue their employer in court.

Employee Involvement

Whatever its popular and political attraction, then, there are marked deficiencies in regulation as a means of providing effective *protection* to workers, relying as this model does on outside lawyers and bureaucrats to represent and press for employee interests on the job. In addition, the regulatory model entirely ignores the independent value of active employee *participation* in the affairs of the workplace. Participation is what the recent employee involvement (EI) movement promises to achieve. Such plans, fashioned by a number of prominent nonunion firms in the seventies, range from modest schemes for job rotation and job enrichment to more extensive efforts to improve the quality of working life and from autonomous production teams to significant levels of employee stock ownership (via ESOPs).

The assumption of the EI movement is that employees want more than just financial and personal protection on the job. They also want the satisfaction of having a voice in their work and in the design of their workplace environment. Advocates of this new style of human resource management say that firms will be able to compete more effectively if they set out to elicit greater employee commitment by tapping the insights and ingenuity that experienced workers can contribute. The result, they say, will be more efficient, higher quality production and a more dedicated, creative work force. That is why in the *Electromation* case I mentioned at the outset, it was the lawyer for the Chamber of Commerce who told the NLRB it was high time to move beyond the anachronistic adversarial structure of the Wagner Act and to interpret our labor laws for the 1990s as *not* "requiring employees to check their brains at the front door when they come to work."

Skeptics, on the other hand, see EI as no more than a tarted-up version of the old company union (McLeod 1990). They object that even though EI programs provide nonunion workers with some measure of participation, the employees still lack any real power, something that is demonstrated quite clearly when a new management decides to abandon or to cut back on the firm's EI program. Tellingly, my Cambridge colleagues at the Harvard or Sloan Business Schools tend to label employee involvement "participatory *management*." The tacit assumption is that the personnel department, now sporting the fancy new designation as Human Resources Division, will assume the job of representing the interests of employees—thereby replacing the "outside" (and supposedly too adversarial) trade union.

To my mind these sophisticated and benevolent forms of partic-ipatory management have secured real benefits for employees in day-to-day relations with managers. That is why I would favor re-peal of Section 8(a)(2) of the NLRA which, on its face, does seem to make this form of employee involvement *per se* illegal. I do strongly oppose any such reform being accomplished on a piece-meal basis, through the NLRB and the courts eviscerating Congress' historic ban on "company unions" via a process of statutory "con-struction." Cutting back on the scope of Section 8(a)(2) should take place only as part of a broader legislative revamping of the entire NLRA, designed to make it easier for employers to embrace the union representation model of involvement if they so desire. Among other things, it is crucial to roll back the managerial exclusion that now denies collective bargaining rights to growing numbers of em-ployees who have even a modest involvement in and influence up-on employer decision making, even if such employer influence is exercised only as part of a group rather than singly (Rabban 1989).

The reason why such a restructured NLRA is important is that recent research (Levine and Tyson 1990; Eaton and Voos 1992; Kelley and Harrison 1992) has demonstrated the intrinsic limits on company-sponsored employee involvement as a mode of worker participation—limits that are as great if not greater than was observed earlier about government regulation as a mode of worker protection. Whatever was true of its origins, as the employee involvement movement has matured it turns out that unionized workers are considerably more likely than their nonunion counter-parts to secure and retain such involvement, and they are far more likely to wield the influence that comes from more searching mod-els of involvement (e.g., from team production systems and labor-management committees rather than small quality circles meeting occasionally with supervisors, or productivity gainsharing plans rather than deferred profit sharing). Ironically, it turns out as well that the union environment, with the guarantees and security that collective agreements provide, is most conducive to employers reaping tangible productivity improvements from such programs.

Nor should one be surprised by these facts. It is problematic to ask employees to entrust representation of their interests to a personnel department that is part of a unified management team ultimately accountable only to the shareholders and their boards of directors. In recent years these limits on participatory management have become vividly apparent in mergers, takeovers, and leveraged buyouts. Firms engaged in such major "restructuring" often increase the value of the shareholders' equity at considerable cost to the stake that employees have built up in their jobs. When put to the test in cases like these—the example of People's Express comes to mind—this more open, participatory style of management has been of little help in defending the vital interests of employees when a Frank Lorenzo takes charge—with his strikingly different human resource philosophy.

A New Model of Employee Representation

Why has neither government regulation nor participatory management been able to satisfy the employee need for either effective protection or constructive participation? The two models each display the same characteristic failing—the absence of an independent and cohesive worker base inside the firm that affords the individual employee a realistic chance to take full advantage of either new legal rights or on-the-job involvement. An apt illustration is the recent plant closing law—the Workers Adjustment and Retraining Notification Act (WARNA)—with its mandatory sixty-day notice of large-scale layoffs. WARNA does have the modest virtue of alerting individual nonunion workers to the need to start looking seriously for another job. But *unorganized* employees will hardly be able to devise and press for constructive alternatives to the employer plan, whether modest work sharing or a full-blown employee buy-out.

Labor Law Reform

By contrast, for all its limits and inadequacies the collective bargaining model does offer workers an organized instrument of their own, one that is far more likely to voice and represent the true needs and priorities of employees than even the most well-meaning government bureaucrat or company personnel manager. Unions can and do serve as a vehicle not just for securing traditional "bread and butter" issues in negotiations, but also helping employees take full advantage of the current trends towards individual employment rights and group involvement on the job. Recognition of these virtues of union representation, along with the flaws so often harped on in the popular press, helps make the case for serious labor law reform that would give American workers a realistic chance of having their interests represented by a labor organization "of their own choosing."

Out of that conviction, I have spent a considerable part of the last decade devising such a reform program—drawing in particular on my personal experience with Canadian legal innovations that helped keep union representation in Canada near the 40 percent mark while it was falling to near 15 percent in this country (Weiler 1980). I have proposed, for example, sharply restricting the length of election campaigns in order to reduce the time during which employers are tempted to use illegitimate tactics to win the hearts and minds of their employees (Weiler 1983). Another suggestion was restraints on permanent replacement of legal strikers struggling to win a first contract from a recalcitrant employer, even though the employer has lost the certification election (Weiler 1984). Here I mention briefly a third proposal, as American as apple pie, to allow the victims of antiunion retaliation access to the ordinary courts—to civil juries of their peers who would decide what are the appropriate damages for the often flagrantly illegal behavior of employers.

The most evident deficiency of the current NLRA system lies in its remedies for unfair labor practices. Under the Act the response to employer violations of the legal rules for the representation contest is far too slow and too modest to provide either meaningful redress or deterrence. For example, an employer prepared to make the necessary expenditures in lawyers' fees to secure all the process which is its due under the NLRA can easily postpone for a thousand days or more the *first* enforceable order of reinstatement of an illegally discharged union supporter, and the monetary awards issued by the Board in such cases now average a mere $2,000 apiece.

For a number of years, many people (including myself) have advocated expedited relief in such cases, perhaps through federal court injunctions that would require reinstatement of the fired employee. If such legal orders could be made available and effective, they would be the ideal method of enforcing the statute and making the victims whole. But I have grown steadily more pessimistic about the capacity of American labor law actually to replace a fired employee safely in his old job in a hostile plant, let alone to install a union as bargaining agent for an ever-changing unit of employees whose primary daily relationship is with their antiunion employer. But the one thing we know that American law can do quite well is force a guilty party to pay money to its victims. Consequently, I propose that we simply remove the current pre-emptive effect of the NLRA on tort claims that could otherwise be brought in state courts by union supporters who have been wrong-fully dismissed in violation of the long-established public policy supporting collective bargaining (Weiler 1986; Gottesman 1990).

The objective of such a step is quite apparent. Instead of the severely limited back pay awards available from the NLRB, a fired union supporter who chose to sue for damages in court instead of petitioning the NLRB for reinstatement could collect not only lost back pay, but also front pay for future earnings losses, compensa-tion for consequential economic and emotional harms, and even punitive damages if the employer's behavior were judged egregious enough. It would take only a few skilled plaintiff's attorneys winning six- or seven-figure jury verdicts to make employers sit up and take more serious notice of their obligations under the NLRA.

The justification for the proposal is also evident. Courts in almost every state now give nonunion workers the right to sue if they are fired for reasons which flout any of a host of public policies. Some of these policies are written straightforwardly into legislation, while others have been discerned by judges in a variety of less explicit sources. Recently the U.S. Supreme Court held that the NLRA did not preclude a unionized worker covered by a collective agreement from suing for a dismissal allegedly made in violation of an external public right—in that case a right arising under workers' compensation legislation (*Lingle* 1988). Historically, the first public policy restraint ever to be imposed on the dismissal prerogative of the employer was the Wagner Act's ban on discharg-ing employees who sought to organize a union. Ironically, present day victims of employer violations of this half-century-old public policy receive far less effective protection from traditional admin-istrative procedures than is enjoyed by claimants suing under stat-utes that are relative newcomers to the legal scene. It is high time, then, that we opened up state courthouse doors to the equally de-serving victims of discriminatory discharges during union cam-paigns.

Beyond Labor Law Reform

I remain thoroughly satisfied that such major alterations in our customary ways of doing things under the NLRA are justified. I am, however, pessimistic about the prospects for labor law reform. This sentiment is due, in part, to the politics of the issue. But I am also concerned about the efficacy of such legal changes even if they could be enacted.

Here again Canada offers some cogent lessons about the limits as well as the possibilities of labor law reform. Underneath the somewhat rosier picture visible in *aggregate* union density in Canada, one finds that union representation in the *private* sector has recently receded to somewhere under 30 percent, and among the private service employees in finance and retail industries—two of the fastest growing employment sectors—union coverage remains under 15 percent (Chaison and Rose 1991). Though these Canadian union levels are still more than twice as high as their American counterparts, the fact is that only a distinct minority of Canadian workers now enjoys any such representation.

The Canadian-U.S. comparison actually highlights the common features of the North American legal regime. In both countries, the "natural" pre-labor law state is for employees to go to work in a bank, an insurance company, or a computer manufacturer, unorganized and unrepresented. To organize a union from that starting point is an arduous, complex, and time-consuming job. Just about every nonunion employer is appalled at the prospect of a union presence in its operations, and management will deploy a variety of tactics designed to head this fate off. In Canada the tactics tend to take the form of obstruction, while in the United States too often they smack of intimidation. And as noted earlier, it takes only a critical mass of employers prepared to fire union supporters in their work force to raise widespread concern among all nonunion employees that they risk being personal victims.

The Catch-22 of the legal situation on both sides of the border is that to establish the necessary employee interest and then to overcome sustained managerial resistance, the organizing campaign must be spearheaded by a large existing union. Only an established union is likely to have the resources for such an undertaking: for example, among the clerical employees at my own Harvard University, and against relatively benign employer opposition, it took several years and several million dollars for the union to win just an eyelash election victory. (One AFL-CIO calculation I have seen puts its affiliates' organizing expenditures at roughly $1,000 for each employee in a newly established unit.) But unions with those

kinds of resources are likely to seem large, distant, and bureaucratic—precisely the kind of organization that a considerable number of
North American workers would rather not be part of, and the
employer very definitely would rather not deal with.

Some fraction of these nonunion employees can rely on their
individual mobility in the job market to better themselves. Others
remain quite satisfied with the representation provided by benevolent human resource management. There is a third group, though,
who feel dissatisfied with the status quo under which they are
locked into their present job, but who are unwilling to join the kind
of big union and to undertake the kind of traumatic organizing
effort that is needed to secure collective action for improved
working conditions.

For precisely these reasons, I am persuaded that we need a more
profound change in our law of the workplace: not just adding more
employment law rights, not just reforming labor laws to make
unions a more accessible option, but mandating a minimum form of
employee participation in all firms. Direct government intervention
in the workplace is no longer considered anathema as a matter of
principle, as it was in the 1930s and 1940s. We think nothing of
adopting new legal regulations that dictate certain substantive
protections for workers—for their health and safety, for example. I
was involved, fifteen years ago, in development by the Ontario
government of an "internal responsibility" alternative to the
American "command and control" model of OSHA: every Ontario
firm, union or nonunion, had to have an in-plant health and safety
committee as a mechanism for reducing on-the-job injuries in ways
that are tailored to the specific features of that workplace (Swinton
1983; Rees 1988). Generalizing from that experience and building on
the West German "works council" model, I now favor requiring
every American workplace above a certain size (say, 25 or 50
employees) to have an employee participation committee (an EPC)
encompassing a broad range of workplace concerns.

As a brief sketch of what I have elaborated in detail elsewhere
(Weiler 1990), a single committee would represent all the
employees in both the plant and the office, including professionals
and lower echelon managers. A proportional electoral system
would be designed to guarantee representation of each of the key
employee constituencies. The committee's jurisdiction would cover
a wide range of employment issues, involving the right to be
consulted before management could make material changes in

workplace conditions (e.g., via the introduction of new technology or the adoption of cost sharing or cost containment programs in health insurance). In addition, the EPC would play the front-line role in administering the growing number of regulatory programs for the workplace, ranging from OSHA to wrongful dismissal rights. (An apt illustration is the new plant closing notification law I mentioned earlier: the EPC would be an employee organization already in place not just to receive the required notice but to try to do something constructive with it—whether job banks, employee retraining, early retirement on pension, perhaps even an employee buy-out.)

Every EPC would be entitled to the extensive information necessary for performing its representation role for the employees, just as management must now provide the data needed by boards of directors representing shareholders. The committee would also be entitled to a defined level of financial resources—contributed jointly by the firm and the employees according to a statutory per capita formula—so that the committee could draw on the advice of people and organizations with experience and expertise in relevant subject matters. A prominent source of such assistance would likely be the trade union in that sector, but so also would be women's action committees, injured worker groups, and the like. Where a union already enjoyed bargaining rights in a workplace, the local union would function as the EPC, assuming the same responsibility and resources to represent the interests of its unit members.

I should emphasize that the immediate focus of this proposal is on employee participation in the office or the plant, not in the corporate boardroom. In the last few years, many people have called for employee representation on boards of directors, or for even greater employee control through ownership of the enterprise via ESOPs (Hyde 1992). This movement has both virtues and risks. To my mind, though, the bare insertion of a few employee director-representatives on a corporate board will make little difference in employees' lives unless there first is a base of employee organization in offices and shops. In allocating our scarce legal and political resources, then, we should give priority to participation in the workplace itself. For one thing, that is where direct contact is made with the daily lives of employees themselves. For another, employee councils at that level could provide meaningful accountability for those people who do purport to act as representatives of nonunion workers in the loftier realms of corporate decision making. That is because effective representation in offices and shops will inevitably require employee committees to become knowledgeable about traditional "management prerogatives," such as capital investment plans and marketing decisions. In that sense, even a "shop floor" model of worker representation requires far greater employee knowledge of what goes on in the boardrooms. Employee participation committees would thus help make ESOPs and other forms of partial worker ownership more meaningful than under current practice, where, unfortunately, the ESOP device has been used mainly as a tool of corporate finance, or as an anti-takeover buffer for entrenched management.

"Compulsory Unionism" or "Company Unionism"?

The foregoing is just a quick sketch of a program whose component parts I have addressed in more detail in *Governing the Workplace* (Weiler 1990). I have learned, though, that simply presenting this skeletal framework is sufficient to evoke sharply different, but equally visceral, reactions from both business executives and union officials.

To management, for example, an EPC is simply a disguised version of compulsory unionism, through which the government would take away from employees themselves this crucial choice about whether they will have such representation on the job. My answer is that, first, an employee participation committee simply is *not* like the unions that are the object of employee choice under traditional labor law—large, national, industrial organizations, engaged in full-fledged collective bargaining, and operating far beyond the confines of any single company. An EPC is no more than an indigenous base of worker representation, of and by employees themselves, built into the structure of every sizable firm. Next, employees do have a real need for the kind of involvement that an EPC would provide. As I observed earlier, this is precisely the direction being taken in the human resource policies of firms (nonunion and, even more so recently, union firms) that are considered the most innovative in North America. Progressive management appreciates that it may be in the interests of the business as well as of the work force to permit much greater involvement by, and thence elicit more commitment from, employees, in order to ensure the firm's survival and success in this demanding economic environment.

One must grant that there are legitimate issues for debate here. But the focus of that debate has to be on the substantive claims made by those who believe the optimal mode of workplace governance is the traditional managerial control over the work force (modified, if at all, only by specific collective agreements negotiated with the management of the union). Suppose one is persuaded, though, that direct democratic participation on the job, like health and safety on th job, is both a benefit that employees should have and one that more and more employers have shown they can provide while remaining productive. From that premise, one should no more be troubled by the broader community adopting as its public policy that this benefit be enjoyed by the employees in *all* sizable firms, than we would be troubled by the fact the community decides what is to be the minimum level of health and safety or pension security to be guaranteed to every worker as a minimum standard of civilized employment.

Indeed, one valuable role for employee participation committees is that they are likely to be the most sensible method of delivering health and safety, pension security, and the like to employees in a manner that also accommodates the needs of firms. Recall what was said earlier about Ontario's "internal responsibility" model of OSHA. The premise of that model is that employees in the firm will serve as principal inspectors and enforcement agents for the province's legal policy, while government agents concentrate on ensuring that this internal responsibility model itself functions properly. Not only does this mechanism promise to enhance the actual presence of the legal regime in tens of thousands of workplaces remote from the center of government, but it can also provide much more flexible adjustment to the needs of particular workplace settings than can be secured from outside bureaucrats and judges. Designed properly, an EPC can actually be made somewhat attractive to firms who realize that their own employees have the right to specify whether certain workplace hazards really are unduly dangerous, or certain discharges really were wrongful, and thence protect the employer from later second-guessing on that score in a courtroom. (The EPC would function, in that respect, along the lines of unions that wield authority to settle individual contract grievances, subject to a reasonably relaxed duty of fair representation [Goldberg 1985].)

However, when this corollary to the EPC idea is spelled out clearly, it only reinforces the objection one hears from so many union leaders and other worker representatives. They tend to characterize the employee participation committee as no more than a modern version of the old "company union": a program designed to give employees the impression that they are participating in firm decisions, yet leaving employees without real power or influence. Worse, it is feared, this kind of in-house representation is likely to distract the nonunion work force from what it really needs—which is to join a large independent union with the strengths and resources to make management sit up and take serious notice of the employees' concerns.

There is something troubling in that line of objection, especially for someone like myself who is generally sympathetic to the premises of the collective bargaining model. Ultimately, however, one must think seriously about the statistics recited earlier: less than 15 percent of private-sector employees currently enjoy full-fledged collective bargaining through an established union. This percentage remains in a free fall state, and there are inherent limits to what (politically elusive) reform of our labor laws can do to close the representation gap.

The question, then, is which path one should follow from that starting point. Using as a concrete reference point the cases alluded to at the outset, should a woman experiencing sexual harassment be left with no organized representation on the job and simply told to consult an outside lawyer and sue (if she dares)? Is it sufficient to rely on the kind of "rap group sessions" sponsored by the personnel department at *Electromation*, a program that management felt might improve the firm's productivity? Or do we think that employees experiencing these and other kinds of workplace problems would be better off—not necessarily *ideally* off, but materially better off—if they could draw upon a system of indigenous employee representation that rested on a legal mandate rather than just managerial discretion? When the choice is squarely faced in those terms, the answer seems quite clear to me.

One reason is that it is a mistake to suppose, as do so many liberal law reformers, that unless the state establishes guaranteed legal rights for workers, it establishes nothing at all. First, as I said earlier, experience and research have graphically demonstrated that writing a law on the books does not guarantee that those rights will live and flourish in practice. Instead, the fate of the law depends on the mode of representation and enforcement afforded those employee rights in the real world of the workplace. At the same time, using scarce legal resources to *reconstruct* rather than *regulate* the workplace itself enhances market sanctions against unfeeling or oppressive management. Employers do face real economic incentives not just to recruit and retain their work forces, but even more to motivate their employees to work hard and intelligently rather than just go through the motions on the job. Those kinds of market incentives will be strongly reinforced if employees, through their employee participation committee, are put in a position where they now realize what their firms should be doing to address employee concerns, but can see that incumbent management simply does not care to do so. The result may well be that as the firm loses productivity, it is management that will lose its jobs.

I suspect that life in such a reconstructed labor market will make many employees perfectly happy with the experience of such direct group dealings with management: these workers won't want anything more. To my mind such cases should be taken as a mark of the success of this new public policy: the aim of this policy, after all, is to improve the condition of *employees*—irrespective of whether doing so will serve the interests of existing labor organizations. Likely, though, the experience of other employees will not be so satisfying. What I observed earlier about "command and control" OSHA regulation in this country has also proved true of the more participatory "internal responsibility" version of OSHA in Canada. In order that an in-house EPC be fully effective in dealing with recalcitrant management teams, employees will often need the experience and the resources they get from membership in a larger union with real bargaining clout. Once employees have been organized by law to exercise just limited collective voice within the enterprise, but have grown dissatisfied with their lack of real influence, many will be more inclined to cast their lot with a full-blown union (Jacoby 1989; Ichniowski and Zax 1990; Jacoby and Verma 1992). At least, that would be true if the union movement were to make itself more inviting to unorganized workers, and labor law were reshaped to make the representation procedure less intimidating an experience than it now is.

Conclusion

That last point underscores my bottom-line position on this topic. There is no one ideal institution for addressing employee needs in our changing workplace. Competitive labor markets, individual legal rights, management-sponsored employee involvement, all have their values as well as their limitations. In quite a number of settings collective bargaining performs favorably by comparison with those alternatives. That is why I continue to hope that we could begin to revamp our federal labor law to give private-sector unionism some prospects of revival in the 21st century. But I am satisfied that priority in expending our scarce political and legal resources should be placed on guaranteeing a basic level of employee organization and representation in every workplace. From that platform American workers might stand a fair chance of taking advantage of what all these institutions promise, including labor law and labor unions.

References

Bartel, Ann P., and Lucy Glenn Thomas. 1985. "Direct and Indirect Effects of Regulation: A New Look at OSHA's Impact." *Journal of Law and Economics* 28, pp. 1-25.

Chaison, Gary N., and Joseph B. Rose. 1991. "The Macrodeterminants of Union Growth and Decline." In *The State of the Unions*, eds. George Strauss, Daniel G. Gallagher, and Jack Fiorito. Madison, WI: Industrial Relations Research Assn., pp. 3-45.

Dertouzos, James N., Elaine Holland, and Patricia Ebener. 1988. *The Legal and Economic Consequences of Termination*. Santa Monica, CA: RAND Institute for Civil Justice.

Dertouzos, James N., and Lynn A. Karoly. 1992. *Labor Market Responses to Employer Liability*. Santa Monica, CA: RAND Institute for Civil Justice.

Donohue, John J., III, and Peter Siegelman. 1991. "The Changing Nature of Employment Discrimination Litigation." *Stanford Law Review* 43, pp. 983-1033.

Dowd, Nancy E. 1989. "Work and Family: The Gender Paradox and the Limitations of Discrimination Analysis in Restructuring the Workplace." *Harvard Civil Rights—Civil Liberties Law Review* 24, pp. 79-172.

Eaton, Adrienne E., and Paula B. Voos. 1992. "Unions and Contemporary Innovations in Work Organization, Compensation, and Employee Participation." In *Unions and Economic Competitiveness*, eds. Lawrence Mishel and Paula B. Voos. Washington, DC: M. E. Sharpe.

Freed, Mayer G., and Daniel D. Polsby. 1989. "Just Cause for Termination Rules and Economic Efficiency." *Emory Law Journal* 38, pp. 1097-1144.

Freeman, Richard. 1992. "Is Declining Unionization of the U.S. Good, Bad, or Irrelevant?" In *Unions and Economic Competitiveness*, eds. Lawrence Mishel and Paula B. Voos. Washington, DC: M. E. Sharpe.

Goldberg, Michael J. 1985. "The Duty of Fair Representation: What the Courts Do in Fact." *Buffalo Law Review* 34, pp. 89-171.

Gottesman, Michael H. 1990. "Rethinking Labor Law Preemption: State Laws Facilitating Unionization." *Yale Journal on Regulation* 7, pp. 355-426.

Heckscher, Charles C. 1988. *The New Unionism: Employee Involvement in the Changing Corporation*. New York: Basic Books.

Hyde, Alan. 1992. "In Defense of Employee Ownership." *Chicago-Kent Law Review*. Forthcoming.

Ichniowski, Casey, and Jeffrey S. Zax. 1990. "Today's Associations, Tomorrow's Unions." *Industrial and Labor Relations Review* 43, no. 1, pp. 191-208.

Ippolito, Richard A. 1986. *Pensions, Economics and Public Policy.* Homewood, IL: Dow-Jones-Irwin.

Jacoby, Sanford M. 1985. *Employing Bureaucracy: Managers, Unions, and the Transformation of Work in American Industry, 1900-1945.* New York: Columbia University Press.

_____. 1989. "Reckoning with Company Unions: The Case of Thompson Products, 1934-1964." *Industrial and Labor Relations Review* 43, no. 1, pp. 19-40.

Jacoby, Sanford M., and Anil Verma. 1992. "Enterprise Unions in the U.S. *Industrial Relations* 31, pp. 137-158.

Kaufman, Bruce, ed. 1988. *How Labor Markets Work: Reflections on Theory and Practice* by John C. Dunlop, Clark Kerr, Richard Lester, and Lloyd Reynolds. Lexington, MA: Lexington Books.

Kelley, Maryellen R., and Bennett Harrison. 1992. "Unions, Technology, and Labor-Management Cooperation." In *Unions and Economic Competitiveness,* eds. Lawrence Mishel and Paula B. Voos. Washington, DC: M. E. Sharpe.

Lalonde, Robert J., and Bernard D. Meltzer. 1991. "Hard Times for Unions: Another Look at the Significance of Employer Illegalities." *University of Chicago Law Review* 58, pp. 953-1014.

Levine, David I., and Laura D'Andrea Tyson. 1990. "Participation, Productivity, and the Firm's Environment." In *Paying for Productivity: A Look at the Evidence,* ed. Alan S. Blinder. Washington, DC: Brookings Institute.

Lingle v. Norge Division of Magic Chef, Inc., 486 U.S. 399 (1988).

McLeod, Wilson. 1990. "Labor-Management Cooperation: Competing Visions and Labor's Challenge." *Industrial Relations Law Journal* 12, pp. 233-291.

NLRB v. Jones and Laughlin Corp., 301 U.S. 1 (1937).

Rabban, David M. 1989. "Distinguishing Excluded Managers from Covered Professionals under the NLRA." *Columbia Law Review* 89, pp. 1775-1860.

Rabin, Robert J. 1991. "The Role of Unions in the Rights-based Workplace. *University of San Francisco Law Review* 25, pp. 169-263.

Rees, Joseph V. 1988. *Reforming the Workplace: A Study of Self-Regulation in Occupational Safety.* Philadelphia: University of Pennsylvania Press.

Swinton, Katherine E. 1983. "Enforcement of Occupational Health and Safety Legislation: The Role of the Internal Responsibility System." In *Studies in Labor Law,* eds. Kenneth P. Swan and Katherine E. Swinton. Toronto: Butterworths, pp. 143-175.

Symposium. 1991. "Drug Testing in the Workplace." *William and Mary Law Review* 33, pp. 1-252.

United States Congress. 1991. *Preventing Replacement of Economic Strikers: Hearings on H.R. 3936 and S. 2112.* Washington, DC: U.S. Government Printing Office.

Viscusi, W. Kip. 1986. "The Impact of Occupational Safety and Health Regulation: 1973-1983." *RAND Journal of Economics* 17, pp. 567-580.

Weil, David. 1991. "Enforcing OSHA: The Role of Labor Unions." *Industrial Relations* 30, pp. 20-35.

Weiler, Paul C. 1980. *Reconcilable Differences: New Directions in Canadian Labor Law.* Toronto: Carswell Press.

_____. 1983. 'Promises to Keep: Securing Workers' Rights to Self-organization under the NLRA." *Harvard Law Review* 96, pp. 1769-1827.

_____. 1984. "Striking a New Balance: Freedom of Contract and the Prospects for Union Representation." *Harvard Law Review* 98, pp. 351-420.

_____. 1986. "Milestone or Tombstone: The Wagner Act at Fifty." *Harvard Journal on Legislation* 23, pp. 1-31.

_____. 1990. *Governing the Workplace: The Future of Labor and Employment Law.* Cambridge, MA: Harvard University Press.

_____. 1991a. "Comparable Worth in United States Antidiscrimination Law." In *Women's Wages: Stability and Change in Six Industrialized Countries,* ed. Steven Willborn. Greenwich, CT: JAI Press.

_____. 1991b. "Hard Times for Unions: Challenging Times for Scholars." *University of Chicago Law Review* 58, pp. 1015-1032.

CHAPTER 3

Union Membership in the United States: The Decline Continues

HENRY S. FARBER AND ALAN B. KRUEGER
Princeton University

The decline of unionization in the private sector in the United States continues unabated. In 1977, 21.7 percent of workers in the private-sector non-agricultural labor force were members of unions or employee associations similar to unions (the private-sector unionization rate). This fell to 15.6 percent by 1984. The private-sector unionization rate fell even further to 11.9 percent by 1991, lower than before the passage of the National Labor Relations Act.[1] The picture is quite different in the public sector where the unionization rate stood at 32.7 percent in 1977, increased to 35.8 percent by 1984, and stood at 36.9 percent in 1991. In fact, by 1991 fully 40 percent of union or employee association members in the United States were in the public sector (compared with 25.9 percent in 1977).[2] Overall, 23.8 percent of the non-agricultural labor force were members of unions or employee associations in 1977. This fell to 19.1 percent by 1984, and it fell further to 16.4 percent by 1991.

There is no disagreement about the dimensions of the decline of labor unions. However, there is an ongoing debate about its causes. Earlier work by Farber (1985) and Dickens and Leonard (1985) suggests that shifts in demographic, industrial, and occupational composition of the labor force away from traditionally heavily unionized types of workers and sectors accounted for less than half of the decline in unionization between the mid-1970s and the mid-1980s. This conclusion is supported by Weiler (1990) and Freeman (1988), who argues (p. 79) that "the anti-union management offensive in the private sector is the key to de-unionization in the United States. . . ."

Freeman bases his conclusion on the facts that (1) unionization has grown in the public sector in the U.S. (where management opposition is more restricted), while declining in the private sector; and (2) unionization has not declined in Canada, where structural shifts in the labor force similar to those in the U.S. have occurred and where the labor law is structured in a way to make private-sector employer resistance more difficult. However, more recent evidence from Canada (e.g., Kumar 1991) shows that the Canadian public sector is much more heavily unionized than the Canadian private sector and that unionization has grown rapidly in the public sector while declining somewhat in the private sector. Thus, it appears that the Canadian experience is not completely at odds with the U.S. experience.[3]

Farber (1987, 1989, 1990) approached the decline of unionization from a different direction. He uses survey data from the 1977 Quality of Employment Survey (QES) and a 1984 survey conducted for the AFL-CIO (AFL) on nonunion workers' preferences for union membership to investigate changes in the demand for union representation and the supply of nonunion jobs relative to demand. The specific information used are the responses of nonunion workers to a question asking if the worker would vote for or against union representation on their current job if an election were held. He finds that there was a decline in the demand for union representation but that the supply of union jobs relative to demand did not change significantly.

Riddell (1991) has examined the demand for and relative supply of union jobs in both the U.S. and Canada using the same 1984 AFL data for the U.S. as Farber and using survey data for Canada from a 1990 survey conducted for the Canadian Federation of Labor (CFL) on a different aspect of workers' preferences for union representation. However, the U.S. and Canadian data are not directly comparable for at least two reasons. First, the questions asked in the AFL and CFL surveys pose potentially very different issues to the respondents. Second, there is a seven-year time difference between the two surveys. Nonetheless, Riddell concludes based on this evidence that most of the difference between the U.S. and Canada is due to a difference in the supply of union jobs relative to demand and that very little is due to difference in the underlying demand for union representation.

In this study we extend this earlier work on the demand for and supply of union representation in several directions. First, we analyze new data for 1991 from the General Social Survey (GSS) on U.S. nonunion workers' preferences for union representation based on responses to the question of how they would vote in a secret-ballot election. This allows us to examine trends since 1984 in demand and supply in the U.S. Next, we examine briefly the public-private differential in union membership in the U.S. using the 1984 AFL data.[4] Finally, we analyze data from a small-scale household survey that we conducted in the U.S. in 1992. In this survey we asked about worker preferences for union representation using both the AFL-style question on voting in a hypothetical election and the CFL-style question on whether the worker would consider joining a union or professional association in the future. This allows us to evaluate systematic differences in responses to the two questions so that we can compare worker attitudes toward unions in Canada and the U.S. in ways that are more reliable than those used in earlier work.

Our main conclusions are summarized quite easily. First, we find that virtually all of the decline in union membership in the United States between 1977 and 1991 is due to a decline in demand as measured by the fraction of the work force that either holds a union job or would vote for union representation on their nonunion job. There was virtually no change over this period in the relative supply of union jobs as measured (inversely) by the fraction of the work force that desires union representation (measured by the vote question) but holds nonunion jobs. Additionally, very little of the decline in unionization in the U.S. can be accounted for by structural shifts in the composition of the labor force. Next, we find that all of the higher unionization rate in the U.S. public sector in 1984 can be accounted for by higher demand for unionization and that there is actually *more* frustrated demand for union representation in the public sector. Finally, we tentatively conclude that the difference in unionization rates between the U.S. and Canada is accounted for in equal measure by differences in demand and in supply between the countries.

A Demand-Supply Framework

Earlier work by Abowd and Farber (1982) and Farber (1983) developed a model of the determination of the union status of workers that allowed for queues for union jobs. In this model, workers might demand union jobs in the sense that they would prefer a union job (or prefer their job to be unionized) without being willing to invest in organizing a union (either on their current job or on another job). This is because the rights to existing union jobs are not owned either by the workers who organize union jobs or by the workers who currently hold union jobs. Outside of a few craft-based unions, employers are free to hire whomever they see fit to fill vacancies in union jobs. While dues and initiation fees are required of union members, these generally are not sufficient to capitalize the flow of benefits of union employment (Raisian 1983). The result is that there is likely to be excess demand for existing union jobs while there may be equilibrium in the market for new union jobs. The quantity of union jobs available depends on the costs of organization (supply) and benefits of organization to workers (demand). This model is presented in more detail by Farber (1983, 1990).

The data requirements for measurement of the demand for and supply of union jobs exceed what are normally available. Ordinarily, data are available on the union status of workers. However, while it is reasonable to assume that all union workers prefer union representation, the queuing model suggests that not all nonunion workers prefer to be nonunion.[5] Nonunion workers fall into two categories: (1) those who prefer nonunion employment, and (2) those who prefer union employment but are not hired by a union employer. The core analyses in this study rely on four surveys that have specific information on the preferences of nonunion workers that can be used to assign them to one of these two categories.

The total demand for union jobs is measured by the fraction of workers who are either union members or would prefer to have union representation. The supply of union jobs relative to demand is measured by the fraction of workers demanding union representation who are actually union members. If there were no queues for union jobs, this fraction would be one. To the extent that there are nonunion workers who prefer union representation, this fraction will be less than one. A direct measure of the size of the queue for union jobs (and, hence, an inverse measure of relative supply) is the fraction of the total work force that demands union representation but are working in nonunion jobs. If there were no queues this fraction would be zero. We focus on this measure of frustrated demand as our (inverse) measure of supply.

To see this more clearly note that a worker is unionized if and only if he/she demands union representation and is hired by a union employer. A probability statement for the likelihood of worker i being unionized is

(1) $\Pr(U_i=1) = \Pr(U_i=1 \mid D_i=1) \cdot \Pr(D_i=1)$,

where U_i is a dichotomous variable that equals one if worker i is unionized and zero otherwise, and D_i is a dummy variable that equals one if worker i desires union representation and zero otherwise. The probability that worker i is not unionized is

(2) $\Pr(U_i=0) = \Pr(D_i=0) + \Pr(U_i=0 \mid D_i=1) \cdot \Pr(D_i=1)$.

This makes clear the two groups that make up the nonunion sector. The first group does not desire union representation, and the second group desires union representation but does not hold union jobs. Finally, note that we can write the probability that i is unionized as

(3) $\Pr(U_i=1) = \Pr(D_i=1) - \Pr(D_i = 1, U_i=0)$.

The first term represents the demand for union representation, and the second term represents frustrated demand or inverse supply. Thus, the probability that a worker is unionized is equal to the probability that he/she desires union representation *minus* the probability that the worker desires union representation but is not hired by a union employer.

This demand/supply framework is extremely useful both for evaluating competing explanations for the decline of unions in the United States and for making the U.S./Canada cross-country comparison. Consider first the U.S. decline. One explanation is that workers are simply less interested in union representation than in the past. This would be reflected directly in $\Pr(D_i=1)$. Another explanation is that more vigorous and effective employer resistance to union organizing efforts makes it more difficult for unions to organize new workers, reducing the relative supply of union jobs. This is an increase in frustrated demand, $\Pr(D_i=1, U_i=0)$.

These explanations are not mutually exclusive, and increased employer resistance might reduce demand in two ways. First, if employers treat their nonunion employees better in order to forestall unionization, this will reduce demand as measured. Second, if employers (legally or illegally) influence their employees in other ways to oppose union representation, demand will also be reduced. To the extent that this latter behavior has increased in recent years, we would attribute a larger share of the decline in union membership to demand than is warranted.

Consider a change in unionization from year s to year t. The change in the probability of unionization can be written as[6]

$$(4) \quad \Pr(U_t=1) - \Pr(U_s=1) = \Big[\Pr(D_t=1) - \Pr(D_s=1)\Big]$$
$$-\Big[\Pr(D_t=1, U_t=0) - \Pr(D_s=1, U_s=0)\Big].$$

The term in the first brackets measures the change in demand between s and t. The term in the second brackets measures the change in frustrated demand or demand in excess of supply.

Now consider the U.S./Canada comparison. One argument for the higher rate of unionization in Canada is that workers in Canada are more favorably disposed toward collective action so that the demand for unionization will be higher in Canada than in the United States (Lipset 1989). An alternative view (Freeman 1988; Weiler 1990) is that the legal framework governing organization and collective bargaining in Canada is more favorable toward unions than that in the United States. It is noted particularly that Canadian unions can organize workers strictly on the basis of the signing of authorization cards and without the secret-ballot election that employers can (and do) request in the United States. To the extent that these legal differences make it more difficult to organize workers in the U.S. relative to Canada, there will be more frustrated demand for union representation in the U.S. than in Canada, but overall demand is likely to be similar.

We can write the U.S./Canada difference in the probability of unionization analogously to equation (4) as

$$(5) \quad \Pr(U_C=1) - \Pr(U_A=1) = \Big[\Pr(D_C=1) - \Pr(D_A=1)\Big]$$
$$-\Big[\Pr(D_C=1, U_A=0) - \Pr(D_C=1, U_A=0)\Big],$$

where the subscript c refers to Canada and the subscript a refers to the U.S. The term in the first brackets measures the difference in demand between Canada and the U.S. The term in the second brackets measures the difference in frustrated demand.

Our plan is to use a measure of demand for union representation among nonunion workers in 1977, 1984, and 1991 in the U.S. to decompose changes in unionization in the U.S. into changes in demand and changes in supply as measured (inversely) by frustrated demand. Similarly, we will use a measure of demand for union representation among nonunion workers in Canada and the United States to decompose changes in unionization into changes in demand and changes in supply.

Data

The key information required for our analysis is information on the preferences of nonunion workers for union representation. There have been three surveys designed to be broadly representative of the nonunion U.S. labor force that have this information. These are the 1977 Quality of Employment Survey (QES), a survey conducted in 1984 by Lou Harris Associates for the AFL-CIO (AFL) and the 1991 General Social Survey (GSS).[7] Additionally, we conducted our own small-scale survey of households in May-June 1992. We refer to this survey as the Farber-Krueger (F-K) survey. The F-K survey was conducted by phone, using a random sample of phone numbers chosen to be representative of exchanges in the continental United States. A total of 201 workers responded to our survey.[8]

The measure of preferences of nonunion workers for union representation is based on the responses to similar questions in all four surveys asking whether the worker would vote for union representation on their current job if an election were held. The precise question on the QES and GSS is

> If an election were held with secret ballots, would you vote for or against having a union or employee association represent you?

The allowed responses are: (1) for, and (2) against. The precise question on the AFL and F-K surveys is

> If an election were held tomorrow to decide whether your workplace would be unionized or not, do you think you would definitely vote for a union, probably vote for a union, probably vote against a union, or definitely vote against a union?

The allowed responses are: (1) definitely vote for a union, (2) probably vote for a union, (3) probably vote against a union, (4) definitely vote against a union, and (5) not sure. For consistency with the QES and GSS, we recode the first two responses as "for" and the third and fourth responses as "against." The fifth response is coded as missing.

Our view is that these two questions are similar enough that the responses can be compared across surveys. This is supported by the fact that the fraction of nonunion workers who give a pro-union response is almost identical on the 1991 GSS (with the first form of the question) and the 1992 F-K survey (with the second form of the question).[9] We interpret the response to these questions as indicating the desire of the worker for union representation *assuming that the worker does not have to bear the cost of organization.*

All but the AFL survey were designed to yield representative samples of the employed work force. The AFL survey departs from representativeness in not including self-employed workers and in systematically undersampling union members. Since we are interested only in workers who are employed by others and in the specific information available for nonunion workers on their preferences for union representation, this is not a problem.[10] Where representative samples of both union and nonunion workers are required, information from the May 1977 Current Population Survey (CPS) and from the Merged Outgoing Rotation Group CPS files for 1984 and 1991 are used.

Samples of workers were derived from the four surveys in an identical fashion. These samples consist of all non-agricultural and non-managerial workers who were not self-employed and for whom complete information was available on the workers' demographic characteristics, industry, occupation, union status, and preference for union representation. The nonunion sample sizes are 663 for the QES, 907 for the AFL survey, 537 for the GSS, and 105 for the F-K survey. The union sample sizes are 298 for the 1977 QES, 231 for the 1984 AFL survey, 117 for the 1991 GSS, and 29 for the 1992 F-K survey. In some of our analyses, we combine the GSS and the F-K survey to yield larger samples for the most recent time period.[11]

In addition to augmenting the recent data on worker preferences, there are two key features of the F-K survey that are important for the analysis. First, we collected information on three dimensions of job satisfaction using questions that are identical to those on the 1977 QES. Since the GSS does not contain comparable questions on these aspects of job satisfaction, our survey enables a more recent comparison of trends in job satisfaction and unionization. This may be important given Farber's (1990) finding that the demand of nonunion workers for union representation is strongly inversely related to job satisfaction. Second, we implemented a "split-ballot" experiment in which we asked the AFL question on union status as well as a related—but different—question that has been used by Riddell (1991) to study worker demand for union representation in Canada. The order of these two questions was randomly interchanged in half of the surveys. Results of this split-ballot experiment are used later in the analysis of U.S./Canada differences in union membership.

We also created samples from the CPS for the relevant years that use identical selection criteria. These samples, weighted by the CPS sampling weights, are used to derive estimates of the population unionization rate.

Table 1 contains summary statistics for the seven samples on the variables used in the analysis. Due to the large underlying sample sizes, the weighted CPS fractions are precise estimates of the population fractions. The data show a decline in the fraction unionized (union membership) from 25.3 percent in 1977 to 20.6 percent in 1984 to 17.7 percent in 1991. The four smaller samples do not line up uniformly with the CPS unionization rates. The QES unionization rate is significantly higher than that derived from the May 1977 CPS.[12] The AFL survey unionization rate is almost identical to that derived from the 1984 CPS, but this should not be the case given the 10 percent undersampling of union members known to have occurred in the AFL survey. The GSS unionization rate lines up very well with that derived from the 1991 CPS. The unionization rate is insignificantly higher in the F-K survey than in the 1991 CPS (p-value = 0.27).

Analysis of Change in Union Membership in the United States

Table 2 contains estimates of the coefficients on year dummy variables from linear-probability and logit models of union membership estimated using the 1977, 1984, and 1991 CPS data. The model without controls for labor force structure simply

EMPLOYEE REPRESENTATION

TABLE 1
Sample Fractions

Variable	1977 QES	CPS	1984 AFL	CPS	1991 GSS	CPS	1992 F-K
Union Member	.310	.253	.203	.206	.179	.177	.216
Female	.387	.443	.468	.472	.520	.483	.537
Married	.649	.620	.639	.585	.543	.569	.537
Married Female	.176	.242	.274	.254	.266	.259	.269
Nonwhite	.118	.119	.118	.136	.164	.151	.164
South	.350	.312	.308	.342	.330	.342	.299
Industry:							
manufacturing	.305	.273	.223	.238	.208	.205	.157
construction	.053	.056	.141	.057	.058	.052	.060
trans., comm. public util.	.084	.067	.092	.077	.075	.076	.082
trade	.158	.195	.138	.218	.171	.219	.179
finance, insur real estate	.044	.049	.060	.056	.063	.057	.067
services	.356	.360	.346	.354	.425	.391	.455
Occupation:							
blue collar	.437	.388	.389	.342	.273	.315	.253
clerical	.176	.209	.215	.198	.202	.197	.172
service	.139	.166	.115	.159	.165	.163	.112
prof, tech	.207	.168	.213	.179	.242	.199	.284
sales	.041	.069	.068	.122	.118	.126	.179
Education:							
<12	.224	.283	.120	.188	.135	.156	.082
=12	.372	.401	.365	.430	.335	.413	.358
13-15	.220	.160	.234	.200	.283	.224	.261
>=16	.184	.156	.281	.182	.247	.207	.299
Age							
<=24	.198	.262	.181	.229	.125	.181	.127
25-34	.310	.259	.341	.298	.301	.294	.276
35-44	.201	.178	.229	.212	.318	.256	.343
45-54	.168	.167	.151	.142	.135	.159	.142
>=55	.123	.134	.098	.119	.121	.110	.112
Nonunion Workers Preferences:							
Pro-union Vote	.386		.331		.337		.352
Sample size:	961	51,624	1138	153,043	654	153,001	134

Note: The CPS data are from May for 1977 and from the merged outgoing rotation group file for 1984 and 1991. The CPS fractions are weighted by the CPS final sample weights. All variables are dummy variables.

replicates the sample fractions in Table 1, and it shows a 4.3 percentage point drop in the union membership rate between 1977

TABLE 2

Linear Probability and Logit Models of Probability of Unionization
1977, 1984, 1991 CPS

Selected Parameters

Variable	(1) OLS	(2) OLS	(3) Logit	(4) Logit
1984 Dummy	−.0478 (.0017)	−.0314 (.0016)	−.271 (.0100)	−.227 (.0113)
1991 Dummy	−.0765 (.0017)	−.0580 (.0015)	−.457 (.0101)	−.442 (.0115)
Labor Force Struc.	NO	YES	NO	YES
R-squared	.0059	.181		
Log-Likelihood n = 357668			−182660.2	−148454.3

Note: The base year is 1977. Self-employed workers, managers, and agricultural workers are deleted from the analysis. Labor Force Structure includes a set of 21 variables representing main effects for sex, marital status, the interaction of sex and marital status, race, region (2 categories), age (5 categories), education (4 categories), public sector, industry (6 categories), and occupation (5 categories). The numbers in parentheses are standard errors.

and 1984. There is a further 2.4 percentage point drop between 1984 and 1991. The central point to note is that when controls for labor force structure (sex, marital status, race, age, education, region, industry, occupation, and public sector) are introduced, the differences in unionization rate by year fall somewhat. About 35 percent of the 4.8 point decline in unionization between 1977 and 1984 can be accounted for by structural changes in the labor force. However, only about 7.3 percent of the 2.9 point drop in unionization between 1984 and 1991 is accounted for by structural changes. Overall, about 25 percent of the 7.7 point overall decline between 1977 and 1991 can be accounted for by structural changes in the labor force.

The demand for unionization among nonunion workers fell between 1977 and 1984 but remained relatively steady between 1984 and 1991. Table 3 contains estimates of the coefficients on year dummy variables from linear-probability and logit models of nonunion-worker demand for union representation estimated using the 1977 QES, 1984 AFL, and the 1991-92 GSS/F-K data. The model without controls for labor force experience indicates a significant 5.5 percentage point drop in nonunion-worker demand between

TABLE 3

Linear Probability and Logit Models of
Probability that Non-Union Worker Desires Union Representation

1977 QES, 1984 AFL, 1991/92 GSS/F-K

Selected Parameters

Variable	(1) OLS	(2) OLS	(3) Logit	(4) Logit
1984 Dummy	−.0554 (.0244)	−.0438 (.0244)	−.241 (.107)	−.205 (.115)
1991/92 Dummy	−.0466 (.0264)	−.0661 (.0266)	−.202 (.115)	−.308 (.126)
Labor Force Struc.	NO	YES	NO	YES
R-squared	.0612	.0808		
Log-Likelihood n = 2212			−1429.3	−1432.0

Note: The base year is 1977. Self-employed workers, managers, and agricultural workers are deleted from the analysis. Labor Force Structure includes a set of 21 variables representing main effects for sex, marital status, the interaction of sex and marital status, race, region (2 categories), age (5 categories), education (4 categories), industry (6 categories), and occupation (5 categories). The numbers in parentheses are standard errors.

1977 and 1984 (p-value = 0.012), and it shows an insignificant 0.9 percentage point *increase* between 1984 and 1991 (p-value = 0.358). Demand remains significantly lower (by 4.7 percentage points) in 1991 than in 1977 (p-value = 0.039).

The results change slightly after controlling for labor force structure.[13] The structural variables account for about 20 percent of the decline in demand among nonunion workers between 1977 and 1984. However, the insignificant increase we found between 1984 and 1991 is now estimated to be an insignificant decrease. The overall decrease between 1977 and 1991, which was estimated to be 4.7 percentage points, actually increases to 6.6 percentage points after labor force structure is accounted for (p-value = 0.007). Overall, we conclude that little if any of the decline in the demand for union representation among nonunion workers can be accounted for by shifts in labor force structure.

With these estimates in hand, we are ready to apportion the decline in unionization to changes in demand and supply. Table 4 contains the levels of key probabilities in 1977, 1984, and 1991 along

TABLE 4

Analysis of Change in Union Membership

Probabilities

(standard errors)

	Level 1977	Level 1984	Level 1991	Change 77 to 84	Change 84 to 91	Change 77 to 91
Pr(U=1)	.253	.206	.177	−.047	−.029	−.076
	(.0019)	(.0010)	(.0010)	(.0022)	(.0014)	(.0022)
Pr(D=1 | U=0)	.386	.331	.340	−.055	.009	−.046
	(.0189)	(.0156)	(.0187)	(.0245)	(.0244)	(.0266)
Pr(D=1, U=0)	.288	.263	.280	−.0256	.0170	−.0085
	(.0048)	(.0032)	(.0033)	(.00582)	(.0046)	(.0059)
Pr(D=1)	.541	.469	.457	−.0725	−.0120	−.0845
	(.0142)	(.0124)	(.0154)	(.0188)	(.0198)	(.0209)

Sources and Definitions:

Pr(U=1): The probability that a worker is a union member. Computed from weighted tabulations of the CPS. Table 1. The standard errors are sampling errors computed as the square root of $p(1-p)/n$.

Pr(D=1 | U=0): The probability that a nonunion worker demands union representation. Computed from tabulations of the "vote" question on the 1977 QES, 1984 AFL survey, 1991/92 GSS and F-K surveys. The standard errors are sampling errors computed as the square root of $p(1-p)/n$.

Pr(D=1, U=0): The probability that a worker demands union representation but is not employed on a union job (frustrated demand). Computed as Pr(D=1 | U=0) · Pr(U=0) from this table. The standard errors are computed by the "delta" method.

Pr(D=1): The probability that a worker demands union representation. This is the sum of the probability that a worker is a union member and the probability that a worker desires union representation but is not employed on a union job (union membership plus frustrated demand). Formally, this is Pr(U=1) + Pr(D=1, U=0) and is computed from this table. The standard errors are computed by the "delta" method.

with computations of changes from 1977 to 1984, 1984 to 1991, and 1977 to 1991. The first row summarizes the changes in the probability of union membership while the second row summarizes the change in nonunion-worker demand for union representation. These are the quantities summarized in Table 1 and analyzed in Tables 2 and 3. The third row of the table uses these quantities to compute frustrated demand, Pr(D=1, U=0), which is defined in terms of the measured quantities as

(6) $Pr(D_i=1, U_i=0) = Pr(D_i=1 \mid U_i=0) \cdot Pr(U_i=0)$.

Frustrated demand seems to have remained fairly constant at about 28 percent of the work force. Finally, the fourth row of the table contains estimates of overall demand for union representation computed as the sum of union membership plus frustrated demand. This is

(7) $\Pr(D=1) = \Pr(U=1) + \Pr(D=1, U=0)$.

Total demand has fallen sharply. Fully 54 percent of the work force demanded union representation in 1977, and this fell to 46 percent by 1991.

As is clear from equation (4), the change in union membership is the difference between the change in overall demand and the change in frustrated demand. By definition, the change in union membership in the first row of Table 4 is fully accounted for by the change in overall demand in the fourth row and the change in frustrated demand (inverse supply) in the third row.

The results of this decomposition are quite striking. *All* of the 7.6 percentage point drop in the unionization rate between 1977 and 1991 is accounted for by a drop in overall demand for union representation. Since demand fell 8.5 percentage points, relative supply actually increased slightly (though insignificantly). Virtually all of the drop in demand seems to have occurred by 1984 (7.25 points of the 8.45 point overall decline). It is interesting that this drop in demand was offset by a significant 2.56 point reduction in frustrated demand between 1977 and 1984. Thus, the relative supply of union jobs actually increased between 1977 and 1984, and the unionization rate would have been even lower in 1984 without this supply increase. Between 1984 and 1991 demand fell insignificantly, but frustrated demand did increase slightly and significantly. Thus, there does seem to have been a small reduction in relative supply between 1984 and 1991.

Overall, virtually all of the decline in unionization between 1977 and 1991 seems to be due to decline in demand for union representation. There is no evidence that any significant part of the decline in unionization is due to increased employer resistance other than the sort of resistance that would be reflected in lower demand for unionization by workers.[14]

Job Satisfaction and Demand for Unionization among Nonunion Workers

Based on our decomposition, understanding the determinants of nonunion workers' demand for union representation is critical for explaining the decline in union membership in the U.S. Farber (1990) presents evidence showing that various aspects of job satisfaction are key determinants of workers' reported desire for union representation. Workers were asked three questions on job satisfaction in the QES, AFL, and F-K surveys: one question concerned overall job satisfaction, another concerned satisfaction with pay, and the third concerned satisfaction with job security. There were minor (and probably inconsequential) differences in the wording of the satisfaction questions between the QES and AFL surveys, but the F-K questions are identical to the QES questions.

Table 5 summarizes and extends Farber's main findings. In each year, nonunion workers are less likely to report that they would vote for a union if they are satisfied with their job overall, satisfied with their pay, or satisfied with their job security. The difference in the proportion who say they would vote for a union between satisfied and unsatisfied workers is quite sizable, and Farber (1990) finds that the gap is not diminished if demographic, industry, and occupation variables are held constant in a probit model.

Farber (1990) further finds that the 1977-1984 decline in demand for union representation could be accounted for almost entirely by an increase in nonunion workers' job satisfaction, particularly with regard to pay and job security. We extend this evidence through 1992 using the F-K survey.

Table 6 presents evidence on trends in worker satisfaction between 1977 and 1992. The overall level of satisfaction has increased slightly for nonunion workers. The 1992 union sample is

TABLE 5

Fraction of Nonunion Workers who would Vote for Union
Representation Broken Down by Year and Job Satisfaction

| | 1977 (n=663) | | 1984 (n=865) | | 1992 (n=125) | |
| | Satisfied? | | Satisfied? | | Satisfied? | |
	No	Yes	No	Yes	No	Yes
Satisfaction with:						
Overall job	.671	.342	.615	.289	.455	.333
Pay	.522	.291	.511	.259	.520	.291
Job Security	.533	.331	.485	.295	.500	.330

Notes: Data set for 1977 is QES, data set for 1984 is AFL-CIO survey, and data set for 1992 is Farber-Krueger survey.

TABLE 6

Job Satisfaction by Union Status

	Nonunion Workers			Union Workers		
	1977	1984	1992	1977	1984	1992
Fraction satisfied with:						
Overall	.867	.894	.903	.879	.853	.903
Pay	.587	.745	.758	.748	.770	.871
Job Security	.729	.850	.880	.762	.783	.774
n	663	865	125	298	217	31

Notes: Data set for 1977 is QES, data set for 1984 is AFL-CIO survey, and data set for 1992 is Farber-Krueger survey.

extremely small, but the results indicate that the overall level of satisfaction for union workers is not terribly different from that for nonunion workers. Different trends between union and nonunion workers emerge when workers are asked to focus specifically on their satisfaction with pay or job security. Between 1977 and 1984 there was a substantial increase in nonunion workers' reported satisfaction with pay and job security. No similar trend is visible for union workers in these years. The F-K survey indicates that nonunion workers report about an equal level of satisfaction in 1984 and 1992, providing further evidence that nonunion workers are reporting higher levels of satisfaction.

Farber (1990) presents evidence that the increase in reported satisfaction can account for the entire decline in demand for union representation among nonunion workers between 1977 and 1984. Note that this is consistent with the finding in Table 6 that the level of satisfaction remained roughly constant between 1984 and 1992 and our earlier finding of hardly any change in the proportion of nonunion workers who desire union representation over this same period.

A critical question is: Why did the proportion of nonunion workers who claim to be satisfied with their pay and job security increase between 1977 and 1984? The increase in reported satisfaction with pay is particularly surprising in view of the fact that real wages were stagnant in this period. These are issues that we leave for further examination.

Why is the Unionization Rate Higher in the Public Sector?

As we noted in the introduction, the unionization rate is much higher in the public sector than in the private sector. Perhaps more importantly, the public-sector unionization rate has been increasing slowly over the same period that the private-sector unionization rate has been falling dramatically. Freeman (1988) and others have argued that this divergence is due to more overt employer resistance in the private sector facilitated by a regulatory structure (the National Labor Relations Act as currently administered) that is less hospitable to union organizing than the regulatory structures prevailing in the public sector (state laws). This is a key part of the basis for the view that reform of the legal structure in the private sector would go a long way toward improving the fortunes of unions in that sector.

In this section we use the data from the 1984 AFL survey and the 1984 CPS to decompose the public-private differential into differences in (1) overall demand for union representation and (2) frustrated demand. Unfortunately, there is no direct information on sector of employment in the 1977 QES or the 1991 GSS, and our 1992 F-K survey has too small a sample of workers in the public sector to yield meaningful results. Thus, we are restricted to the 1984 cross-section.

The view that the sectoral difference in unionization rates is due to differences in employer resistance suggests that there is more frustrated demand in the private sector and no sectoral difference in overall demand. Table 7 contains the decomposition of the public-private difference in unionization.

Based on weighted tabulations from the 1984 CPS, the unionization rate is over twice as high in the public sector as in the private sector (35.5 percent versus 15.6 percent). Using the responses to the vote question on the 1984 AFL survey, we also find that there is substantially more demand for union representation among nonunion workers in the public sector than in the private sector (43.6 percent would vote for union representation in the public sector versus 28.8 percent in the private sector). On this basis, overall demand for union representation is much higher in the public sector. Fully 63.6 percent of workers in the public sector prefer union representation compared with only 39.9 percent in the private sector. What is even more striking is that the level of

TABLE 7

Analysis of Difference in Union Membership
1984 Public-Private Comparison

Probabilities
(standard errors)

	Level Private	Level Public	Public- Private
Pr(U=1)	.156 (.001)	.355 (.0027)	.199 (.0029)
Pr(D=1 | U=0)	.288 (.017)	.436 (.031)	.148 (.035)
Pr(D=1, U=0)	.243 (.0026)	.281 (.011)	.038 (.0015)
Pr(D=1)	.399 (.0141)	.636 (.0203)	.235 (.0247)

Sources and Definitions:

Pr(U=1): The probability that a worker is a union member. Computed from weighted tabulations of the 1984 CPS MOGRG file. The standard errors are sampling errors computed as the square root of $p(1-p)/n$.

Pr(D=1 | U=0): The probability that a nonunion worker demands union representation. Computed from tabulations of the "vote" question on the 1984 AFL survey. The standard errors are sampling errors computed as the square root of $p(1-p)/n$.

Pr(D=1, U=0): The probability that a worker demands union representation but is not employed on a union job (frustrated demand). Computed as $Pr(D=1 \mid U=0) \cdot Pr(U=0)$ from this table. The standard errors are computed by the "delta" method.

Pr(D=1): The probability that a worker demands union representation. This is the sum of the probability that a worker is a union member and the probability that a worker desires union representation but is not employed on a union job (union membership plus frustrated demand). Formally, this is $Pr(U=1) + Pr(D=1, U=0)$ and is computed from this table. The standard errors are computed by the "delta" method.

frustrated demand is slightly but significantly higher in the public sector (p-value of 3.8 percentage point difference = 0.01).

This simple analysis does not support the attribution of the relatively high unionization rate in the public sector to strong employer resistance in the private sector. The results suggest that *all* of the 19.9 percentage point difference in unionization is due to an even larger difference in worker demand for union representation that is actually offset by a higher level of frustrated demand for union representation (lower relative supply of union jobs) in the public sector.

Although there is evidence that the union-nonunion wage differential is smaller in the public sector than in the private sector (e.g., Lewis 1988), it may not be surprising that workers in the public sector are more likely to demand union representation. Unions in the public sector play a different role in some important dimensions than unions in the private sector. First, the interest of public-sector unions in lobbying for funding and legislative support is clear and of real benefit to public-sector workers. Second, unions in the public sector replace (or augment) a civil service system that provides wage structures not far different from the sort that unions typically provide. We are thinking specifically of standardizing wages and attaching wages to jobs rather than to specific individuals. Thus, public-sector workers have a choice between an administered wage system set by the government (the civil service) and an administered wage system set through the collective bargaining process. In contrast, private-sector workers typically have a choice between a more individualized market-oriented wage system and an administered wage system set through the collective bargaining process. When viewed in this light, it seems plausible that public-sector workers would be more likely to opt for an administered wage system where they have some control (union) while private-sector workers would be more likely to opt for a more individualized system (nonunion). It may simply be that public- and private-sector workers have different alternatives.

U.S.-Canada Comparison

Often cited evidence against a demand-side explanation of the low unionization rate in the U.S. comes from a comparison between the U.S. and Canada (e.g., Weiler 1990 and Freeman 1989). The argument relies on the facts that (1) the unionization rate has fallen dramatically in the United States at the same time that it has grown or remained stable in Canada, and (2) the U.S. legal environment is less favorable to union organization than is the Canadian legal environment.[15] Since the legal environment fundamentally affects the supply of union jobs, these facts are used to justify a supply-side explanation for the low U.S. unionization rate.

In an interesting recent paper, Riddell (1991) investigates U.S.-Canadian differences in supply and demand directly using information on U.S. and Canadian workers' responses to questions concerning their preferences for unions. The Canadian data were collected from a survey sponsored by the Canadian Federation of Labor (CFL). Riddell compares the 1990 CFL survey to the 1984 AFL survey. Columns 1 and 2 of Table 8 present Riddell's main results. For the nonunion sample, Riddell finds that Canadian workers are slightly less likely than American workers to say they desire union representation. Following Farber (1990), Riddell focuses on the ease of obtaining a union job given that a worker desires a union job ($Pr[U=1 \mid D=1]$) as a measure of relative supply. Primarily because the union rate is much higher in Canada than in the U.S., Riddell finds that there is far more frustrated union demand (less relative supply) in the U.S. than in Canada. He interprets this as providing support for a supply-side explanation of the divergence between Canadian and U.S. union rates.

Notice that Riddell's estimate of the union rate is 48 percent for Canada. In contrast, the Canadian Labor Market Activity Survey (LMAS) for 1990 indicates a union rate of 36.2 percent. This prompted us to reanalyze the CFL data (see column 3 of Table 8). Our estimates are similar, but not identical, to Riddell's. As far as we can tell, the reason for the extremely high union rate in Canada based on the CFL survey is that union and "professional association" members are included together. When they are

TABLE 8

Canada-U.S. Comparison of Union Preferences
Riddell's Results based o 1990 CFL and 1984 AFL Surveys

	Riddell Estimates		Farber-Krueger Estimates	
	1990 CFL (1)	1984 AFL (2)	1990 CFL (3)	1991/2 GSS/F-K (4)
Number of observations				
Union	250	196	242	146
Nonunion	267	694	270	642
Total	517	890	512	788
$Pr(U=1)$	.48	.22	.47	.19
$Pr(D=1)$	.64	.50	.65	.46
$Pr(D=1 \mid U=0)$	.30	.36	.33	.34
$Pr(U=1 \mid D=1)$	.76	.44	.74	.40
$Pr(D=1, U=0)$	.16	.28	.18	.27

Source: Columns 1 and 2 are from Table 3 of Riddell (1992). Columns 3 and 4 are authors' calculations.

separated, 17 percent of the CFL sample are members of a professional association and 35 percent are members of a union.[16] Since many professional associations bear little resemblance to unions, we use the LMAS estimate of 36.2 percent for the Canadian union membership rate in our calculations later in this section.

A key variable to compare between Canada and the U.S. is the fraction of nonunion members who desire a union.[17] Riddell finds that 30 percent of nonunion Canadian workers desire union representation, compared to 36 percent of nonunion American workers. Calculations based on Riddell's tabulations, contained in the first two columns of Table 8, show that of the 26 point difference between Canadian and U.S. unionization rates, 14 points are due to a difference in total demand and 12 points are due to a difference in supply (frustrated demand).

One potential problem with Riddell's comparison of union demand among nonunion workers is that he compares Canadian data from the 1990 CFL survey to U.S. data from the much earlier 1984 AFL-CIO survey. Therefore, it is difficult to separate out temporal differences from true cross-country differences. Additionally, our reanalysis of the CFL data suggests that 33 percent of nonunion workers desire union membership in Canada.[18] In order to address these problems, the third and fourth columns of Table 8 contain our tabulations of the 1990 CFL survey and the 1991/92 GSS/F-K surveys. Since demand for unionism remained relatively constant between 1984 and 1991 in the U.S. and because our tabulations of the CFL survey are very close to Riddell's, neither problem turns out to be of much consequence.

Perhaps more importantly, the Canada-U.S. comparison is imperfect because Canadian workers were asked a considerably different question regarding their desire for unions than their American counterparts. The key question from the CFL questionnaire is:

> Thinking about your own needs and your current employment situation and expectations, would you say that it is very likely, somewhat likely, not very likely, or not likely at all that you would consider joining or associating yourself with a union or a professional association in the future?

Recall that the exact wording of the AFL question is:

If an election were held tomorrow to decide whether your workplace would be unionized or not, do you think you . would definitely vote for a union, probably vote for a union, probably vote against a union, or definitely vote against a union?

The CFL question is broader than the AFL question, encompassing both unions and employee associations. In addition, the commitment on employees' part is vague in the CFL question; workers are asked whether they would "consider joining or associating" themselves with a union. Finally, the CFL question pertains to the current job or a future job, whereas the AFL question is focused on considering how an individual would vote if an election were held tomorrow. We suspect that these considerations are likely to bias the estimate of $Pr(D=1 \mid U=0)$ upwards in the CFL survey.

The AFL question makes little sense in the Canadian labor market where union representation is decided by card signings, not elections. The Canadian question does make sense in the U.S. context, however.

Here we investigate how the Canada-U.S. comparison is affected by the different questions used in the two nations' surveys. Specifically, in our survey (the F-K survey) we asked each respondent the CFL question as well as the AFL question. Furthermore, in order to examine whether the ordering of the questions influences our conclusions, we randomly selected half of the questionnaires and reversed the order in which the CFL and AFL questions were asked. We separated the AFL and CFL questions with questions on demographic and employment-related outcomes.[19]

Table 9 presents basic results for nonmanagerial, non-self-employed workers from our survey. The sample used to create this table includes all observations, regardless of the order in which they were asked the CFL and AFL questions.[20] The results indicate that nonunion workers are more likely to answer the CFL question favorably than the AFL question (41 percent vs. 35 percent), but the difference is not statistically significant (p-value = 0.373).

As the following table makes clear, the order of the AFL and CFL questions has a dramatic impact on the responses to the CFL

TABLE 9

Farber-Krueger Union Preference Survey

	Question Style	
	CFL	AFL
Number of observations		
Union	31	29
Nonunion	117	105
Total	148	134
Pr(U=1)	.199	.199
Pr(D=1)	.534	.493
Pr(D=1|U=0)	.410	.352
Pr(U=1|D=1)	.377	.414
Pr(D=1, U=0)	.328	.282

Note: Sample consists of nonmanagerial, non-self-employed workers who reported union status.

question, but no discernible effect on the responses to the AFL question.

Percent Responding Favorably to Union Representation

Question	AFL question asked first	CFL question asked first	Absolute t-ratio for difference
CFL	.550	.263	3.268
AFL	.358	.346	.131

Workers are much more likely to respond favorably to the vague CFL question on future union membership if it follows the more focused AFL question on how workers would vote in an hypothetical election held tomorrow. The AFL question, however, is notably robust to the order in which it is asked. When asked of American workers, the gap between the CFL-style question and the AFL-style question is +20 points or −9 points, depending on the order of the CFL question.

This finding raises some question about the validity of responses to the CFL survey. If the CFL questionnaire is more like the version of our survey in which the CFL-style question is asked first, then somewhat fewer workers seem to respond favorably to the CFL-style question than they would to an AFL-style question. In other words, for a given proportion of workers desiring unions based on the CFL question, we would expect a higher fraction to respond favorably to unions if they were asked the AFL question. This would tend to diminish the cross-country difference in the relative size of the queue of workers seeking union jobs. On the other hand, the CFL questionnaire asks four questions concerning general views towards unions before asking the question on workers' likelihood of joining a union. This may lead the CFL questionnaire to behave like the case in which the CFL question is asked second and would suggest an even larger gap in frustrated union demand between the U.S. and Canada than Riddell estimates.

The following cross-tabulation shows that there is considerable disagreement between individuals' responses to the AFL and the CFL questions.

		CFL Question:	
		No	Yes
AFL	No	51	15
Question	Yes	9	27

A majority of individuals give the same answer to the two questions.[21] However, nearly one-quarter of workers answer the AFL and CFL questions differently (24/102). If the CFL question is asked first, responses on the off-diagonals tend to be cases in which workers respond positively to the CFL-style question but negatively to the AFL-style question; if the AFL question is asked first, the opposite is the case.

We have searched for various factors that might be associated with the difference between individuals' responses to the AFL and CFL questions. Specifically, we estimated exploratory regressions using as the dependent variable the difference between the AFL and CFL union preference variables $(-1, 0, 1)$. The only right-hand-side variables that significantly affected this difference was the order in which the questions were asked and the respondent's gender. Men were relatively more likely to answer the AFL question unfavorably and the CFL question favorably. A worker's industry, occupation, region, marital status, age, and education have little power in explaining the difference between the AFL and CFL variables.

Issues of noncomparability in questionnaire design aside, we can decompose the Canadian-U.S. union gap using the supply and demand framework outlined above and presented in equation (5). In 1990, the difference in union density between Canada and the U.S. was 18.5 points (=36.2%−17.7%) using the tabulations from the LMAS in Canada and the CPS in the United States.

If we take our CFL estimate of $Pr(D=1 \mid U=0)$ at face value, then $Pr(D_c=1, U_c=0) = .33 \times (1−.362) = .211$. The corresponding figure for the U.S. based on the 1991/2 GSS-F-K survey is $Pr(D_A=1, U_A=0) = .340 \times (1−.177) = .280$. Therefore, about 7 points of the 18.5 point gap in union density between the U.S. and Canada is attributable to differences in frustrated demand, perhaps due to the differences in the legal environment between the countries. The remaining 11.5 points is attributable to greater worker demand for unions in Canada than in the U.S. In other words, 38 percent of the Canada-U.S. gap in union density is attributable to supply-side differences between the countries, and 62 percent is attributable to demand-side differences.

As we have emphasized, the estimate of $Pr(D=1 \mid U=0)$ based on the CFL question may not be directly comparable to the estimate based on the AFL question. Ignoring question order, we find that the average response to the CFL question is about 6 points higher than the average response to the AFL question in our survey of U.S. workers. As a rough gauge of the sensitivity of the supply-demand decomposition, we have recalculated the decomposition assuming the $Pr(D=1 \mid U=0)$ is 6 points lower for Canada (i.e., using .27 instead of .33). In this scenario, we find that 58 percent of the Canada-U.S. gap in union density is due to supply-side differences and 42 percent is due to demand-side differences. This small change reverses the relative importance of supply and demand factors.

To sum up, our exploration leaves us somewhat skeptical of the plausibility of the Canadian-U.S. comparison based on the AFL and CFL surveys. The placement and wording of the CFL question seem to have a substantial effect on workers' responses. Nevertheless, the most careful literal interpretation of our results suggest that *both* supply- and demand-side factors contribute to the higher union density in Canada than in the U.S. Past analyses that attribute the entire divergence between the Canadian and U.S. union rates to supply-side factors may be misleading.

Summary and Conclusion

Our analysis of the decline in unionization in the U.S. and comparisons with Canada relies on a demand-supply framework. We measure total worker demand for unions as the sum of union members and nonunion members who say they would vote for a union if a hypothetical election were held at their workplace. We measure supply inversely as frustrated demand (nonunion workers who would vote for union representation). Using this framework, we reach a number of conclusions.

First, we dismiss the argument that industrial and demographic shifts account for the decline in unionization in the U.S. Only about one-quarter of the decline in the union membership rate can be accounted for by these factors. Second, we find that a decline in demand-side factors can account for virtually all of the decline in the union membership rate since 1977. Virtually none of the decline seems to be due to changes in the relative supply of union jobs as measured by frustrated demand.

The reasons for the decline in workers' demand for union representation need to be investigated further, but our brief analysis suggests that nonunion workers are more likely to report being satisfied with their jobs in 1984 and 1992 than in 1977. This, in turn, can account for much of the decline in the demand for union representation. Another possibility is that demand for union representation has declined because the services unions provide are no longer perceived as valuable by nonunion workers, or that unions have not been able to convince workers of the value of union representation, perhaps t cause of poor public relations. The potential causes of a decline in demand, as well as the reasons for the increase in reported work satisfaction, are worthy topics of further research.

Next, we use our framework to investigate the 20 point differential in union membership between the public and private sectors. Our results are very clear. All of the higher unionization rate in the U.S. public sector in 1984 can be accounted for by higher demand for unionization; there is actually more frustrated demand for union representation in the public sector. These findings are inconsistent with recent work that has attributed the relatively high public-sector unionization rate to more employer resistance to unionization in the private sector.

Finally, we apply our demand-supply framework to try to explain the nearly 20 point differential in union membership between Canada and the U.S. Although our split-ballot survey casts some doubt on the comparability of different opinion questions regarding demand for union representation across countries, our best estimate is that approximately half of the Canada-U.S. gap in the union membership rate is due to supply-side factors and half is due to demand-side factors. This conclusion is at odds with several recent studies that have concluded that the entire Canada-U.S. union gap is a result of supply-side factors.

Although we show that the demand for traditional forms of union representation has declined, our analysis does not address the potential demand for alternative forms of worker representation (e.g., Freeman 1991; Freeman and Rogers 1993). Nevertheless, the door may be open for the growth of new forms of representation. How successful such alternatives might be remains unresolved.

Acknowledgments

We thank W. Craig Riddell for providing us with one of the data sets used in this paper. We thank Bruce Kaufman, Morris Kleiner, Daniel J. B. Mitchell, and participants at workshops at Cornell University and the NBER Labor Studies Program 1992 Summer Meetings for comments. The analysis and conclusions drawn in this paper are those of the authors and do not reflect those of the Canadian Federation of Labor, Decima Research, or any other organization that was involved in collecting data that we analyze. Financial support for the collection of our survey and general research support was provided by the Industrial Relations Section, Princeton University. Farber acknowledges support from the National Science Foundation. Krueger acknowledges support from the Sloan Foundation.

Endnotes

[1] These frequencies are based on weighted tabulations of the relevant Current Population Surveys (CPS). The 1977 data come from the May 1977 CPS. The 1984 and 1991 data come from the CPS merged-outgoing-rotation groups files for those two years. Starting in 1977, the CPS asked whether workers were members of a union or an employee association similar to a union. The earlier CPS data on union status (May 1973 through May 1976) asked only about union membership and thus are not directly comparable.

[2] Only 17.6 percent of the work force was employed in the public sector in 1991 compared with 18.8 percent in 1977.

[3] Troy (1992) takes this as evidence that structural shifts in the labor force do account for the decline in unionization in the U.S. This is not supported either by the studies cited above or by our research.

[4] Unfortunately, neither the 1977 QES nor the 1991 GSS contains direct information on sector of employment.

[5] Survey evidence on the preferences for union representation of union members from a number of sources (the 1991 GSS used in this study, the 1992 household survey we conducted and used in this study, the 1980 wave of the National Longitudinal Survey of Young Men, and the 1982 National Longitudinal Survey of Young Women) implies that between 80 and 90 percent of union members would vote for union representation in a hypothetical election.

[6] Note that we suppress the individual i subscript on these probabilities here and in what follows. Think of these probabilities as representing group averages.

[7] See Quinn and Staines (1979), Lewis Harris and Associates (1984), and Davis and Smith (1991) respectively for detailed information on the three surveys.

[8] Nonresponding households were called back at least four times to try to elicit a response. The response rate for working phone numbers was 40 percent. This response rate is computed excluding households that did not have an employed individual between age 18 and 65 (191), businesses (59), and disconnected numbers (110). It includes refusals (141), terminated interviews (4), deaf individuals or non-English speakers (15), answering machines (39), and no answers (99). Further details of the survey are available on request.

[9] This tabulation is at the bottom of Table 1.

[10] See Farber (1990) for an analysis of the AFL data that explicitly accounts for the undersampling of union members using a choice-based sampling framework.

[11] Chi-squared tests fail to reject the hypothesis that the distributions of characteristics are the same in the GSS and the F-K survey for any of the characteristics used in this study. This includes the unionization rate, the measure of nonunion worker demand for union representation, and all demographic characteristics listed in Table 1. No p-value is less than 0.27.

[12] See Farber (1990) for a more detailed discussion of this deviation.

[13] The labor force structure variables are the same as those used in the analysis of union membership with one exception. No control for public sector is included because the QES and GSS do not have direct information on sector. See the note to table 3 for a more detailed list of variables.

[14] As mentioned earlier, higher wages or better working conditions offered by employers hoping to avoid unionization or fear of job loss by workers as a result of unionization would be reflected in lower demand as measured by our "vote" question.

[15] As noted in the introduction, the presumption that the private-sector unionization rate in Canada grew over the last 15 years is open to some question. Kumar (1991) finds that the union membership rate fell by two points between 1977 and 1988 in Canada, while the union rate among government workers in Canada increased in this period.

[16] These do not sum to the total fraction that belong either to a union or professional association because some workers report belonging to both.

[17]Unfortunately, the question on workers' desires for union representation was only asked of individuals who were not members of either a union or a professional association. If the nonunion/nonassociation sample is representative of the professional association sample, estimates of $pr(D=1 \mid U=0)$ will not be affected.

There were 64 workers in the CFL sample who were not union members but were professional association members. This is about one-fourth the number of workers (270) who were not members of either unions or professional associations.

[18] It is interesting that our tabulation of the AFL data, shown in Table 1, yields the same 33 percent share of nonunion workers desiring union representation.

[19] A copy of our questionnaire is available on request.

[20] The tabulations of the two questions have different numbers of observations because of missing responses. The nonresponse rate is greater for the AFL-style question than the CFL-style question: 16 percent of the sample failed to answer the AFL question, whereas 6.4 percent of the sample failed to answer the CFL question.

[21] A chi-squared test of the hypothesis that the responses to the AFL and CFL questions are independent of each other overwhelmingly rejects the null of independence (p-value < .00001).

References

Abowd, John M., and Henry S. Farber. 1982. "Job Queues and the Union Status of Workers." *Industrial and Labor Relations Review* 35, no. 3 (April).

Davis, James Allan, and Tom W. Smith. *General Social Surveys, 1972-1991*: [machine-readable data file]. Principal Investigator, James A. Davis; Director and Co-Principal Investigator, Tom W. Smith. NORC ed. Chicago: National Opinion Research Center, producer, 1991; Storrs, CT: The Roper Center for Public Opinion Research, University of Connecticut, distributor. 1 data file (27,782 logical records) and 1 codebook (989 p.).

Dickens, William T., and Jonathan S. Leonard. 1985. "Accounting for the Decline in Union Membership, 1950-1989." *Industrial and Labor Relations Review* 38 (April), pp. 323-34.

Farber, Henry S. 1983. "The Determination of the Union Status of Workers." *Econometrica* 51, no. 5 (September), pp. 1417-37.

_____. 1985. "The Extent of Unionization in the United States." In *Challenges and Choice Facing American Labor*, ed. T. Kochan. Cambridge, MA: MIT Press.

_____. 1987. "The Recent Decline of Unionization in the United States." *Science* 13 (November), pp. 915-20.

_____. 1989. "Trends in Worker Demand for Union Representation." *American Economic Review* 79 (May), pp. 166-71.

_____. 1990. "The Decline of Unionization in the United States: What Can Be Learned from Recent Experience?" *Journal of Labor Economics* 8 (January), pp. S57-S105.

Freeman, Richard B. 1988. "Contraction and Expansion: The Divergence of Private Sector and Public Sector Unionism in the United States." *Journal of Economic Perspectives* 2 (Spring), pp. 63-88.

_____. 1989. "On Divergence of Unionism Among Developed Countries." NBER Working Paper No. 2817 (January).

_____. 1991. "Employee Councils, Worker Participation, and Other Squishy Stuff." *Proceedings of the 43rd Annual Meeting of the IRRA* (December 1990), pp. 328-37.

Freeman, Richard B., and Joel Rogers. 1993. "Who Speaks for Us? Employee Representation in a Non-Union Labor Market." In *Employee Representation: Alternatives and Future Directions*, eds. B. Kaufman and M. Kleiner. Madison, WI: IRRA.

Kumar, Pradeep. 1991. "Industrial Relations in Canada and the United States: From Uniformity to Divergence." Queens's Papers in Industrial Relations No. 1991-2 (March).

Lewis, H. Gregg. 1988. "Union/Nonunion Wage Gaps in the Public Sector." In *When Public Sector Workers Unionize*, eds. R. B. Freeman and C. Ichniowski. Chicago: University of Chicago Press, pp. 169-94.

Lipset, Seymour Martin. 1989. Continental Divide: *The Values and Institutions of the United States and Canada*. New York: Routledge.

Quinn, Robert P., and Graham L. Staines. 1979. *The 1977 Quality of Employment Survey: Descriptive Statistics with Comparison Data from the 1969-70 and 1972-73 Surveys*. Ann Arbor, MI: Institute for Social Research.

Raisian, John. 1983. "Union Dues and Wage Premiums." *Journal of Labor Research* (Winter), pp. 1-18.

Riddell, W. Craig. 1991. "Unionization in Canada and the United States: A Tale of Two Countries," Department of Economics, University of British Columbia, mimeo.

Troy, Leo. 1992. "Convergence in International Unionism, etc. The Case of Canada and the USA." *British Journal of Industrial Relations* 30 (March), pp. 1-43.

Weiler, Paul C. 1990. *Governing the Workplace: The Future of Labor and Employment Law*. Cambridge, MA: Harvard University Press.

Chapter 4

Evolving Modes of Work Force Governance: An Evaluation

Thomas A. Mahoney and Mary R. Watson
Vanderbilt University

Work force governance is, in general form, the focus of the essays in this volume. The present analysis addresses the subject of governance in perhaps a different context than other essays. We conceive of work force governance as the structure for making rules and decisions regarding conditions of employment, the structure of rights and reciprocal obligations in the employment relationship. These rules and decisions range from specification and standards of performance for work to be performed through employee selection, job assignment, promotion, compensation, and termination; in short, the entire system of human resource management. Our evaluation of modes of work force governance is set within the context of implications for performance of the employing organization.

Absent collective bargaining, the system for work force governance typically is not set forth explicitly within organizations. The rules and policies for human resource management may be stated more or less explicitly, while the procedures for influencing those rules tend to remain implicit in analysis of HRM policies.

The rights and obligations of the employment relationship in American industry have evolved and changed over time. Typically the initiation of change is attributed to management, a union representing the work force or, at times, social interests expressed in public policy. Changes in those rights and obligations both reflect and impact upon the governance structure. Any such change exhibits change in the governance structure, and influences exerted within it often also alter the governance structure by constraining or enlarging the scope of future decisions and the relative influence of different interests.

We approach the analysis of changing forms of work force governance in American industry through a review of trends in systems for HRM, the various policies setting forth employment rights and responsibilities, and infer from those changes the accompanying changes in work force governance of systems of HR decision making. We evaluate alternative approaches to work force governance in the context of implications for organizational performance. Towards that end, we begin with models from organization theory supplemented with constructs from economics and social psychology, then review trends in HRM including governance implications, and finally evaluate the variations in governance systems identified in light of implications for organizational performance. Our review is restricted primarily to American HR systems and work force governance, although parallels and comparisons with foreign experience are possible.

Organization Theory Framework

What is termed organization theory is a broad collection of conceptual frameworks attempting to explain different phenomena relating to organizations and to guide the design and management of organizations. The conceptual frameworks range from economics to industrial and social psychology, sociology, and political science. One general unifying theme, however, is a focus upon a structure of relationships and an assumption that this structure of relationships relative to key exogenous influences determines relative performance of the organization. A once common search for the single best method of organization has given way to specification of contingent relationships of performance with structure and exogenous influences.

One such conception of organizations views them as people participating within a structure and employing some technology to accomplish a mission defined in the context of an exchange with the environment (Thompson 1967). In general terms, that mission involves some input from the environment, transformation of that input, and an exchange of output with the environment. Definition of the relevant task environ ent(s) and of the exchanges to be undertaken constitute the mission of the organization. In any event,

FIGURE 1
Model of organization adapted from Thompson (1967).

Environment

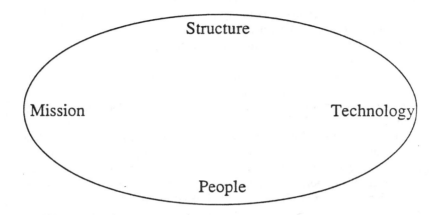

the exchanges must result in some net benefit in order to sustain the organization and maintain its participants.

Technology is viewed broadly as the process of tasks and work performed in the transformation of inputs into outputs. It may range from routine sequential processing of tasks to unique craft and professional application of skills, individual processing to group or team interactive work, interaction with physical inputs to interaction with cognitive and/or human inputs, and from stable to dynamic and changing processes (Perrow 1986). Technology is viewed as the work of the organization whether performed by machine or people. People must be involved at some stage in the technology, however, and the design of technology thus determines the roles, tasks, and jobs for employee performance.

Definition of participants in the organization will vary depending upon the purpose of analysis (e.g. employees, linked suppliers and customers, stakeholders) (Freeman and Reed 1983). For our analysis, we focus upon employees as the primary participants in the organization. There is an obvious interaction between characteristics of the technology and characteristics of the employee participants, the work force of the organization. Employee participants are to perform the work of the organization defined in the context of the technology employed. Views as to which, technology or the work force, is dominant have changed over time. The concept of a technological imperative that determines the work and structure of the organization has given way to socio-technological approaches that address the interactive influences of employee participants and technology upon performance and, in certain instances, to design of technology to exploit some valuable and rare work force capability (Trist 1981).

Structure in the simple organization model refers to authority and decision making relationships, the structure for coordination of activities of work force participants (Thompson 1967). Classical organization theory viewed authority as vested in the management function and then delegated as appropriate throughout the organization. This delegation of decision making is cast as creating differentiated sub-units of the organization, sub-units with varying authority to make decisions. Two forms of differentiation, horizontal and vertical, are considered. Horizontal differentiation (functional organization) is considered appropriate when the relevant influences are different (e.g. patent law, labor law, tax law) and vertical differentiation (decentralization) is considered appropriate when the relevant influences are unstable and require local knowledge and information. The guiding principle is to differentiate or delegate decision making to the location with the best available knowledge and information to make decisions. Differentiation or decentralization of decision making creates counter problems of coordination, and increased decentralization requires advanced forms of coordination or integration as overlays upon the decentralization (Lawrence and Lorsch 1969).

Obviously the structure, technology, and work force should co-align with each other and with the mission of the organization. Change in any one of the components calls for complementary change in the other elements.

Two common criteria for organizational performance are effectiveness and efficiency of performance (Barnard 1938; Thompson 1967). Effectiveness is defined in terms of accomplishing mission objectives, and efficiency is defined in terms of resource utilization, the overall productivity of performance. These criteria are imposed within the context of the task environment of the organization. An organization must be effective in order to serve a purpose in the relevant task environment and thus survive. The efficiency criterion then is a measure of health and a second test of survival. Note that the criteria of effectiveness and efficiency are measures of survivability and not social approval.

A criterion of equity often raised in the context of labor relations typically is unstated in organization theory and derives only implicitly in the context of the employment exchange generalized to all organizational stakeholders (March and Simon 1958). Stakeholders are defined as all of those groups and individuals that can affect, or are affected by, the accomplishment of organizational purpose (Freeman and Reed 1983). Stakeholders vary in their objectives for the organization and in terms of power derived from organizational dependence upon them. Typically those in most direct exchange with the organization (suppliers of capital, labor, materials, and customers) exercise most influence upon the organization. The relative power of stakeholders varies within the group and over time with circumstances of dependence. The management function can be characterized as building and maintaining coalitions of support from stakeholders.

Organization participants contract to provide contributions in exchange for some set of inducements (Barnard 1938; Simon, Smithburg, and Thompson 1950). In the context of work force participants, employees exchange their work for economic and noneconomic inducements. The employment exchange is somewhat different from exchanges with other participants in so far as it involves acceptance of an authority relationship; the employment exchange establishes a zone of indifference to submission to managerial authority (March and Simon 1958). Equity, in the context of the employment exchange, is a negotiated exchange acceptable to both parties. An effective organization must be able to secure the cooperation of the necessary work force and thus at minimum provide inducements sufficient to secure the desired contributions. The realization of equity in the employment exchange is of instrumental value only to the employing organization and thus is not a primary objective in this model.

The topic of work force governance is not addressed directly in traditional organization theory. It arises only implicitly in the context of structure of decision making and the employment exchange. Simple consideration of effectiveness and efficiency would dictate that decision making, including HR decisions, should be centralized for coordination and decentralized only as dictated by the diffusion of relevant knowledge and information. Terms of the employment exchange, similarly, should be standardized except as needed to cope with differentiated occupations, jobs, and unique skills. Equity considerations, not explicit in classical theory, would presumably occur in the negotiation of the employment exchange. Completed exchange agreements by presumption achieve equity as perceived by the negotiating parties.

As elaborated below, however, contributions from the disciplines of economics and social psychology elaborate and modify the simple framework above. Certain models for decision making, for example, argue for decentralization of decision making beyond that dictated by the diffusion of knowledge and information (Maier 1963; Vroom and Yetton 1973). Effective decisions are cast as a joint function of technical quality of the decision and acceptance of the decision. And delegation and participation may be prescribed for purposes of increasing acceptance even where they do not contribute to technical quality.

The simple concept of negotiated employment exchange presumes no form of organizational governance. Terms of the exchange are constrained, however, by the discipline of a competitive market. Employee participants have the options of exit behavior and limited voice in the negotiation process (Hirschman 1970). Both options are constrained, however, by competitive aspects of the market. Decisions concerning human resources in the organization not specified in the exchange agreement are implicitly relegated to the management function. The governance or decision making system can pursue efficiency goals without regard for equity considerations except as dictated by market pressures.

Barnard noted that "cooperation" is among the contributions sought in the employment exchange, a cooperation which extends beyond formally stated work requirements and which is difficult to encompass in the economic framework of employment contract (Barnard 1938). The importance and value of this "beyond contract" cooperation varies among organizations and among individual employees in a single organization. Models of social exchange, elaborated below, are particularly relevant in conceptualizing an employment exchange where desired contributions are implicit and difficult to state explicitly in contract form.

A rationally ordered structure for decision making, and thus HR governance, as implied by classical organization theory may well be appropriate in seeking effective and efficient performance within a requisite norm for equity; however, the relevant decision variables and relationships are more complex than typically considered in simple rational decision models resulting in a model of bounded rationality decision making. Further, there is no explicit concern for equity in the rational structure for decision making and some equity norm must be specified exogenously.

Employing organizations are engaged in economic activity and are organizations of interacting people. Not surprisingly, constructs from both economics and social psychology influence organization theory and contribute to our analysis of HR governance. Selected constructs from economics and social psychology which figure in our analysis are reviewed below.

Economic theory constructs. The simple economic theory of the firm is a theory of entrepreneurial decision making in a competitive market environment. Rational behavior directed towards the goal of optimizing self-interest, usually cast as profit, is assumed. Profit maximization is sought through economic efficiency, a traditional goal attributed to organizations (Milogram and Roberts 1988).

The constructs of competitive market and of contracting are central to the theory of the firm. The firm, analyzed as an extension of the owner/entrepreneur, is the primary unit of analysis, but the firm acts in a competitive market which constrains choices of the firm. The firm is cast as a contracting agent, contracting with resource suppliers, including human resources, and with customers. At the extreme, what is viewed as the firm is merely a "bundle of contracts." The construct of contracting implies considerable freedom to negotiate from self-interest, yet the market construct implies competitive pressure constraining the options for contracting available to the firm.

The contracting construct assumes rational individual pursuit of self-interest and likely difference of interests between the contracting parties, particularly as each strives to maximize return to self (Jensen and Meckling 1976). One purpose of the contract is to constrain the discretion available to the other party which might permit decisions and actions detrimental to one's self-interest. The contract is cast in a legalistic framework where details of the exchange are specified and penalties are available for nonperformance.

In this same vein, adversarial relationships are assumed along with a mode of distributive bargaining and negotiations. In extreme form, deceit in both negotiations and contracted performance is admitted and assumed in so far as it advances self-interest. Implicitly, detailed contract specification and monitoring of performance are necessary to assure receipt of the desired exchange between contracting parties.

This characterization of the contracting construct is difficult to apply to long-term contracting (Williamson 1975). Circumstances change over time requiring change in the contracted exchange. In consequence, the economic contracting construct connotes short-term contracts. While a continuing relationship might emerge, it would take the form of a string of short-term contracts with no commitment for future contracts.

The concept of economic exchange which emerges is that of a short-term exchange negotiated between adversaries seeking self-interest and bargaining in a distributive mode. Only what is specified in the contract is exchanged and, due to self-interest, the possibility of cheating in the absence of monitoring is likely.

The role of contracting in the framework of HRM is illustrated in the principal-agent relationship in economics. The principal (owner) contracts with an agent to exercise authority in decision making and constrains discretionary authority to pursue the agent's self-interest at the expense of the principal's self-interest. In similar fashion, presumably, agents acting as principals contract with subordinate agents in a framework analogous to hierarchical delegation (Macneil 1980). The underlying theme, however, is one of control and constraint of discretion.

Economic efficiency is the assumed goal of the organization, and organizational concerns for equity and justice are not stated as organizational goals. What might be viewed as equity or justice is provided by the discipline of a competitive market. Organizational participants seek the best alternative available, and terms of exchange for comparable participants converge due to competition. This is a consequence of market competition, however, not a consequence of explicit attention to norms of justice and equity. Further, due to market imbalances and available alternatives, the relative power of negotiating parties often differs considerably with individual employees possessing relatively little power to influence the terms of negotiation.

Similarly, HR governance is not addressed explicitly and, by inference, emerges from the discipline of competition. Work force participants engage in exit behavior if a better alternative is perceived, forcing convergence among employers in terms and conditions of employment. These terms and conditions are not viewed as just or unjust; they either do or do not conform to competitive market consequences. Reliance upon the discipline of market competition ignores subjective norms and standards for equity which arise in social and political settings.

Social psychological constructs. As in economics, exchange is a key construct in social psychology; the conceptualization of exchange is quite different, however. The process of dyadic exchange (exchange within a two person relationship) is the fundamental unit of analysis (Thibaut and Kelley 1959), and the principle of dyadic exchange can be extended to exchanges conducted between individuals and groups.

The process of dyadic exchange, within social psychology, is viewed as discrete episodic exchange transactions which occur within continuing, long-term relationships (Kelley and Thibaut 1978; Emerson 1990). Since an exchange relationship is assumed to continue indefinitely until terminated by one or both of the parties, the analysis of exchanges from a social psychological perspective does not necessarily proceed from strict assumptions of individuals maximizing self-interest in each discrete exchange. Rather, the relationship within which episodic exchanges occur, not the conditions for specific transactions of exchange within the relationship, is of paramount concern. When making decisions about exchange behavior, individuals consider not only immediate outcomes anticipated from the current episodic exchange, but also anticipate future interactions and forecast trends in outcomes of those interactions (Thibaut and Kelley 1959). The individual transactions within the continuing exchange are influenced and bounded by the expectation of a continuing relationship. The expectation of long-term benefit from the relationship, not the benefit of individual transactions, is central to maintenance of the continuing exchange relationship. This focus upon a continuing relationship rather than upon individual transactions shapes many of the differences between the analyses derived from economics and from social psychology.

Power to influence negotiation outcomes is viewed in the economic model in terms of relative opportunity costs of the transaction to the two parties. If either party estimates opportunity costs will exceed expected return, that party will withdraw from the transaction. However, power in the social psychological model is viewed in terms of relative dependence within the continuing relationship rather than in each episodic transaction. The social psychological model, therefore, allows for the possibility that an individual may participate in an episodic transaction which will result in an outcome below that possible through available alternative episodic transactions.

There are three situations where this type of participation is expected. First, an individual with a relative power advantage in the long-term relationship may accept a suboptimal episodic outcome because long-term benefit from the relationship is expected. Second, an individual who has low power in a long-term relationship may be forced to accept a suboptimal episodic outcome because of dependence on the continuing relationship. Third, an individual with high power to influence an individual transaction may choose not to exploit the situation because of relative lack of power in the continuing chain of transactions. In the social psychological model, the individual frames choices based on alternatives available to the long-term relationship, not alternatives to each episodic transaction. Further, while dependence is crudely analogous to opportunity cost, in the social psychological model it extends to include subjective and affective considerations as well as objective terms of exchange.

Social psychology distinguishes between economic exchange and social exchange. Economic exchange is viewed as contractual, containing explicit definitions for equivalence, a distinct timetable for the exchange, and terms which are discussable, negotiable, and enforceable. Social exchange is viewed as noncontractual, lacking explicit definitions of equivalence, and having terms which are not explicit. The terms are cast as expectations which typically are not discussed, and where explicit negotiation is viewed as inappropriate (Brown 1986). Because of the ambiguity surrounding what, where, when, and how the exchange occurs, explicit contracting is not feasible. Rather, mutual expectations of trust are necessary to ensure that each party fulfills obligations to the other. This mutual exchange of trust creates a unique social exchange, a psychological contract which is not encompassed in the formal economic contract.

Contrary to the economic contract which constrains the discretion of the contracting parties, discretion is inherent in the social exchange construct. Each party is trusted, and thus obligated, to be attentive to the other party's desires and objectives and to assist in their fulfillment. Trust and discretion are obverse sides of the coin. The employment exchange, while it clearly involves economic exchange, also typically involves some form of social exchange (Fox 1974).

Social psychology elaborates another construct particularly relevant to exchanges, the construct of justice or equity. Exchange relationships must be judged beneficial by both parties in order to continue. In addition, the resulting exchange relationship is evaluated in terms of the criterion of fairness or justice. Social psychology identifies two aspects of justice, distributive and procedural, which are evaluated when making judgments of fairness. The aspect of distributive justice dictates that the relative outcomes of the exchange are judged by the involved parties to be fair. The aspect of procedural justice dictates that the criterion and process for determining outcomes are perceived as fair.

Within dyadic exchanges, distributive justice is most relevant and is considered in the context of expected benefits of a continuing relationship. Exchange will generally continue as long as the net result of the continuing relationship meets distributive justice standards. Procedural justice concerns are less relevant because individuals generally possess considerable control over the process of the exchange. However, perceptions of procedural injustice may arise, particularly in situations of relative power imbalance. In this case, exchanges viewed as unjust by one party may well be terminated even though alternatives are viewed as less beneficial in some objective sense.

In order to manage exchange within the organization as a whole, *systems* must be developed which institutionalize the exchange process. Just as in the dyadic exchange, individual perceptions of both distributive (outcome) and procedural (process) justice determine assessment of the fairness of the exchange system and are critical to maintenance of the exchange relationship. Evaluation of the fairness of relative outcomes determines perceptions of distributive justice. Perceptions of perceived justice of the exchange system are particularly critical in an organizational setting because the individual possesses less power to shape and influence that system than in the dyadic exchange (Thibaut and Walker 1975).

Considerable research in recent years indicates that perceived justice in organizational exchanges influences individual behavior and thus organizational performance (Lind and Tyler 1988). Employees, for example, maintain group membership when they perceive likely long-term benefits of association and when they judge the exchange system as just. Procedural justice is often viewed as more critical than distributive justice resulting from exchange, distributive injustice being more readily accepted in the presence of procedural justice. Procedural justice is cast as enhancing satisfaction, compliance with rules and decisions, and reducing conflict, even in the presence of distributive injustice (Lind and Tyler 1988).

Within the economic model, the organization is viewed as having a unitary goal of efficiency. However, the social psychological model suggests that while individuals, groups, and coalitions may have goals, a unitary goal criterion of efficiency is not inferred for all organizations. Rather, equity figures more prominently as a common goal because it is required to maintain organization membership and stimulate increased performance. Thus, a realization of justice in the organization can enhance organizational efficiency and effectiveness, and perceptions of injustice can be detrimental to the attainment of these goals. By inference, the long-term health and performance of an organization depend upon satisfying justice expectations of all parties, particularly expectations of procedural justice.

Issues of HR governance arise only indirectly in social psychology in the examination of justice of rules and decisions concerning human resources. Procedural justice in social exchange is most likely to be realized as parties to the exchange accept the reciprocal obligations of trust and seek to accommodate mutual interests. Procedural justice is less likely to be realized through arbitrary specification of rules limiting discretion or through adversarial negotiation and contracting. Rather, social psychological theory suggests that norms of procedural justice in social exchange are different from the norms for economic exchange; the system for decision making should be framed in general principles with provision for discretionary judgments in individual transactions over the life of a continuing relationship.

While economic and social exchange are posed here in extreme form, there is opportunity for combinations of them in the employment exchange. (A related distinction is made by Macneil [1980] between discrete and relational contracts.) Certainly either, in extreme form, contradicts the other. Yet a relaxed form of economic exchange may constitute a base for the employment exchange upon which forms of social exchange are built. An economic exchange enhanced with expectations of a continuing relationship, the extension of trust between the parties, and the reciprocal acceptance of non-negotiated obligations elaborates a social exchange which extends beyond the economic exchange in employment. It is this enhancement of social exchange in the employment exchange which elicits the critical "beyond contract" contributions vital to organizational effectiveness and efficiency (Fox 1974).

Evolving Human Resource Management

Human resource management (HRM) encompasses all of the decisions and actions regarding employees of an organization. While these practices might be grouped on some basis for simplification, historically there was no conceptual model relating them. Rather, they formed a collection of practices for recruiting, managing, and maintaining a work force. Dunlop, in his "system of industrial relations," addressed these practices as rules and provided one such framework (Dunlop 1958). He identified three components, rules regarding (1) procurement, (2) compensation, and (3) the making of rules. This "web of rules" constitutes what we analyze as a human resource system including work force governance (Dunlop 1948).

More recently, Beer and colleagues utilized a framework of four components of the HRM system: policies regarding (1) flows, (2) rewards, and (3) influence (analogous to Dunlop's components), and also (4) work design (Beer, Spector, Lawrence, Mills, and Walton 1985). Dunlop's "rules for making rules" and Beer et. al's system for "influence" constitute what we focus upon as work force governance in a strictly limited sense. However, "influence" appears throughout the HR system and cannot be limited to merely "rules for making rules." The policies and rules for making continuing decisions regarding work design, work force flows, and rewards constitute work force governance in the broad sense. The decisions made within each of the components of HRM determine the expected work contributions of employees and their reciprocal rewards. The policies for making these decisions affecting work force participants constitute work force governance in the full sense employed here. Our review of the evolving form of HRM addresses changes in the form and content of rules or policies governing work force decisions regarding work design, HR flows, and rewards, and thus addresses implicitly the changes in actual work force governance.

Work Design. Interestingly, the design of work and the definition of jobs and/or roles for performance was not considered in the framework employed by Dunlop (1958) and his peers yet it appears today in the framework of HRM. We will argue that this conceptual evolution following change in practice is significant in effect upon the full range of HR governance. It is also notable that work design was not considered in the context of human resources earlier in light of its role in organization theory. The design of work into jobs and roles frames one side of the employment exchange; it specifies the nature of expected contributions from employees.

Work design traditionally has been addressed in the context of technological effectiveness and efficiency and not within the context of equity and the employment exchange. Consistent with traditional organization theory, decisions about the design of work were made by management utilizing efficiency as the decision criterion and reflecting what was known as the "technological imperative"; given a choice of technology, the design of work into jobs was an exercise in rationality. Also, consistent with concepts of contracting in economics, jobs were designed to minimize the need and opportunity for employee discretion (Taylor 1911).

Socio-technical considerations in organization theory and industrial experimentation challenged the concept of technological imperative (Trist 1981). Increasingly the motivational effects of work design and the effects of social configuration of work upon safety, quality, and productivity have been recognized. Much of this experimentation and theory argues for enlarging task variety and worker discretion subject to the limits of employee ability. The design of work into jobs and roles and the implicit development of rules for performance has moved from a rational managerial/ engineering context to a human resource context (Hackman and Oldham 1976).

Faced with product market competition and lagging quality and productivity, the design of work for efficient and effective performance has received increased attention. And consistent with models for organizational decision making, considerable authority for redesigning work has been decentralized to the involved employees. Continuous improvement, for example, relies upon initiation of change in performance at the level of individual work operations and is dependent upon recommendations for change by individual employees (Walton 1986). Further, the introduction of flexible technologies and the development of work force skill levels both argue for increased discretion in work performance and decentralization of decisions concerning work design in order to achieve efficiency.

At the same time, increased discretion in work design and performance transforms the employment exchange from a strict economic exchange to incorporate aspects of social exchange (Fox 1974). Increased discretion communicates heightened trust, trust which creates a reciprocal obligation and reciprocated trust. Reciprocal obligations evolve for the exchange of inducements and contributions beyond those specified in explicit contractual form. This delegation of authority, employee participation in traditionally management decisions, has been termed the "high-involvement organization" and often offers improved quality of work design decisions and improved implementation (Lawler 1986).

Other noted changes in work design concern the development of cross-functional and self-managed teams (Wellins, Byham, and Wilson 1991). Both of these, in one sense, are attempts to improve the integration of work decisions, particularly given differentiation in decision making. Increases in individual discretion are balanced, where necessary, with teamwork and discretion shared within the team.

Obviously there is no one single best system for work design. The well-publicized changes discussed here appear to have been driven by demands of changing and competitive environments, particularly the product market and technological environments. Other organizations more isolated from external influences perceive less need for and probably would benefit less from change in work design systems. It is interesting to note, however, that innovative change in systems for human resource flows and rewards tends to be associated with change in work design (Rankin 1990). The changes in work design appear to have driven change in the broader system of HRM.

HR Flows

Policies governing the flow of people into, through, and out of organizations have always been central to the achievement of both organizational effectiveness and efficiency and the equity perceptions of the work force. These flow policies impact directly upon the efficiency of job performance and at the same time control employee access to economic and psychological rewards associated with employment and work assignments.

The varying nature of human resource flow systems was noted some years ago in the characterization of "internal labor markets" (Kerr 1954). Essential characteristics of the internal labor market were degree of openness to the external labor market, channels for movement among jobs within the organization, and the criteria for movement (Doeringer 1967). Two ideal models, the "open" and "closed" internal labor markets, were identified and a third variant, a casual and/or low-wage market, has since been identified. Choice among alternative flow policies serves ideally to best relate resources in the external labor market and the structure of technology and work design of the organization and will be influenced by both. Thus, for example, a relatively open internal market is feasible only when available external skills match jobs of the organization, and a relatively closed market might be dictated when the structure of jobs does not match external supplies.

A relatively open internal labor market characterized most firms in the period of industrialization and mass production. Relatively low skills were demanded, little discretion was permitted, and an ample supply of labor was available. A high degree of discretion for personnel decisions was delegated throughout management with often negative impact upon employee perceptions of equity as decisions often appeared arbitrary, capricious, and contradictory. There likely was little direct effect upon efficiency due to the high replaceability of labor. Interestingly, industries such as automobile and steel evolved towards a closed internal market with the development of collective bargaining, a concession, presumably, to work force demands for fairness and equity rather than as a response to the redesign of work and jobs. Criteria and rules for movement became more specific and illustrated a move towards balancing of efficiency and equity considerations as in the specification of joint criteria of ability (efficiency) and seniority (equity) for access to higher paid jobs. Freeman and Medoff (1984) argue that these equity considerations impact indirectly upon effectiveness and efficiency of performance; introducing equity into the employment exchange elicits commitment and loyalty as would be predicted by the social exchange model.

Aspects of both simple models, open and closed, appear today in many organizations, one occupation or division conforming more to the open and another more to the closed model. Also some organizations distinguish between a core or permanent work force managed in a closed internal market and a flexible or temporary work force managed in an open market; core employees are provided a measure of employment security beyond that provided to temporary employees, and core employees experience social exchange beyond that extended to temporary employees.

Flow policies evolve and change in response to changes in work design. For example, increasing use of team work dictates that employees be capable of team interaction and problem solving, introducing new criteria for selection. Often self-managed teams are provided with discretion in the selection of new members as well as training and counseling members. Changes in the organization of work also change career paths, and many organizations increasingly seek to implement lateral career moves to replace previous skill linked vertical career ladders.

Other changes in flow policies can be related to change in the supply of labor resources. Opportunities for family leave are provided as well as flex-time and job sharing to accommodate external demands upon employees.

Finally, various changes in flow policies have been in response to public policy, nondiscrimination policies of selection, promotion, and termination, for example.

Many of the organization-initiated changes in flow policies appear to involve relaxation of rigidly specified and applied rules for flow. Flows based upon shifts among rigidly specified jobs in a job structure are being replaced with informal shifts among tasks and skills within a more loosely defined structure of work, for example. This relaxation of rules and criteria aligns with differentiated decision making to permit rapid and unique changes in the organization. As such, they should contribute to achievement of effective and efficient performance. Interestingly, there has been at the same time greater provision for limited direct participation of the work force in making these decisions. Team involvement in selection, training and counseling of team members, peer training and coaching in skill-based organizations, and individual initiation of job bids, flex-time schedules, and job sharing all provide opportunity for direct participation in flow decisions.

Direct participation in HR flow decisions, however limited, likely influences work force perceptions of both procedural and distributive justice. The opportunity to participate in flow decisions provides limited opportunity to influence decisions regarding one's work assignments and career aspects of employment. This opportunity to express individual voice should enhance perceptions of procedural justice. Distributive equity may or may not be realized, but there is greater likelihood of achieving individually desired outcomes because of the greater access to opportunities. On balance, one would expect enhanced perceptions of justice as a consequence of direct participation, however limited, in flow decisions.

HR Rewards

Just as policies of work design relate most clearly to the contributions element of the employment exchange, so reward policies relate clearly to the inducements element. And reward policies have changed as work design and flow policies have changed.

Organizational reward systems are subject to the mutual considerations of efficiency and equity. The employing organization seeks to obtain participant services as economically as possible, yet this is conditioned upon acceptance of the reward system as just and equitable (Livernash 1957). Key characteristics of the system are the basis(es) for differentiation in rewards, the extent of differentiation, and the form of rewards, all of which have changed in recent years.

The common conceptual basis for reward differentiation is contributions of work. Change in the conceptualization of work embodied in work design has occasioned change in reward systems (Mahoney 1989). An essentially job-based reward system common

in most organizations has been supplemented or replaced by skill-
or knowledge-based and performance-based systems in many
organizations. Similarly, the basis for distributive justice in the
reward distribution has changed with revision in the conceptualization of work design. Highly differentiated job structures which once
provided the basis for reward differentiation are replaced with skill,
knowledge, and performance based differentiation.

Work rotation and job enlargement have, in many instances,
eliminated the basis of specific job based differentials, resulting in
less differentiation in the reward structure. Individuals rotate
among related assignments without associated changes in compensation. At the same time there has been a move to implement
organization performance-based rewards resulting in greater
variability of rewards over time (Mitchell and Broderick 1991). By
and large these changes have been implemented for reasons of
effectiveness and efficiency, relaxing highly structured compensation systems which constrained changes in work design and flows in
the organization. Whether or not perceived justice of the changed
reward systems is achieved depends in large part upon acceptance
of the logic of change in work design. Norms of justice, once
established in tradition, may be particularly resistant to dramatic
change. Probably for this reason these changes in reward systems
are most common in relatively newer organizations without long
traditions of a job-based structure of work.

Other less heralded changes in reward systems are illustrated in
the introduction of individual flexibility in reward form as seen in
flexible benefit plans. While a primary logic for flexible benefits lies
with the efficiency criterion, maximizing individual returns within a
constrained total benefit cost, flexible benefits likely also enhance
individual perceptions of distributive equity. Individuals apply
their own assessments of benefit equity in making benefit choices.
Flexible benefits also provide opportunity for individual discretion
and participation in the reward system. Flexible benefits thus also
enhance perceptions of procedural equity in benefit compensation.

The relaxation of reliance upon a job-based reward system and
the provision of alternative reward sources also provides
opportunity for limited individual participation. Individuals queue
for flow into higher paying jobs, often on the basis of seniority, in
the job-based reward system. Advancement is less attributable to
individual action than to system structure. Opportunities for

increased rewards due to skill enhancement and/or performance accomplishments provide more control to individual employees who are free to act individually to qualify for increased rewards.

Governance

Changing forms of work force governance can be observed in two respects; the first relates to the structure of decision making to design HRM policies, and the second relates to the structure of HR decisions within that policy framework, many of which were noted in the reviews above. For purposes of comparative analysis, we blend these two perspectives and utilize three broad characterizations of governance for comparison. As in the preceding sections, these characterizations reflect evolving practice in HR governance. The first characterization of governance we consider is authoritarian which connotes management control of governance decisions, typically in centralized decisions. The second characterization is that of collective bargaining between management and a union representing the work force. The third characterization is termed employee involvement and connotes influence of employees, individually and in groups, in decision making. As with any set of characterizations, these three are presented in extreme form and doubtless will vary in detail in application; further, aspects of several may be combined in application.

Authoritarian Model. What we term the authoritarian model has direct roots in concepts of principal-agent relationships of economics and so-called classical management theory (Massie 1965). Authority, in both of these traditions, derives from ownership. A scalar model of decision making evolves in the economic tradition through principal-agent contracting with subordinate agents serving as principals in subordinate contracting (Macneil 1980). This chain of contracts, although evolved in a market context, presumably serves to align subordinate decisions with principal objectives. The scalar principle in management theory evolved rationally based upon the need to coordinate decisions and upon the limited capacity of individual offices to coordinate and to monitor subordinate actions. Authority, in this tradition, is delegated from superior to subordinate only as necessary to make decisions coordinated within the constraints of superior established policies and parameters. The theme underlying the hierarchical structure in the economics tradition is control of performance consistent with owner/principal objectives, while the management tradition supplements that theme with assumptions of breadth of knowledge related to the hierarchy. Both traditions, however, seek effectiveness and efficiency of performance.

The economics tradition assumes divergent self-interests of parties and adversarial relationships; the purpose of the employment contract is to constrain subordinate discretion where possible or provide incentives to utilize discretion to further the principal's objectives. Classical management theory would also constrain subordinate discretion, but based more upon assumptions concerning knowledge and discretionary ability than upon self-interest considerations (Barnard 1938).

Both the traditions of economics and management theory pose constraints upon managerial decision making, constraints which arise through negotiation. The economics tradition casts the market as a disciplining influence; employees seek alternative employment if dissatisfied with managerial decisions, exhibiting Hirschman's "exit" behavior (Hirschman 1970). In practice, of course, this discipline is more or less relaxed depending upon structure of the market. In a similar manner, organization theory attributes the discipline of decision making to the negotiation of the employment exchange in which employees negotiate the limits to acceptable management authority (March and Simon 1958). By inference, the power of negotiation is influenced by market alternatives.

The extreme centralized authoritarian mode of decision making can work efficiently in both human resource systems and other management systems of an organization in circumstances where the assumptions of rational self-interest and/or limited complexity are realized. Complications are introduced as the organization becomes more complex—multiple products, locations, and client/customer groups—but can be addressed through differentiation of decision making and improved methods for coordination. Rapidity of change in differentiated environments introduces still more complications as well.

The authoritarian mode of governance, particularly viewed within the framework of an economic exchange, clearly attempts to limit discretion. Subordinate agents are distrusted to exercise discretion, and discretion is provided only as necessitated by possession of knowledge and information. The constraints upon discretion, derived from lack of trust, are reciprocated with mutual lack of trust and disinterest in performing beyond the requirements of the contracted exchange. Enlargement of discretion through decentralization of decision making would be a rational approach to achieving effective and efficient performance. Decentralized decision making will be limited to that necessitated by the diffusion of knowledge and information.

The authoritarian model is subject to criticism in achieving equity, particularly in the extreme centralized mode. In extreme form, there is no opportunity for employee voice in workplace governance and the only available response to governance decisions is in the form of exit. There is no assurance that employee norms and expectations will be reflected in decisions. There are, however, mechanisms for voice participation (opinion surveys, open forums, suggestion systems) which can provide the opportunity for realizing some degree of equity. Given the relative power imbalance in the individual-organization employment exchange, realization of employee norms of justice is dependent upon authoritarian recognition of and responsiveness to employee concerns.

Differentiated decision making within the human resource system can raise potential challenges to the equity criterion for decisions. Employee participants assess both the distributive justice provided and the procedural justice of decision making, and differentiated decision making often results in decisions which may be locally rational and just but which appear globally inequitable. For example, the criteria for distribution of compensation increases may differ between adjacent departments and, while locally just, may appear inequitable to employees in another department. There is likely to be constant tension between the desire to decentralize HR decisions for purposes of efficiency and to centralize them for purposes of equity.

Collective bargaining model. Negotiation between management and a union representing the interests of the work force provides an alternative mechanism for work force governance. The exchange traditions of economics and rganization theory are continued but major characteristics of the exchange are negotiated by management and the union. The exchange is between the collective work force, not individual employees, and the employer. Individual employees are denied the opportunity to negotiate individually and are constrained to exit behavior. Only indirect participation in decision making is provided through union representation.

The collective bargaining model casts unionization and collective negotiations as an alternative for employees dissatisfied with and angered by management decision making (Wheeler and McClendon 1991). The option of collective negotiations is thus viewed as providing opportunity for a form of "voice" behavior, a form of indirect voice (Freeman and Medoff 1984).

Collective bargaining takes the form of constraining management decision making since it stems from reaction and dissatisfaction. In legalistic form, agreements are expressed in explicit written form which limits and constrains discretion. Consistent with the economics tradition, the parties are cast as having divergent interests and negotiations take the form of distributive bargaining. The exchange is cast in terms of simple economic exchange with no pretense of a social exchange. Of necessity, collective bargaining addresses those issues which can feasibly be contracted: hours of work, pay, bases for job assignment, and the like. Open-ended trust and undefined reciprocal obligations which characterize social exchange cannot be contracted.

Involvement of a union in negotiating decision rules for human resource management is viewed as potentially constraining effectiveness and efficiency of performance. Differentiation of decision making authority and flexibility of response to local conditions are constrained by centralized negotiation of standard rules. The relative effect of these constraints upon organizational performance will, of course, depend upon the stability and uniformity of relative environments which dictate the desirability of varied responses.

Participation of a union in the design of human resource policies does provide a form of voice for the work force and should thereby contribute to perceptions of both distributive and procedural justice. Given that union organization typically proceeds from employee frustration and anger over authoritarian decisions, collective bargaining provides the opportunity to better realize employee objectives. Collective bargaining does enhance the power of employees, albeit collectively, to influence terms of the employment exchange. To the extent that bargaining results in policies viewed as more desirable by the work force (e.g. higher wages), perceptions of distributive justice should be enhanced.

Further, the opportunity for at least indirect participation in collectively bargained decisions and negotiation of a grievance appeal system should provide enhanced perceptions of procedural justice.

Indirect participation through union negotiations results in a leveling effect upon terms of the employment contract and application of human resource policies, however (Freeman and Medoff 1984). Minimizing management discretion and the explicit prescription of rules for human resource decisions assures uniformity of treatment contributing to this leveling. The resulting uniformity, interestingly, may well result in perceptions of internal distributive inequity, particularly among minority interest employees. These employees, denied the opportunity for direct voice and participation, may also experience procedural inequity. Collective bargaining, often hailed as providing equity in the employment relationship, may provide collective equity at the expense of individual equity in both distributive and procedural terms.

The collective bargaining model is consistent with the traditional hierarchical model of decision making. It merely challenges the typical management authority in the hierarchical model and provides for joint management and union participation in the determination of rules. Decision making within the constraint of the collective agreement remains hierarchical and authoritative. The collective bargaining model also constrains the devolution of authority and discretion possible in the hierarchical model; centralized joint decision making sets rules for treatment throughout the organization which cannot be altered or modified for local conditions.

The collective bargaining model thus is a potential constraint upon effective and efficient performance of the organization. Otherwise rational decisions to achieve effectiveness and efficiency may be constrained by equity considerations advanced in the collective agreement. While it can be argued that acceptance of negotiated rules will be more enthusiastic and perceptions of equity higher thus contributing to improved performance, this must be qualified. The collective agreement negotiated in distributive bargaining reinforces the perception of a simple economic exchange and lack of trust beyond terms of the agreement. Further, the limited term of contracts inhibits the development of expectations concerning a longer term relationship and the trust which accompanies it. The benefits of social exchange beyond the economic exchange contract are not pursued. A social exchange may develop between negotiators for management and labor, but development of a social exchange between the organization and individual employees will likely be frustrated. Acceptance of negotiated rules will doubtless be greater than acceptance of disliked and arbitrarily imposed rules, but negotiated rules are unlikely to facilitate full development of a social exchange.

In general, realization of an equity norm probably is advanced through collective participation in the negotiation of a contract since unionization proceeds from anger and frustration. However, the resulting contract specifies common rules without provision for discretionary application. The realized collective equity may frustrate realization of individual equity which is at least conceivable in the hierarchical model with a responsive management.

Employee involvement model. Newer forms of work force governance which have been evolving take a variety of forms, many of which provide for limited direct involvement of employees in human resource decisions. Note that these forms have developed in organizations also employing the management hierarchy and/or collective bargaining models, and the newer forms may complement either mode. We analyze these varied forms as a class, despite differences, since all involve some direct participation of members of the work force.

The concept of direct individual involvement in work force governance appears incongruous in an organization employing hundreds and thousands of people. Yet the changing practices of human resource management sketched above all involve increased participation of individuals and work teams in making those decisions that affect the design of the work they perform, their individual career flows, and the form and amount of rewards they receive. These changing practices in the three subsystems of human resource management have the effect of relaxing highly specific standard rules for more general decision criteria and decentralizing individual decisions (Rankin 1990). General policies and decision criteria may be established within the hierarchical or collective bargaining model with the involved individuals making personal decisions within that framework. Examples of this limited employee involvement include individual and team redesign of work practices, scheduling task rotation, selecting, training and counseling team members, seeking skill enhancement, bidding for movement to other assignments, taking personal leave for family and other reasons, scheduling work hours in a flex-time system, designing personal benefit allocations, investing in deferred compensation, and scheduling pre-tax earnings for health and family care expenses.

Direct individual participation in human resource decisions has its most apparent effect upon the criterion of equity. The collective equity provided in the general decision policies is enhanced by increased individual equity realized through individual decisions. Enhanced perceptions of distributive equity are likely due to individual choices based upon attractiveness of outcomes, and enhanced perceptions of procedural equity are likely due to the greater exercise of individual influence and choice.

These provisions for individual participation expand the discretionary content of the employment exchange and communicate trust in employee decisions. The reciprocal extension of trust and discretion creates a social exchange of obligations which extend beyond those in the economic exchange of the employment contract (Fox 1974). These experienced obligations should be evidenced in loyalty, commitment, and dedication to the work of the organization.

Direct participation in work design decisions typically arises due to recognition of the potential contributions of those performing work tasks, particularly as they contribute to continued improvement. Direct participation in work design decisions thus is intended to impact directly upon effective and efficient performance. Equity implications of direct participation in work design decisions are not quite so apparent.

The implications of direct participation in flow and reward decisions for the effectiveness and efficiency performance criteria are less apparent than the implications of participation in work design. One consequence should be flexibility for management decisions due to relaxation of rules and the extension of discretion and trust. Also, we would expect greater acceptance and commitment to changes in practice due to participation and the enhanced social exchange relationship. And as noted earlier, direct participation in flow and reward decisions should enhance perceptions of both procedural and distributive justice due to individual shaping of both flow and reward outcomes to better match individual needs.

The employee involvement model described here involves individual work force participants making decisions about their individual terms and conditions of employment within a broader framework of policies, what Kerr described as "free individuals and controlled organizations" (Kerr 1979). Individual employees are less likely to participate directly in the establishment of those policies. Thus direct participation is more likely to evolve from a centralized hierarchical model than from a centralized collective bargaining model. The centralized hierarchical model evolves to direct participation through decentralization of decision making in response to change in technology and work design for effective and efficient performance and as a means of moving from mere economic exchange to incorporate more social exchange. Direct participation is less likely to evolve from the collective bargaining model which is cast as mere economic exchange and which strives to eliminate discretion. Further, direct employee involvement contradicts the collective orientation of collective bargaining and often is viewed as a challenge to the union representing the work force (Kochan, Katz, and Mower 1984).

Recent experiments such as Saturn and NUMMI suggest, however, that employee involvement, individually and in work teams, is feasible within a collective bargaining framework although these experiments are relatively rare in the American experience. Turner (1991) also reports illustrations of increasing direct employee involvement, particularly work team involvement through works councils independent of both management and union, within a collective bargaining framework in Germany. Apparently, direct employee involvement and collective bargaining need not be contradictory.

Evaluation

What approach to work force governance holds most promise for achieving the joint criteria of effective and efficient performance and justice and equity for the participants? Alternatively, what approach to human resource management holds most promise? While limited evaluations are implicit in our analyses above, we attempt here an overall summary evaluation. The correct answer to evaluation is, as always, "It depends." The three extreme modes of governance identified here present different advantages and disadvantages, and the relative importance of these differences will vary among situations. Note that our evaluation proceeds from the standpoint of the employing organization, not an individual, a total economy, or society. Thus the equity criterion of evaluation is cast instrumentally as realizing the equity norms of the work force sufficient to elicit the necessary and desired contributions from them.

What we termed the authoritarian mode offers the advantage of control and coordination of decision making for direct pursuit of performance objectives. Assuming management exercise of authoritarian governance, employees can be deployed as resources in the most efficient manner to achieve the organization's mission. Justice and equity are addressed instrumentally only in so far as necessary to obtain membership and cooperation of the work force. The power of employees to influence decisions is limited to organization dependence upon "beyond contract" cooperation and will vary with the nature of technology and the role of employees in that technology. The model of economic exchange is applied, and human resource policies are standardized for efficiency and convenience. This mode appears most appropriate for relatively smaller unitary organizations, either the total organization or a relatively self-managed plant or division, with relatively simple, routine, and stable technology, and a relatively homogeneous work force with relatively little dependence upon individual work force participants for skill, knowledge, or cooperation. Since the work force adds relatively little value beyond the performance of routine tasks and is easily replaced, the criteria of justice and equity, while perhaps important to employees, have little relationship with effective and efficient performance. Alternatively, a homogeneous work force may permit realization of perceived justice with standardized rules determined by a perceptive management.

The collective bargaining mode alters the power relationship and establishes collective power for the work force. Collective bargaining introduces constraints upon authoritarian governance, constraints intended to assure a sense of collective justice and equity. Negotiated policies and constraints upon management decisions inevitably constrain managerial pursuit of effective and efficient performance. While it can be argued that the provision for collective equity is likely to elicit greater cooperation of the work force, this expectation is diminished by the context of economic exchange, legalistic formulation of rules limiting discretion, and the typical adversarial roles of the parties. Turnover may be reduced by limiting managerial discretion, but the context of an extreme economic exchange is unlikely to elicit "beyond contract" performance and contributions (Fox 1974). Collective bargaining provides an alternative to authoritarian management governance, however, which can be useful in achieving both distributive and procedural justice for work force participants and provides a mechanism for limited voice in governance.

Given the traditional adversarial orientation of collective bargaining in negotiation of an economic exchange, this mode of governance inevitably limits the flexibility of management decision making. The performance implications of these constraints are most serious for organizations in dynamic and changing market and technological environments. The traditional collective bargaining mode is probably most appropriate in environments conducive to authoritarian governance but where there is some collective dependence upon the work force and where the management function fails to address distributive and procedural justice. To the extent that perceptions of justice are necessary to recruit and maintain a work force, it may be easier and more efficient to have collective representation of work force expectations.

What we have termed the employee involvement mode offers the opportunity for evolution of a social exchange in addition to economic exchange. Direct participation requires relaxation of highly specific policies for more general principles permitting greater discretion in individual applications. These more general principles may conceivably be achieved through the authoritarian or collective bargaining modes but are unlikely to be established through direct participation. Individual employees possess relatively little power to influence broad policies requiring consideration of issues at a more general level of analysis. Rather, limited direct participation occurs at the individual or team level of application.

Direct participation with the evolution of social exchange and mutual trust certainly offers greater flexibility and ease of response to varied and changing environments (Rankin 1990). Direct participation also should enhance organizational performance through improved quality of decisions, particularly in organizations with diffused knowledge and skill. Realization of social exchange, however limited, also should elicit individual performance beyond that specified in the employment contract. Finally, the opportunity for direct participation in making decisions about one's own specific employment conditions should contribute to a greater sense of individual justice and equity than can be achieved in either of the other modes. By inference, direct participation offers most promise to organizations in dynamic and changing environments and where skill, ability, and likely, individual aspirations are varied and diffused throughout the organization.

Employee involvement and direct participation, however limited, do have costs which must be considered. We have linked direct participation with the evolution of social exchange, an exchange which involves trust within the framework of a continuing relationship. At least implicit commitment to a continuing relationship is a prerequisite for development of a social exchange. This commitment is unlikely in organizations with short-term missions and/or highly fluctuating cycles of activity. A true social exchange, while extending discretion to the parties, also requires trust in the exercise of discretion which imposes implicit constraints and costs. Individual decisions are less constrained, but the balancing of a stream of individual decisions to the benefit of all parties is required to maintain trust. Perhaps the greatest threat to development of a social exchange with the work force is the threat of job loss. Lack of trust in the management function to place a high priority upon and strive to provide economic security will hinder development of a social exchange with "beyond contract" contributions from the work force.

The less adversarial social exchange mode offers flexibility for management response to changing conditions and imposes the obligation of not exploiting work force trust. Exploitation of trust in a continuing relationship by downsizing and layoff can terminate the social exchange with loss of work force trust and contributions beyond contract. The social exchange mode thus offers opportunity and at the same time imposes constraints upon the exercise of that opportunity. Paradoxically, a dynamic environment requires social exchange behavior in response to changing conditions, yet also encourages collectively bargained long-term contractual agreements that prohibit behavior viewed as necessary for survival of the organization.

One solution may lie in developing a long-term broad framework which satisfies security needs of the work force, coupled with compensating short-term flexibility which allows for adaptability by both management and labor. It is conceivable that the direct participation mode might evolve from either the authoritarian or collective bargaining modes of governance, and examples of both are available. However, it would appear to be less likely to evolve from collective bargaining. The entrenched traditions of economic exchange, adversarial pursuit of self-interest through distributive negotiations, lack of trust between the contracting parties, and the mutual constraint of discretion, all discourage the evolution of direct participation and social exchange. Most likely, direct participation in the collective bargaining mode will be constrained to governance aspects not commonly negotiated, the design of work. Direct participation in decisions specified through collective negotiations is prohibited by tradition and public policy.

There is evidence of forms of direct participation in unionized as well as nonunionized firms (Eaton and Voos 1992). Many of these attempts at direct participation have evolved in recent years as organizations strive for survival in more competitive markets. Interestingly, while we might have expected the management function to be less willing to extend direct participation during stressful competitive times, the extensions appear to be attempts to secure the beyond contract benefits of social exchange. Similarly, union willingness to participate in the extensions of direct participation often derives from desires to protect jobs in a competitive environment. The common rule of industry agreements has given way to enterprise bargaining and the common rule of enterprise contracts may be relaxed to permit individual direct participation. It may be questioned whether or not the mode of direct participation will survive a return to less competitive markets.

Realization of the social exchange benefits of direct participation is possible only within an exchange system that is perceived as just and equitable. The provision for justice in a system that provides opportunities for individual variation in contributions and inducements in the employment exchange requires some broad overlying policies guaranteeing, particularly, procedural justice. Although less common in the U.S., reports of workplace governance in some industries in Germany indicate that the collective bargaining mode can provide that structure while yet relaxing the common rule philosophy to permit individual and work team direct participation (Turner 1991). Turner reports that collective bargaining in the German automobile industry has provided "external certainty" in the form of broad policy constraints while permitting "internal flexibility" where works councils, independent of management and union, negotiate constantly over details of organizational operations. Such an approach to governance challenges the traditional collective bargaining mode as practiced in the U.S.

Of the three modes of governance reviewed here, some form of direct involvement appears to offer most benefit for organizational functioning and performance. There is opportunity, however, for incorporating a modified form of collective bargaining with direct involvement which could provide greater assurance of justice while also permitting development of social exchange with beyond contract exchanges. Evolution towards increased direct involvement has occurred as a consequence of heightened market competition. Threats to the survival of organized labor also have encouraged evolution of change in traditional collective bargaining. Continued adaptation in modes of work force governance would appear beneficial for employing organizations and their employee participants. There is a definite role for collective bargaining in this evolution, a role notably different from that of traditional collective bargaining.

The apparent lack of congruence between direct involvement and traditional collective bargaining is in some respects unfortunate. Direct participation, as it is evolving, requires establishment of a broader framework of policies within which individuals participate. Lacking collective bargaining, there is no immediate alternative to development of broad policies but a relaxed form of authoritarian governance. All three modes of work force governance will continue to be appropriate and effective for different organizations and environments. From an economic and social view it would appear desirable to be able to shift more easily from one mode to another as appropriate than now appears to be the case. Present pressures of competitive markets, rapidly evolving technologies and products, and the increasing diversity of the work force suggest that limited direct involvement holds current promise for the achievement of effective and efficient performance. An alternative form of collective bargaining could help to assure a just governance system.

References

Barnard, Chester. 1938. *The Functions of the Executive*. Cambridge, MA.
Beer, Michael, Bert Spector, Paul R. Lawrence, D. Quinn Mills, and Richard E. Walton. 1985. *Human Resource Management*. New York: The Free Press.
Brown, Roger. 1986. *Social Psychology*. New York: The Free Press.
Doeringer, Peter B. "Determinants of the Structure of Industrial Type Internal Labor Markets." *Industrial and Labor Relations Review* 20, pp. 206-20.
Dunlop, John T. 1948. "The Development of Labor Organization: A Theoretical Framework." In *Insights into Labor Issues*, eds. Richard Lester and Joseph Shister. New York: Macmillan, pp. 163-93.
_____. 1958. *Industrial Relations Systems*. New York: Holt.
Eaton, Adrienne E., and Paula B. Voos. 1992. "Unions and Contemporary Innovations in Work Organization, Compensation, and Employee Participation." In *Unions and Economic Competitiveness*, eds. Lawrence Mishel and Paula B. Voos. Armonk, NY: M.E. Sharpe, pp. 173-216.
Emerson, Richard M. 1990. "Social Exchange Theory." In *Social Psychology, Sociological Perspectives*, eds. Morris Rosenberg and Ralph H. Turner. New York: Basic Books, pp. 30-65.
Fox, Alan. 1974. *Beyond Contract: Work, Power, and Trust Relations*. London: Farber and Faber Limited.
Freeman, Richard B., and James L. Medoff. 1984. *What Do Unions Do?* New York: Basic Books.
Freeman, R. Edward, and David L. Reed. 1983. "Stockholders and Stakeholders: A New Perspective on Corporate Governance." *California Management Review* XXV (Spring), pp. 88-106.
Hackman, J. Richard, and Greg R. Oldham. 1976. "Motivation Through the Design of Work: Test of a Theory." *Organizational Behavior and Human Performance* 16 (August), pp. 250-79.
Hirschman, Albert O. 1970. *Exit, Voice, and Loyalty: Responses to Declines in Firms, Organizations, and States*. Cambridge, MA: Harvard University Press.
Jensen, Michael C., and William H. Meckling. 1976. "Theory of the Firm: Managerial Behavior, Agency Costs and Ownership Structure. *Journal of Financial Economics* 3, pp. 305-60.
Kelley, Harold H., and John W. Thibaut. 1978. *Interpersonal Relations: A Theory of Interdependence*. New York: Wiley Interscience.
Kerr, Clark. 1954. "The Balkanization of Labor Markets." *Labor Mobility and Economic Opportunity*. New York: John Wiley and Sons, pp. 92-110.
_____. 1979. "Introduction." In *Work in America: The Decade Ahead*, eds. Clark Kerr and Jerome M. Rosnow. Scarsdale, NY: Work in America Institute.
Kochan, Thomas A., Harry C. Katz, and Nancy R. Mower. 1984. *Worker Participation and American Unions*. Kalamazoo, MI: W.E. Upjohn Institute for Employment Research.
Lawler, Edward E. 1986. *High Involvement Management: Participative Strategies for Improving Organizational Performance*. San Francisco: Jossey-Bass.
Lawrence, Paul R., and Jay W. Lorsch. 1969. *Organization and Environment*. Homewood, IL: Richard D. Irwin.
Lind, E. Allan, and Tom R. Tyler. 1988. *The Social Psychology of Procedural Justice*. New York: Plenum Press.
Livernash, E. Robert. 1957. "The Internal Wage Structure." In George W. Taylor and Frank C. Pierson, eds., *New Concepts in Wage Determination*. New York: McGraw-Hill, pp. 143-72.
Macneil, Ian R. 1980. *The New Social Contract*. New Haven, CT: Yale University Press.

Mahoney, Thomas A. 1989. "Multiple Pay Contingencies: Strategic Design of Compensation." *Human Resource Management* 28 (Fall), pp. 337-47.

Maier, Norman. 1963. *Problem-Solving Discussions and Conferences.* New York: McGraw-Hill.

March, James F., and Herbert A. Simon. 1958. *Organizations.* New York: John Wiley and Sons.

Massie, Joseph L. 1965. "Management Theory." In *Handbook of Organizations*, ed. James G. March. Chicago: Rand McNally and Company, pp. 387-422.

Milogram, Paul, and John Roberts. 1988. "Economic Theories of the Firm: Past, Present and Future." *Canadian Journal of Economics* 21 (August), pp. 95-58.

Mitchell, Daniel J.B., and Renae F. Broderick. 1991. "Flexible Pay Systems in the American Context: History, Policy, Research, and Implications." In *Advances in Industrial and Labor Relations*, eds. Donna Sockell, David Lewin, and David B. Lipsky. Greenwich, CT: JAI Press, pp. 95-149.

Perrow, Charles. 1986. *Complex Organizations: A Critical Essay.* New York: Random House.

Rankin, Tom. 1990. *New Forms of Work Organization: The Challenge for North American Unions.* Toronto: University of Toronto Press.

Simon, Herbert A., Donald W. Smithburg, and Victor A. Thompson. 1950. *Public Administration.* New York: Knopf.

Taylor, Frederick W. 1911. *The Principles of Scientific Management.* New York: Harper and Brothers.

Thibaut, John W., and Harold H. Kelley. 1959. *The Social Psychology of Groups.* New York: John Wiley and Sons.

Thibaut, John, and Laurens Walker. 1975. *Procedural Justice: A Psychological Analysis.* Hillsdale, NJ: Lawrence Erlbaum Associates.

Thompson, James D. 1967. *Organizations in Action.* New York: McGraw-Hill.

Trist, Eric L. 1981. "The Sociotechnical Perspective." In *Perspectives on Organizational Design and Behavior*, eds. Andrew H. Van de Ven and William F. Joyce. New York: Wiley.

Turner, Lowell. 1991. *Democracy at Work.* Ithaca, NY: Cornell University Press.

Vroom, Victor H., and Philip Yetton. 1973. *Leadership and Decision Making.* Pittsburgh, PA: University of Pittsburgh Press.

Walton, Mary. 1986. *The Deming Management Method.* New York: Dodd, Mead, and Company.

Wellins, Richard S., William C. Byham, and Jeanne M. Wilson. 1991. *Empowered Teams.* San Francisco, CA: Jossey-Bass.

Wheeler, Hoyt N., and John A. McClendon. 1991. "The Individual Decision to Unionize." In *The State of the Unions*, eds. George Strauss, Daniel G. Gallagher, and Jack Fiorito. Madison, WI: Industrial Relations Research Association, pp. 47-84.

Williamson, Oliver E. 1975. *Markets and Hierarchies: Analysis and Antitrust Implications.* New York: The Free Press.

Chapter 5

Representatives of Their Own Choosing: Finding Workers' Voice in the Legitimacy and Power of Their Unions

Patricia A. Greenfield
University of Massachusetts at Amherst

Robert J. Pleasure
George Meany Center for Labor Studies and Antioch University

[T]he labor movement [is] "the most articulate, indeed, the only voice of the front-line worker in America."

—Robert Reich, Secretary of Labor, quoted in *The New York Times*, February 17, 1993.

In the opening chapter of their classic work, *Industrial Democracy* (1902), Beatrice and Sidney Webb find the beginnings of primitive industrial democracy in England in the trade clubs of the latter part of the 18th and early part of the 19th centuries. The English clubs were reluctant to recognize any authority other than "the voices" of the workers themselves (p. 3); "what concerns all should be decided by all," and the means to find that common concern were periodic general membership meetings (p. 8). As the trade clubs and their functions expanded or formed federal unions, they developed representative governance structures. The broader based trade unions, the Webbs reported, sought the appropriate balance between administrative efficiency and popular control, between the need for a union to transact its business on behalf of its constituents in an effective manner and the requirement that the institution provide mechanisms to hear "the voices" of their members and use those mechanisms to ascertain and advance the will of their constituents. The representative body, then, took the place of "pure" or, as the Webbs labeled it, "primitive" democracy and through the transformation became a more efficient mechanism for the expression of worker voice.

Superficially, this concept of worker voice, familiar to most trade unionists as an ideal description of the purpose and function of a trade union, appears consistent with the definition of voice developed initially by Hirschman (1970) and applied to industrial relations by Freeman and Medoff (1984). Hirschman defines voice as "any attempt at all to change . . . an objectionable state of affairs, whether through individual or collective petition to the management directly in charge, through appeal to a higher authority with the intention of forcing a change in management, or through various types of actions and protests, including those that are meant to mobilize public opinion" (p. 30). Citing Hirschman, Freeman and Medoff refer to voice as "the use of direct communication to bring actual and desired conditions closer together" (p. 8). In industrialized economies and large enterprises, they note, "A trade union is the vehicle for collective voice—that is, for providing workers as a group with a means of communicating with management" (p. 8).

In the burgeoning literature on employee voice, however, a significant, consistent and troubling underlying assumption appears: that voice is desirable primarily or solely insofar as it creates or contributes to the efficiency of the firm. Hirschman describes voice as a control which, in concert with exit and loyalty, acts to maintain the efficiency of a firm in an insufficiently competitive market. While he notes in passing that voice in the context of worker representation can maintain the responsiveness of the labor union to its membership in the context of rival unions battling for a worker's loyalty (pp. 79-80), he does not use "voice" as a construct to describe worker representation in the workplace. Hirschman describes the boycott, again in market terms, as a "hybrid" of voice and exit (p. 86); the boycott, Hirschman asserts, "combines the characteristics of exit, which causes losses to the firm or organization with those of voice, which is costly in time and money for the member-customers" (p. 86). Freeman and Medoff distinguish the voice "face" of unions from the monopoly "face," the latter characterized by the "harmful economic effects" unions can cause when they use their monopoly power to raise wages above market-determined levels. This face of unions, Freeman and Medoff assert, is to be condemned, as opposed to the voice function which they contend should be lauded for its creation of "the possibility for improved labor contracts and arrangements and higher economic efficiency" (p. 11). Ironically, to a trade unionist the ability to use power in the labor market to "take wages out of competition," or to improve workers' benefits and working conditions above what the employer argues the market will bear, is an essential part of providing effective voice for workers. To its members, a trade union achieving such goals through use of collective action would be viewed as successful in providing workers with an effective and powerful exercise of voice.

An examination of the literature inspired by Freeman and Medoff demonstrates that the bulk of the discussion and empirical examination of voice has focused upon the capacity of traditional union voice mechanisms, such as grievance procedures, to enhance firm productivity (Lewin and Mitchell 1992, 12-15). Grievance procedures, then, are not evaluated to determine whether the goals of the members are achieved through the prosecution of a grievance, but whether ultimately the grievance process or result enhances firm efficiency.

But the grievance and arbitration procedure, established through a collective bargaining agreement, is part of a system of workplace democracy through which workers have an opportunity to give effective voice to their grievances. Clearly the fundamental issue is not the efficiency of the firm; a union does not bring a grievance for the purpose of improving the firm's productivity. That unions should act solely for constituent workers and not for the sake of firm efficiency is a notion deeply ingrained in U.S. law and tradition. Indeed, a union officer who acts otherwise may be in breach of fiduciary duty under the Landrum-Griffin Act; may, by such conduct, show a union breach of the duty of fair representation; and may provide evidence of unlawful employer assistance or domination of the union under the NLRA. It is important that measures of worker representation use yardsticks other than contributions to firm efficiency.

In making this point, we do not reject the value of workplace efficiency nor suggest that the productivity of a firm is of no significance to unions. In fact many unions have worked closely with management to improve productivity to enhance an organization's competitive strength. Empirical studies by Freeman and Medoff and others establish that unions can and often do contribute to efficiency and productivity. We have no quarrel with the evaluation of efficiency and productivity relative to a union's presence or to unions working on such issues. But efficiency and productivity must be put in their proper perspective when examined in connection with fundamental union goals.

The central activity of a union is the legitimate and powerful expression of the collective voice of the workers. In a particular time, place, union, or industry, that voice may be directed to the improvement of production; in another context it may be the establishment of a particular system of industrial justice. Goals may vary over time and issue, and multiple objectives may exist. The key is that these objectives are set by the members themselves through collective voice. While researchers can certainly discuss and debate whether the members are "right" or "wrong" in their choice of goals to which they employ their collective voice, it is inappropriate to impose a normative set of objectives on a union or particular union function and then evaluate that expression of voice on the basis of that externally imposed set of values.

We contend that the appropriate and necessary yardsticks, familiar to courts and unionists alike, for assessing whether any entity, including unions, provides "true" voice for workers, are legitimacy and power. Is the voice expressed being expressed by the legitimate representative of the workers? Is the nature of the voice expressed such that it carries with it the power to effectively voice workers' concerns (i.e., does this voice have the capacity to effectively influence decisions with which the workers are concerned?)

We begin with the contention that the appropriate definition of "collective voice" in a labor context is communication that has power to effect the represented workers' purposes and is the legitimate expression of their collective aims. Our definition of "collective voice" is drawn from political theory and the observations of political actors and empirical researchers who have studied and observed worker collective action. "Collective voice" so defined also comports with common usage, particularly voice as "a right or power to take part in the control or management of something, chiefly in the phr. *to have a v.* in. 1835" (*Oxford Universal Dictionary* 1955, 2368).

When we use the term "legitimacy" to apply to the collective voice of a worker organization, we mean an organization of the workers' own choosing. In that sense "legitimacy," as discussed below, implies general consent of the workers to the representative capacity of the organization carrying collective voice. "Power" of an organization carrying collective voice encompasses a wide range of capacities including persuasiveness, influence, and control, depending on the purposes of the workers represented (see discussion below).

In this chapter we explore the concepts of power and legitimacy and their relationship to the definition of voice, particularly voice as applied to unions. We then examine this more developed definition of voice in the context of legislation and existing empirical studies. Finally, we suggest how the constructs of power and legitimacy can be used in future examinations of worker voice.

"Voice" in Political Theory

We contend that the voice debate should be shifted from neo-classical economic analysis back to its original home, democratic political theory, which focuses on voice as a necessary element in the operation of representative democratic processes. (Derber 1970, 16-21.) The fundamental issue to be examined is the relationship of worker voice to a workplace democracy in which employees can express views and exercise the ordinary rights and powers of the governed. And what, then, is the most effective mechanism or sets of mechanisms for expressing worker voice in order to achieve workplace democracy? We look initially to concepts of political theory relating to representation and governance in order to understand the political bases of the concept of worker voice.

The system of exclusivity and majority rule in North American industrial relations is exceptional and relevant to an understanding of the application of political theory (including the concepts of legitimacy and power) to union voice in the United States. "Legitimacy," "power," and "voice" are concepts drawn from political theory. The decisive historical fact that makes those concepts central to an understanding of union activity in the U.S. was the enactment in federal labor law of a structure that made the workplace, upon the choice of the workers, a polity. Howard Dickman in his work, *Industrial Democracy in America* (1987), observed:

The affinity of exclusive representation to *political* rule is neither casual nor accidental. On the contrary, it is the climax of a long-standing and deeply rooted impulse to democratize, that is to *politicize*, the workplace. Workers, many felt, ought to and must have "a voice in determining the laws within industry and commerce which affect them, equivalent to the voice which they have as citizens in determining legislative enactments which shall govern them"—a voice which, the proponents of unionism argued, they did not have in a regime of individual bargaining. (Dickman 1987, 11 citing American Federation of Labor Reconstruction Program, 1918, quoted in David Saposs ed., *Readings in Trade Unionism* [New York: George H. Doran, 1926], p. 46.)

Dickman points out that the philosophical argument in trade union theory favoring exclusivity is based on the workers' bargaining disadvantage. Specifically, there is apprehension of economic coercion; the coercion, it is reasoned, results from unequal bargaining power inherent in capital ownership and control over the source of workers' survival enabling managers to dictate the terms of the employment contract:

Social theorists who championed market transactions over legal controls were mistaken, because the distribution between voluntary exchange for material benefit and unilateral political coercion is nebulous, if not wholly illegitimate. . . . The employment relationship is a political one; "industry," the dean of American reform economists wrote in the 19th century, is a "despotism" (Dickman 1987, 12, citing Richard T. Ely, *An Introduction to Political Economy* [New York: Chatauqua Press, 1889], p. 236).

Mark Perlman, in *Labor Union Theories in America* (1958), describes the development of American trade union theory among Henry C. Adams, John R. Commons, and Selig Perlman as distinct from earlier German and British theories of political democracy applied to the workplace. The Americans, Perlman asserts, "fall conceptually somewhere between the English who tended to regard the state as an evil, and the Germans who tended to regard it as an end in itself" (p. 162). Adams, Commons, and Selig Perlman found in America a "scene, where social and political power rested on a complex network of economic bargaining groups and a constitutional tradition of limited governmental powers. There was in America no simple legal or productive 'leviathan'" (p. 162). Mark Perlman clearly places Adams, Commons, and Selig Perlman among those theorists who regarded unions "as critical elements of the historical democratic process, and . . . essentially bargaining institutions, aimed at increasing the social status, and particularly the economic liberty of working people" (p. 162). Perlman's choice of the words "economic liberty" rather than "economic outcomes" is apt. The central focus of trade union theorists of Commons' era was ". . . to give proprietary significance to job rights; the material benefits coming from the collective bargaining process were desirable, but not inherently necessary by-products" (p. 162). But, Selig Perlman and J.R. Commons were institutional economists describing trade union theory as it was developed by an articulate movement led by Samuel Gompers, Frank Morrison, Peter McGuire, Adolf Strasser, and others.

To Gompers and Morrison, worker representation through unions of their own choosing was linked to democracy. Just as legitimate government is self-government in a democracy, representation of workers through their own organizations has appeared to unionists to be the articulation in the workplace of just principles of democratic theory. In the 1920s Samuel Gompers and Frank Morrison, President and Secretary respectively of the American Federation of Labor in 1921, would regularly publish the pamphlet, *Trade Unions: Their Origin and Objects, Influence and Efficacy*, by the English economist William Trant. In the postscript to the 19th edition published in that year, as in previous editions, Gompers and Morrison ask rhetorically, "Which is the best form of organization for the people, the workers? We unhesitatingly answer: 'The organizaton of the working people, by the working people, for the working people—that is the trade unions'" (Gompers and Morrison 1921, 61).

Gompers chaired the drafting committee for the labor sections of the Treaty of Versailles and participated in securing acceptance of trade union rights in the body of international law (Gompers 1925, 487-500). The right of workers to form their own organizations and to speak and act through trade unions was established as a matter of international law first by the Treaty of Versailles after the first World War and by the Universal Charter of Human Rights after the second. Convention 87 of the International Labor Organization specifically guarantees the right of workers to form trade unions and to maintain their own structures and internal rules, free from interference. The same documents—the Treaty of Versailles, the UN Charter, and ILO Convention 87—also define labor not to be merely a commodity. (See generally, Alcock 1971.)

It is against this international legal framework and the nearly universal practice of industrialized countries to provide protection for the expression of collective voice through trade unions (with important interruptions by totalitarian systems), that the old arguments for state- and employer-sponsored alternatives to unions of the workers' own choosing are advanced. And it is against these international expressions of both trade union legitimacy and the special character of labor as distinct from a commodity, that the now discredited notions of trade unions as merely trusts and labor's alleged monopolistic practices are resurrected. Powerless employee involvement programs and quality circles are advanced often not as additional forums through which collective voice may be heard, but as substitutes for unions of the workers' own choosing.

There is a category of representative, a trustee, who acts for a beneficiary and who may be appointed by the state or the creator of a trust. In such case there is no consent, express or implied, between the trustee and the beneficiary. The specific idea of a trusteeship was the essence of welfare capitalism in the United States. According to David Brody,

> The flawed performance of welfare capitalism was not a true measure of its significance. Welfare capitalism exceeded the sum of its parts. It was also an idea that management accepted the obligation for the well being of its employee. In May 1929 Charles Schwab reminded the American Iron and Steel Institute of "the responsibilities that repose upon us in the steel industry . . . a real trusteeship . . . for hundreds and thousands of families. We seek to prosper ourselves but above all we seek the welfare, progress and happiness of our people (applause)." That promise, more than all of its actual programs, constituted the essence of welfare capitalism (Brody 1980, 61).

In sharp contrast to Schwab, Gompers rejected the notion of trusteeship. In a pamphlet published in 1915 by the AFL, Gompers asserted: "Doing for people what they can and ought to do for themselves is a dangerous experiment. In the last analysis the welfare of the workers depends upon their own initiative" (Gompers 1919, 16). For Gompers the idea of the workers' representative role was clearly one of agency, not trusteeship: "Class is no assurance of genius, ability or wisdom. No man is fit to control the lives of his fellows. The trade unions are the agencies through which wage earners are working out their destinies and interposing a check on arbitrary power in industry" (Gompers 1919, 22).

The Concept of Legitimacy

Legitimacy is an important concept for purposes of assessing competing claims for the exercise of power in governmental and representation systems because legitimacy, put most simply, is the right to exercise power. Further, "the right to carry out an action exists if and only if there is a general consensus that the particular actor in question has the right to carry out that action" (Coleman 1990, 470). Collective voice, to extend Coleman's discussion to labor, is the authoritative expression of the purposes of the workers.

Further, legitimacy for purposes of the representation of workers means consent to representation by a collective agent. The situation is not precisely that of principal and agent because the members must be both active participants and commit to solidarity behind the collective voice of the union. Authority within unions is often more fluid as between officers and members than it is within Weber's highly differentiated and stratified corporate structure (Weber 1958, 151-52). The requirement within unions to mobilize members in voluntary activity as the source of its power manifests itself in a set of beliefs about legitimacy which will often require (1) direct membership contract ratification, (2) direct membership voting on local union officers, (3) direct membership strike votes, (4) consideration by the committee of the whole of any financial change requiring an increased payment by members, and (5) that the officers and staff will be drawn from among the members and will have worked "at the trade" or within the work jurisdiction of the labor organization. Thus, the legitimacy of a labor union's representative capacity is not fully encompassed by the usual legal description of principal and agent because of the practical requirement in unions of continuous reinforcement of collectivity, mobilization, and solidarity as sources of legitimacy and power.

There are valuable new efforts at refinement of the concept of legitimacy as it is applied to unions. Chaison, Bigelow, and Ottensmeyer (1992) draw from organizational theory literature (e.g., Meyer and Rowan 1977; Pfeffer and Salancik 1978), and define legitimacy "as a status conferred on organizations whose objectives, goals and structures conform to values and expectations, both of society at large and of key constituencies" (p. 3).

Ahlen (1992) emphasizes the idea of procedural and substantive legitimacy: "Procedural legitimacy refers to the organization's 'form', its organizational structure and processes. In contrast, substantive legitimacy is 'the range of activities an organization may engage in and still maintain its legitimacy' . . . together with the legitimacy of the goals to which these activities are directed and the legitimacy of the priorities given among these goals. . . . Unions' procedural legitimacy derives, therefore, from the extent to which they conform to notions of democracy" (p. 7). Ahlen proposes a method for evaluating legitimacy of a particular union or union activity by testing the degree to which decision making is accomplished through membership participation. She emphasizes that her focus on participation rather than representative democracy is due to the strong Swedish bias in favor of maximum membership participation (p. 8).

While the Chaison et al. and Ahlen essays are helpful refinements of legitimacy, their focus is on the vitality and survival of established unions. They describe a way to measure likelihood of survival and union effectiveness at mobilizing workers through an assessment of level of membership participation in decision making. What is not evaluated by Chaison et al. and Ahlen is the choice between an organization of the workers' own choosing and one that is not; an organization governed by a set of bylaws established by workers and an organization whose framework is determined by the state or an employer. While it is clear Chaison et al. and Ahlen believe unions can sacrifice legitimacy through undemocratic practices, they appear to find it self-evident that an organization not of the workers' choosing is, in its inception, illegitimate.

The Concept of Power

Power is often described as "the ability to bring about outcomes you desire" (Ryan 1984, 21, citing Pfeffer and Salancik 1977). The ability is not seen as inherent in a person but rather as the outcome of relationships between persons, groups, or institutions. There is debate as to whether to distinguish power, persuasion, authority, influence and control (Ryan 1984, 22). As we have noted, our definition of power allows for a range of capacities, including the ability to exercise significant workplace power—what Freeman and Medoff refer to as "monopoly power." In the political theory literature, one of the analogies we find most apt to the workplace and labor relations systems is the division of power by intention, as in a tricameral or bicameral system, and it is one that describes power as influence which produces bargaining.

"The political structure in an organization," according to Ryan (1984), "can be seen as arising out of the division of labor" (p. 30). Dependence and interdependence can create power distributions that result in bargaining. Expressed differently, Ryan (1984), quoting Tushman, points out: "If there is no need for joint decision making (i.e., no interdependence) and there is no resource scarcity, then the subunits can make independent decisions. But, if the groups are interdependent and must share scarce resources, they must engage in joint decision making. Under these ubiquitous conditions the political perspective has the most relevance" (p. 30). The notion of interdependent entities developing ways to bargain over scarce resources provides us with a useful framework for examining the labor-management relationship, for it is a well-recognized characterization of the collective bargaining process (Chamberlain and Kuhn 1986, 445-57).

This pluralism has been applied to government structures by Neustadt (1990) who defines a kind of power called persuasion. Neustadt's definition of the power to persuade hinges on the conception of a government "not of separated powers, but of separated institutions sharing powers" (p. 332). Focusing on presidential powers, he comments:

> The separateness of institutions and the sharing of authority prescribe the terms on which a President persuades. When one man shares authority with another, but does not gain or lose his job upon the other's whim, his willingness to act upon the urging of the other turns on whether he conceives the action right for him. The essence of the President's persuasive task is to convince such men that what the White House wants of them is what they ought to do for their sake and on their authority (p. 332).

Neustadt clearly does not mean that persuasive authority hinges on charm or reasonable arguments. He is quick to add that persuading others that they ought to do as he proposes requires that the others "fear some acts by him on his own responsibility" (p. 332). Further, "[t]he power to persuade is the power to bargain. Status and authority yield bargaining advantages. But in a government of 'separated institutions sharing powers', they yield them to all sides" (p. 333). In the sphere of congressional relations, Neustadt comments that "what he demands, the others can resist. The stage is set for that great game, *much like collective bargaining,* in which each seeks to profit from the other's needs and fears. It is a game played catch-as-catch-can, case by case. And everybody knows the game, observers and participants alike" (p. 334, emphasis added).

The Link Between Power and Legitimacy

Power within organizations when legitimately exercised is, as discussed supra, authority. "The crux of authority is seen as the voluntary acceptance of it by those over whom it is exercised . . ." (Ryan 1984, 33). Collective voice, as a form of authority, does not derive its legitimacy from employers or the state but from its own constituencies (Ahlen 1992; Chaison et al. 1992). While legitimacy is drawn originally from internal constituencies, in our view, that legitimacy can be broadened and made authoritative within a larger system of industrial relations owing to a consensus established by law or voluntary recognition of the union as collective bargaining agent. A union's legitimacy is not, however, diminished by denial of recognition. But in the larger community the exercise of collective voice may be perceived as power of a coercive nature because it is not recognized.

When collective voice seeks control of entry into the work force or seeks to limit the hiring of replacement workers or seeks to organize all workers in a labor market, a neoclassical economist may choose to describe those practices as potentially inefficient and thereby seek to delegitimize collective voice when it has what they describe to be a monopolistic purpose. However, that is simply a value, and a value that describes interests other than those represented by a trade union. To a trade unionist, labor market control is not only "good" but necessary to accomplish fundamental trade union goals; this control is crucial to the exercise of effective collective voice. An adequate understanding of the social interaction between employers and workers must account for conflicts in the interests of various stakeholders rather than submerging them in a value-laden assertion of a community interest in efficiency.

Values, Assumptions, and The Monopoly Power Debate

As Ryan (1984) points out, "Talcott Parsons has been criticized for basing his analysis of social structure on a theory of consensus of values, ignoring the conflicts of interests between groups, and therefore political processes, and in his later writings for trying to show that all power is legitimized . . ." (p. 33). The treatment of unions as monopolies by Freeman and Medoff results from the same kind of uncritical fusion or merger of social interests and values in the manner of Parsons two generations earlier, except that now economists rather than sociologists assert a kind of hegemony of values. Today it is efficiency that Freeman and Medoff submit is a commonly shared social value that led them to conclude "[w]hile our analysis, and that of other researchers has found the monopoly costs of unionism to be relatively small to the society as a whole, even small social costs should, when possible, be cut. As the principal weapon against monopoly power is competition, we favor continued governmental efforts to reduce industry (and therefore union) monopoly power through deregulation; we oppose efforts to reduce foreign competition for the purpose of bailing out particular sectors . . ." (Freeman and Medoff 1984, 249).

In a review of *What Do Unions Do?*, Lipsky (1985) assesses Freeman and Medoff's "surprisingly uncritical . . . view that unions do have a monopoly face." Lipsky comments:

> To [Freeman and Medoff], whether unions are primarily monopolistic or primarily voice institutions is entirely an empirical question. In my judgment, however, the utility of considering unions as monopolies is more than an empirical question; it is a critical conceptual and theoretical issue. At best, the monopoly model of unions is a useful metaphor; at worst, it is an utter distortion of the nature of unionism.
>
> Clearly, unions are not *literally* monopolies; to cite only a few of the well-known flaws of the monopoly model, unions cannot be monopolies because they do not actively

sell the services of their members; they are not profit maximizers (nor is it evident that they engage in any form of maximizing behavior); they lack meaningful cost functions; they do not (in the absence of a closed shop) control the supply of labor; and as Freeman and Medoff themselves emphasize, they adhere to the precept of the standard wage rather than engaging in price (wage) discrimination, as true monopolies do (p. 252).

The distinctions that Lipsky makes between unions and monopolies are not new, nor is the characterization by Freeman and Medoff of unions as monopolistic new. Indeed, the concept of unions as collective voice rather than as monopolies or trusts is well established in American trade unionism. In 1907 Gompers argued against the particularly corrosive miscasting of unions as trusts (corrosive because of the vehemence in Anglo-American legal practice with which antitrust laws were applied to union activities.) Gompers argued:

> Let me reiterate most emphatically here and now that *the trade union* is not, *and from its very nature cannot be, a trust*. It is sometimes derisively called a trust by those who expose their ignorance of economic first principles in making such a statement.
> The union is the *voluntary association of the many for the benefit of all* the community. The trust is the voluntary association of the few for their own benefit. The trade union puts no limit upon its membership, except that of skill and character, it welcomes every wage-worker. In fact, its strength and influence rest in its universal adoption by the wage-workers as the permanent and potent method of voicing their needs. . . .
> Trusts consist of organizations for the control of the products of labor. Laborers possess their labor power; that is, their power to produce (Gompers 1919, 15-16; emphasis in original).

The power of unions and their legitimacy resided, for Gompers, in a voluntarist notion in which, as he said, "strength and influence [would] rest in [their] universal adoption as the permanent and potent method of voicing [workers'] needs . . ." (Gompers 1919, 15.) In the Gilded Age context in which Gompers operated in the 1890s, "the courts' very sway made common law and constitutional discourse beckon as the surest framework within which to contend for legitimacy and relief" (Forbath 1991, 7).

The AFL's effort which took on a generally anti-statist approach from the 1890s through the 1920s resulted in legislative enactment of antitrust exemptions and anti-injunction statutes at the state level. (For a full discussion of the development in the AFL of a voluntarist and highly legal and constitutional approach to trade union legitimacy and power see Forbath 1991, 7.) It was not until 1928, when Felix Frankfurter and other reformist lawyers drafted a successful substitute bill to the AFL-sponsored federal anti-injunction act, that a positive national labor charter was sketched in the early draft of the preamble to the 1932 Norris-LaGuardia Act, discussed in detail in the following section of this chapter.

These reformist lawyers had earlier drafted the 1926 Railway Labor Act which protected the right to organize and elect bargaining representatives. These students of the reformist tradition of Frankfurter and others, according to Forbath, were drafters of the National Labor Relations Act through which an administrative structure was erected to supplant the courts with a board (p. 164). However, Forbath concludes, "If the old guard grossly underestimated the good that would flow from the new order, they were not wrong about the possibility that within it many of the old common law restraints on collective action might reassert themselves" (p. 165).

While the legislature may have intended otherwise, "Courts continue to treat labor and labor protest on marketplace terms" (Forbath 1991, 166). Thus, while the legitimacy of the exercise of power by unions is now enacted in statute, the judicial and neoclassical economists' understanding of unionism remains limited by common law and market theory. (On this point, in addition to Forbath, see also Atleson 1983.)

"Representatives of Their Own Choosing": Legitimacy, Power and Voice in the Evolution of U.S. Labor Policy

Despite the influence of such judicial and neoclassical interpretations, the concepts of power and legitimacy, intertwined with the need for workers to have representatives of their own choosing, were embodied in federal statutes in the U.S. in the late 1920s and the early to mid-1930s. This legislation was enacted in the wake of the Depression and the collapse of the "welfare capitalism" of the prior decade. As Brody (1980, 48-81) documents, a number of prominent business leaders in the 1920s adopted the welfare capitalist philosophy, asserting that business had the inclination and ability to provide for workers' needs and that these needs could be met through a system of enlightened, humane, management practices and labor-management cooperation.

The centerpiece of welfare capitalism was the employee representation plan (Brody 1980, 58). Created, assisted, and, at times, dominated by management, these structures, sometimes taking the form of a company union, sought to provide workers with a vehicle for making suggestions to management and airing grievances (Bernstein 1960, 170-89; Brody 1980, 48-81). Management often instituted these plans in response to the threat of or as a direct substitute for unionization (Bernstein 1960, 170; Brody 1980, 58) and operated them under the theory that the employees should interact not with other workers in the industry, but with the firm as "an island, cut off from contact with other companies in the same labor market or same industry" (Bernstein 1960, 170).

Workers did not need a "third party" such as a broad-based trade union and would naturally benefit from these management-created structures because, as one observer contended in 1929, "modern business acted on the 'sincere belief that the interests of the employer and employee are mutual and at bottom identical'" (Brody 1980, 51). Trade unionists of the time voiced concern that workers had been "lulled" into thinking that the employer was their "protector" and that, therefore, trade unionism was unnecessary (p. 78). Bernstein contends that such plans reflected management's desire to deprive workers of the bargaining power available only through a trade union.

> The company union lacked authorization to strike, had no funds to finance a stoppage, and was incapable of coordinating its acts with organizations at other firms in the industry. Its only sanction, if it may be called that, was persuasion. A second shortcoming was inability to bargain over the basic employment issues, wages, and hours. At Jersey Standard . . . the representation meetings during the twenties largely degenerated into repeated employee requests for a wage increase, with continued management promises that they "would be looked into" (Bernstein 1960, 173).

Historians debate whether welfare capitalism would have fallen of its own weight based upon its failure to provide "a system of shop government placed in a climate of political democracy and universal suffrage" or whether it had a fundamental appeal and would have continued if not for the economic havoc wreaked by the Depression (Brody 1980, 78; Bernstein 1960, 187-88; see also, Millis and Brown 1950, 19-20).

No matter which theory one accepts, the Depression did bring an abrupt end to these experiments, and the labor legislation of the 1930s clearly repudiated the concepts of identical employer-worker interests, finding employer-established and controlled worker organizations to be, ultimately, illegitimate. As Bernstein notes, labor relations scholar William Leiserson's comments presaged these significant shifts. Leiserson argued that management failed to recognize the governmental and political considerations involved in labor-management relations: "self-determination, the consent of the governed, and a voice for the wage earner" (Bernstein 1960, 187).

It was these concerns that came to the fore in the labor legislation of the 1930s. In actuality, the earliest statutory support for the concept of noninterference with workers' choice of their own representatives had come in the Railway Labor Act of 1926 which, in the context of establishing mediation and arbitration procedures to reduce industrial unrest in the railway industry, gave railway workers the right to bargain collectively. In an industry rife with company unions, however, section two of the Act was almost revolutionary:

> Representatives . . . shall be designated by the respective parties in such manner as may be provided in their corporate organization or unincorporated association, or by other means of collective action without interference, influence, or coercion exercised by either party over the self-organization or designation of representatives by the other (Railway Labor Act 1926).

In 1930 the Texas and New Orleans Railroad's legal challenge to the RLA reached the Supreme Court. The railroad had refused to recognize or bargain with the Brotherhood of Railway Clerks, choosing instead to deal with a company-sponsored and dominated union. In declaring the Act constitutional, the Court rejected the company's claim that the Act violated the Constitution's guarantee of due process:

The Railway Labor Act does not interfere with the normal exercise of the right of the carrier to select its employees or to discharge them. The statute is not aimed at this right but at the interference with the right of employees to have representatives of their own choosing. As carriers subject to the Act have no constitutional right to interfere with the freedom of the employees in making their selections, they cannot complain of the statute on constitutional grounds (281 U.S. at 571).

This ruling, with its recognition of workers' right to collective bargaining through representatives they choose, was crucial in paving the way for 1930s' labor legislation (Taylor and Witney 1987, 148; Bernstein 1960, 406). The opinion particularly encouraged Senator George Norris (Bernstein 1960, 496) who, along with Representative Fiorello LaGuardia, introduced the Norris-LaGuardia Anti-Injunction Act in 1932. Section 2 of Norris-LaGuardia recognized that "the individual unorganized worker is commonly helpless to exercise actual liberty of contract and to protect his freedom of labor, and thereby to obtain acceptable terms and conditions of employment." Therefore,

it is necessary that he have full freedom of association, self-organization, and designation of representatives of his own choosing, to negotiate the terms and conditions of his employment, and that he shall be free from the interference, restraint, or coercion of employers of labor, or their agents, in the designation of such representatives or in self-organization or in other concerted activities for the purpose of collective bargaining or other mutual aid or protection . . . (Norris-LaGuardia Act, 1932).

This same underlying philosophy was reflected in the National Labor Relations Act (or the Wagner Act) passed in 1935. Senator Robert Wagner, chief architect and sponsor of the Act, saw worker voice as fundamental to the preservation of the American system: "the [workers'] struggle for a voice in industry through the process of collective bargaining is at the heart of the struggle for the preservation of political as well as economic democracy in America" (Gross 1985, 10, quoting Keyserling). The link between democracy and voice, however, was ensured only through voice expressed by legitimate representatives of the workers—representatives they themselves had chosen. Wagner, reflecting on the Act two years after it passed, stated that democracy in industry required "fair participation by those who work in the decisions vitally affecting their lives and livelihood" and that workers "can enjoy this participation only if allowed to organize and bargain collectively through representatives of their own choosing" (Derber 1970, 321).

The National Labor Relations Act reflected Wagner's thinking, combined with statements similar to those expressed in the RLA and Norris-LaGuardia. The "Findings and Policy" section dealt directly with the power issue, acknowledging the "inequality of bargaining power between employees who do not possess full freedom of association or actual liberty of contract and employers who are organized in the corporate or other forms of ownership association." Equality of bargaining power can be restored, this section went on to note, through legal protection "of the right of employees to organize and bargain collectively." Thus, it concludes:

> It is hereby declared to be the policy of the United States to eliminate the causes of certain substantial obstructions to the free flow of commerce . . . by encouraging the practice and procedure of collective bargaining and by *protecting the exercise by workers of full freedom of association, self-organization, and designation of representatives of their own choosing,* for the purpose of negotiating the terms and conditions of their employment or other mutual aid or protection (National Labor Relations Act 1935, emphasis added).

While there is debate over the exact impact of the Taft-Hartley amendments and the addition of newer policies to the original Wagner Act statements cited above (Gross 1985), these policies remain as the preface to the Act. The acknowledgment of the worker's *own* organization, not one controlled by the employer, as the legitimate entity recognized under the Act is further emphasized in Sections 7 and 8(a)(2). Section 7 echoed the policy statement of the Act:

> Employees shall have the right to self-organization, to form, join, or assist labor organizations, to bargain collectively through representatives of their own choosing, and to engage in concerted activities, for the purpose of collective bargaining or other mutual aid or protection.

Finally, Section 8(a)(2) made it an unfair labor practice for an employer "[t]o dominate or interfere with the formation or administration of any labor organization or contribute financial or other support to it."

The 1935 debate over 8(a)(2) in the Senate Labor Committee took a predictable form. Management defended the company union as a reflection of the mutual interests of employers and workers, while labor and other supporters of the bill argued that company unions denied workers their fundamental right of freedom of association (Bernstein 1970, 332-33, 338). Wagner noted that in "free . . . elections workers had voted overwhelmingly for trade unions over company unions" (Bernstein 1970, 333). And echoing Samuel Gompers' discussion of trade unions as agents almost three decades previously, William Leiserson questioned how the legislation could allow the employer to be "in the position of the customer dictating who should be the sales agent of the fellows who have goods to sell" (Bernstein 1970, 333).

The Current Debate Over 8(a)(2)

As Morris (1991, 18-29) notes, the 8(a)(2) bar to employer-dominated or assisted unions was central to Wagner's vision of national labor policy. This philosophy was shaped, in part, by the short-lived experience of the National Industrial Recovery Act which, while supporting worker choice of representation under Section 7(a), allowed company unions. Reacting to the enormous growth in company unions—surpassing trade union growth—(Morris 1991, 22-23), Wagner introduced the NLRA with a diatribe against company unionism, noting that "only representatives who are not subservient to the employer with whom they deal can act freely in the interest of the employee" (Morris 1991, 23, quoting NLRA legislative history).

The 8(a)(2) question reemerged briefly in the statutory limelight in 1947 when employers attempted to amend Taft-Hartley to allow a broader definition of a labor organization (Section 2[5] of the Act) which encompassed employer-created committees. The amendment was defeated, and, in the 1959 *Cabot Carbon* case, the Supreme Court made it clear that other Taft-Hartley language was not intended to alter the statutory ban on such committees. The court also recognized that the clear distinction between those shop committees and a truly independent union lay in the "unfettered power of the [union] to insist upon its requests" (*Cabot Carbon* 1959, 360 US 203, 214).

The proliferation of employer-created shop committees and experiments with cooperative labor-management programs during the past decade has reignited the 8(a)(2) debate (and the related 2[5] debate concerning the proper definition of a "labor organization"). Most recently, the Board considered the issue in the *Electromation* case (1992). As in 1935 labor, management, and labor relations scholars have taken sides in the debate (Morris 1991; Zurofsky 1992; Hutson 1992). The facts are uncontested. Management created employee action committees to make recommendations to management on a number of different issues. A Teamster organizing drive began soon after. The union filed unfair labor practice charges on the basis of the committees during the campaign and after they lost the election. No antiunion animus was alleged, and no serious dispute existed as to management's domination of these committees.

As Morris notes, this issue is not new. The administrative law judge's decision finding that the committees constituted a violation of the NLRA was "ordinary" (Zurofsky 1992, 381). The NLRB agreed in a December 1992 ruling striking down Electromation's committees as violative of 8(a)(2). While the Board noted in its opinion that it was not finding all labor-management committees to be unfair labor practices, the basic discussion reinforces the notion that concepts of legitimacy and power remain the foundation of our nation's labor policy supporting labor organizations independent of employer control. Use of an employer-controlled entity to exercise workers' voice "makes a sham of equal bargaining power," Robert Wagner noted in 1934. And, as illustrated by our previous discussion, the employer-controlled or assisted entity is illegitimate when used as the sole or primary form of worker voice for, as Wagner also stated, it is "generally initiated by the employer; it exists by his sufferance; its decisions are subject to his unimpeachable veto" (cited in Morris brief, p. 23). Board member Devaney's concurring opinion in *Electromation* underscored the Wagner Act's original concern: "by creating the illusion of a bargaining representative without the reality, [company unions] denied employees wishing representation the service of an effective and loyal agent and . . . frustrated employees' impulses toward genuine self-organization and the security of a representative of their own choosing" (p. E-10).

Voice, Legitimacy and Power: Empirical Examinations

Part of Robert Wagner's motivation for emphasizing the need for legitimate and powerful trade unions was his strong belief that

> the highest degree of cooperation between industry and labor is possible only when either side is free to act or to withdraw, and that the best records of mutual respect and mutual accomplishment have been made by employers dealing with independent labor organizations (Morris 1991, 24).

Wagner's belief that the trade union model was the most beneficial for cooperation and "mutual accomplishment" has been borne out by empirical work on the impact of unions as vehicles for employee voice. According to a recent study by Kelley and Harrison (1992), workplaces with employee involvement or employee participation plans *and* a union are more likely to produce productivity gains than nonunion workplaces, while unionized workplaces with no such plans are even more highly productive. Plants without unions are the least efficient (pp. 268-69). In addition, the presence of a union "provides greater employment security to employees in the form of a lower probability that managers will engage in outsourcing" and provides blue-collar workers with "a significantly better chance of having their jobs redesigned to include the new skill-enhancing responsibility of programming" (p. 277). Their empirical results support their theory that the difference is due, in part, to the union's function as an effective vehicle for employee voice, which they would expect "to influence management decision making in ways that enhance the power of the membership" and thus to reflect strongly "the blue-collar work force's concerns, particularly with respect to employment security and control over new technology." In support of this point, they cite a review of studies finding that where a positive relationship between employee participation plans and productivity exists, the plant or firm usually has "institutional arrangements commonly associated with the presence of a union," including "relatively narrow wage differentials, long-term employment guarantees, and rules protecting workers from unjust dismissal by management" (pp. 254-55).

Kelley and Harrison discuss additional reasons based upon voice, for expecting a link between unions and efficiency. Their definition of voice includes the recognition of the significance of power and influence. Voice, they state, is "the power to ensure that managers will treat them more fairly and to otherwise influence management decisionmaking" (p. 256). The opportunity to exercise voice, they note, combined with the union's ability to provide higher average wages (through their exercise of what Freeman and Medoff label the monopoly face of unions but which we have argued above is integral to the exercise of effective employee voice) attracts and retains more experienced and highly skilled workers, creates higher morale and, therefore, creates a more productive work force (p. 256). Overall, they conclude, successful collaborative problem solving requires the possibility that employees may "achieve outcomes that also empower them" (p. 277). Clearly, their findings establish that the existence of a union is the crucial element that provides such a possibility.

Kelley and Harrison's work is notable not only for their results, but for their discussion that makes a careful and crucial distinction between the central goals of unions in exercising collective voice— e.g., higher wages, job security, job enhancement, and, in general, the ability to limit unilateral managerial control—and the byproduct that often results, that is, increased worker productivity. Productivity and efficiency, as we noted in our introductory discussion, may often be a union goal. Unlike its clear and consistent link with common notions of proper managerial interests, productivity and efficiency do not go to the fundamental purpose of a trade union, and thus are neither the sole nor oftentimes appropriate criteria by which a trade union should be measured. (In addition, it is likely that nationally based labor unions with stakes in the long-term industry-wide prosperity and the health and security of a trained work force, will define productivity and efficiency differently than a narrowly interested firm under conventional neoclassical notions of efficiency.)

Consistent with our discussion of Freeman and Medoff above, it is clear that in the post-*What Do Unions Do?* research era, most researchers examine and value only the variable of worker productivity and firm performance. For example, Lewin and Mitchell (1992) trace the body of economic and industrial relations research in the much-examined area of grievance procedures. The "vast bulk" of this research, they note (and as we discussed in our introduction), "focuses on the effects of unionized grievance procedures on measures of establishment and firm performance. . . . [L]ittle of the aforementioned research directly considers the question of whether, and to what extent, grievance procedures provide an effective voice mechanism or, more fundamentally, industrial democracy to unionized workers" (p. 14).

The issue of effective voice, Lewin and Mitchell (1992) note, is examined most directly by labor law scholars such as Aaron, who found that "*independent* representation" of employees and arbitration is the best evidence of effective voice; i.e., voice imbued with power and utilizing legitimate representatives (pp. 14-15, emphasis in original). Similarly, in their survey of research on nonunion grievance procedures, Lewin and Mitchell note that legal scholars find that the central characteristic of nonunion grievance procedures—the fact that management retains ultimate decisional power in resolving the grievance—is *per se* evidence of their limited capacity to provide effective worker voice and industrial democracy. They also find powerful voice absent in their survey of the literature on codetermination. Citing, among others, Hammer's findings that workers felt their representatives inadequately communicated and represented their interests and Kassalow's illustrations of the bypassing of worker board representatives, Lewin and Mitchell suggest that "it is one thing to mandate voice . . . but quite another thing to mandate *effective* voice" (p. 7).

The impact of unions in creating that effective voice is clearly illustrated in Weil's (1992) research on the role of unions in enforcement of the Occupational Safety and Health Act (OSHA). In a study using the complete inspection history of federally run OSHA programs, Weil finds that unionized workplaces are more likely to be inspected by OSHA (pp. 27-28), and that the inspectors give greater scrutiny to inspections of unionized workplaces due, in large part, to the more frequent existence of employee "walk-around" rights in union establishments (i.e., the right of a worker or workers to accompany the inspector throughout the plant, pointing out actual and possible violations) (pp. 28-29). Weil also finds that union workplaces pay higher penalties for health and safety violations (pp. 31-33). While finding similar results in a specific examination of the unionized construction industry, Weil also establishes that unionized construction establishments are required to remedy their health and safety violations more quickly than nonunion operations (p. 128).

Weil's research underscores the points illustrated in these other studies: unions are the entities capable of creating true and effective voice for workers. The worker participating in the health and safety inspection by virtue of collectively bargained and enforceable walk-around rights is often a union-trained member of a union health and safety committee and/or an elected union official. That member's role is primarily or solely to represent the interests of the workers in pointing out health and safety problems. He or she represents the legitimate and protected voice of the workers. The power of the voice is evident in the union's ability to produce positive outcomes for its members in the critical area of occupational safety and health.

The presence of union representation is critical to the expression of true worker voice. As Marshall (1991) has noted in a discussion of experiments in labor-management cooperation, legitimate representation and power are crucial elements in labor-management relations:

> Workers will not go all out unless they have independent representation in the process. Labor history will confirm that point. . . . We had [employee representation plans] all over this country, and it worked well—when everything was going well. The ERP is organized as though the workers were in the House of Representatives, the foremen were in the Senate, and the management was the Executive. They would cooperate and pass legislation. When they got into trouble, the Executive proposed a wage cut, and it passed the Senate and failed in the House. But management put it in anyway. When they did that, the workers went out and built a union. They call it the Steelworkers now. The Communications Workers of America also grew out of that kind of conflict.
>
> Another proposition, also borne out by history, is that it's very hard to have a cooperative relationship between parties with unequal power. Sooner or later the party with more power will exert it, and then there is no cooperative relationship anymore (p. 130).

Conclusion

In this chapter we have attempted to formulate a concept of voice consistent with the realities of the labor relations context. In articulating such an approach, we find that power and legitimacy constitute the two crucial definitional elements. Without power and legitimacy, the concept of voice is rendered virtually meaningless for it can be used to describe anything from a suggestion box that is ignored to coordinated bargaining in the electrical industry. Without power and legitimacy, any individual or collective worker statement can be labeled voice, even if that voice is, in reality, muffled or inaccurate, stifled or distorted.

Thus, it is on these terms—power and legitimacy—that all voice mechanisms should be evaluated. We have defined workers' voice as a communication that has the power to persuade and is a legitimate expression of the collective aims of those workers. We urge researchers to employ this definition of voice in order to allow a careful and critical examination and evaluation of whether an entity truly gives voice to workers. This sort of discriminating analysis will allow researchers to distinguish among voice mechanisms and ask significant questions concerning the nature of varying modes of communication.

We believe that as scholars begin to employ a definition of voice encompassing the concepts of legitimacy and power, it will be clear that unions are the natural and primary vehicle for the expression of worker voice. Only autonomous worker organizations have the capacity and flexibility to coalesce and frame the goals of workers on the workers' own terms and thereby acquire a special legitimacy and power not possessed by employer- or state-created entities.

References

Ahlen, Kristina. 1992. "Union Legitimacy: Members' Preceptions of Union Government." Paper presented at the Symposium on Emerging Union Structures: An International Comparison, Worcester, MA.

Alcock, Anthony. 1971. *History of the International Labor Organization.* New York: Octagon Books.

Atleson, James B. 1983. *Values and Assumptions in American Labor Law.* Amherst, MA: The University of Massachusetts Press.

Bernstein, Irving. 1960. *The Lean Years.* Boston, MA: Houghton Mifflin Company.

————. 1970. *Turbulent Years.* Boston, MA: Houghton Mifflin Company.

Brody, David. 1980. *Workers in Industrial America.* New York: Oxford University Press.

Cabot Carbon Co. 117 NLRB 1633, *enforcement denied,* 256 F.2d 281 (CA5, 1958), *reversed and remanded,* 360 U.S. 203 (1959).

Chaison, Gary N., Barbara Bigelow, and Edward Ottensmeyer. 1992. "Unions and Legitimacy: A Conceptual Refinement." In *Advances in the Sociology of Organizations,* eds. Bacharach, Seeber, and Walsh. Worcester, MA: Clark University Graduate School of Management. Forthcoming.

Chamberlain, Neil W., and James W. Kuhn. 1986. *Collective Bargaining,* 3rd ed. New York: McGraw-Hill.

Coleman, James S. 1990. *Foundations of Social Theory.* Cambridge, MA: The Belknap Press of Harvard University Press.

Derber, Milton. 1970. *The American Idea of Industrial Democracy, 1865-1965.* Chicago: University of Illinois Press.

Dickman, Howard. 1987. *Industrial Democracy in America: Ideological Origins of National Labor Relations Policy.* LaSalle, IL: Open Court.

Electromation, Inc.; International Brotherhood of Teamsters, Chauffeurs, Warehousemen and Helpers of America, Local Union No. 1049; and Action Committees. 1992. *Daily Labor Report* (December 18), pp. E1-E23.

Forbath, William E. 1991. *Law and the Shaping of the American Labor Movement.* Cambridge, MA: Harvard University Press.

Freeman, Richard B., and James L. Medoff. 1984. *What Do Unions Do?* New York: Basic Books.

Gompers, Samuel. 1919. *Labor and the Common Welfare.* New York: E.P. Dutton & Company.

————. 1925. *Seventy Years of Life and Labor.* New York: E.P. Dutton & Company.

Gross, James A. 1985. "Conflicting Statutory Purposes: Another Look at Fifty Years of NLRB Law Making." *Industrial and Labor Relations Review* 39, No. 1 (October), pp. 7-18.

Hirschman, Albert O. 1970. *Exit, Voice and Loyalty.* Cambridge, MA: Harvard University Press.

Hutson, Melvin. 1992. "Electromation: Employee Involvement or Employer Domination." *The Labor Lawyer* 8, No. 2 (Spring), pp. 389-404.

Kelly, Maryellen R., and Bennett Harrison. 1992. "Unions, Technology, and Labor-Management Cooperation." In *Unions and Economic Competitiveness*, eds. Lawrence Mishel and Paula B. Voos. New York: M.E. Sharpe, Inc., pp. 247-86.

Lewin, David, and Daniel J.B. Mitchell. 1992. "Systems of Employee Voice: Theoretical and Empirical Perspectives." Paper presented at 45th Annual Meeting of the Industrial Relations Research Association, New Orleans (January).

Lipsky, David B. 1985. "What Do Unions Do?" *Industrial and Labor Relations Review* 38, No. 2 (January), pp. 250-53.

Marshall, Ray. 1991. "The Future Role of Government in Industrial Relations." Seminar: Employee Rights in a Changing Economy. Washington, DC: Economic Policy Institute, pp. 119-34.

Millis, Harry A., and Emily Clark Brown. 1950. *From the Wagner Act to Taft-Hartley.* Chicago: The University of Chicago Press.

Morris, Charles J. 1991. Brief of Amicus Curiae. *Electromation, Inc.; International Brotherhood of Teamsters, Chauffeurs, Warehousemen and Helpers of America, Local Union No. 1049; and "Action Committees."* Case No. 25-CA-19818.

National Industrial Recovery Act. 48 Stat. 198 (1933).

National Labor Relations Act. 29 U.S.C. §§ 151-169 (1982 ed).

Neustadt, Richard E. 1990. "The Power to Persuade." In *Classic Readings in American Politics*, eds. Pietro S. Nivola and David H. Rosenbloom. New York: St. Martin's Press, pp. 331-39.

Norris-LaGuardia Act. 47 Stat. 70 (1932), 29 U.S.C. §§ 101-15 (1964).

Oxford Universal Dictionary, 3rd ed. 1955. Oxford: Oxford University Press.

Perlman, Mark. 1958. *Labor Union Theories in America: Background and Development.* Evanston, IL; White Plains, NY: Row, Peterson and Company.

Railway Labor Act. 44 Stat. 577 (1926), 44 U.S.C. §§ 161-63 (1964).

Reich, Robert. 1993. In Peter T. Kilborn, "Labor Secretary Sees a Vital Role for Unions in Economic Growth," *The New York Times*, February 17, p. 13.

Ryan, Margaret. 1984. "Theories of Power." In *Power, Politics, and Organizations: A Behavior Science View*, eds. Andrew Kakabadse and Christopher Parker. New York: John Wiley & Sons, pp. 21-45.

Taylor, Benjamin J., and Fred Witney. 1987. *Labor Relations Law*, 5th ed. Englewood Cliffs: Prentice-Hall.

Texas & New Orleans R.R. Co. v. Brotherhood of Railway and Steamship Clerks. 281 U.S. 548 (1930).

Trant, William. 1921. *Trade Unions.* Washington, DC: The American Federation of Labor.

Webb, Sidney, and Beatrice Webb. 1902. *Industrial Democracy.* London: Longmans, Green and Co.

Weber, Max. 1958. *The Theory of Social and Economic Organization*, ed. Talcott Parsons. New York: The Free Press.

Weil, David. 1992. "Building Safety: The Role of Construction Unions in the Enforcement of OSHA," *Journal of Labor Research* XIII, No. 1 (Winter), 121-32.

_____. 1991. "Enforcing OSHA: The Role of Labor Unions," *Industrial Relations* 30, No. 1 (Winter), pp. 20-36.

Zurofsky, Bennet D. 1992. "Everything Old is New Again: Company Unions in the Era of Employee Involvement Programs," *The Labor Lawyer* 8, No. 2 (Spring), pp. 381-88.

CHAPTER 6

Joint Governance in the Workplace: Beyond Union-Management Cooperation and Worker Participation

ANIL VERMA
University of Toronto

JOEL CUTCHER-GERSHENFELD
Michigan State University

Recent developments in industrial relations have raised many questions about the efficacy of traditional forms of collective bargaining in meeting the social and economic aspirations of employees and employers. The ensuing debate over the future prospects of collective bargaining as an institution has intensified in recent years in both Canada and the United States (Chaykowski and Verma 1992; Weiler 1990; Heckscher 1988; Kochan, Katz, and McKersie 1986). The decline of collective bargaining and the labor movement, especially in the U.S., and mounting competitive pressures of international trade have put this debate in sharper focus. In this chapter we discuss an emergent and relatively newer form of collective negotiations and interaction, namely joint governance— where labor and management share joint decision-making authority on matters of mutual concern—which offers one alternative to traditional collective bargaining.

In practice most worker participation programs and union-management cooperation initiatives in North America are limited in scope. They are primarily advisory mechanisms in which final decision-making authority still resides with management. There are a limited number of instances, however, where the parties have expanded beyond the traditional boundaries of participation and

cooperation. In these cases, workers and/or their unions share varying degrees of decision-making power with management. The
scope of decision making varies from a single issue (such as worker
training) to a broad range of workplace decisions (all of which
might be embodied in a "living agreement").

The North American experience with joint governance differs
sharply from the European in that it is not legally mandated. The
cases that we discuss are also different from the Japanese joint
decision-making forums which are essentially consultative in nature
with no executive authority to make decisions. While consultative
forms of joint governance can be found in many enterprises in both
Canada and the U.S., our focus is on joint arrangements which
come about through private mutual agreement and are vested with
decision-making power and authority.

What makes joint governance both useful and challenging within
the Wagner Act framework is that it is simultaneously an extension
of traditional bargaining and a significant departure from the traditional separation of management and labor roles in governance.
This makes joint governance unique among various alternatives to
traditional collective bargaining discussed in this volume.

Politically, joint governance can appeal to those who want to
preserve the essence of the collective bargaining system because of
its emphasis on joint decision making. On the other hand, because
of its departure from traditional, arm's-length forms of governance,
it offers new opportunities to manage in a flexible, high-involvement, high-skill, value-added workplace—which is the challenge
facing most organizations in North America in the 1990s. Thus, joint
governance could be of interest to all parties within the industrial
relations system.

Despite these potential advantages, joint governance remains
limited in its diffusion in both Canadian and U.S. industrial relations. As with any change process, the evolution of joint governance
faces many hurdles—institutional, political, and attitudinal. The
small number of joint governance arrangements that have evolved
over the last dozen years or so provide a very useful window on
their feasibility and utility. From the early experiments we need to
learn more about conditions that facilitate these arrangements and
their consequences for the parties as well as for collective bargaining itself. For example, under what conditions will parties agree to
joint governance (given that it is not required by law)? How well

does it serve the distinct, but overlapping interests of unions, employees, and employers? How compatible is it with traditional aspects of collective bargaining on one hand and the demands of flexibility, quality, and cost containment on the other hand?

In this chapter we examine the experience of nine organizations that have adopted, through mutual agreement, some form of joint governance. First, we provide a conceptual framework for joint governance identifying it within the larger industrial relations system and specifying four key dimensions of joint governance. The second part of the paper presents empirical data from these nine sites on the scope and dynamics that characterize each case. The last section summarizes the learning from these nine "experiments" across the four dimensions and offers propositions on the antecedents, the dynamics, and the consequences of joint governance for theory and practice. Our objective in this research has been to use the limited amount of currently available field data to generate a series of hypotheses that can be put to more rigorous examination at a larger number of field sites in the future.

A Conceptual Framework for Joint Governance

In many ways joint governance is not a new concept. Labor law in both Canada and the U.S. is permissive in letting labor and management arrive at new rules or arrangements to meet their needs. But it is a historical fact that the evolution of collective bargaining over the last fifty years has weighed heavily in favor of substantive rules rather than in negotiating procedural arrangements (Slichter, Healy, and Livernash 1960). There are two ostensible exceptions to this generalization.

First, the grievance procedure, now ubiquitous in collective bargaining, is a good example of joint governance applied to disputes. However, because of its orientation around substantive rules, grievance procedures can become more legalistic and adversarial—with little of the intended joint dialogue at early stages of the procedure. As a result, many grievance procedures in practice involve little or no actual joint governance of disputes.

Second, labor-management committees (LMCs) and various forms of employee involvement (EI) have been used by the parties since the earliest days of collective bargaining. However, LMCs and EI efforts do not necessarily engage in joint decision making. A closer look at these joint initiatives reveals that the vast majority of them have little or no decision-making power. Typically their role is advisory or consultative in nature. We have argued elsewhere (Cutcher-Gershenfeld, Kochan, and Verma 1991) that employee involvement initiatives are unstable as a purely advisory structure—either they must diffuse and expand to encompass some measure of what is here termed joint governance (one path), or else the joint efforts will erode and deteriorate over time (an alternate path). This chapter thus extends our earlier analysis by providing a more complete portrait of the joint governance path.

Joint Governance: A Definition

It is important to define exactly what we mean by joint governance. For the purpose of our analysis, joint governance is an ongoing formal process where workers and their immediate supervisors or union and management leaders bear *joint* responsibility for making decisions. The scope of decision making may be narrow (i.e., it may involve a single issue), or it may be broader, covering a whole range of issues. In addition, there may or may not be formal procedures for resolving disputes that arise in the joint decision-making process.

By adopting this definition, we are limiting the scope of joint governance in this paper in two significant ways. First, we consider only those cases where the joint process has been *formalized* in some way—whether in the collective agreement, through letters of understanding, or through legal arrangements. Thus informal arrangements made orally or through private understandings among individuals and other such arrangements are excluded.[1] Second, the term *joint* is used to imply sharing decision-making power *equally*. Theoretically it is possible to envisage joint governance with unequal sharing of power. We exclude those arrangements from our analysis because the dynamic of unequal power sharing is likely to be very different from those involving relatively equal power. The relative power of the parties, in practice, depends on a wide range of factors including technology, markets, etc. In this paper we use the term "equal power" in the more circumscribed context of formal decision making in a mutually agreed to sphere. Thus, if a joint committee charged with making decisions were to consist of equal numbers of labor and management representatives or if it were to operate on a consensus basis, it would fall within the purview of our study.

To further sharpen the concept of joint governance used in this chapter, it is useful to contrast it with other well-known forms of governance. Joint governance may be compared with, among others, traditional nonunion systems, high employee involvement nonunion systems, traditional collective bargaining, labor-management committees, labor representation on the board of directors and German-style works councils. The contrast with traditional nonunion systems, which usually have no employee input, is quite obvious. In recent years many nonunion firms have introduced a variety of employee involvement programs with apparent effectiveness (Wellins, Byham, and Wilson 1991). Despite involvement of workers at the shop-floor level in production and quality matters, rarely do these programs give them any decision-making power. With only rare exceptions, these programs place employees in an advisory role, which in some firms may be an influential voice but it is still far short of sharing decision-making power. Japanese-style quality circles are a good exemplar of this form of governance.

In traditional collective bargaining the governance system consists of collective negotiations, the collective agreement, and the administration of the agreement through the grievance procedure. Although there is joint decision making at the bargaining table on bargainable issues, there is little evidence that joint decision making characterizes labor-management interaction thereafter and on other issues. In the same spirit, labor-management committees, which have been ubiquitous in unionized firms for many years, have played mostly an advisory role, with only a few exceptions, and that too on lesser decisions.

Labor members on the board of directors could constitute a form of joint governance if labor's representation were equal to that of the employer. No system in the English-speaking world has ever come even close to it.[2] Only one law anywhere in the world, the Coal, Iron, and Steel Industry Co-determination Law of 1951 enacted in (the former West) Germany, provides for parity (i.e., equal) representation of labor on the board. Our experience with unequal representation on the board in several countries suggests that joint governance objectives are seldom met under this regime. Although unequal representation is better than no representation, we have excluded treatment of this form of governance because the prospects for such arrangements in North America remain dim in the near term.

German-style works councils are the best example of the concept of joint governance as we have defined it. What distinguishes them from our cases is that works councils in Germany are legally mandated. A second distinction is that works councils have a broad mandate over workplace issues. North American experiments, which are mutually agreed to, bilateral, decision-making forums, tend to have a more limited scope, at least for now.[3]

Historical Background

The point of departure for our discussion of joint governance is the unilateral control that the employer has traditionally exercised in the workplace. Historically unilateral employer control was characterized by repression, coercion, and sporadic violence. Even in the earliest stages of industrialization, management's unilateral control was recognized by scholars as the most central issue in employment relations and workplace governance. As the Webbs put it:

> The issue turns essentially on whether or not the employers are prepared to forgo their dictatorships inside their own workshops and honestly submit the conditions of employment to an effective joint control, whether by collective bargaining or otherwise (Webb and Webb 1897).

In the four decades following the passage of the Wagner Act in the U.S. (1935-1975) and the passage of similar legislation in Canada, the institutionalization and incremental expansion of collective bargaining became the primary vehicle for bilateral exchange.

To counter management's unilateral control, unions sought to put limits on management prerogatives through the collective agreement. Management responded by seeking limitations to the scope of collective bargaining within the law. Successive iterations of these strategies over the years led to increasing specificity within bargaining and the collective agreement within a bounded domain of issues. Over time, rule making aimed at mutual containment became a viable middle ground for a political union and a hierarchical management. For example, the initial contract between General Motors and the UAW was 39 pages long while the current contract totals over 500 pages (with an even smaller typeface).

Conceptual Dimensions of Joint Governance

Joint governance in its essence is joint decision making under relatively equal power-sharing arrangements. What distinguishes it from other forms of governance? In this section we discuss the core dimensions of the underlying processes and outcomes that can be used to understand joint governance. These dimensions are rooted in both industrial relations theory and in political theories of governance.

We propose four dimensions that describe and distinguish the key processes of joint governance. First, joint governance involves a mixture of conflict and cooperation—reflecting underlying cooperative and conflictual interests in the employment relationship (Walton and McKersie 1965; Cutcher-Gershenfeld 1988; Verma 1991). Thus, we are interested in how joint governance arrangements build on (or relate to) advisory forms of labor-management cooperation. Similarly, what is the relationship between joint governance and preexisting vehicles for conflict resolution? Finally, what are the interactions (in the context of joint governance) between concurrent patterns of cooperation and conflict?

Second, joint governance can be structured as a representative form of participation (e.g., a labor-management committee or collective bargaining) or as a direct form of participation (e.g., a workplace team). Where there is some measure of joint governance, there will often be multiple representative structures coexisting in a single workplace. How then would representative forms of joint governance interact with those that involve direct participation?

Third, joint governance functions in conjunction with the collective agreement which itself contains many work rules about workplace affairs. Dunlop (1958) drew the distinction between procedural work rules and substantive ones. Joint governance is an example of a set of procedural work rules whereas the collective agreement is typically crowded with substantive work rules. What is the relationship between coexisting procedural and substantive work rules? Also, how does joint governance, as a procedural set of work rules, affect the ability of the firm (on the one hand) to meet market demands of quality and productivity and the employee/union (on the other hand) to address concerns of job security, institutional stability, and higher standards of living?

Lastly, we discuss the demands that joint governance makes on the parties' skills and abilities. What kinds of competencies are required to participate in joint governance? The union is typically savvy at political skills because it manages a political organization. Management is usually competent in administrative skills because it

TABLE 1

Joint Governance and Other Governance Forms

Dimensions	High-Involvement Nonunion Systems	Traditional Collective Bargaining	Traditional Labor-Management Committees	Labor Representatives on the Board	German-style Works Councils	Mutually-agreed-to Joint Governance
Conflict vs. Cooperation	Heavy emphasis on cooperation; only interpersonal avenues for conflict resolution	Formal conflict resolution procedures with limited emphasis on cooperation	Cooperative forum with no decision-making role and no formal conflict resolution procedure	More of a cooperative forum; some room for expressing conflict	Potential for cooperation; conflicts can be taken to labor courts	Potential for cooperation and room for surfacing and resolving conflicts
Procedural vs. Substantive Workrules	Few formal workrules; heavy emphasis on informal resolution	Heavy reliance on substantive rules enforced by the grievance procedure	Procedural rule-making	Procedural decision-making	Heavy emphasis on procedural decision-making	Heavy emphasis on procedural decision-making
Direct vs. Indirect Participation	Heavy emphasis on direct participation	Mostly indirect; little emphasis on direct participation	Mostly indirect; little emphasis on direct participation	Indirect	Indirect; informal direct participation	Indirect; creates pressures to introduce direct participation
Administrative vs. Political Skills	Administrative skills taught to employees at all levels	Management concentrates on administrative skills; union on political skills	Some overlap but lack of decision-making role prevents further diffusion	Labor representatives develop administrative skills but only marginal diffusion of political skills among management	Labor develops administrative skills; plant management develops political skills	Labor develops administrative skills; management develops political skills

TABLE 1 (*Continued*)
Joint Governance and Other Governance Forms

Dimensions	High-Involvement Nonunion Systems	Traditional Collective Bargaining	Traditional Labor-Management Committees	Labor Representatives on the Board	German-style Works Councils	Mutually-agreed-to Joint Governance
Joint & Equal Decision-making power	No	Yes, but in bargainable issues and at bargaining time only	May contain equal number of labor & management reps but, equality is less significant because the role is mostly advisory	No, with the exception of the German law of 1951 covering the iron, steel, and coal industries	Yes	Yes

manages a hierarchical organization. How do these skills come to mesh where a system of joint governance is in place?

Table 1 shows a comparison of joint governance with other forms of governance discussed earlier along these dimensions. In procedural terms German-style works councils come closest to the joint governance forms discussed in this chapter. As mutual bilateral arrangements which are not mandated by law, joint governance remains unique in this comparison.

We will elaborate on each of these four dimensions later in this chapter—utilizing the experience from our nine cases to illustrate and clarify points. First, however, we will review the cases and compare their structure and antecedents.

Selected Cases of Joint Governance

In order to clarify what we mean by joint governance and to more fully develop the concepts presented above, we will summarize nine handpicked cases of different forms of joint governance in the U.S. and Canada. These sites were selected to represent a variety of different forms of joint governance, different industries, and different locations. Some of these parties entered into joint governance more than ten years ago. Other cases are more recent but even the most recent case has been in place for at least three years. Thus, although these cases are not a perfectly random sample, in our view, they provide a very useful sample of current practice for our subsequent task of inductively developing several theoretical propositions on the dynamics of joint governance.[4]

Case Summaries

The section below provides a brief overview of the key developments in each case discussed in this chapter. The summaries are intended to illustrate a broad range of possible joint governance arrangements.

B.C. Telephone and Telecommunications Workers' Union (TWU)[5]

The Contracting Out and Technological Change Committee. More than a decade of conflict between the parties peaked in 1977-78 with a long and bitter strike. In the contract concluded after the strike, the parties agreed to form a joint committee with decision-making powers and a formal dispute resolution procedure to oversee cases of contracting out and technological change. The basic provision in the collective agreement was that "no regular employees who attain two years of regular service will lose their employment as a result of technological change." An umpire plays the role of a mediator-arbitrator. The early years of the committee were characterized by a heavy reliance on the umpire. This has declined substantially over the years because the parties can resolve most issues among themselves with only an occasional dispute going to the umpire in the late 1980s and early 1990s.

Work Jurisdiction Committee. For more than ten years the parties have disputed each other's claims of whether certain jobs belong inside or outside the bargaining unit. This problem has been exacerbated by advances in technology over the years. Ultimately the dispute was put to arbitration. The arbitrator, realizing that the nature of the dispute did not lend itself to a fixed formula, awarded the parties a joint committee to resolve such disputes. Thus this committee, in contrast to other cases, is not an example of voluntarism. Overseen by a permanent umpire, the committee has had difficulty in resolving disputes in the first few years of its existence. The parties, nonetheless, have taken steps to make it more effective. Both parties remain committed to the process both in principle and practice.

The Forest Industrial Relations Ltd. (FIR) and IWA Canada

Joint Contracting Out Review Committee. After a bitter, industry-wide, four and a half-month strike in 1986 over job security issues, the parties decided to form a joint review committee to address the issue of subcontracting. The industry-wide committee investigates local disputes in the role of factfinder and mediator. If the issues remain unresolved, they are submitted to an arbitrator. The number of disputes going to arbitration has declined significantly over time. According to the parties, previous arbitration awards have clarified areas of ambiguity, thus providing local parties with more guidelines on making subcontracting decisions.

Ford Motor Company and the United Automobile Workers (UAW)[6]

UAW-Ford National Joint Training Center. During the early 1980s, sales and employment at Ford Motor Company declined dramatically. From 1980 through 1982 Ford lost over $4 billion in its

U.S. operations, and the UAW-represented work force had been reduced by close to 100,000—a loss of 50 percent of the work force. Thousands of UAW members faced the prospect of being laid off and never seeing the inside of an auto plant again.

In response, union and management leaders in 1982 negotiated the establishment of a joint training fund to be supported at a rate of five cents per hour worked by each worker. A UAW-Ford National Joint Training Center was established to administer the fund. It features a joint governance structure at every level—including union and management approval of expenditures.

The initial use of the funds was to provide training and placement assistance to displaced workers. However, by the mid-1980s the level of the training fund had expanded threefold, and the focus shifted to address the training needs of the active work force (as well as the then smaller number of workers facing displacement). The joint training fund was never intended to replace existing management support for worker training and education, but the joint umbrella has come to cover a wide range of activities including literacy and math skills, prepaid tuition, pre-retirement planning, computer awareness, interpersonal skills, labor history, and global competition.

Employee involvement and other participative structures. In 1979 joint Employee Involvement (EI) was negotiated. Soon thereafter many plants established joint problem-solving groups. These groups were only an advisory vehicle and did not constitute joint governance as we have defined it here. By the late 1980s and the early 1990s, however, selected Ford plants featured locally negotiated "Modern Operating Agreements" that called for team-based work systems with few job classifications and pay-for-skill compensation. The team-based systems utilized many of the problem-solving and group principles forged in EI as well as utilizing many of the former union and management EI facilitators for training and support purposes. These workplace teams feature shop-floor, self-governance by workers and hourly team leaders on matters such as job assignments, work scheduling, monitoring inventory, quality control, minor maintenance—much of which would traditionally be handled by a supervisor. Additionally, most facilities with these agreements feature a joint plant steering committee that has some degree of shared administrative responsibilities for training, diffusion, and other aspects of the team activities.

Manitoba Telephone System (MTS) and Communications and Electrical Workers of Canada (CWC)[7]

After reports of shock-like incidents to employees throughout 1986 and 1987, several investigations were conducted without success to identify their cause. In 1988 the parties agreed to form a joint task force to develop ways to reduce stress on the job on the assumption that the shock-like incidents were partly attributable to job stress. The task force came up with 22 recommendations in the area of work redesign, employee involvement, and related changes. Nine of these recommendations were accepted by a joint board of trustees and ratified by each side. These are now being implemented including small work groups, elimination of remote monitoring, cross-training, dedicated training, and better communication, among other recommendations. This successful experimentation in joint work has led to two other joint committees, one on scheduling and another on modernization of technology for operators. None of these arrangements are codified in the collective agreement but each has been formalized by a letter of understanding.

National Steel (Great Lakes Division) and the United Steelworkers of America (USWA)[8]

Joint training in the context of a cooperative partnership. The National Steel Company is a joint venture by Great Lakes Steel and NKK Corporation, Japan's second largest steelmaker. Massive Japanese investment in the mid-1980s helped to assure the future of the mill, but it was contingent on indications of positive labor-management relations. In 1986 a dramatic labor agreement was negotiated for the integrated, seven-mile-long steel facility in Ecorse, Michigan. Dubbed the "Cooperative Partnership," the agreement featured a no-layoff pledge for the existing work force, a reduction to just one production classification and three skilled trades classifications, and a pay-for-skill compensation system notable in particular for combining skilled trades classifications. The overall joint structure established under the contract features a facility-wide Joint Labor-Management Cooperation Committee, process area groups in the six major parts of business, intermediate groups and shop-floor groups. Also a joint training center was established to facilitate the cross-training required under the contract—which involved full apprenticeships of over 1,000 hours each in multiple new trades for skilled trades workers. Our focus is on the joint governance of employee development training, including cross-training in job skills.

Saturn Corporation (a Division of General Motors) and the United Automobile Workers (UAW)

A *living agreement and comprehensive joint governance structure*. In 1984 the General Motors Corporation set aside an initial investment of $3.2 billion and established a planning team to design a complete automotive company (from design to manufacturing to sales) using a "clean slate" approach. From the outset the initial planning included UAW representatives. The result is the Saturn Corporation, a highly autonomous division of General Motors which features a far-reaching joint governance structure with the UAW in its design and manufacturing operations. UAW representatives are formally included on the Strategic Action Council (SAC), which handles long-term planning and external relations for the business; the Manufacturing Action Council (MAC), which makes operational decisions for the entire manufacturing and assembly complex; business unit groups, which comprise functional areas such as stamping, assembly, powertrain, etc.; and work unit teams, which are integrated groups of 6-15 work unit members. At each level, decision making is in the hands of union and management officials jointly. Perhaps the most remarkable feature of this system of joint governance is the parties' commitment to consensus decision making at all levels. Thus even though there may be fewer union representatives than managers in a particular meeting, they have equal ability to block a consensus until they are satisfied with a decision.

Shell (Sarnia Plant) and the Energy and Chemical Workers' Union (ECWU)[9]

A *living agreement and comprehensive joint governance structure*. Located in Sarnia, Ontario, this chemical facility for the production of polypropylene and isopropyl alcohol was designed in keeping with sociotechnological principles. ECWU officials joined the initial organizational design task force in 1977—prior to construction of the plant. The plant, which was completed in 1979, is run on a 24-hour-a-day basis by six process teams, each of which features 18-20 members and one 18-person craft team. There is very little direct supervision by management. The members of the process teams are also cross-trained in support functions such as quality control, scheduling, warehouse, and maintenance. A computer expert system helps operators record the output associated with combinations of temperature, pressure, materials, etc., and assess cost implications of current operations. Operators are paid on a pay-for-skill basis. The internal structure of the union reflects the participative plant structure, including a governing board that consists entirely of rank-and-file members (unpaid officers).

Xerox Corporation and the Amalgamated Clothing and Textile Workers' Union (ACTWU)[10]

The emergence of a broad range of joint governance activities over a decade. In the early 1980s Xerox and ACTWU had a well-established employee involvement program that was advisory in nature. As the company experienced a dramatic loss of market share in world-wide copier revenues (from 82 percent in 1976 to 41 percent in 1982), the company's initial responses included a unilateral decision to subcontract about 180 wire harness assembly jobs to nonunion operations. The union countered that such a unilateral decision was inconsistent with the principles of jointness emphasized in the context of the participation program. In response a joint study team was established, and six months later, suggestions were presented that projected over $3.7 million in savings—enough to equal anticipated savings from the proposed subcontracting. The work was kept in-house and most of the noncontractual changes were made.

In the 1984 negotiations the parties were faced with study team recommendations concerning flexible work rules and other matters. Not only were these changes granted, but new contract language was drafted indicating that all future subcontracting decisions would be subject to a joint study team—converting a key management right into a subject where there was a measure of joint governance. During the same negotiations, management agreed to a no-layoff pledge for the manufacturing work force in Rochester, New York. Building on this foundation, joint governance has emerged at the shop-floor level in a number of work areas where the employees have petitioned to operate as semiautonomous work teams (a right granted to groups of employees in 1986).

At an administrative level, the parties have established (1) joint processes for providing benefits information to employees; (2) joint informal processes designed to resolve grievances prior to being reduced to writing; (3) joint agreements to allow flexibility in the utilization of bargaining unit employees, as part of simultaneous engineering design processes; and (4) a joint training program for the training and implementation of the corporate-wide Leadership Through Quality (LTQ) program. At a strategic level, the parties have established a joint structure for long-term human resource planning (termed "Horizon Teams") and a joint task force responsible for the redesign of a plant for manufacturing toner for use in copiers. Although the parties did not begin with a long-term plan of extending the concept of joint governance to so many domains, the process evolved (sometimes following key confrontations) to the point that each side respects the distinctive competence that the other brings to the consideration of employment issues.

Zehrs Markets and United Food and Commercial Workers
Local 1977 (UFCW)

Training Trust Fund. As early as 1981 the union negotiated a one-cent-an-hour contribution to a union-run education fund. After the contributions were increased over the next two bargaining rounds, the parties decided to form a joint Training Trust Fund in 1987 managed by a joint board of trustees. The trust is a separate legal entity that operates the Clifford Evans Training Center (named after the union's former Canadian director). The Training Center offers programs in new skills as well as in updating and upgrading skills. Its resources allow for training roughly six hundred employees a year. The current contribution level in the collective agreement is 15-cents an hour. The center has also received some initial support from the provincial and federal governments.

Overview of Case Characteristics

These cases were selected to illustrate a diverse range of joint governance arrangements. The following tables illustrate a range of possible characteristics associated with joint governance systems. Table 2 offers a general overview of the cases indicating the key parties and other relevant data. Of note is the range of industries (public utilities, forestry products, auto manufacturing, electronic office products, steel, and telecommunications) and work-site sizes (from bargaining units of 138 to over 100,000) included in this sample. Also the chart indicates the many topic areas that are the focus of joint governance activities, including training, team-based work systems, contracting out, ergonomics, and HRM strategic planning. This suggests that joint governance is a phenomena that has potential for broad application across many sectors of an economy and across many subject areas.

As Table 3 indicates, the joint governance structures in seven of our cases are rooted in "enabling" language found in the collective bargaining agreement. Of these seven, two of the cases (Saturn and Shell) feature "living" agreements where the entire contract codifies comprehensive joint governance arrangements rather than just one or a few provisions on the matter. In one case, B. C. Tel's Work Jurisdiction Committee, the joint procedure came from an arbitrator's award. In another case, Zehrs' training venture with UFCW is run by a Training Trust Fund which is a separate legal entity but its funding is enshrined in the collective agreement.

In some cases representative forms of participation coexist with direct forms of participation, but joint governance did not always extend to the direct forms. In fact, in one case (B. C. Telephone), the joint governance committees on contracting out and work jurisdiction coexist with quality circles that are opposed by the union. With the exception of three sites, there were direct participation programs at all the other sites.

A formal process to resolve disputes was directly or indirectly available in all the cases. In some cases a special procedure has been established for the resolution of disputes that arise with the joint governance system. In other cases resolution via the grievance procedure is available for issues specifically delineated in the collective bargaining agreements. In case of the Zehrs' joint Training Trust Fund with the UFCW, the trustees would resolve disputes under the constraints of legislation governing trusts. The parties could also raise and resolve disputes about financing within the collective agreement. In the case of MTS-CWC joint task forces, there is no formal process to resolve disputes. Both parties have subscribed to decision making by consensus with the understanding that either side has the right to pull out of the process if the process does not meet their needs.

Finally, it may be noted that nearly all of the cases feature some degree of economic or relationship crisis driving the parties to explore joint governance options—though none involved economic

TABLE 2

Case Profiles

| Site | Union | Number of Employees at the site | | Products | Area of joint governance | Year Started |
		Company	Bargaining Unit			
B.C. Telephone	Telecommunications Workers' Union (TWU)[a]	14,997	11,990	Telephone & Related Services	A. Contracting out and technological change B. Work Jurisdiction	1978 1988
Ford Motor Company, North American Operations	United Auto Workers (UAW)	142,000	96,500	Vehicle Manufacturing & Assembly (cars and trucks)	A. Education & Training B. Employee Involvement	1982 1979
Forest Industrial Relations Ltd. (FIR)—bargaining agent for employers in the industry	IWA (Canada)	—	14,000	Logging and Lumber	Contracting out	1988
Manitoba Telephone System (MTS)	Communications & Electrical Workers of Canada (CWC)[b]	5,308	612	Telephone & Related Services	Ergonomics & other work-related issues	1988
National Steel (Ecorse Mill)	United Steelworkers of America (USWA)	4,800	4,000	Integrated Steel Mill	Training for Skill Combinations	1986

TABLE 2 (Continued)

Case Profiles

Site	Union	Number of Employees at the site		Products	Area of joint governance	Year Started
		Company	Bargaining Unit			
Saturn	United Auto Workers (UAW)	5,500	4,000	Auto Manufacturing & Assembly	Wide variety of work operations	1985
Shell Canada (Sarnia Plant)	Energy & Chemical Workers Union (ECWU)[b]	200	138	Petroleum Products	Wide Variety of work operations	1978
Xerox— Manufacturing	Amalgamated Textile and Clothing Workers Union (ACTWU)	50,000	4,100	Manufacturing & Assembly of Electronic Office Products	Employee Involvement; Outsourcing; Strategic HRM Planning; etc.	1980
Zehrs Markets	United Food & Commercial Workers (UFCW)	5,400	4,000	Retail Food Supermarkets	Training	1987

Notes:

[a] An independent union

[b] Three unions, the CWC, the ECWU and the Canadian Paperworkers' Union (CPU), merged in November 1992 to form the Communications, Energy, and Paper Workers Union (CEP).

pressures so extreme that the firm faced bankruptcy or imminent collapse. Walton (1980) has called this the "golden middle" of competitive pressure.

The picture that emerges from the sample of nine cases highlighted in this chapter suggests that joint governance systems remain grounded in collective bargaining, but that they are a complex and multifaceted phenomena. Given this diversity, what can we learn about the dynamics and dimensions of joint governance?

Deriving Propositions for Theory, Practice, and Policy

Four broad aspects of joint governance were highlighted in the second part of this chapter. Drawing on the cases, we see that important insights emerge along each of the dimensions of joint governance.

Joint Governance: Conflict or Cooperation?

A core assumption of this chapter is that employment relations are mixed motive in nature—featuring a mixture of common and competing motives or interests among stakeholder groups. Thus we assume that there will always be areas of conflict between labor and management, *and* that there will always be areas of common interest. The issue then centers on how the conflicts are resolved and whether the common interests are realized.

Building on this assumption, we find that in these cases joint governance arrangements add a conflictual dimension to what would otherwise be cooperative efforts with a purely advisory role. At the same time, we find that joint governance adds a cooperative dimension to what would otherwise be an institutional arrangement oriented around conflict resolution. In both cases the relations become more complex but potentially more fruitful (Savoie and Cutcher-Gershenfeld 1992).

There are many advisory institutions and initiatives designed to foster labor-management cooperation, including quality circles or employee involvement groups, joint task forces on specific issues (such as health-care cost containment), and labor-management committees (on issues such as health and safety, training, apprenticeships, United Way campaigns, etc.). In these instances issues are presumed to involve many commonalities between labor and management. When deep conflicts surface both parties retain the option

TABLE 3

Characteristics of Joint Governance

Site	Forces Driving Joint Governance	Basis for Joint Governance	Forms of Direct Participation	Representative Participation through Committee	Coverage	Dispute Resolution Procedure
B.C. Tel - TWU						
A. Contracting Out & Tech Change Committee	-Tech Change -Conflictual relations	Collective Agreement Article XXII	Employer initiated Quality Circles - Opposed by the union	4 - union 4 - management 1 - umpire	Company-wide	Med-arb by permanent umpire
B. Work Jurisdiction Committee	-New Technology	Arbitrator's Award				
FIR - IWA Joint Contracting Review Committee	-Nonunion Alternatives -Response to Strike	Collective Agreement Article XXV	None	4 - union 4 - Industry (mgmt)	Industry-wide	Arbitration by external third party
Ford - UAW	-International Competition	Collective Agreement (various provisions) and letters of understanding	Individual Career Planning, Employee Involvement Groups; Team-Based Work Systems; *Ad Hoc* Task Forces on Quality, Health & Safety			Many issues subject to grievance procedure; specific programs excluded from grievance procedure
A. National Joint Training Center	-Employee Education, Training & Career Needs			National Joint Training Center	National; Plant	
B. Employee Involvement and Team-Based Work Systems	-Changes in Work Systems			Plant Committees	National; Plant	

TABLE 3 (*Continued*)

Characteristics of Joint Governance

Site	Forces Driving Joint Governance	Basis for Joint Governance	Forms of Direct Participation	Representative Participation through Committee	Coverage	Dispute Resolution Procedure
MTS - CWC Trustee Group and Joint Taskforces	-Safety Issues	Letters of Understanding	None	Equal numbers from both sides; size varies	Operator services throughout the province	None - either party can pull out
National Steel - USWA	-New Technology -International Competition -Joint Partnership with NKK of Japan	Collective Agreement Articles - various provisions	Cross-Utilization of Workers	Plant Steering Committee and Joint Training Committee	Company-wide	Many issues subject to grievance procedure
Saturn - UAW Joint Committees	-International Competition -"Clean Slate" opportunity	Entire Collective Agreement— "Living Contract" (28 pages)	Entire Work System	Entire Organizational Structure	Company-wide	Many issues subject to grievance procedure
Shell - ECWU	-"Clean Slate" Opportunity	Entire Collective Agreement— "Living Contract"	Entire Work System	Entire Organizational Structure	Plant-wide	Many issues subject to grievance procedure

TABLE 3 (*Continued*)
Characteristics of Joint Governance

Site	Forces Driving Joint Governance	Basis for Joint Governance	Forms of Direct Participation	Representative Participation through Committee	Coverage	Dispute Resolution Procedure
Xerox - ACTWU	-International Competition -Past History of Joint Activities	Collective Agreement Articles II(B), XII, XIV, XV, XIX	Business Area Work Groups; Outsourcing Study Teams; *Ad Hoc* Task Forces; Semi-Autonomous Work Groups	Four Building Steering Committees; HRM Horizon Strategic Planning Teams; New Plant Design Teams	Manufacturing at four plants in Rochester, N.Y.	Many issues subject to grievance procedure
Zehrs Markets - UFCW Joint Training Center	-Employee Career Needs	Training Trust Fund (separate legal entity)	None	2 - Employer 2 - Union 2 - Rank-&-file	Company-wide	In accordance with law regulating trust funds

of not addressing these matters in the context of the cooperative effort. One study of health and safety committees has found, for example, that conflicts of interests often undermined the joint activities (Kochan, Dyer, and Lipsky 1977). However, the movement to a joint governance arrangement converts the advisory discussions into decision-making procedures, which generally broadens the parties' responsibility for dealing with difficult issues.

For example, an advisory joint committee on worker training might sidestep disputes over whether supervisors allow employees time off from work for scheduled training. The joint committee might well classify such a dispute as an internal hierarchical issue for management to address—beyond the scope of the joint committee's advisory role in recommending appropriate training. The situation is very different, however, at National Steel where a joint committee has full budgetary responsibility for the administration of certain types of training (such as movement through a skill certification ladder in a pay-for-skill system). In these cases, the alleged recalcitrant supervisors are impairing the operations of the committee and the issues are as likely to be surfaced by union appointees to the training staff as by managers on the training staff (though they are not necessarily any easier to resolve).

Similarly conflicts among co-workers can often be ignored in the context of a quality circle or employee involvement group that meets for one or two hours on a once-a-week (or less frequent) basis. In contrast, at Saturn these issues could not be ignored in the context of the team-based work system that grants workers decision-making authority on matters such as job assignments, quality, materials coordination, etc. Thus, the union worked jointly with management to ensure that employees were trained in conflict resolution and consensus decision-making skills. As well, the role of the steward (termed the committeeman in the UAW system) has been redefined in ways that encompass these areas of dispute resolution.

The two primary vehicles for addressing conflict in a traditional labor-management relationship are collective bargaining and the grievance procedure. Even in the traditional context, there has always been an integrative dimension to collective bargaining (Walton and McKersie 1965) and a willingness of some parties to voluntarily take a problem-solving approach to grievance administration (Taylor 1948). However, the operation of these two institutional arrangements changes dramatically in the context of joint governance—especially when it is centered on a comprehensive "living contract." Parties will often utilize grievance mediation processes and interest-based or mutual gains-oriented approaches to collective bargaining. Under these procedures, the parties take it upon themselves to identify and address the other side's interests as well as their own, looking for "win-win" options wherever possible. As such the adversarial quality of traditional grievance handling and collective bargaining is replaced with a problem-solving approach. Conflicts still exist and are recognized, but the attempt is made to treat the conflict as a joint problem to be solved.

For example, in the context of traditional collective bargaining the issue of health-care cost containment might surface in the form of a management demand for employee copayment of a portion of health-care costs. There would follow a positional back and forth over whether employees would contribute and then over what the amount would be. This is the way the issue first surfaced in the early 1980s at Xerox. In the context of the extensive system of joint governance that has since emerged at Xerox, however, the issue of health-care costs now involves a full sharing of information on health-care costs and utilization. Further, there is more brainstorming of options, some of which then involve joint analysis. Naturally there are many aspects of the problem solving that involves deep disagreements, but the focus is always on finding mutually acceptable solutions.

Thus we see that advisory forms of labor-management cooperation may sidestep contentious issues that can't be ignored in the context of joint governance. Similarly, problem-solving approaches to grievances and collective bargaining may be optional in the context of a traditional system, but they are essential in the joint governance context. In both cases joint governance arrangements lead parties to be more fully engaged in the mixed-motive nature of employment relations—which makes matters more complex, but the resolutions potentially more comprehensive.

Joint Governance: Direct vs. Representative Participation

In political theory there is a longstanding distinction between representative and direct forms of democracy. The experience in the workplace is directly analogous. On the one hand, there are labor-management committees and task forces in which union leaders or workers (volunteer, elected, or appointed) attempt to represent the interests of a larger group of the work force. On the other hand, there are employee participation processes that involve the direct input of employees. Both forms of participation can often be found in a single workplace. For example, in a majority of our sites there are team-based work systems or employee involvement programs that feature regular meetings of employee groups or work teams (direct participation) and there are also regular meetings of elected or appointed team/group leaders and overarching steering committees (representative participation). In addition there may be multiple forms of direct or representative participation in a given workplace. For example, there may be multiple labor-management committees in operation—each charged with addressing different issues. Further, the concurrent activities of the many labor-management committees will occur in parallel with collective bargaining—another representative form of participation.

Thus, where a workplace features some measure of joint governance we are interested in knowing three things about the form of participation: (1) Where joint governance processes are established as representative forms of participation, how do they interact with direct forms of participation? (2) Conversely, where joint governance processes are structured as direct forms of participation, how do they interact with representative forms of participation? and (3) How do the joint governance processes (whether direct or representative) interact with other coexisting (advisory) participative forms?

In political theory, representative and direct democratic forms are often cast as being in tension with one another—with each representing a potential encroachment on the other's decision-making territory. For example, the town meeting in the New England area of the United States (a direct form of democracy) is often seen as being in tension with the activities of elected town councils (a representative form). In industrial relations theory, by contrast, the linkage hypothesis advanced by Kochan, Katz, and McKersie (1986) would call for the necessary coordination of participative forms (especially across "levels") if any set of cooperative relations (let alone a system of joint governance) is to be viable.

We have found that there are both tensions (as highlighted in political theory) and mutually reinforcing linkages (as highlighted in industrial relations theory) across coexisting participative forms. For example, work teams have been established in some Ford plants at the shop floor through pilot local contracts or informal union-management agreements that allow a broad latitude in work practices. Even though there is active involvement by local union leaders and managers in jointly overseeing the experiments, they have not always established formal representative plant-wide steering committees for teams (since that involves a complicated decision over redefining existing employee involvement (EI) steering committees or creating new, parallel committees). As a result, team-level activities in some sites are well advanced at the time that a representative body is created to oversee the activities. Key policy decisions have already been made around issues like the selection of team leaders (appointed or elected) or the interface between teams and functional departments (engineering, quality control, etc.). The representative body will not always concur with the prior decisions made by the direct participants, which then prompts the beginning of a crucial joint governance dialogue regarding the respective scope and influence of the representative and direct participative initiatives.

Further, we have found that the management or coordination of these tensions and linkages engages parties in a process of bargaining over how to bargain (Cutcher-Gershenfeld, McKersie, and Walton 1989) where the parties are shaping the institutional structures within which they will then interact. For example, the TWU and B. C. Telephone chose to utilize a permanent umpire when they were addressing issues of contracting out and technological change—even though most unions and employers are loathe to bring "outsiders" into their daily affairs. In making this choice the parties were agreeing to change the way they interacted with one another. Similarly, the ACTWU and Xerox bargaining committees have found it helpful on some issues to invite a facilitator to join them during collective bargaining to help foster a problem-solving approach.

The tensions across participative forms are particularly salient in the case of B. C. Telephone and the TWU. In this case, the parties have agreed to a measure of representative joint governance around issues of new technology and subcontracting. At the same time, the union is opposed to quality circle efforts by the company—a direct form of participation which is advisory.

Joint Governance: Substantive vs. Procedural Work Rules

In examining rule making in industrial relations, Dunlop (1958) distinguished procedural work rules and substantive ones. While most of Dunlop's subsequent analysis centered on substantive rules, we observe an interesting development in the context of joint governance. Many of the substantive rules that typically accumulate in a collective bargaining agreement are set aside by parties and replaced with broad statements regarding how they will relate to one another around various issues. Centering a system of relations on procedural (rather than substantive) rules affords the parties a great deal of flexibility, but it raises fundamental dilemmas regarding the management of variation in practice.

Management is typically the moving party in seeking to reduce or eliminate substantive work rules. Ironically, it was management (in the 1920s) that first advanced substantive work rules as a complement to the Tayloristic segmentation of work (Jacoby 1985). Unions accepted the idea since it provided a check on what was then termed "the arbitrary rule of the foreman." In time, however, this solution to one problem has come to be seen as a problem itself. As firms have abandoned elements of the mass production system in favor of work systems that emphasize flexibility and quality, the detailed work rules have proven to be a barrier to innovation and continuous improvement. Of course some firms have also joined on the bandwagon and just sought to eliminate work rules without having concurrently redesigned work processes around flexibility and quality.

The first movement toward procedural rules will often occur without the replacement of substantive rules (and prior to the establishment of joint governance). This movement takes the form of contract language agreeing to establish an advisory joint committee—such as a health and safety committee. The rights and responsibilities of parties regarding their actions on such a committee are generally only spelled out in the broadest terms. But the joint advisory activities do not generally involve the replacement of existing substantive rules. For example, the joint task force involving the Manitoba Telephone System and the CWC developed recommendations for a joint Board of Trustees, but did not, itself, require changes in substantive rules.

As the capacity for joint governance is established, however, relevant substantive rules can be replaced. Where joint governance is limited to a single issue—such as training—the substantive rules on just that issue might be relaxed or replaced. We have observed this, for example, at National Steel where rules around training policies and procedures have been jointly modified. Similarly, the recommendations of the joint committee at Manitoba Telephone System involved increased flexibility in certain work rules. Further, the initial joint committee has led to two additional committees which are likely to point toward further changes.

Where the joint governance is broadly focused, it becomes possible for major areas of a traditional collective bargaining agreement to be replaced. At the extreme, for example, the initial collective bargaining agreement for Saturn is only 28 pages long (in a small six-by-three-and-a-half-inch book)—in contrast to the national agreement for the rest of GM which is 527 pages long. On the one hand, the Saturn agreement devotes five of the 28 pages to Saturn's joint structure and consensus decision-making process—all procedural matters. On the other hand, there are only short paragraphs on what would normally be major substantive issues—such as shift assignments, leaves of absence, working hours, and job classifications (one for production and 3-5 for skilled trades). Further, the language in these short paragraphs is broad in scope. For example, Section 23 on working hours states: "To fulfill the objective of the Saturn philosophy and mission, it will be necessary to have flexible hours of work that meet the needs of the individual as well as Saturn." That is the complete text of Section 23; nothing further was specified in this initial contract about working hours.

While movement to a system of procedural rules affords the parties greater flexibility, it also brings the likelihood of increased variation in practice (Cutcher-Gershenfeld 1988). Thus, contract administration becomes less a matter of the systematic enforcement of specific negotiated language and more a matter of the clinical application of jointly derived principles. This case-by-case approach fundamentally changes the roles of shop stewards and supervisors (Cutcher-Gershenfeld, McKersie, and Wever 1988; Klein 1988) and surfaces the traditional historical concern with special treatment for some parts of the work force.

For example, at Xerox union stewards report having to regularly meet with one another to stay informed of patterns of informal resolution—since there are no written records and the other alternative is to learn about inequity issues in the form of worker complaints. A standard is even emerging regarding what issues require being reduced to writing even if they could be settled informally—which are matters that have direct implications for multiple work areas. Thus, we see the balance between substantive and procedural rules shifting, but bounded by the underlying tension between the need for flexibility and the need for consistency.

Joint Governance: Political vs. Hierarchical Skills

Unions are political organizations, while corporations are hierarchical organizations. These are truisms in the teaching of industrial relations. Managers are reminded to be sensitive to the political pressures faced by an elected union leader. Union leaders are reminded to be aware of the hierarchical constraints faced by a manager.

In the context of joint governance the reality becomes more complex—in reciprocal ways. As unions enter joint governance arrangements, they are taking on a daily (joint) responsibility for one or more topic areas. With the responsibilities comes staff and a hierarchical chain of command, all of which involves building new or expanded administrative capabilities. As managers enter joint governance arrangements, they become enmeshed in the political realities of their union counterparts—which involves building new or increased political savvy regarding the factions and dynamics across the work force. Also, political contests within management become both more complex and more visible.

For both union leaders and managers, the increased awareness and capabilities bring risks and dilemmas. For union leaders the administrative roles bring accountability for the results of joint governance activities. For example, when training opportunities at Zehrs are restricted to a limited number of "slots" in a session, it is the union leaders as well as the managers who are held responsible by disgruntled members. Thus, there is the dilemma for union leaders that they will have to make an increasing number of administrative decisions in which there will be winners and losers. There is also a risk for union leaders which is that they will sound like managers as they present justification for the decisions and will thus be charged with having "sold-out" and become too much like management (Cutcher-Gershenfeld, McKersie, and Wever 1988).

Alternatively, where union leaders do bow to the politics, the joint initiative suffers. For example, the pay-for-skill system at National Steel was negotiated in a setting with an existing, high-seniority work force. In order for them to ratify the agreement, these workers were "grandfathered" into the system and are paid at the top rate. They are still required to learn all of the skills, but this political reality has taken away a major incentive that usually helps drive a pay-for-skill system.

The implications of joint governance for union operations have reached into the very structure of the union local in Sarnia. Members bring the union activities the same high levels of commitment and insistence on input and influence that they bring to the plant. In fact, as noted earlier, the local union's governing board is comprised entirely of hourly members.

For managers the risks and dilemmas are more subtle but no less salient. As they come to appreciate all of the internal politics among workers—particularly in the context of organizational change initiatives—managers face the dilemma of not being able to provide the administrative system the sort of specificity that is usually expected. Managers are supposed to provide their supervisors with specific performance objectives and business plans. In the context of joint governance, however, they will instead be reporting on broad statements of intent and ongoing processes. The risk, of course, is that a manager's career development will suffer.

A further set of risks and dilemmas for management arises around job assignments. For example, at Ford and at many other large corporations, promising plant managers are asked to change jobs every two or three years (and sometimes more often). As these individuals become involved in joint governance arrangements, however, they realize that the processes depend on shared understandings among union and management leaders. As a result, they report concluding that spending less than five or six years in the position would seriously undermine the institutionalization of the new processes. Some have turned down new "career-building" assignments in order to support joint governance initiatives, while others have moved and added complexity to joint activities left behind.

The combined dilemmas facing union and management leaders became salient at Saturn as the assembly operation began to approach full levels of production volume. Previously, there had been a number of years of initial planning and trial production runs during which great attention was given to joint processes and consensus decision making. As the volume increased, however, there emerged tensions between the highly consultative process and production requirements. The response was a reassertion of joint processes in the form of investigative task forces and extended union-management dialogue. While there are still unresolved tensions around these issues, the solution has required union leaders to be more supportive of the production demands of the system (than would be typical for a union leader), *and* it has required managers to be more sensitive to the transitional tensions in the work force (than would be typical for line managers).

Thus, joint governance arrangements require union leaders to take on administrative responsibilities that bring risks and dilemmas vis-à-vis their members, while joint governance arrangements require managers to build political sensitivity that brings risks and dilemmas vis-à-vis the larger corporation. In both cases we have to revise the old truisms about unions being political organizations and corporations being hierarchical organizations. Now both organizations look a bit more like the other, which makes people uncomfortable in each.

Learning from the Case Studies

The research reported in this chapter was undertaken with the objective of improving our understanding of joint governance processes. There are many lessons imbedded in the case studies that we have presented in the preceding sections. These must stand up to the scientific standards of reliability and validity before we can place any confidence in them. There is a problem, however, in meeting the requirements of these tests in the immediate term. There are only a handful of joint governance sites and, until larger samples are available, we cannot fully assess the lessons suggested above. Yet the need to derive some generalizations is very important for both research and practice.

In this spirit and with the caveats offered above, we present the following generalizations as propositions that need to be tested in future research. These propositions are divided into three sections—focusing on the antecedents, dynamics, and consequences of joint governance arrangements.

Propositions on the Antecedents of Joint Governance

1. Some degree of "crisis" cajoles the parties into joint governance. But joint governance is unlikely, as a volunteer effort, if the degree of "crisis" is too low or too high.
2. Some degree of relationship building (informal or formal) through advisory joint programs is a necessary but not sufficient condition for joint governance.

3. Some degree of strategic bargaining to draft "enabling legislation" is a necessary but not sufficient condition for joint governance.

Propositions on the Internal Dynamics of Joint Governance

4. Under joint governance, the surfacing and resolution of conflict is a necessary condition for effective (and far-reaching) cooperation. In the absence of effective conflict resolution, cooperation will be undercut.
5. Under joint governance, the identification and pursuit of common interests is a necessary condition for effective (and comprehensive) dispute resolution. In the absence of meaningful cooperation, conflicts will escalate out of control.
6. Linkages or consistencies between representative and direct forms of joint governance will aid the institutionalization of the joint governance procedures (and the lack of such linkages—or direct contradictions—will be a barrier to institutionalization).

Propositions on the Consequences of Joint Governance

7. Without direct participation, representative forms of participation will have limited impact on workplace outcomes; without representative forms of participation, direct forms of participation would create new tensions in the employment relationship.
8. Joint governance will promote procedural rule making as parties get used to joint decision making. This will gradually reduce the emphasis and reliance on substantive rules.
9. Joint governance will steer the union—a political institution—to build administrative competence at the shop floor and at higher levels. Similarly, it will steer the management—a hierarchical institution—to build political competence at the shop floor and at higher levels.

These propositions are phrased in the language of research, but they also can have direct value for practitioners. Each represents a core strategic issue to be considered in the context of a joint governance undertaking.

Conclusion

This paper has examined the nature and dynamics of joint decision-making arrangements between labor and management in a small but significant number of cases in Canada and the U.S. These joint decision-making arrangements are of particular interest since they are not mandated by law in either country. Contrary to popular apprehension of such power-sharing arrangements, the joint decision-making process appears to have generally "worked out" for the parties. Their experiences have not been without problems but the majority of those we spoke to believe that creation of joint decision-making forums was the best solution to their problems.

Such evidence presents a paradox. If the arrangements have generally "worked out" for the parties, why is it that we see so few of them? In this paper we have tried to sort out from among the possible answers by offering a theoretical view of the underlying processes in joint governance. As with every innovation, only a few parties would initially experiment with it. To those willing to take the risk, the period of experimentation yields valuable insights about problems and opportunities inherent in the innovation. Initial successes help develop a knowledge base and legitimize the innovation for other parties. In this sense joint governance is currently at the initial experimental stage. Until such time that a knowledge base and greater legitimacy are established, it is unlikely to spread rapidly to other organizations.

Since the industrial revolution, the authority for decision making has resided primarily with management. It seems remarkable that any manager would give up this authority willingly. It seems equally remarkable that elected union leaders would agree to join management in making day-to-day decisions. But the experience at the sites discussed in this chapter suggests that some managers and union leaders, who are searching for new ways of managing, are willing to assume the risks of joint decision making in some areas of governance. In most of the cases, the alternatives, though less risky, had less to offer in accomplishing newer or higher goals. The evidence shows that many of these arrangements have been effective in meeting the needs (for achieving higher goals or newer challenges) of both parties.

The biggest obstacle to joint governance lies in the traditional separation of roles between labor and management. Corporate laws and labor laws reinforce this separation. Company managers risk their career progress and union leaders risk losing elections when they innovate in the area of shared decision making. At least in the short run, the traditional route looks safer. Even if there is a willingness to assume these risks, a further obstacle to joint governance is the limited number of established and documented examples on which the parties could draw upon to engineer their own arrangements. Interested union and management leaders must forge new institutional arrangements to fit their context with only the most general of templates and road maps to guide them.

Despite the advantages that the evidence suggests, joint governance remains on the fringes of North American collective bargaining practice. Its incidence alone, however, cannot be judged as an indicator of its promise. The potential of joint governance for transforming traditional collective bargaining may never be known unless these experiences are carefully examined for their underlying processes and dynamics. There is an underlying public interest in joint governance to the extent that it can enhance productivity and stability in the economy. For supporters of the collective bargaining system, it offers a chance to innovate within the framework of the existing industrial relations system.

A better understanding of the problems and prospects of joint governance will help overcome many doubts and apprehensions that hold parties back from such solutions. Thus, there is an urgent need to focus more research on the processes underlying joint governance. Among other aspects, we need to examine the broader social and economic implications of jointly made decisions at establishment, firm, and industry levels. More research would help the parties with better implementation as well as guide public policy in this area.

There is no doubt that legally mandated joint governance—like that found in many parts of Western Europe—would diffuse much faster across industries and firms. However, the political climate in North America may not be conducive at the present time to such considerations. Increased prominence for joint governance initiatives and the attendant public debate might help shift the climate. Most major legal innovations are preceded by a set of economic and social events that build a constituency for legislative intervention. In the five years preceding the Wagner Act, collective bargaining with unions and the use of labor boards by government to mediate employment disputes had become increasingly more common (Jacoby 1985, 217-228). These events created the required political momentum for the passage of the Wagner Act. Joint governance does not yet have a large enough constituency or the political momentum that could aid reform minded lawmakers. Yet if joint governance is to be encouraged through changes in the law, the precedent-setting successful innovations are needed to demonstrate that it is a viable form of governance that helps us improve upon the old methods.

Typically, policymakers choose from among an array of "innovative" practices. In this case the experience with joint governance brings us full circle back to the initial debates over the Wagner Act. At the time Wagner advocated an adversarial model based on independent unions. The key alternative, championed by Cyrus Ching, embraced multiple forms of representation including, among others, what we would now term enterprise unions that gave greater prominence to joint decision making. (See the *Congressional Record* [1935] for further details.) Of course, it was Wagner who carried the day. Yet the experiences we have documented in this chapter on joint governance point toward a reopening of parts of the earlier debate. If joint governance holds the promise indicated by these cases, then the challenge before us is to craft public policies that facilitate, if not require, such joint decision making by labor and management.

Acknowledgments

The authors wish to thank Roy Adams, Anthony Smith, Tiziano Treu, and Kirsten Wever for helpful comments on an earlier draft and Peter Seidl for valuable research assistance. Financial support from the Social Sciences and Humanities Research Council of Canada is gratefully acknowledged under the Structural Change in Industrial Relations project at the Center for Industrial Relations, University of Toronto. Additional support is appreciated from the School of Labor and Industrial Relations and the Institute for Public Policy and Social Research—both at Michigan State University.

Endnotes

[1] This limitation reflects our belief that informal processes, though worthy of study, deserve their own separate treatment. There is reason to believe that the dynamic of informal arrangements is different from that of formal arrangements.

[2] Employee-owned firms do have a majority of the board of directors appointed by employees. However, this is not an exception to the norm, but rather in conformance with the general case in which the board is controlled by the majority shareholders.

[3] Some joint governance cases, such as Saturn or NUMMI, reach far beyond works councils.

[4] Our cases are but a sample of joint governance arrangements in the U.S. and Canada. There are many other notable instances of joint governance that are not included. For example, we present the case of Saturn and the UAW, but not the case of NUMMI and the UAW or the case of the Steelworkers and I/N Tek and I/N Kote, though either of the other two cases would be illustrative of a union that is deeply enmeshed in the daily decision making for a large-scale industrial plant. Similarly, we present the case of the UAW-Ford National Joint Training Center but not the case of UAW-GM National Human Resource Center or the ATT-CWA Alliance—both of which are also large-scale national joint training initiatives.

[5] See Verma and Weiler (1992) for a more detailed description of this case.

[6] See Tamasco and Dickinson (1991) for a more detailed description of this case.

[7] See Verma and Weiler (1992) for a more detailed description of this case.

[8] See McHugh and Cutcher-Gershenfeld (1991) for a more detailed description of this case.

[9] See Rankin (1990) for more detail on this case.

[10] See Cutcher-Gershenfeld (1988) for a more detailed description of this case.

References

Chaykowski, Richard P., and Anil Verma, eds. 1992. *Industrial Relations in Canadian Industry*. Toronto: Holt, Rinehart & Winston.

Cutcher-Gershenfeld, Joel. 1988. *Tracing a Transformation in Industrial Relations: The Case of Xerox Corporation and the Amalgamated Clothing and Textile Workers Union*. Washington, DC: Bureau of Labor-Management Relations and Cooperative Programs, U.S. Department of Labor (BLMR 123).

Cutcher-Gershenfeld, Joel, Thomas Kochan, and Anil Verma. 1991. "Recent Developments in U.S. Employee Involvement Initiatives: Erosion or Diffusion." In *Advances in Industrial and Labor Relations* (Vol. 5), eds. Donna Sockell, David Lewin, and David Lipsky. Greenwich, CT: JAI Press, pp. 1-32.

Cutcher-Gershenfeld, Joel, Robert B. McKersie, and Richard Walton. 1989. "Negotiating Transformation: Negotiations Lessons from Current Developments in Industrial Relations." In *Academy of Management Best Papers Proceedings*, ed. Hoy. Washington, DC: Academy of Management.

Cutcher-Gershenfeld, Joel, Robert B. McKersie, and Kirsten Wever. 1988. *The Changing Role of Union Leaders*. Washington, DC: Bureau of Labor-Management Relations andCooperative Programs, U.S. Department of Labor (BLMR 127).

Dunlop, John. 1958. *Industrial Relations Systems*. New York: Henry Holt and Company.

Heckscher, Charles. 1988. *The New Unionism: Employee Involvement in the Changing Corporation*. New York: Basic Books.

Jacoby, Sanford M. 1985. *Employing Bureaucracy*. New York: Columbia University Press.

Klein, Janice. 1988. *The Changing Role of First-Line Supervisors and Middle Managers*. Washington, DC: Bureau of Labor-Management Relations and Cooperative Programs, U.S. Department of Labor (BLMR 126).

Kochan, Thomas, Lee Dyer, and David Lipsky. 1977. *The Effectiveness of Union-Management Safety and Health Committees*. Kalamazoo, MI: The W. E. Upjohn Institute for Employment Research.

Kochan, Thomas, Harry Katz, and Robert McKersie. 1986. *The Transformation of American Industrial Relations*. New York: Basic Books.

Rankin, Tom. 1990. *New Forms of Work Organization: The Challenge for North American Unions*. Toronto: Univesity of Toronto Press.

Savoie, Ernest J., and Joel Cutcher-Gershenfeld. 1991. "The Governance of Joint Training Initiatives." In *Joint Training Programs: A Union-Management Approach to Preparing Workers for the Future*, eds. Louis Ferman, Michele Hoyman, Joel Cutcher-Gershenfeld, and Ernest Savoie. Ithaca, NY: ILR Press.

Slichter, Sumner, James Healy, and Robert Livernash. 1960. *The Impact of Collective Bargaining on Management*. Washington, DC: The Brookings Institution.

Tamasco, Elizabeth S., and Kenneth K. Dickson. 1991. "The UAW-Ford Education, Development and Training." In *Joint Training Programs: A Union-Management Approach to Preparing Workers for the Future*, eds. Louis Ferman, Michele Hoyman, Joel Cutcher-Gershenfeld, and Ernest Savoie. Ithaca, NY: ILR Press.

Taylor, George. 1948. *Government Regulation of Industrial Relations*. New York: Prentice Hall.

Verma, Anil. 1991. "Restructuring in Industrial Relations and the Role for Labor." In *Labor in a Global Economy: A U.S.-Canadian Symposium*, eds. Margaret Hallock and Steve Hecker. Eugene, OR: University of Oregon Books, pp. 47-61.

Verma, Anil, and Joseph P. Weiler. 1992. "Industrial Relations in the Canadian Telephone Industry." In *Industrial Relations in Canadian Industry*, eds. Richard P. Chaykowski and Anil Verma. Toronto: Holt, Rinehart & Winston.

Walton, Richard E. 1980. "Establishing and Maintaining High Commitment Work Systems." In *The Organizational Life Cycle*, eds. J. R. Kimberly and R. H. Miles. San Francisco: Jossey-Bass.

Walton, Richard, and Robert McKersie. 1965. *A Behavioral Theory of Collective Bargaining*. New York: McGraw-Hill Book Company.

Webb, Sidney, and Beatrice Webb. 1897. *Industrial Democracy*. London: Longmans.

Weiler, Paul C. 1990. *Governing the Workplace*. Cambridge, MA: Harvard University Press.

Wellins, Richard S., William C. Byham, and Jeanne M. Wilson. 1991. *Empowered Teams*. San Francisco: Jossey-Bass.

Chapter 7

Does Strategic Choice Explain Senior Executives' Preferences on Employee Voice and Representation?

David Lewin
UCLA

Peter D. Sherer
University of Pennsylvania

The notion that employee voice and representation (EVR) can or does play a role in the formulation or implementation of the business strategy of U.S. enterprises has largely gone unexplored. Most U.S. industrial relations literature equates EVR with unions and sees them as a collective agent to which the firm reacts (Strauss 1984). The business strategy literature at times similarly relegates the role of EVR to unions and sees them as a force for firms to contend with (Porter 1980), or it recognizes but does not fully address the role of EVR in the formulation or implementation of the business strategy (e.g., Ansoff 1988).

The continuing decline of unionization in OECD countries, the rise and diffusion of new forms of EVR in firms, the emerging integration of human resource management into business strategy, and the growing interest in strategic choice in the industrial relations and human resource literatures all suggest the time is ripe to explore the conceptual and empirical roles of EVR in firms' business strategies. With this in mind, we examine key strategic decision makers—senior executives in American and Japanese firms both operating in the U.S.—preferences on the form and scope of EVR. We find that executives from Japanese firms view employees as more important stakeholders than do executives from U.S. firms.

The executives from the Japanese firms also see more of a role for EVR than do the executives from the U.S. firms, but not on all matters or forms of EVR. Most striking, the executives from the Japanese firms attach greater importance to EVR in the formulation of business strategy, while those from the U.S. firms attach more importance to EVR in the implementation of the business strategy.

A strategic choice framework and series of equations was developed to explain these findings. Environmental and resource differences among firms and differences in personal characteristics among senior executives served as controls. Strategic choice was addressed through senior executives' rankings of the importance of employees as firm stakeholders relative to other groups. The results suggest that strategic choice, so defined, plays a role in explaining senior executives' preferences on the form and scope of EVR. The finding also persisted that executives from the Japanese and U.S. firms differ in their preferences on the form and scope of EVR, thus suggesting that strategic choice operates through country and cultural differences.

The Classical/Traditional Firm and the Emerging Alternative

From very different theoretical perspectives, there is something of a consensus about how to characterize the classical/traditional firm. A fundamental building block of this characterization rests on the employment relationship. From a behavioral and administrative science perspective, Simon (1958) proposes that employment is essentially an authority relationship: an employee allows an employer to exercise authority over him within some feasible set of commands in exchange for the guarantee of a wage. From an information economics perspective, Alchian and Demsetz (1972) argue that the key to the employment relationship in the classical firm is the role designated for a specialist monitor. This specialist gives work assignments, tells employees what to do and how to do it, measures effort in input and work output, allocates rewards, and enforces discipline. Finally, from a radical or neoMarxist perspective, Edwards (1979) suggests that the role of an employer is to be a controller who directs and tells employees what is to be done, evaluates them on how well they have done their assignments, and rewards and disciplines them. In short, a variety of perspectives tell us that the employer engages in hierarchical or vertical coordination and control, be it as an authority, monitor, or controller.

In the classical firm, vertical coordination and control were taken to be functionally appropriate because they ensured that information flowed from the top to the bottom of the organization; the boss gave orders and subordinates executed them. Horizontal coordination and control mechanisms, such as those found in certain labor-management partnerships or in firms like Volvo, which have autonomous work teams, were seen as exceptions to competitive rules that favored hierarchy. Informal or individual bargaining took place as a market means for adjusting wages, but the role of formal EVR was secondary, irrelevant, or at odds with the efficiency properties of vertical coordination and control.

Moving from superior-subordinate relationships to the business as a whole revealed that the organizational structure of the classical firm had centralized decision making and control. Each vertical reporting relationship was part of another vertical relationship, with the end product being a pyramid where ultimate control and coordination rested with a very few. In this traditionally structured or functional organization, decisions were made by a small number of senior executives, orders were carried out by those in the lower ranks of the organization, and information flowed from the top to the bottom of the organization.

It would be difficult to overstate the importance of this classical form of organization to the operation not only of business enterprises, but of government, nonprofit, and voluntary enterprises. Indeed, this organizational form had its roots in religious and military enterprises, including those which long predated the development of industrialized economies and modern business corporations (Blau and Scott 1962). Prototypes of modern business enterprises with traditional "command and control" organizational structures included such leading manufacturing firms as General Motors Corporation (GM), International Business Machines Corporations (IBM), and American Telephone and Telegraph Company (AT&T).

During the 1980s and continuing into the 1990s, many large U.S. business enterprises, including GM, IBM, and AT&T, began to depart from the hierarchical form of organizational coordination and control. These firms came to advocate and adopt flatter organizations, more participative decision-making processes in which information also flows from the bottom to the top, and the "empowerment" of lower ranking organizational members to make decisions rather than merely to execute the decisions made by other, higher ranking, organizational members. Horizontal coordination and control thus seemed to have come of age during the 1980s and reflected a new organizational structure characterized by relative flatness, decentralized (and fewer layers of) management, and diffuse decision-making responsibilities (Lawler 1986; Simmons and Mares 1985).

A major implication of these developments was that employees in teams often took on some of the coordination and control role by making decisions previously reserved to management and supervisors. Thus, it was not that control and coordination had ended, but that vertical coordination and control was supplanted by its horizontal counterpart (Sherer and Lee 1993). Critical to the success of horizontal coordination and control is getting all employees—not just managers and supervisors—to share values, habits of the mind, and other ways by which employees come to think alike. Such "jointness" is seen as key to achieving goal congruity, that is, the integration of the individual and the firm's goals and objectives. It is, therefore, not surprising that nonunion (U.S.) business enterprises that moved toward this new organizational form clothed it in a "cultural jacket." In such enterprises, especially those with strong-minded, entrepreneurial-type leaders, major programs were often undertaken to socialize employees into the central "values" of the enterprise—employees become "cultural carriers" of these values. Apple Computer Corporation, for example, publishes a list of nine key Apple values and conducts mandatory training and orientation programs to apprise employees of and inculcate employees in these values.[1] More generally, the term "partnership," which has a narrow legal significance as a form of joint ownership, took on a broader symbolic meaning and growing importance to indicate that jointness and sharing were critical.

In nonunion (U.S.) business enterprises, initiatives at self-management, empowerment, and centrally shared corporate values are aimed directly at employees who are without representation under the National Labor Relations Act (NLRA) or other labor law. In unionized (U.S.) enterprises, initiatives at self-management, empowerment, and centrally shared corporate culture/values typically are aimed at or negotiated with representatives of employees.

Such changing conceptions of the role of both nonunion and union employees in the decision making of the firm are also more clearly formalized in recognition of employees as stakeholders: "An identifiable group or individual who can affect the achievement of an organization's objectives or who is affected by the achievement of an organization's objectives" (Freeman and Reed 1983, 91). While unions through their bargaining power have always been able to affect business organizations in their achievement of goals, that role was circumscribed by the NLRA through its specification of what issues were bargainable. Moreover, since the responsibility for achieving outcomes is so much more diffuse and decentralized in this alternative to the classical firm, recognition has been growing that firms need to "configure" their objectives to consider employees more fully (Ansoff 1988). This has led some scholars to conclude that industrial relations/human resources now constitute a key strategic element or choice varia. .e in the firm's planning and decision-making processes (Kochan, Katz, and McKersie 1986; Lewin 1987).

In light of these developments, we may ask "Does strategic choice enter into and explain senior executives' preferences on the scope and form of EVR?" We will attempt to answer this question later in this paper by analyzing primary data on senior executives' preferences on the form and scope of EVR. Initially, we identify and define various forms of EVR.

Forms of Employee Voice/Representation in the Enterprise

Employee voice refers to any means by which employees express their views and provide firms or other interested parties (e.g., regulatory agencies such as the National Labor Relations Board) with information that pertains to their employment condition. The institutional arrangement of a union as a collective agent or representative of employees has been the primary mechanism recognized in the U.S. for expressing voice (Freeman and Medoff 1984). However, the extent of unionism and explicit collective employment contracting among the U.S. work force has declined markedly in recent decades. The proportion of the U.S. private-sector work force that belongs to labor organizations stood at about 11.5 percent in 1992, which compares with a high of over 35 percent in the mid-1950s. Moreover, the decline in the "demand" for unionism and union services has occurred throughout OECD countries (Blanchflower and Freeman 1992). For the U.S., which has always had a comparatively low rate of employee unionization, the recent proportionate decline in work force unionization underscores what has always been true—that the majority (now the vast majority) of U.S. workers are not formally represented in enterprises in which they are employed (Bognanno and Kleiner 1992).

Yet, unionization is only one form of EVR in the business enterprise. Other forms of EVR in the enterprise are employer initiated and include organizational teams and conflict resolution procedures. To illustrate, many U.S. businesses have recently initiated team-based employee involvement programs featuring task forces or committees to study and advise senior management about such workplace issues as productivity, product quality, work organization, work methods and labor costs (Nadler et al. 1992). The membership on such committees is solicited on a voluntary basis, though occasionally committee members are regarded as "representing" the views of the larger units, departments, or workplace groupings with which they are associated.

Another employer-initiated form of EVR in the enterprise is the formal appeal, complaint, grievance or grievance-like procedure. Such procedures, long common to unionized firms, have grown markedly in nonunion U.S. businesses in recent years and are intended to provide employees with a mechanism for surfacing and resolving disagreements with their employers over a variety of employment, workplace, and organizational issues. As with employer-initiated employee involvement programs, plans, and committees, employer-initiated grievance(-like) procedures constitute a form of individual rather than collective voice in the enterprise. Further, employees voluntarily decide whether or not to file "grievances" under these types of conflict resolution procedures (Lewin 1990; Lewin and Mitchell 1992).

Employee involvement programs and grievance-like procedures thus constitute the two main types of initiatives recently undertaken by U.S. firms, especially nonunion firms, and both of these arrangements can be said to provide particular forms of employee participation in business enterprises (Delaney, Lewin, and Ichniowski 1989). Especially notable about such initiatives is that they apparently cover far larger proportions of the U.S. work force than those that belong to or are represented by labor organizations.

Outside of the U.S., especially in western Europe, mandatory or legally required systems of employee voice/representation in the business enterprise are common. One such mandated system is the works council, which typically is composed of elected representatives of employees, supervisors, and middle managers and with which senior management consults over a wide range of business decisions, including acquisitions, divestitures, plant closings, plant relocations, and work force reductions. Works councils prevail in Austria, Belgium, Denmark, France, Germany, Greece, Italy, Luxembourg, the Netherlands, and Norway; they can exist at the corporate, divisional, and plant/facility levels of an enterprise. Such councils almost always have rights to information, usually have rights to consultation, and occasionally have rights to joint decision making with senior management.[2]

Another type of mandatory or legally required system of EVR is codetermination, which refers to the representation of employees on company managing boards and/or boards of directors. Codetermination laws prevail in Austria, Denmark, Germany, Ireland, Luxembourg, the Netherlands, Norway, Sweden, and Spain. Unlike elections for works council representatives in which all employees are eligible to vote, employee directors are often selected by unions as, for example, in Sweden, Luxembourg, and Germany—and, in the rare case where voluntary codetermination exists, in the U.S.[3]

A final type of legally mandated EVR in the business enterprise, found primarily in western Europe, is legislated protection against dismissal from the job. Such legislation prevails in Belgium, France, Ireland, Italy, Luxembourg, Portugal, and the United Kingdom. It typically requires that the terms and conditions of an individual's employment be written and supplied to the employee by the employer. In some countries, such as Great Britain, dismissal for economic reasons (or redundancy) is treated differently from dismissal for disciplinary reasons (or cause). Western European-type unjust dismissal legislation more or less requires an employer to justify or "prove" that a dismissal is warranted, whereas so-called wrongful termination suits filed by employees against U.S. businesses require the employee to "prove" that the dismissal was illegal based on very narrow definitions of unlawful conduct. For example, dismissal for whistle-blowing typically results in reinstatement only if the whistle was blown on a clearly unlawful act by the firm. Nonetheless, the challenge to the doctrine of employment-at-will in the U.S. represented by such wrongful termination litigation can be seen as constituting another form of EVR in the business enterprise.

In western Europe, works councils, codetermination, and legislative protection against unjust dismissal typically coexist with employee unionism, which means that an individual employee has multiple forms of EVR in the decisions of business enterprises. In the U.S., by contrast, mandated works councils, codetermination, and legislative protection against job dismissals do not exist, and employer-initiated employee involvement programs and grievance(-like) procedures are, generally speaking, substitutes for employee unionism—though employee involvement programs can be found in both unionized and nonunion firms (Boroff and Lewin 1991; Ichniowski and Lewin 1988; Feuille and Delaney 1993). Each of the above forms may be regarded as providing a certain degree of employee "voice" and "representation" in the decisions of business enterprises.

The Linkage of Employee Voice/Representation to Business Strategy

Central to the practice of modern business strategy is a series of steps that begin with an environmental analysis and a resource analysis, followed by a comparison of these two analyses (see, for example, Kotler and Bloom 1984). In an environmental analysis, a firm scans its internal environment (i.e., key internal stakeholders), factor market (e.g., suppliers), public interest and regulatory environments (e.g., Nader's Raiders, the NLRB), competition, and the macroeconomic environment or large scale forces that influence all organizations. The process of identifying these environmental forces includes an assessment of the threats and opportunities that they present and are likely to present to the business—sometimes referred to as a threat (or risk) and opportunity analysis. In a resource analysis, an organization analyzes and identifies its resources, capabilities (capacity to act), distinctive competencies (those which the organization is strong in), and differential advantages (those which the organization is strong in relative to the competition). The comparison of the environmental and resource analyses leads to goal formulation—the specification of the goals consistent with the overall mission and objectives of the firm.

In the steps leading up to and including goal formulation, EVR can play an important role. Unions often will be a key consideration in a threat analysis and may at other times show up in an opportunity analysis. Furthermore, employee input into the capability set of the firm and the need to mobilize employees towards achievement of the goals suggest that EVR may be an important consideration in the resource analysis and in the actual specification of goals, mission, and objectives.

Once goals have been formulated, the choice of a strategy is made. A firm might, for example, choose to take a strategy of overall cost leadership by keeping costs low and volume high (Porter 1980). Or, a firm might take a strategy of differentiation by creating a product or service that is novel in some way.

The implementation of the business strategy follows. This process is most often discussed in terms of aligning the organizational structure to the strategy, although culture and people in the organization are sometimes discussed as alignment points. Most discussions of strategy implementation suggest that structure follows from strategy in some fit or contingency sense, with the assumption being that there is one best structure for a given strategy. Missing or at least not fully addressed in discussions of strategy implementation is the role of EVR.

The form and scope of EVR is one of several potential choices a firm makes in strategy formulation and implementation. The form and scope of EVR in the goal formulation phase may be important in gaining input from employees on goals and it also may be critical for getting employees to "sign on" at the front end to the business strategy. Similarly, the form and scope of EVR in strategy implementation may be important in getting employees to provide input on how the strategy will be accomplished at the workplace level and in getting employee support at the workplace level in accomplishing the formulated strategy.

Stakeholder analysis, the process of identifying the key interest groups that influence or are likely to influence a business enterprise, allows for a more formal way of assessing the strategic role of EVR (Freeman and Reed 1983). Typically the key stakeholders include shareholders (in public-held businesses), customers, suppliers (including suppliers of capital and credit), regulatory agencies, community groups and, of particular relevance for purposes of this chapter, employees. Much of stakeholder analysis is devoted to assessing the power or bargaining power and potential impact of stakeholders on the achievement of business objectives. For key stakeholders, the business enterprise seeks to define and manage ongoing relationships.

Dore (1987) has cogently argued that Japanese firms located in Japan have gone much further than U.S. firms to embrace a multiple stakeholder model of the firm. Central to the Japanese stakeholder model is: (1) a consensus that there are many stakeholders in the firm and thus that the firm is a community, (2) a conviction that employees are key members of the community, and (3) a commitment to employees as key community members who should be provided with a long-term relationship and are in a relational exchange with the firm, and who therefore are entitled to have a say or voice in firm matters that will affect them.

The view that dominates in the U.S. is that management has a fiduciary responsibility to the corporation. This responsibility has often been equated with maximizing shareholders' value. From this view, it follows that an employer should provide employees with voice and representation when it reduces costs or fosters revenue generation and potentially increases shareholder wealth.

The differing emphasis paid to employees as stakeholders in U.S. and Japanese firms can be explained at least in part by the national environments in which these firms operate. The legal system in Japan as compared with that of the U.S. seems to be more favorable toward employees (Dore 1987). Japanese corporate law specifies several groups in its definition and conception of the firm. Japanese bankruptcy law requires that employees receive debt payments ahead of other creditors. The capital market in Japan as expressed through stock and stockholders also plays less of a role in firms gaining access to capital as compared with in the U.S. Friendly banks provide a significant portion of the equity capital that Japanese firms require. As a result, stockholders in Japan have not received higher dividends presumably at the expense of employees (Dore 1987).

Dore, however, cautions that these legal and market differences can be overstated and it is wrong to see them as determinative in their own right. They are manifestations of underlying cultural differences or choices made about what is the firm and who are its members.

We examine senior executives' views on EVR in both U.S. firms and Japanese firms located in the U.S., controlling for environmental and resource differences among these firms as well as various personal characteristics of the senior executives. The conceptual and statistical experiment is as follows: After controlling for differences among firms and executives, if there is a relationship between the executive rankings of employees as stakeholders and their preferences on the form and scope of employee, we can conclude that strategic choice on EVR operates among these senior executives.

Modeling the Sources for Employee Voice/Representation in the Firm

We offer the following model of EVR in the enterprise:

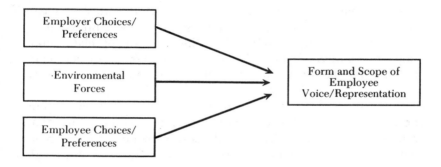

This model suggests that the form and scope of EVR in the enterprise are shaped by environmental forces and by choices/preferences of employers and employees. The environment includes the legal (e.g., bankruptcy law and labor law), political (e.g., relationship of the political party to labor), and social conditions (e.g., period of social crisis or conformity) in a society. At any given point in time and within a particular society, such as that of the U.S., legislation pertaining to employee representation in the enterprise is fixed, whereas choices and preferences for employee representation will vary among employers and employees. Thus, for example, we would expect that employees with long-term career/occupational attachments and/or long-term employer attachments are more likely to prefer representation in business decisions than employees with short-term career/occupational or employer attachments. We would also expect that employers who regard employees as a major stakeholder in the business have stronger preferences for employees to have voice/representation in phases of the business strategy than employers who regard employees as a minor or negligible stakeholder in the business.

The form and scope of EVR include a wide range of activities about which employer and employee choices/preferences may vary greatly. Some employers and employees may prefer representation in a wide range of business decisions, while other employers and employees may prefer representation in a narrow, closely circumscribed set of business decisions. Similarly, some employers and employees may prefer representation at high organizational levels, including the board of directors, while other employers and employees may prefer representation at lower organizational levels, such as the department or workplace level. Finally, some employers and employees may prefer representation as a continuing institutional feature of the employment relationship, while other employers and employees may prefer representation to exist only for the short term (and only for the resolution of narrow issues).

In this paper we focus on employers' views of EVR. In part our choice is based on recent industrial relations literature that emphasizes the newly active role of management in bringing about changes in employer-employee relationships (Cappelli and Singh 1992). Our sample of senior executives are the key strategic decision makers in firms and thus their choices/preferences are likely to be of particular influence in their firms. We have also chosen a sample of senior executives because much less is generally known about top management's as opposed to supervisory personnel's views of EVR. Most prior research has addressed the views of first-line supervisors and middle managers who are in direct contact with employees and union officials on the "shop floor" (Purcell 1983).

To test the full range of propositions that could be generated from our model would require a larger data base drawn from samples of employers and employees across a wider range of countries than was available to us. However, it is our hope that this more limited study will nevertheless generate additional research on EVR, including in other countries.

Research Design and Empirical Testing

A research design was developed to obtain primary data from senior executives in a sample of publicly held U.S. firms and in a sample of Japanese firms that own and operate at least one business (plant, office, or facility) in the U.S. As noted earlier, there is a widespread belief that executives of Japanese firms place greater emphasis than executives of U.S. firms on employees as stakeholders in the business and are thus more likely than U.S. executives to favor employee representation in business decisions (Lewin and Zhuang 1992). This proposition along with others concerning employer preferences for employee representation in business decisions can be empirically tested using within-country (in this case, U.S.) data which, in effect, hold constant relevant legislation as well as other external environmental factors.

To implement this research design, a mail survey questionnaire was constructed and administered in mid-1990 to senior executives of 2,115 U.S. businesses and 384 Japanese businesses that operate in the U.S. The questionnaire was designed specifically to elicit senior management views of and preferences for EVR. A total of 438 fully usable questionnaire responses were received from executives of U.S. businesses, or 20.7 percent of the original sample, while 107 fully usable questionnaire responses were received from executives of Japanese businesses operating in the U.S., or 27.9 percent of the original sample. These response rates are somewhat higher than those generally obtained from surveys of senior business executives, which perhaps reflects the use of a double follow-up procedure that featured a second mailing and telephone calls to firms that did not respond to the initial survey.

The starting point for our empirical analysis is the weight or value that executives of U.S. and Japanese businesses place on employees as stakeholders in the business. The executive respondents to our survey questionnaire were asked specifically to rank the importance of employees as a stakeholder in relation to other stakeholders, in particular, shareholders, customers, suppliers, government regulatory agencies, and community groups; these rankings are shown in Table 1. Senior executives of U.S. firms ranked employees as the fourth most important stakeholder group behind shareholders, customers, and suppliers; senior executives of Japanese firms operating in the U.S. ranked employees as the second most important stakeholder group behind customers.

TABLE 1

Senior Executive Rankings of Stakeholder Group Importance, 1990
(Ranked on a scale with 1 = most important
to 6 = least important)

Rank by Importance	Executives of U.S. Firms	Executives of Japanese Firms Operating in the U.S.
First	Shareholders M = 1.38 SD = 0.21	Customers M = 1.43 SD = 0.31
Second	Customers M = 1.97 SD = 0.37	Employees M = 1.83 SD = 0.29
Third	Suppliers M = 2.73 SD = 0.33	Suppliers M = 2.66 SD = 0.28
Fourth	Employees M = 3.78 SD = 0.37	Government Regulatory Agencies M = 3.59 SD = 0.34
Fifth	Government Regulatory Agencies M = 4.62 SD = 0.56	Shareholders M = 4.54 SD = 0.38
Sixth	Community Groups M = 5.59 SD = 0.40	Community Groups M = 5.67 SD = 0.36
N =	384	107

M = Mean ranking
SD = Standard deviation

The two sets of executives then rated the importance of EVR in the enterprise on a scale in which one equaled "not at all important" and five equaled "extremely important." For this purpose, EVR was first defined as "any formal or informal mechanism by which employees participate or are consulted in business decisions." As shown in Table 2, the senior executives of U.S. firms rated this definition of EVR in the enterprise at a mean of 3.65, whereas the senior executives of Japanese firms operating in the U.S. rated this definition of EVR in the enterprise at a mean of 4.16. The difference between these mean ratings is statistically significant at $p < .05$.

The two sets of executives next rated the importance of EVR in the enterprise where EVR was defined as "a formal role for employees in business decisions, such as through unionization,

TABLE 2

Senior Executive Ratings of the Importance of Employee
Representation in the Enterprise, 1990
(Mean rating on a scale with 1 = not at all important,
5 = extremely important)

Item	Executives of U.S. Firms		Executives of Japanese Firms Operating in the U.S.	
	Mean	Standard Deviation	Mean	Standard Deviation
Any formal or informal mechanism by which employees participate or are consulted in the business	3.65°,+	1.13	4.16°,++	0.52
A formal role for employees in business decisions, such as through unionization, works councils, or codetermination	1.56°°,+	0.44	2.04°°,++	0.81
N =	384		107	

° = Significantly different at p = < .05.
°° = Significantly different at p = < .05.
+ = Significantly different at p = < .01.
++ = Significantly different at p = < .01.

works councils, or codetermination." As also shown in Table 2, the senior executives of U.S. firms rated this definition of EVR in the enterprise at a mean of 1.56, while senior executives of Japanese firms operating in the U.S. rated this definition of EVR in the enterprise at 2.04. The difference between these mean ratings is again statistically significant at p < .05.

Respondents were then asked to rate the desirability of specific types of EVR, including unionization, works councils, codetermination, written grievance procedures, legal challenges to employment-at-will, and various team-based initiatives such as quality circles, quality-of-work-life improvement programs, autonomous work teams, and problem-oriented committees. Respondents were asked to rate each of these arrangements on a scale in which one equaled "not at all desirable" and five equaled "completely desirable."

The very striking differences for these items are shown in Table 3. Executives of U.S. firms rated legal challenges to employment-at-will, codetermination, and unionization as the least desirable forms

TABLE 3

Senior Executive Ratings of the Desirability of Forms of Employee
Representation in Business Decisions, 1990
(Mean rating on a scale with 1 = not at all desirable,
5 = completely desirable)

Item	Executives of U.S. Firms		Executives of Japanese Firms Operating in the U.S.	
	Mean	Standard Deviation	Mean	Standard Deviation
Unionization	1.42°	0.34	1.82°	0.46
Works Councils	1.84	0.52	2.02	0.51
Codetermination	1.34°	0.19	1.78°	0.38
Written Grievance Procedure	2.86°°	0.82	1.68°°	0.23
Legal Challenges to Employment-at-Will	1.27°	0.16	1.79°	0.18
Quality Circles	2.95°°	0.56	3.73°°	0.31
Quality-of-Work-Life Improvement Programs	3.02°	0.68	3.58°	0.41
Autonomous Work Teams	4.11°	0.81	3.45°	0.54
Problem-Oriented Committees	3.83°	0.62	3.21°	0.59
N =	384		107	

° = Significantly different at p = < .05.
°° = Significantly different at p = < .01.

of employee representation in business decisions. The executives of
Japanese firms operating in the U.S. rated grievance procedures
and legal challenges to employment-at-will as the least desirable
forms of employee representation in business decisions. Executives
of U.S. firms rated written grievance procedures as substantially
more desirable than did executives of Japanese firms operating in
the U.S. Both groups of executives regarded team-based initiatives
as relatively desirable, although the executives of U.S. firms gave
higher desirability ratings than executives of Japanese firms to
autonomous work teams and problem-oriented committees,
whereas the executives of Japanese firms gave higher desirability
ratings than executives of U.S. firms to quality circles and quality-
of-work-life improvement programs.

The executives then rated the desirability of employee representation in specific areas of business decision making, including

business acquisition, business divestiture, plant/facility closing, plant/facility relocation, work force downsizing, customer satisfaction, product quality, technological change, work flow, job design, compensation, job security, and performance appraisal. The rating scale used here again ranged from one equalling "not at all desirable" to five equalling "completely desirable."

The findings about EVR in these areas of business decision making are shown in Table 4. Executives of U.S. firms generally regarded employee representation as more desirable for such workplace level issues as job design, compensation, job security, and

TABLE 4

Senior Executive Ratings of the Desirability of Employee
Representation in Specific Business Issues, 1990
(Mean rating on a scale with 1 = not at all desirable,
5 = completely desirable)

Item	Executives of U.S. Firms		Executives of Japanese Firms Operating in the U.S.	
	Mean	Standard Deviation	Mean	Standard Deviation
Business Acquisition	1.27°°	0.21	2.36°°	0.31
Business Divestiture	1.19°°	0.11	2.81°°	0.34
Plant/Facility Closing	1.68°	0.35	2.48°	0.22
Plant/Facility Relocation	1.74°°	0.39	2.55°°	0.19
Work Force Downsizing	1.96°	0.44	2.41°	0.23
Customer Satisfaction	1.83°	0.37	2.36°	0.29
Product Quality	2.32°°	0.29	3.46°°	0.23
Technological Change	1.94°°	0.45	2.76°°	0.30
Work Flow	2.04	0.33	1.95	0.45
Job Design	3.04	0.62	2.87	0.52
Compensation	3.35°	0.41	2.62°	0.42
Job Security	3.24°	0.38	2.55°	0.31
Performance Appraisal	2.92	0.32	2.74	0.49
N =	384		107	

° = Significantly different at p = < .05.
°° = Significantly different at p = < .01.

performance appraisal than for such strategic-level issues as business acquisition and divestiture and plant closings and relocations. The executives of Japanese firms operating in the U.S. give higher desirability ratings to employee representation in strategic-level issues than in workplace-level issues—ratings which are both striking and significantly different from those given by senior executives of U.S. firms.

These results suggest that Japanese executives believe it is important to have EVR in strategy formulation, but have a weaker preference for EVR at the workplace level where the strategy is implemented on a day-to-day basis. By contrast, U.S. executives attach more weight to EVR as a component of strategy implementation than of strategy formulation.

Multivariate Analysis

To examine more fully employer preferences for EVR in business decisions, ordinary least squares equations were specified and tested. The first of these equations examines the determinants of U.S. and Japanese executives' rankings of the importance of stakeholder groups to the firm. While executives' ranking of employees as stakeholders were used to form the dependent variable, the following served as independent variables:

Demographic Variables

—Executive age, in years

—Executive experience with current business, in years

—Executive schooling, in highest year of school completed

—Executive foreign assignments, in number of assignments outside of company's home country

—Executive country of origin, with U.S. = 0, Japan = 1

Firm Characteristics

—Size of firm, in assets (1990) dollars

—Age of firm, in years since founding

—Unionization, in percent of employees covered by collective bargaining agreements

—Globalization, in number of countries in which the firm owns/ operates plants, offices, or facilities

—Capital/labor ratio, in capital investment to payroll expenditures (in 1990 dollars)

—Economic sector, with nonmanufacturing = 0, manufacturing = 1

—Home country of firm, with U.S. = 0, Japan = 1

The results for this analysis are shown in Table 5. Among the demographic variables, the (number of years of) experience and

TABLE 5

Regression Coefficients on Senior Executive Ranking of
Employee Stakeholder Group Importance
(standard errors in parentheses)

Independent Variable	Coefficient
Constant	3.13° (1.42)
Executive Age	0.40 (0.29)
Executive Experience	0.51° (0.24)
Executive Schooling	−0.15 (0.09)
Executive Foreign Assignments	0.69° (0.32)
Executive Country of Origin	0.43° (0.20)
Firm Size	0.31° (0.14)
Firm Age	0.33 (0.20)
Unionization	−0.79°° (0.30)
Globalization	0.63° (0.29)
Capital/Labor Ratio	−0.41 (0.26)
Economic Sector	0.56° (0.25)
Home Country of Firm	0.84°° (0.32)
N =	491
R^2	0.46

° = Significantly different at p = < .05.
°° = Significantly different at p = < .01.

(number of) foreign assignments of senior executives are significantly and positively related to their ranking of employees as stakeholders in the firm. Senior executives born outside of the U.S. are significantly more likely than senior executives born in the U.S. to rank employees highly as stakeholders in the firm. Among firm characteristics, size of firm, location in the manufacturing sector, and globalization are significantly and positively associated with senior executive rankings of employees as stakeholders, while the proportion of employees covered by collective bargaining agreements (a proxy for unionization) is significantly and negatively related to senior executive rankings of employees as stakeholders in the firm. Most notable in Table 5, however, is the finding that senior executives of Japanese-headquartered firms are significantly more likely than senior executives of U.S.-headquartered firms to assign employees a high ranking as a stakeholder group.

In the second set of equations in this analysis, senior executives' ratings of the importance of broad and narrow EVR in business decisions served as the dependent variables. Recall that broad representation refers to "any formal or informal mechanism by which employees participate or are consulted in the business," and narrow representation refers to "a formal role for employees in business decisions, such as through unionization, works councils, or codetermination." In these equations, firm characteristics and personal characteristics of senior executives served as controls although we believe they too contain information about both individual and firm strategies (firms select certain types of individuals, socialize them to certain views, and provide them with certain experiences and exposures).[4] However, we test for strategic choice more narrowly and conservatively by entering into these equations as an independent variable the senior executives' ranking of the importance of employees as a stakeholder group in the firm.

The results of these regression equations are reported in Table 6. They show that senior executive ratings of the importance of broad EVR in business decisions are significantly and positively related to an executive's ranking of the importance of employees as a stakeholder group in the firm. These executives' ratings of the importance of broad EVR in business decisions are also significantly and positively related to an executive's tenure with the business, an executive being born in Japan, the number of foreign assignments an executive had, globalization of the firm (measured by the number of countries in which the firm owns or operates

TABLE 6

Regression Coefficients on Determinants of Executive Ratings
of Broad and Narrow Employee Representation
in Business Decisions
(standard errors in parentheses)

Independent Variable	Broad EVR	Narrow EVR
Constant	2.12°° (0.78)	2.01°° (0.74)
Executive Age	0.99 (0.62)	0.45 (0.31)
Executive Experience	1.97° (0.84)	1.10 (0.60)
Executive Schooling	− 0.29 (0.16)	− 0.21 (0.12)
Executive Foreign Assignments	2.08° (0.92)	1.77° (0.76)
Executive Country of Origin	1.51° (0.68)	1.39 (0.85)
Executive Ranking of Employees as Stakeholders	2.36°° (0.84)	1.99° (0.81)
Firm Size	0.71 (0.51)	0.51 (0.35)
Firm Age	1.03 (0.64)	1.68° (0.77)
Unionization	− 1.16° (0.47)	− 1.39° (0.62)
Globalization	1.80° (0.82)	1.73° (0.78)
Capital/Labor Ratio	−1.33° (0.60)	−1.44° (0.62)
Economic Sector	1.72° (0.77)	1.05 (0.61)
Home Country of Firm	2.34°° (0.88)	2.29°° (0.85)
N =	491	491
R^2	0.43	0.38

° = Significant at $p = < .05$.
°° = Significant at $p = < .01$.

plants, facilities, or offices), and location of the firm in the manufacturing sector. Senior executive ratings of the importance of EVR are significantly and negatively correlated with the extent of unionism (collective bargaining coverage) in the firm and the firm's capital/labor ratio. Senior executives of firms headquartered in

Japan are significantly more likely than senior executives of firms headquartered in the U.S. to assign high importance ratings to broad EVR in the firm.

Senior executive ratings of the importance of narrow EVR in business decisions via the formal mechanisms of unionization, works councils, or codetermination are significantly and positively correlated with a senior executive's ranking of the importance of employees as a stakeholder group in the firm. Senior executive ratings of the importance of narrow EVR in business decisions are also significantly and positively correlated with the number of foreign assignments experienced by an executive and the globalization of the firm. These findings suggest that personal experience with foreign assignments and expansion of the firm to foreign locations lead to higher senior executive ratings of the importance of narrow EVR in business decisions. Senior executive ratings on the importance of narrow (or formal) EVR in the firm are significantly negatively correlated with the extent of unionism in the firm. Senior executives may believe that employees have effective (perhaps too effective) voice through the union, or they may have soured on EVR because of their experiences with unions, or union environments may be associated with certain kinds of work and technologies that require relatively less EVR. This last interpretation is consistent with the negative sign on the capital/labor ratio in the regression analysis on narrow EVR, although we cannot rule out the possibility that lower cost labor (in terms of blue-collar relative to white-collar and professional labor) is seen by senior executives as requiring more EVR.

As was the case with broad EVR, senior executives of firms headquartered in Japan assign significantly higher ratings to narrow EVR in the firm than do senior executives of firms headquartered in the U.S. Taken together, these two findings seem to provide strong evidence that senior executives of Japanese firms regard EVR as more important than do senior executives of U.S. firms.

Regression analyses were also conducted in which executive ratings of the desirability of several specific forms of EVR—e.g., unionization, codetermination, grievance procedures, and autonomous work teams—in business decisions served as the dependent variables. To summarize without reporting in detail the results of these analyses, senior executive experience with the firm and number of foreign assignments held by a senior executive are significantly and positively associated with the desirability of codetermination and significantly and negatively associated with the desirability of unionization; senior executive age is significantly and negatively correlated with the desirability of autonomous work teams; and globalization of the firm is significantly negatively correlated with the desirability of unionization. It thus appears that an executive's and a firm's exposure to industrial relations systems outside of the home country lead to higher desirability ratings of most forms of EVR, but to lower desirability ratings of unionization as a specific form of EVR. Also, relatively younger senior executives appear to have a stronger preference for autonomous work teams as a form of EVR than do older senior executives.

Senior executives of Japanese firms rate the desirability of most forms of EVR significantly higher than do senior executives of U.S. firms, except in the case of grievance procedures where the relationship is reversed. Among all senior executives of the firms included in this study, however, senior executives' ranking of the importance of employees as stakeholders is significantly and positively associated with senior executive ratings of the desirability of all specific forms of EVR, except unionization and legal challenges to employment-at-will. These findings suggest that senior executives who believe that employees are an important stakeholder group in the firm will have a high rating for the desirability of EVR in the firm. However, senior executives of Japanese firms are less likely than senior executives of U.S. firms to prefer forms of EVR that are most explicitly adversarial or conflict-oriented—in particular, grievance procedures and legal challenges to employment-at-will.

Finally, a set of regression analyses was performed in which senior executive ratings of the desirability of EVR in strategic-level issues and workplace-level issues served as the dependent variables. Strategic-level issues included business acquisition, business divestiture, plant/facility closing, and plant/facility relocation. Workplace-level issues included job design, compensation, job security, and performance appraisal. Separate indices of strategic-level and workplace-level issues were constructed by combining the senior executives' ratings of the desirability of EVR on the scales used to measure each of the four issues in each of the two categories.

The results of these regression analyses are summarized in Table 7 (minus the control variables used in the equations). Senior executive

TABLE 7

Regression Coefficients on Senior Executive Ratings of
the Desirability of Employee Voice and Representation
in Strategic and Workplace-level Issues
(standard errors in parentheses)

Independent Variable	Strategic Issues	Workplace Issues
Executive Rankings of Employees as Stakeholders	1.92° (0.88)	2.02° (0.91)
Home Country of Firm	2.12°° (0.82)	−1.72° (0.77)
N =	491	491
R²	0.41	0.39

° = Significant at p = < .05.
°° = Significant at p = < .01.

ranking of employees as an important stakeholder group was significantly and positively related to senior executive ratings of the desirability of EVR in both strategic-level and workplace-level issues. However, senior executives of Japanese firms had a significantly higher preference than the senior executives of U.S. firms for EVR in strategic-level issues; senior executives of U.S. firms had a significantly higher preference than senior executives of Japanese firms for EVR in workplace-level issues. These findings are especially notable because other factors contributing to senior executive ratings of the desirability of EVR in the firm were controlled—firm characteristics and personal characteristics of the executives. These results thus suggest that strategic choice, as proxied through the executives' rankings of employees as stakeholders, partly explains executives' preferences for EVR. However, the separate effect for home country of the firm suggests that strategic choice also operates through culture.

Discussion and Conclusions

From a U.S. perspective, unionization has historically been the most significant form of EVR in business decisions, though even at its peak modern unionism (during the 1950s) represented only a minority of employees who actually participated in the decisions of firms. Moreover, the scope of issues in which unionized U.S.

employees have been and are represented is relatively narrow, largely confined to immediate workplace issues of pay, work load, job assignments, and other terms and conditions of employment. Unionization as a form of employee representation in the business enterprise emerged, grew, and remained mainly in those businesses where unionized labor represented a major (strike) threat. Today, this threat is seen by business executives and managers to be modest, and the opportunities to avoid or escape unionism are seen by business executives and managers to be large.

Yet, the traditional model of command and control that is found in hierarchical organizations is under attack and appears to be in decline. Senior executives of large enterprises in particular have sought to push responsibility for decision making down to lower organizational levels and members, with self-management and team management having become more popular. Such initiatives as quality circles, quality-of-work-life improvement programs, semi-autonomous and autonomous work teams, joint labor-management committees, project teams, task forces, and the like constitute evidence of this developing movement away from centralized decision making in business enterprises.

Can these new forms of employee involvement in business decisions be regarded as forms of meaningful EVR in the enterprise? For those who believe that voice/representation is synonymous with the election of individuals to represent employees in negotiations with management, the answer is no; for them, representation is elected representation (Aaron 1992; Weiler 1990). For those who believe that employee representation in business decisions is more multifaceted than the "election model" of representation implies, newer forms of employee involvement also provide elements of representation. As the U.S. experience shows, employee representation in business decisions can occur through involvement in team-based organizations (Heckscher 1988; Lawler 1985). Further, grievance procedures and various forms of alternative dispute resolution for nonunion employees as well as wrongful termination challenges to the doctrine of employment-at-will constitute other new forms of employee voice/representation in business decisions—though admittedly forms of after-the-fact representation without collective voice. Whether or not employee voice in the enterprise can be effective without formal representation, especially elected representation, is a question which continues to be debated among industrial relations scholars.

Another question which has been debated among industrial relations scholars is whether or not executives and managers of enterprises exercise strategic choices over human resource/ industrial relations (HR/IR) policy and practice. Much of the research on strategic HR/IR choice is nonempirical (for exceptions, see Kochan and Chalykoff 1986; Fiorito, Lowman, and Nelson 1987; Arthur 1992), and case studies constitute the bulk of the work that has been done in this area to date (see, for example, Verma 1985; Kochan, Katz, and McKersie 1986; Kalwa 1987). This body of work has been criticized for failing to reject the null hypothesis that executives and managers of enterprises largely react to external environmental forces in determining HR/IR policy and practice (Lewin 1987; Block, Roomkin, Kleiner, and Salsburg 1987; Chelius and Dworkin 1990).

The present study has sought to isolate the determinants of strategic choice in EVR by, in effect, holding constant environmental and demographic variables expected to influence such choice. Among the sample of senior executives of U.S. and Japanese firms operating in the U.S. included in this study, the executives of Japanese firms view employees as a more important stakeholder in the firm than do the executives of U.S. firms. Furthermore, senior executives of Japanese firms operating in the U.S. favored EVR in the formulation of business strategy (so-called strategic-level issues), while senior executives of U.S. firms favored EVR in the implementation of business strategy (so-called workplace-level issues). These findings were partly explained by a strategic choice model that proxied choice through stakeholder rankings. There continued to be an effect for home country of the firm, suggesting that strategic choice also operates through culture. Hopefully, the approach and findings of this study will spur wider interest and provide something of an empirical bedrock for future research on strategic choice and EVR and, more generally, research on strategic choice and HR/IR practices and policies.

Endnotes

[1] The idea that business enterprises have an organizational or corporate culture not only emerged during the 1980s, but grew with a vengeance to the point where a majority of large publicly held business enterprises include a statement of organization/corporate culture in their strategic business plans (Nadler, et al. 1992). Such statements typically identified and described the central "values" of the business enterprise, the most prevalent of which were the provision of excellent products and service to the customer, and the high value of employees to the enterprise (most often phrased as "people are our most important asset").

[2] There is considerable variation in the scope of employees, scope of issues, and specific rights vested in works councils, just as there is variation in these respects under unionism, employer-initiated employee involvement programs, and grievance-like procedures in U.S. firms (Bain 1992).

[3] While codetermination legally provides workers with the types of business information that permits them to participate in making long-term strategic decisions for the business enterprise, empirical evidence indicates that such variables as employee directors' technical training, acceptance by other board members, and dual (and possibly split) loyalties to employer and employee organizations significantly influence the long-term versus the short-term orientation of employee directors as well as the scope of issues over which they participate (Bain 1992).

[4] A more complete model of strategic choice and EVR would decompose the coefficients for variables into portions due to (a) strategic choice and (b) simple contingencies.

References

Alchian, Armen A., and Harold Demsetz. 1972. "Production, Information Costs and Economic Organization." *American Economic Review* 62 (December), pp. 777-795.

Ansoff, Igor H. 1988. *The New Corporate Strategy*. New York: John Wiley and Sons.

Aaron, Benjamin. 1992. "Employee Voice: A Legal Perspective." *California Management Review* 34 (Spring), pp. 124-138.

Arthur, Jeffrey B. 1992. "The Link Between Business Strategy and Industrial Relations Systems in Steel Minimills." *Industrial and Labor Relations Review* 45 (April), pp. 488-506.

Bain, Trevor. 1992. "Employee Voice: A Comparative International Perspective," Paper presented to the Forty-Fourth Annual Meeting, Industrial Relations Research Association, New Orleans, LA, January.

Blanchflower, David G., and Richard B. Freeman. 1992. "Unionism in the United States and Other Advanced OECD Countries." *Industrial Relations* 31 (Winter), pp. 56-79.

Blau, Peter W., and Richard W. Scott. 1962. *Formal Organizations*. San Francisco, CA: Chandler.

Block, Richard N., Morris M. Kleiner, Myron Roomkin, and Sidney W. Salsburg. 1987. "Industrial Relations and the Performance of the Firm: An Overview," in *Human Resources and the Performance of the Firm,* eds. M. Kleiner, R. Block, M. Roomkin, and S. Salsburg. Madison, WI: Industrial Relations Research Association, pp. 319-343.

Bognanno, Mario F., and Morris M. Kleiner. 1992. "Introduction: Labor Market Institutions and the Future Role of Unions." *Industrial Relations* 31 (Winter), pp. 1-12.

Boroff, Karen, and David Lewin. 1991. "Loyalty, Voice, and Intent to Exit a Nonunion Firm: A Conceptual and Empirical Analysis." Los Angeles: UCLA Institute of Industrial Relations Working Paper #211, August.

Bureau of National Affairs. 1993. "Union Membership: Proportion of Union Members Declines to Low of 15.8 Percent." *Daily Labor Report* 24 (February 9), pp. B3-B7.

Cappelli, Peter, and Harbir Singh. 1992. "Integrating Strategic Human and Strategic Management," in *Research Frontiers in Industrial Relations and Human Resources,* eds. David Lewin, Olivia S. Mitchell, and Peter D. Sherer. Madison, WI: Industrial Relations Research Association, pp. 165-192.

Chelius, James R., and James B. Dworkin. 1990. *Reflections on the Transformation of Industrial Relations*. New Brunswick, NJ: Institute of Management and Labor Relations, Rutgers University.

Dickens, Linda, Moira Hart, Michael Jones, and Brian Weekes. 1984. "The British Experience Under a Statute Prohibiting Unfair Dismissal." *Industrial and Labor Relations Review* 37 (July), pp. 497-514.

Delaney, John Thomas, David Lewin, and Casey Ichniowski. 1989. *Human Resource Policies and Practices in American Firms.* Washington, D.C.: U.S. Department of Labor, Bureau of Labor-Management Relations and Cooperative Programs, Bulletin #137.

Dore, Ronald. 1973. *British Factory—Japanese Factory: The Origins of National Diversity in Industrial Relations.* Berkeley, CA: University of California Press.

————. 1987. "Japan's version of managerial capitalism." Unpublished manuscript, Department of Political Science, MIT.

————. 1986. *Flexible Rigidities: Industrial Policy and Structural Adjustment in the Japanese Economy, 1970-80.* Stanford, CA: Stanford University Press.

Edwards, Richard C. 1979. *Contested Terrain: The Transformation of the Workplace in the Twentieth Century.* New York: Basic Books.

Feuille, Peter, and John Thomas Delaney. (forthcoming.) "The Individual Pursuit of Organizational Justice: Grievance Procedures in Nonunion Workplaces," in *Research in Personnel and Human Resources Management,* eds. George Farris and Kenneth W. Roland. Greenwich, CT: JAI Press.

Fiorito, Jack, Christopher Lowman, and Forest B. Nelson. 1987. "The Impact of Human Resource Policies on Union Organizing." *Industrial Relations* 26 (Spring), pp. 113-126.

Freeman, Edward, and David Reed. 1983. "Stockholders and Stakeholders: A New Perspective on Corporate Governance." *California Management Review* 25 (Spring), pp. 88-106.

Freeman, Richard B., and James L. Medoff. 1984. *What Do Unions Do?* New York: Basic Books.

Heckscher, Charles C. 1988. *The New Unionism: Employee Involvement in the Changing Corporation.* New York: Basic Books.

Ichniowski, Casey, and David Lewin. 1988. "Characteristics of Grievance Procedures: Evidence From Nonunion, Union, and Double-Breasted Businesses." *Proceedings of the Fortieth Annual Meeting, Industrial Relations Research Association.* Madison, WI: IRRA, pp. 415-424.

Kimberly, John R., Robert H. Miles, and Associates. 1980. *The Organizational Life Cycle.* San Francisco, CA: Jossey-Bass.

Kalwa, Richard W. 1987. "Collective Bargaining in Steel: A Strategic Perspective." *Proceedings of the Thirty-Ninth Annual Meeting, Industrial Relations Research Association.* Madison, WI: IRRA, pp. 257-263.

Kochan, Thomas A., and John Chalykoff. 1986. "The Effects of Corporate Strategy and Workplace Innovations on Union Representation." *Industrial and Labor Relations Review* 39 (July), pp. 487-501.

Kochan, Thomas A., Harry C. Katz, and Robert B. McKersie. 1986. *The Transformation of American Industrial Relations.* New York: Basic Books.

Kotler, Philip and Paul N. Bloom. 1984. *Marketing Professional Services.* Englewood Cliffs, NJ: Prentice-Hall.

Lawler, Edward E., III. 1986. *High-Involvement Management.* San Francisco, CA: Jossey-Bass.

Lewin, David. 1987. "Industrial Relations as a Strategic Variable." in *Human Resources and the Performance of the Firm,* eds. M. Kleiner, R. Block, M. Roomkin, and S. Salsburg. Madison, WI: Industrial Relations Research Association, pp. 1-41.

————. 1990. "Grievance Procedures in Nonunion Workplaces: An Empirical Analysis of Usage, Dynamics, and Outcomes." *Chicago-Kent Law Review* 66(3), pp. 823-844.

Lewin, David, and Daniel J.B. Mitchell. 1992. "Systems of Employee Voice: Theoretical and Empirical Perspectives." *California Management Review* 34 (Spring), pp. 95-111.

Lewin, David, and John Zhuang Yang. 1992. "HRM Policies and Practices of U.S. and Japanese Firms Operating in the U.S." *Proceedings of the Forty-Fourth Annual Meeting, Industrial Relations Research Association.* Madison, WI: IRRA, pp. 344-351.

Nadler, David, Marc S. Gerstein, Robert B. Shaw, and Associates. 1992. *Organizational Architecture: Designs for Changing Organizations*. San Francisco, CA: Jossey-Bass.

Porter, Michael E. 1980. *Competitive Strategy: Techniques for Analyzing Industries and Competitors*. New York: Free Press.

Purcell, John. 1983. "The Management of Industrial Relations in the Modern Corporation: Agenda for Research." *British Journal of Industrial Relations* 21 (March), pp. 1-16.

Rumelt, Richard P. 1984. "Towards a Strategic Theory of the Firm," in *Competitive Strategic Management*, ed. Robert Lamb. Englewood Cliffs, NJ: Prentice-Hall.

Sherer, Peter D., and KyungMook Lee. 1993. "Variation from the Standard-Form Employment Relationship: The Character and Determinants of Risk Involved Teams, Contracting-In Retirees, and Altered-Time Arrangements." Unpublished Manuscript, The Wharton School, University of Pennsylvania.

Simmons, John, and William Mares. 1985. *Working Together: Employee Participation in Action*. New York: New York University Press.

Simon, Herbert A. 1958. *Administrative Behavior*. New York: Free Press.

Strauss, George. 1984. "Industrial Relations: Time of Change." *Industrial Relations* 23 (Winter), pp. 1-15.

Verma, Anil. 1985. "Relative Flow of Capital to Union and Nonunion Plants Within the Same Firm." *Industrial Relations* 24 (Fall), pp. 395-405.

Weiler, Paul C. 1990. *Governing the Workplace: The Future of Labor and Employment Law*. Cambridge, MA: Harvard University Press.

Chapter 8

Employee Representation Through the Political Process

John Delaney and Susan Schwochau
University of Iowa

Fairness at the workplace is important to people. Perceptions of fairness depend both on the outcomes of resource allocation decisions and the procedures used to achieve those outcomes (Sheppard, Lewicki, and Minton 1992; Greenberg 1990). Research on organizational decision processes suggests that employees who are given meaningful input into certain organizational procedures view the process as fairer than employees who have little or no input (Folger and Greenberg 1985). Thus, there appears to be a link between workers' perceptions of fairness and their ability to have input into organizational decision making.

Employees may have input in decision making through direct voice mechanisms or through representatives. The traditional form of representation at work is unionization. Although unionization has been declining for some time, in recent years there has been an increase in the willingness and ability of employers to undertake tactics to avoid unionization (Kochan, Katz, and McKersie 1986) and thwart unionization attempts (Lawler 1990). In addition, there has been a rise in the extent to which government regulation affects workers and the workplace (Weidenbaum 1977), reducing employees' perceived need to seek union representation as a voice mechanism. Unions are formed or joined by fewer and fewer employees because it seems as if the costs of unionization are increasing and the perceived benefits of organizing are declining.

Competitive pressures and the apparent success of management techniques used in other countries have led American employers to

experiment with other mechanisms that provide voice or representation to employees, ranging from communication systems and suggestion boxes to the "team" approach and employee involvement
programs. While the literature is replete with studies of and testimo-
nials to these mechanisms, it is unclear how many employees
actually have these voice or representation mechanisms available to
them (see Delaney, Lewin, and Ichniowski 1989).

Moreover, there are some fundamental differences between
these "newer" forms of voice and representation and unionization
that may affect the degree to which they contribute to employees'
perception of having meaningful input. First, as workplace voice
and representation systems, all but labor unions are established
voluntarily by employers in the U.S. (though individual employees
often may choose whether or not to participate in them). For example, there is no law mandating works councils or employee involvement programs. Second, in many nonunion systems, management
retains final decision-making authority over issues. Thus, employees
may be able to offer opinions, suggestions, or state their interests,
but there is no guarantee that their views will be considered in
formulating outcomes.

This leaves open the possibility that many employees do not
have input in decisions regarding their working environment.
Indeed, one reason why individuals might practice political action is
to ensure that they receive fair treatment at work. Because
employers are not always willing to provide true representation or
voice to workers, the political process is often the only forum that
remains for ensuring the establishment of meaningful self-rule at
work. American employers are legally permitted wide latitude in
how they manage the workplace and employees. Abuse of that
latitude or unresponsiveness to employees' concerns may lead
workers to seek governmentally imposed limits on firms' workplace
discretion. Such limits would be achieved through the political
process. Thus, we examine individuals' and workers' participation
in the political process.

Accordingly, this chapter examines the extent to which individuals use the political process and the methods that they use to
achieve input into the governmental process in general and to
secure self-determination at the workplace in particular. People can
choose to participate directly in the political process or to ignore it
entirely. Direct participation can occur through individual action or

collective action. Individuals choosing to ignore the political process may do so because of indifference, because the costs of direct participation outweigh the benefits, or because existing groups (collectives) provide sufficient representation. We constructed three major data sets to provide information on the extent to which each of these options is employed: One is a random sample of individuals that contains information on their political interests and sentiments; a second data set contains information on key votes in Congress compiled by the AFL-CIO over the years 1977-1991; and the final data set includes information on the political positions and views of a variety of American interest groups. Below, after describing the data sets, we discuss workers' alternatives for securing political representation and we examine the extent to which individuals use these alternatives.

Data

Three major data sets were developed for the analyses. First, to assess individuals' views on various political issues and the extent to which they engage in political action, we created an extract from the General Social Survey (GSS), a government-sponsored annual survey of Americans that focuses on social, demographic, political, and topical issues. The GSS has been administered via face-to-face interviews to a national probability sample of individuals 18 years of age or older each year since 1972 (with the exception of 1979 and 1981).

The GSS survey contains three types of items: (1) "core" items that are included in each year's survey, (2) "secondary" items that are excluded every third or fourth year, and (3) items within special modules that are included only in certain years. Core items include most demographic characteristics, while opinion items fall largely into the "secondary" category. In addition, in several years, a split-half sample design was employed, with each subsample responding to items that were differently worded or differently sequenced within the survey. Because of these characteristics, we have focused on three data years (1985, 1987, and 1990) and have designed our analysis so that variables correspond to identical item wording where respondents were split into subsamples (that is, we have not pooled split samples).

Examination of GSS descriptive statistics for the three years for both the total sample and subsamples of employed individuals indicates that males are generally underrepresented in these samples, and that sample sizes vary by characteristic (for example, in 1990, only 65.5 percent of the participants were asked whether they belonged to a labor union). Despite these limitations, the data permit a crude assessment of the extent to which individuals engage in political efforts to serve their interests and the views and opinions that they have about certain national issues. Although it is unclear whether the GSS samples approximate the American population, the general design of the GSS permits cautious generalizations to be drawn from it. (An Appendix containing the GSS descriptive statistics is available from the authors.)

Second, we collected information on the political issues that unions indicated to be most important over the years 1977-1991. The issues were extracted from the AFL-CIO's annual *Report on Congress*, which rates federal legislators. The ratings are a useful (albeit imperfect) indicator of unions' views and success in Congress. The 1977-1991 time period was selected because it included votes taken during the Carter administration, when Democrats controlled the executive and legislative branches of government, votes taken during the first six years of the Reagan administration, when Republicans controlled the executive branch and the U.S. Senate, and the 1987-1991 period, when Democrats controlled Congress and Republicans controlled the executive branch. In addition, the time period is recent and overlaps with the administration of the GSS. Systematic examination of the political issues emphasized by unions and the extent to which those issues received legislative support can provide insight into whether unions advocate issues of interest to workers generally or to union members and unions specifically.

Third, we developed a data base on political issues emphasized by other interest groups that advocate positions on issues relevant to working people—groups that may compete or cooperate with labor unions. Although there are many organizations active in the political process, we focused on national organizations that are large (and thus have more potential political power), allow any individual to become a member, and charge yearly dues of $50 or less. To gauge the nature and breadth of issues emphasized by these groups, we gathered materials indicating their political positions and conducted interviews with group officials. This information was supplemented with data on the positions of selected groups on key votes published by *Congressional Quarterly*. Comparison of this information with data from the GSS permits us to assess the extent to which these groups advocate interests similar to those expressed by individuals. In turn, this allows speculation about the extent to which these major interest groups serve workers' interests in the political process. Before proceeding with the analysis, however, one caveat is noteworthy.

Workers' political interests are extremely diverse, in part because individuals have interests related and unrelated to work or the workplace. As a result, it would be extremely difficult and probably impossible for one organization to represent workers' political interests in a generic fashion. Even with respect to work-related issues, there is variance in employees' interests. For example, steel import quotas likely increase work for American steelworkers, but may reduce work for American dockworkers. The work interests of employees do not easily lend themselves to a "single issue" approach to political action. (Other issues are more easily separated out, such as gun ownership and control, and give rise to interest groups, such as the National Rifle Association [NRA] that have a simple and single objective.) In some instances, organizations that usually oppose each other work together to achieve an outcome that is perceived to be jointly beneficial. Accordingly, it does not seem appropriate to conceptualize the process of political representation by assuming that some group, such as a union, represents certain employee interests that other interest groups, such as employer organizations, regularly ignore. Instead, it is necessary to identify the positions of a variety of interest groups on work-related and other political issues and to ascertain whether those positions generally coincide with the views of workers.

Individuals, the Political Process, and Employee Representation

In a democracy, individuals have three primary options for representing their interests in the political process. First, they can attempt to serve their own interests by gathering information, lobbying, and engaging in political activities on an individual basis. They can use their right to vote to select candidates that they as individuals believe would serve their (or society's) best interest.

This is the principle of democracy, where individuals use their informed judgment to select and monitor officials. This ideal is not always met in reality, however, because some individuals may feel that their vote does not matter. This feeling may be particularly great for individuals who are not similar to the "average voter." Indeed, the notion that it is not rational for an individual to vote in elections has been well developed in the academic literature (see Knoke 1986; Downs 1957).

Second, individuals may choose to band together in organizations or associations made up of people having similar interests. For example, individuals can join unions, trade and professional associations, political organizations, and a wide variety of special interest groups that are involved in politics. These organizations can then engage in political action with the strength of numbers that make politicians pay more attention to them than they might to any individual citizen acting alone. To some extent, an individual may be able to express his or her voice more powerfully through an organization of similar individuals and this may increase the likelihood that the individual's political preferences are expressed in government decisions. People who are not similar to the "average voter" may be especially willing to express themselves through organizations because they may see collective action as the only way to realize their preferences (see Knoke 1990).

Third, individuals may choose to abandon the political process altogether as a waste of their time. If people feel that there is no difference between candidates on average or that it does not matter who gets elected anyway, they may opt to ignore voting and political citizenship. Such people may feel that existing interest groups will protect their interests without their active participation or that no one looks out for them anyway. Regardless of which view is held, however, the withdrawal of voters from the political process makes the actions of interest groups, associations, and organizations more important in the political arena. This occurs because the withdrawal of voters from political citizenship reduces the spectrum of views that the average elected official is exposed to and increases the dependence of politicians on the groups that are active in the political process. Examination of information on the political activities of individuals and selected work-related organizations will shed light onto the political options chosen by individuals and the representation that they receive as a result of their choices.

Individuals' Interest in Politics and Participation in Political Processes

To assess individuals' and workers' participation in the political process, we focus on GSS data collected in 1987. In that year, the survey included a social and political participation module that asked participants about their membership in various organizations and the extent to which they had engaged in different political activities. Where information was not available in the 1987 data, we report statistics for 1985. Respondents to each survey are similar in age, education, gender, race and religious affiliation. Although the 1987 sample contains a larger percentage of union members than the 1985 sample (15.5 percent versus 13.9 percent), the difference is not statistically significant. About 80 percent of respondents in the samples of employed persons held full-time jobs. Those not employed were primarily retired persons and persons "keeping house."

We have argued that individuals may express their views in three ways: by individual action (such as voting, contributing to campaigns, lobbying, and working on behalf of candidates in elections); by collective action (joining existing groups, or forming new collectives); or by allowing the actions of other individuals and collectives to provide representation for them (free riding). Two preconditions appear necessary if individuals are to participate directly in political processes. First, individuals must have some interest in politics or national affairs. Absent such interest, a person would likely ignore political participation. Second, individuals must perceive that involvement leads to some benefit—that political action on their part is worthwhile.

Preconditions for Political Participation

Interest in politics. We use several GSS variables to assess interest in politics or national affairs. One of the items in the 1987 survey queried participants on how interested they were in these subjects. Responses were coded on a four-point scale ranging from "very interested" to "not interested." Because of the social response bias likely inherent in these data, we also examined whether survey participants could name the governor of the state in which they resided, the congressional representative from their district, and the head of their local school system. Table 1 reports results of these analyses.

TABLE 1

GSS Respondents' Interest in Politics, 1987[a]

Political Variables	Total Sample	Employed	Not Employed	Non-Members[b]	Union Members[b]
Interest in politics					
Very interested	23.0	23.3	22.6	23.9	20.2
Somewhat interested	42.6	44.3	39.6	44.2	44.8
Only slightly interested	25.8	25.5	26.3	24.9	28.4
Not interested	8.4	6.9	11.2	7.0	6.6
Don't know	.1	0.0	.4	0.0	0.0
Sample size	1,459	941	518	756	183
Governor's name?					
Correct answer	79.1	82.3	73.3	81.2	86.9
Incorrect answer or doesn't know	20.9	17.7	26.7	18.8	13.1
Sample size	1,455	939	516	754	183
Congressman's name?					
Correct answer	37.6	37.4	38.0	36.9	39.3
Incorrect answer or doesn't know	62.3	62.6	62.0	63.1	60.7
Sample size	1,433	925	508	740	183
Head of the local school system?					
Correct answer[c]	31.8	32.4	30.8	31.9	34.4
Incorrect answer or doesn't know	68.2	67.6	69.2	68.1	65.6
Sample size	1,440	930	510	745	183
Political Efficacy Score					
Mean	3.948 (2.685)	4.020 (2.729)	3.796 (2.588)	3.980 (2.707)	3.778 (2.600)
Sample size	654	443	211	547	90

Notes:

[a] Table entries are percentages unless otherwise noted. Data for Political Efficacy score are from 1985. Political Efficacy Score standard deviations are in parentheses.

[b] Union members and nonmembers include only employed individuals.

[c] Name of school superintendent or head of school board counted as correct.

On average, respondents to the 1987 survey were "somewhat interested" in politics or national affairs (42.6 percent gave that response). Only 23 percent of the respondents indicated they were "very interested" while another 25.8 percent said they were "only slightly interested." Employed respondents indicated more interest than those not employed. A significantly larger percentage of employed individuals said they were somewhat interested in politics (Z = 1.74, p < .10), while a significantly smaller percentage said they were not interested in politics (6.9 percent relative to 11.2 percent of those not employed; Z = 2.83, p < .01). Employed respondents were also more likely to know the governor's name (82.3 percent to 73.3 percent; Z = 4.04, p < .01). In general, just over one-third of the sample knew their representative's name, and slightly less than one-third knew the name of the head of the local school system. There were no differences between the employed and those not employed on these variables. Interestingly, only 19.1 percent of the GSS respondents could correctly name all three political representatives.

Perceived value of political action. To assess individuals' perceptions of the value of political action, we constructed a "political efficacy" measure using 10 items from the 1985 GSS survey (no information on this construct was available in the 1987 data). GSS respondents were asked whether they agreed or disagreed with statements such as "The public has little control over what politicians do in office," "The average citizen has considerable influence on politics," and "The government is generally responsive to public opinion." Responses to these items were recoded so that agreement equalled one and disagreement or "can't choose" equalled zero. Two items were reverse coded so that larger values corresponded to perceptions of benefits to political activity. The responses were then summed to foi ı a political efficacy scale ($\alpha = .77$), which is also presented in Table 1.

Respondents to the 1985 sample had fairly low scores on the political efficacy scale. The average score for the sample was 3.95 out of a maximum possible score of 10. Employed respondents had a somewhat higher score (4.02) than those not employed (3.80), but the difference was not statistically significant.

Implications. Overall, findings relevant to each of the preconditions for political action suggest that the average individual in the GSS is not likely to be politically active. Though most say they are at least slightly interested in politics, over 20 percent could not correctly identify the governor of their state, and two-thirds of the respondents could not name their representative to Congress. In general, there seems to be more disagreement than agreement with statements indicating the value of individuals' political action. The relatively low scores on the political efficacy scale suggest a fair amount of disillusionment among respondents. Other GSS data may be used to verify the conclusion that Americans, on their own, are unlikely to participate actively in the political process.

Political Participation of Individuals

To assess the extent to which individuals engage in political action, we examined responses to six items in the 1987 GSS. The pattern of responses in Table 2 generally confirms that individuals are not politically active. Over half of the respondents indicated they never try to sway another person's vote, and 72.8 percent said they had never done any other work (outside of swaying votes) for one of the parties or candidates in elections. Only 19.1 percent of the total sample had attended a political rally or meeting in the last three or four years, and only 22.9 percent indicated they had contributed money to a political party, cause, or candidate in the same period. About 35 percent of the respondents said they had personally gone to see, spoken to, or written to some member of local government on some need or problem, and about 30 percent indicated they had done such lobbying at higher levels of government.

Closer analysis indicates that employed persons are more politically active than those not employed. While employed individuals were no more likely to work in elections, they were more likely than those not employed to say they often try to sway another person's vote ($Z = 1.74$, $p < .10$); to have attended political rallies ($Z = 3.02$, $p < .01$); to have contributed money ($Z = 3.13$, $p < .01$); and to have lobbied at both the local level ($Z = 2.76$, $p < .01$) and levels above the local government ($Z = 4.51$, $p < .01$).

If these data are combined with the fact that only about half of the eligible population votes in presidential elections (and that turnout is even lower in off-year elections), it is reasonable to conclude that large segments of the population do not express political opinion through individual action (see Abramson and Claggett 1991). Moreover, it is not surprising that individuals are less likely to lobby or work for candidates than to vote in elections, given the additional costs involved (particularly in the form of opportunity costs).

The GSS also provided limited data on the extent to which individuals join existing organizations or form new collectives. Participants in the 1987 survey were asked if they belonged to any

TABLE 2

Individuals' Political Activities, 1987[a]

Political Variables	Total Sample	Employed	Not Employed	Non- Members	Union Members
SWAY					
Often	9.5	10.5	7.7	10.4	11.4
Sometimes	22.4	23.1	21.1	23.1	22.8
Rarely	14.1	16.2	10.4	15.5	19.0
Never	53.9	50.2	60.7	51.0	46.7
Sample size	1,456	939	517	753	184
WORKELC					
Most elections	2.6	2.9	2.1	2.9	2.7
Some elections	9.7	9.0	10.8	9.0	9.2
Only a few	14.9	15.5	13.7	14.2	20.7
Never	72.8	72.6	73.3	73.9	67.4
Sample size	1,457	940	517	754	184
RALLIES					
Yes	19.1	21.4	14.9	20.7	23.9
Sample size	1,456	941	516	755	184
MONEY					
Yes	22.9	25.4	18.2	25.2	26.6
Sample size	1,457	941	516	755	184
LOCLOB					
Yes	34.8	37.4	30.2	37.2	38.0
Sample size	1,458	941	517	755	184
OTHLOB					
Yes	29.8	33.8	22.5	33.4	35.3
Sample size	1,457	941	516	755	184

Notes:

[a] Table entries are percentages unless otherwise noted.

SWAY - "During elections, do you ever try to show people why they should vote for one of the parties or candidates? Do you do that often, sometimes, rarely, or never?"

WORKELC - "Have you done (other) work for one of the parties or candidates in most elections, some elections, only a few, or have you never done such work?"

RALLIES - "In the past three or four years, have you attended any political meetings or rallies?"

MONEY - "In the past three or four years, have you contributed money to a political party or candidate or to any other political cause?"

LOCLOB - "Have you ever personally gone to see, or spoken to, or written to—some members of local government or some other person of influence in the community about some needs or problems?"

OTHLOB - "What about some representatives or governmental officials outside of the local community—on the county, state or national level? Have you ever contacted or written to such a person on some need or problem?"

of 16 different types of organizations, including political clubs, sports groups, church-affiliated groups, labor unions, veterans' groups, professional or academic societies, and "any other group" (complete results are available from the authors). In this context, "organizations" referred to groups that had characteristics such as newsletters, dues, and meetings. Of the 16 different groups, respondents were most likely to say they belonged to church-affiliated groups (30.4 percent), sports groups (19.0 percent) and labor unions (15.7 percent). Only 4.4 percent of the total sample indicated membership in political clubs. Only nationality groups and farm organizations had smaller membership percentages than political organizations.

About 31 percent of the sample did not belong to any group. Employed individuals were more likely to say they belonged to at least one organization (73.9 percent) than those not employed (59.1 percent; Z = 5.83, p < .01). Only for church-affiliated groups were the not employed more likely than employed persons to report membership. There were no differences between the employed and those not employed in the percentage indicating membership in political clubs. On average, individuals belonged to 1.68 groups. Of those belonging to at least one group, the average was 2.45 group memberships.

These data suggest that while a majority of individuals belong to some organization, the organizations to which they belong are typically related to work (professional or academic societies, unions), to religious affiliation, or to leisure activities (sports groups, hobby/garden clubs, literary or art groups). The findings are consistent with the reasons given by nearly 4,400 people surveyed by Knoke (1990, 124-27) as to why they belonged to one or more of a wide variety of American associations. Although some organizations may engage in political activities, it is noteworthy that few individuals belonged to organizations solely devoted to political action—that is, political clubs.

GSS respondents were also asked about their efforts to solve local problems. While data regarding formation of groups intended to lobby at the federal level are unavailable, individuals were asked whether they had taken part in the formation of a new organization or group to solve a community problem. We examined this item to assess individuals' general willingness to form collectives. Only 17.2 percent of the total sample had taken part in the establishment of a new group or organization. Employed people were more likely to have engaged in such activity (19.2 percent) than those not employed (13.5 percent; $Z = 2.76$, $p < .01$).

In short, although individuals can express political opinions in any of three ways, GSS data strongly suggest that one approach predominates. Neither individual political activities nor collective political efforts, through an existing group or the formation of a new group, are widely employed. Instead, the average GSS respondent is politically inactive—the average individual allows others who are politically active to speak for him or her. This may be due to a lack of sufficient interest (though relatively few GSS respondents expressed *no* interest in politics), or to the perception that the benefits of political action do not outweigh its costs. Although employed persons are more likely to engage in political activities than those who are not employed, the data still suggest that the average person does not seek voice individually or form groups to secure it. That the average individual avoids the political process clearly allows active individuals and groups effectively to have a "larger voice" on issues important to them that arise in political arenas.

Union Involvement in the Political Process

Many interest groups are involved in the American political process. In 1991 there were more than 14,500 registered lobbyists in Washington, D.C. (Close, Bologna, and McCormick 1991) and thousands more in state capitals around the nation. The information provided in the GSS suggests that many individuals, employed and not employed, choose not to directly participate in political processes. This choice may be seen as rational if existing interest groups adequately represented their views in political arenas.

As a vehicle for employee representation, unions are unique in that they are active in both the workplace and the political arena. Unions in the United States are primarily collective bargaining organizations. Although there is some evidence that workers consider political instrumentality when deciding whether or not to join a union (Fiorito 1987), political activity is usually considered to be secondary to bargaining in the industrial relations literature (see Masters and Delaney 1987b). Nonetheless, the American labor movement has long claimed to represent the political interests of working people generally (see Rehmus, McLaughlin, and Nesbitt 1978). While some observers have disputed this claim, insisting that labor serves its own interests in the political process (Heldman and Knight 1980), others have shown union political action to have broad emphases (Masters and Delaney 1987a; Rehmus et al. 1978). Further, debate about union political efforts has been amplified by an absence of relevant research (for a review, see Masters and Delaney 1987b). Accordingly, we have compiled information on unions' legislative efforts over the years 1977-1991 to identify political issues recently emphasized by the union movement. To the extent that available data permit, we also speculate as to whether or not organized labor has achieved its political objectives.

Our primary source of data on union legislative emphasis is the *AFL-CIO News*. In its newspaper, the AFL-CIO regularly publishes articles and reports on political issues and voting records of members of Congress. The analysis relies on two different types of information. The primary data are the legislative issues used to rate the extent to which members of Congress were "friends of labor" during the years 1977-1991. These issues are a useful starting point because the AFL-CIO urges union members to base their voting decisions on the legislative records of elected officials. In addition, issue selection biases that might be introduced by researchers are minimized because the AFL-CIO selects the important labor issues. A recent time period was examined to ensure that the issues emphasized by unions are timely and the data cover three presidential administrations to increase the representativeness of the ratings.

The secondary data are legislative issues indicated by the AFL-CIO to be of most concern during the 1990s. These issues are reported in the *AFL-CIO News* in part to galvanize rank-and-file lobbying activities. We supplement the legislative ratings data with these legislative concerns because the list of concerns tends to be somewhat broader than the legislative ratings information; some issues of interest to unions do not make it to the floor of Congress for a vote. Consequently, examination and comparison of these union data provide much insight into the political issues foremost in the minds of American union leaders. These data, however, are not without problems.

First, the data are published by the AFL-CIO, but may not represent the position of every U.S. union. It has been reported that in a few cases individual unions take conflicting positions on issues (Masters and Delaney 1987a). More importantly, certain issues (such as prevailing wage laws) are more important to some unions than others, and thus an examination of AFL-CIO ratings may not accurately reflect the perspectives of specific unions. While research shows that these data reflect the views of the labor movement in general, caution must be exercised in generalizing the results to specific unions.

Second, the willingness of unions to raise issues in Congress is influenced by the existing political climate. Unions are usually unwilling to raise certain issues at times when Congress seems unfriendly to the position that labor endorses. Moreover, the political climate likely influences the nature of the issues raised in Congress to which unions are forced to respond. For example, unions appear to raise different issues during a "friendly" administration than during an "unfriendly" one (Masters and Delaney 1987a).

Third, the legislative ratings and concerns data presented by the AFL-CIO are self-selected. While this reduces researcher-introduced bias, there is a possibility that issues were selected to project a certain image of success (that is, certain roll calls could be selected or excluded to inflate or deflate the legislative success ratings—what has been termed "the ratings game"). This is confounded by the fact that any manipulation of issues rated is probably not constant over time. In essence, the data present a broad picture of union legislative concerns, but one that is not amenable to precise statistical analysis.

Fourth, efforts to keep legislation or issues in committee and off the floor of Congress can be critical to unions' ability to secure its political interests. But such efforts do not appear in published legislative ratings. To the extent that the published ratings diverge from the behind-the-scenes work done by union lobbyists, the ratings may not be perfectly correlated with labor's political efforts. As better data are not available, we turn to an examination of legislative ratings to develop a picture of union political efforts.

Union Legislative Priorities, 1977-1991

Ratings of Legislators' Votes. Table 3 reports a summary of the 485 congressional votes used by the AFL-CIO to rate legislators during the years 1977-1991. (An Appendix reporting the data summarized in Table 3 is available from the authors.) The pattern of results in the table suggests some interesting observations about

TABLE 3
Unions' Legislative Issues, 1977-1991

Legislative Issues by Category	U.S. House of Representatives				U.S. Senate			
	Number of Occurrences	% of Total	Number Won by Labor	% Won	Number of Occurrences	% of Total	Number Won by Labor	% Won
Enhancements of Workers' Rights and Protections	21	8.6%	13	61.9%	25	10.4	8	32.0%
Limitations on Workers' Rights and Protections	37	15.2	30	81.1	44	18.3	27	61.4
Enhancements of Union Interests and Rights	10	4.1	8	80.0	8	3.3	2	25.0
Limitations on Union Interests and Rights	8	3.3	7	87.5	11	4.6	10	90.9
Other Union Interests	6	2.4	4	66.7	6	2.5	4	66.7
Trade and Economic Issues	48	19.7	32	66.7	27	11.2	15	55.6
International Issues	9	3.7	9	100.0	11	4.6	5	45.5
Tax Policy	9	3.7	2	22.2	14	5.8	4	28.6
Social Security	3	1.2	0	0.0	9	3.7	1	11.1
Budget Policy	21	8.6	10	47.6	15	6.2	7	46.7
Energy Policy	12	4.9	8	66.7	11	4.6	6	54.5
Social Issues	48	19.7	37	77.1	41	17.0	19	46.3
Environmental Issues	4	1.6	2	50.0	3	1.2	2	66.7
Other Governmental Issues	8	3.3	5	62.5	16	6.6	5	31.3
All Issues	244	100.0	167	68.4	241	100.0	115	47.7

union legislative priorities and unions' success in achieving those priorities.

First, unions have focused on a wide variety of issues in their legislative ratings. Issues explicitly related to the priorities of unions and unionized workers comprised 39 percent of the issues rated in the U.S. House of Representatives and 42 percent of the issues rated in the U.S. Senate. More than half of the votes included in the legislative ratings were indirectly related to unions (for example, votes on jobs legislation) or unrelated to unions (for example, votes on voter registration reforms or sanctions against South Africa). Labor also took positions supporting the interests of those members of American society who are least well off (for example, the AFL-CIO opposed Reagan administration efforts to cut food stamps benefits for the poor). Nearly 20 percent of the votes rated in each chamber of Congress involved social issues. On the other hand, unions advocated positions on many bills that affected the job interests of workers and union members directly or indirectly. For example, 20 percent of the votes in the House and 11 percent of the votes in the Senate involved trade or economic issues. With regard to those issues, the AFL-CIO has consistently endorsed positions supporting the preservation of American jobs and the use of "fair trade" practices by other countries. Overall, however, unions seem to emphasize issues related to unions and to workers' job interests.

Second, issues specifically connected with union interests can be divided into votes on bills extending or enhancing the rights of workers and unions, and bills restricting or eliminating existing rights enjoyed by workers and unions. Taking this division into account, nearly 60 percent of the votes involving explicit union interests were on bills that would have imposed new limitations on workers or unions (55 percent in the House and 59 percent in the Senate). Moreover, the percentage of votes on union-related issues that would impose new restrictions rose after the election of President Reagan. As a result, while labor's political efforts helped defeat most attempts to impose restrictions, unions have been in a defensive mode in Washington for the past decade.

Third, there is a difference across the chambers of Congress in the extent to which union-favored positions have been achieved in the votes comprising the legislative ratings. Overall, unions "won" 68 percent of the votes rated in the U.S. House and 48 percent of the votes rated in the U.S. Senate. The disparity is most obvious during the years 1979-1986, a period when the Labor Law Reform Act was defeated during the last two years of the Carter administration and when Republicans held control of the Senate from 1981-1986. Even when Democrats were in control of the Senate and the union position was supported by a majority of senators, many union-supported bills were defeated by filibusters (which require 60 votes to invoke cloture on debate). For example, in 1978, a prolonged filibuster prevented a vote on the Labor Law Reform Act, which, among other things, would have made changes in the National Labor Relations Act to lessen employers' ability to cause delays in the election process. Partly because of defeats in the Senate, unions have had very little success in securing enhancements or extensions of union-related legislation in recent years. At the same time, support in the House of Representatives has ensured that existing rights of unions or workers have not been restricted.

Fourth, even when labor-backed bills have been passed by both chambers of Congress, presidential vetoes have regularly prevented them from becoming law. For example, nearly four years passed (January 1989-October 1992) before Congress was able to override any of President Bush's vetoes. As a result, the union "win" rates reported in Table 3 overstate the extent to which labor-backed bills have become law and hence the extent to which unions have won political battles.

Fifth, some specific issues not broken out in Table 3 reveal interesting insight into the political efforts of labor. The three most frequent types of votes rated involved prevailing wage laws (26 votes involving the Davis-Bacon or Service Contract Acts), omnibus budget bills (26 votes, especially during President Reagan's first term), and "Jobs" legislation (21 votes). Prevailing wage laws have been bitterly contested in recent years, to some extent becoming a symbol of unions that is under attack. Union-backed positions on such laws have prevailed in almost every vote (23 of 26), but that success has seemed only to inspire more frequent challenges to prevailing rates. The position of unions on jobs bills has prevailed in most cases too (15 of 26 votes), though key failures on other bills that affect American jobs (such as losing the "fast track" vote on the North American Free Trade Agreement—technically a "trade" bill) suggest that the record overstates unions' ability to secure legislation protecting American workers' jobs. In contrast, unions have been less successful on omnibus budget bills, winning 11 of 26 votes.

Because many of those bills contained budget reductions and rearranged budget priorities in a way that unions did not support (such as increasing spending on defense and reducing spending on social and entitlement programs), the inability to achieve success on them was a clear defeat for the labor movement.

Finally, during the 1977-1991 period several attempts were made to reduce the political activity of unions and to maintain restrictions on the political activities of certain public employees. Votes on such measures occurred 16 times. The AFL-CIO opposed restrictions on the political activities of any worker in all cases, and the union position prevailed 12 times (75 percent of the cases). While the union movement was able to prevent an erosion of its political rights over the years studied, there is ongoing pressure to reduce unions' political power, and that pressure threatens organized labor's ability to remain a strong political force. For example, in response to the Supreme Court's decision in the *Beck* case (*Communications Workers of America v. Beck* 487 U.S. 735 [1988]), President Bush issued an executive order requiring federal contractors to post notices that nonmembers who are covered by a collective bargaining agreement have the right to request a refund of union dues that are spent on activities unrelated to collective bargaining. Moreover, *Beck* and other recent court decisions have imposed restrictions on unions' political spending, but have not similarly restricted corporate political spending (see Delaney 1991).

In general, Table 3 suggests that the American labor movement supports a broad array of legislative issues and has had mixed success in its political efforts. Unions have taken positions on many issues that do not directly benefit organized labor; those positions often benefit the job interests of workers or the general interests of disadvantaged segments of society. Unions have been more successful in the House and when they are attempting to protect existing rights than they have been in the Senate or when they have attempted to extend existing rights or secure new rights. It is clear, however, that the performance reflected in Table 3 is an overstatement of union success, in part because the table does not reflect the actions of the executive branch of government.

The legislative agenda proposed by the AFL-CIO at the start of 1991 included 42 widely ranging issues (AFL-CIO 1991). In addition to the type of bills included in unions' legislative ratings, organized labor was interested in legislation involving asbestos removal, national minimum collective bargaining rights for public employees, revision of the National Labor Relations Act, restrictions on employers' right to monitor employees electronically at work, universal health coverage for all Americans, and elimination of Hatch Act restrictions on federal employees' political activities. The breakdown of issues was generally similar to the categorization presented in Table 3. Although many of the legislative issues would directly or indirectly benefit unionized workers or unions if enacted into law, examination of the full list shows that unions publicly advocated a variety of issues that benefit others, especially working-class people, members of protected classes, and the poor. Consistent with patterns of results in the 1980s, however, unions had little success in achieving their legislative agenda in 1991.

Individuals' Views on Selected Political Issues

If workers are to rely on the AFL-CIO to represent their interests, then it is necessary for organized labor's political positions to be consistent with employees' views on political issues. Therefore, it is useful to examine questions in the GSS that indicate individuals' positions on selected issues. This examination relies primarily on the 1985 and 1990 data samples, though some information in the 1987 sample is relevant to the analysis. The GSS included several items tapping individuals' views on issues such as abortion, government spending priorities, capital punishment, and gun control. Interest groups regularly take positions on some of these issues.

The GSS responses are not directly comparable to the published preferences and ratings of interest groups because GSS respondents were asked questions that differed from the measures rated by groups such as the AFL-CIO and the GSS sampling design systematically excluded sets of questions from subsets of the participants. A cautious use of the GSS, however, provides a crude picture of the views of individuals generally and workers particularly on a broad array of issues.

Jobs. GSS respondents seemed to favor a limited role of government in the job creation process. In 1985 and 1990, a majority of them said it probably or definitely should not be the government's responsibility to provide a job for everyone who wants one. Of those not employed, 53.5 percent expressed this opinion in 1985, while 47.2 percent did so in 1990. A significantly larger percentage of the employed sample (66.6 percent in 1985 [Z = 3.26, p < .01] and 57 percent in 1990 [Z = 3.21, p < .01]) voiced this opinion. But other results indicate that nearly 70 percent of the respondents were in favor of government financing of projects to create jobs. In the total samples and each subsample, a larger percentage of respondents favored government support of declining industries to protect jobs than opposed such support.

Government regulation and support of industry. The modal response for both the total samples and the employment-status subsamples was to favor less government regulation of business. Interestingly, between 1985 and 1990, there appears to have been a sizeable change in the percentage of the total sample indicating support for deregulation. By 1990, a significantly larger percentage of the employed sample than the not employed sample indicated opposition to deregulation (20.1 percent to 15.7 percent; Z = 1.85, p < .10). Over two-thirds of respondents in all samples favored government support of industry to develop new products and technology, though working people were significantly more likely to express this sentiment than those not employed in 1990 (Z = 3.30, p < .01).

Government Spending. Over three-fourths of all respondents favored cuts in government spending. Over time, however, the percentage of the total sample favoring such cuts declined. Moreover, individuals generally favored spending on certain issues. For example, when asked about Social Security, retirement benefits, health care, education, law enforcement, drug rehabilitation, and aid to the poor, individuals were most likely to respond that government was spending too little. In many cases, differences of opinion existed between those who were employed and those who were not employed. In each year, and for each question, employed individuals were more likely than those not employed to favor increased spending on education. Further, a majority of GSS respondents indicated that the government should spend more on the environment, even if such spending meant that taxes had to rise. Between 1985 and 1990, support for government spending on the environment increased substantially. Employed individuals were always more likely than those not employed to say that the government should spend more in this area (the difference was statistically significant in all cases except one of the 1985 subsamples). These findings reflect the paradox that lawmakers face today, as individuals indicate a preference for less government spending in general at the same time that they want more spending on programs they favor. On the other hand, there was sentiment among GSS respondents for spending cuts in some areas, especially national defense and aid to foreign countries.

"Moral" Issues. The average GSS respondent does not have a consistent liberal or conservative ideology, especially when responses to questions about "moral" issues are examined. Some results suggest that respondents are conservative. For example, on average, a substantial majority of respondents favored the death penalty, with employed individuals significantly more likely to favor capital punishment than those not employed in 1987 ($Z = 2.82$, $p < .01$) and 1990 ($Z = 2.12$, $p < .05$). Similarly, a majority of respondents seemed to favor prayer in public schools and employed persons were significantly more likely than those not employed to hold such views in each year. On average, GSS respondents favored some limits on the ability of a woman to receive an abortion, though employed persons were significantly less likely than those not employed to favor such restrictions in each year (1985, $Z = 3.48$, $p < .01$; 1987, $Z = 4.97$, $p < .01$; 1990, $Z = 3.15$, $p < .01$). And while GSS respondents generally opposed busing, employed individuals were slightly, though insignificantly, more likely to favor busing than those not employed.

On the other hand, results suggest that respondents hold some liberal positions. Nearly eight of ten respondents favored a law requiring a police permit in order to purchase a handgun. In each year, however, working people were less likely to favor gun control than those not employed (the difference was significant in 1985). Further, about six out of ten respondents believed that "people with high incomes should pay a larger share of their income in taxes than those with low incomes."

Comparing Political Views of Workers and the AFL-CIO. Some of the questions asked to individuals surveyed in the GSS addressed issues or bills that were of interest to organized labor in its legislative ratings. Again, it is not possible to make precise comparisons because questions asked to individuals and votes rated by organized labor were not exactly similar. It is possible, however, to make some careful comparisons of selected issues and votes. GSS respondents' views on spending for various purposes, for example, may be compared to AFL-CIO ratings. In general, a great majority of GSS respondents (nearly 90 percent) opposed reductions in spending for highways and bridges, a position echoed by the AFL-CIO in its ratings of various highway appropriations measures. At least 75 percent of GSS respondents in each data year indicated that the amount spent on mass transportation was too little or about right. This view is consistent with organized labor's consistent opposition to votes proposing cuts in mass transit. Consistency of opinion can also be seen on the subject of social security. Nearly 90 percent of GSS respondents in each year agreed that spending on Social Security was either too little or about right. In a question worded slightly differently, more than 40 percent of respondents indicated that more should be spent on social security, even if it meant that taxes had to be increased. These positions were very consistent with AFL-CIO efforts in the 1980s to restore cost of living adjustments to social security payments and with union opposition to President Reagan's proposed cuts in social security. Overall, it appears that there is general consistency between the positions of individuals, especially working people, and organized labor on a wide variety of issues.

Given the decline in union membership and the imposition of restrictions on union political activities by the courts, it is necessary to examine alternative forms of political representation that may serve as substitutes for union activities. To gain perspective on the extent to which different interest groups represent the views of American workers, we turn to an analysis of nonlabor groups having interests that may overlap with workers.

The Political Involvement of Other Interest Groups

To determine the scope of issues advocated by prominent interest groups, we examined information on selected organizations that employed registered congressional lobbyists (Foundation for Public Affairs 1988). Specifically, because many interest groups seek to influence public policy, we focused on organizations that indicated an interest in issues relevant to working people and had no membership restrictions. As a result, some organizations (such as the National Rifle Association) were excluded because their stated objectives were narrow (gun ownership). The method produced an initial list of 76 associations. Organizations that seemed inaccessible to individuals were then eliminated. For example, associations of companies or employers (such as the National Association of Manufacturers) were eliminated, as were "think tanks" (such as the Hoover Institution) and groups that charged excessive dues (such as Health Research Group—$20,000 annual dues—or Catalyst—$190,000 annual dues). This produced a list of 39 associations that varied greatly in membership size (from 750—Americans for Generational Equity—to 31 million—American Association of Retired Persons or AARP) and interest orientations.

    To isolate major interest groups, we restricted the sample to the 19 associations that had at least 100,000 members or published ratings of U.S. legislators. We conducted telephone interviews of an official of each of the associations that had working telephone numbers. In the interviews, which lasted from 15 minutes to one hour, we requested information on each group's purpose, focal issues, size, structure, tax status, method of operation, funding sources, dues structure, and publications, as well as the official's estimate of the effectiveness and political orientation of the group. In addition, we asked groups that published ratings of lawmakers to send us a copy of recent ratings. While this approach did not produce an exhaustive list of relevant associations, we believe that the final sample is representative of major nonunion interest groups. Selected results are presented in Table 4.

    The data in Table 4 suggest several observations. First, relatively few Americans are members of these major associations. About 43 million people belong to the 16 organizations listed in the table, though 31 million of them are members of one organization, the American Association of Retired Persons (AARP). Assuming that membership across these organizations is mutually exclusive, about 15 percent of Americans belong to these national organizations. Even if it is assumed that comparable numbers of Americans who do not belong to these organizations belong to smaller national associations and to local groups, the data suggest that a large majority of Americans are not members of associations that emphasize work-related issues.

    Second, to achieve its objectives, each of the organizations listed in Table 4 emphasizes activities that are political in nature, including lobbying, grass roots organizing, political polling, and media campaigns. Many of the associations have ideological orientations (liberal or conservative). This may allow a small number

TABLE 4
Selected Interest Groups Involved in the Political Process

Interest Group	Members (thousands)	Staff Size	Yearly Dues	Membership Requirements	Political Orientation	Publish Ratings	Method of Operation	Current Political Issues
AARP	31,000	1,300	$ 5	Age 50+	Neutral/Issue	No	Lobbying, ads	Age discrimination, health care
Citizen Action	3,000	20	$ 5	None	Liberal/Issue	Some	Grass roots	Health care, toxic waste
American Legion	2,900	246	$17	Veteran	Neutral/Issue	No	Lobbying, polls	Aging veterans, youth programs
National RTW Committee	1,750	64	Free	None	Conservative	Some	Legal help, ads	Hobbs Act, RTW, political spending
U.S. PIRG	1,500	12	$25	None	Neutral	No	Lobbying, polls	Campaign reform, toxic waste
Amnesty International	400 (U.S.) 1,100 (Total)	79	$25	None	Neutral/Liberal	No	Demonstrations	Human rights, torture
NAACP	500	100	$10	None	Liberal	No	Lobbying	Economic development, EEO
Clean Water Action Project	400	60	$24	None	Consumer	Some	Polls, lobbying	Toxic wastes, right to know laws
People For the American Way	270	80	$15	None	Liberal	No	Local help, ads	Education, First amendment rights
NOW	252	28	$30	None	Liberal	No	Media, lobbying	Economic rights, EEO, ERA
ACLU	250	126	$ 5	None	Neutral/Liberal	Yes	Legal help	Censorship, reproductive freedom
NTU	200	17	$15	Taxpayer	Conservative	Yes	Lobbying, ads	Balanced budget, tax limits, social security reform
U.S. Chamber of Commerce	180	1,200	Varies	None	Conservative	Yes	Ads, awards	Budget and regulatory reform
ACU	100	6	$15	None	Conservative	Yes	Lobbying, ads	Strategic defense initiative, waste in government
ADA	40	9	$40	None	Liberal	Yes	Political, ads	Civil rights, privacy rights
League of Conservation Voters	30	9	$25	None	Neutral/Liberal	Yes	Political, ads	Mine safety, nuclear waste siting

Notes: (1) Abbreviations: AARP = American Association of Retired Persons; National RTW Committee = National Right-to-Work Committee; U.S. PIRG = U.S. Public Interest Research Group; NAACP = National Association for the Advancement of Colored People; NOW = National Organization for Women; ACLU = American Civil Liberties Union; NTU = National Taxpayers Union; ACU = American Conservative Union; and ADA = Americans for Democratic Action. (2) Dues figures are approximate.

of ardent supporters to have a greater effect on the organization's activities or positions than would normally occur in groups of comparable size.

Third, although a variety of issues—including issues relevant to workers—are stressed by the groups, each group seems to emphasize a few related issues or a group of issues consistent with an overall organizational purpose. For example, groups focus on issues of concern to retired and older persons (AARP), taxation (NTU), environmental issues (Clean Water Action Project), and women's issues (NOW). The narrow issue focus taken by most of these groups suggests that an individual might have to join more than one group to support all issues of interest to him or her.

Fourth, about one-half of the associations publish ratings of legislators. Six of the 16 publish ratings regularly and another three associations publish ratings on some occasions. One of those three associations calculates ratings on important votes and circulates them internally (National Right to Work Committee), one rates legislators in selected states through local affiliated organizations (Clean Water Action Project), and the other organization publishes ratings "only when issues require it" (Citizen Action).

Recent ratings published by five of the associations provide some insight into the nature of those organizations and the breadth of their interests, as well as a clue to the limitations of published ratings. In particular, the associations display different orientations and methodological approaches to the selection of issues and construction of ratings. For example, the U.S. Chamber of Commerce indicated a primary interest in improving the American business climate. It rated legislators in 1990 using 14 votes that "were selected as a fair representation of floor votes on issues important to business, including large and small firms" (U.S. Chamber of Commerce 1991, 2A). The issues rated were broad, including votes on alternative fuel requirements, the Clean Air amendments, regulation of railroads, Davis-Bacon Act changes, and a windfall profits tax on oil companies, as well as a presidential line item veto, public financing of political campaigns, a balanced budget amendment, the Civil Rights Act of 1990, and tax limitations. In general, the Chamber opposed measures that restricted American businesses or could conceivably impose a cost on businesses.

In contrast, the National Taxpayers Union (NTU) takes a narrow focus, examining legislators' votes on spending issues and annually publishing a "Congressional Spending Score" for each representative and senator. The score reflects the extent that an individual legislator supports lower government spending. In 1990, the NTU also indicated how a representative voted on the proposed Balanced Budget Amendment to the U.S. Constitution because "this was the most important vote on fiscal responsibility in the House in 1990" (National Taxpayers Union 1991, 2).

The American Conservative Union (ACU) is interested in the use of conservative economic and social approaches by the government (Foundation for Public Affairs 1988, 618). The ACU's conservatism is evident in its recent support for aid to the contra rebels, funding for the strategic defense initiative program, and capital punishment. In contrast to the ACU, the Americans for Democratic Action (ADA) is devoted to "formulating liberal domestic and foreign policies based on the realities and changing needs of the American democracy" (Americans for Democratic Action 1987, 1). The centerpiece of ADA's ratings is a legislator's "liberal quotient," or the extent to which he or she supports the liberal position in congressional votes. Like the Chamber of Commerce and the ACU, the ADA calculates ratings based on a wide variety of bills, including budget bills, the balanced budget amendment, civil rights legislation, worker protection legislation, human rights issues (such as the granting of most favored nation status to China), military spending and weapons measures, abortion rights legislation, nominations to the federal courts (such as the Clarence Thomas nomination), and environmental protection bills.

The League of Conservation Voters reports the views of the American environmental movement in its "national environmental scorecard." The League is somewhat like the NTU in the sense that it has a singular focus (maintaining and improving the quality of the environment) that is clear in its ratings. In 1990 it rated bills affecting smog control, the Clean Air Act, standards on emission of radioactive particles, the national forests and the everglades, water subsidies to agriculture, global warming, and the elevation of the Environmental Protection Agency to a cabinet-level department.

Comparison of Interest Groups' Legislative Efforts

It is risky to compare interest groups using their published ratings and positions because they often emphasize different congressional issues. To compare interest group positions more fairly and directly, we tabulated the positions of four groups— ACU, ADA, Chamber of Commerce, and AFL-CIO—on overlapping "key votes" in 1985, 1986, 1988, and 1990 that were reported by the editors of *Congressional Quarterly*. The votes were chosen by the interest groups themselves as those best reflecting their stances and priorities. Although we focus primarily on votes chosen by at least two of the groups, note that a review of the issues rated by only one group may suggest interesting insight into the character of that group. Because votes are used to rate legislators, the caveats described previously also apply here.

The positions of these groups on selected bills and issues are presented in Table 5. Across the years chosen for comparison, the ACU selected a total of 167 key votes on which to rate legislators, the ADA selected 155 votes, the AFL-CIO identified 116 votes, and the Chamber chose 139 votes. The issues included in the table are those on which positions of more than one interest group could be ascertained, based on the key votes. To be represented, more than one group had to identify the issue as important by selecting a specific vote (in the House or Senate) as a key vote. Thus, the information reported in the table is not a comprehensive list of the positions of the four groups on every issue, but rather is a sample of the issues deemed important over a fixed time frame.

Despite these limitations, Table 5 suggests some interesting observations. First, not surprisingly, the ADA and the AFL-CIO often hold similar positions, and positions opposite those of the ACU and the Chamber. This is not to say that the Chamber and the AFL held opposite views on all issues. Both opposed cuts in funding for the National Endowment for Democracy. It is also likely that the Chamber and the AFL-CIO held similar positions on other votes that were not identified as key votes and thus were excluded from this analysis. For example, other information indicates that the Chamber favored trade law reform, a position consistent with that of the AFL-CIO and ADA. At the same time, the AFL-CIO and the ACU rarely held similar political positions and the ADA and the ACU virtually never agreed.

Second, the ADA and ACU typically choose votes that encompass a broader spectrum of issues than those selected by the AFL-CIO and Chamber. For example, the ADA and ACU rated legislators' votes on abortion funding, defense projects, the death penalty, foreign military aid, gun control, AIDS research, and

TABLE 5

Comparison of Political Positions of Selected Interest Groups

Legislative Issues by Category	Interest Groups and Positions (O = Opposed Measure; S = Supported Measure)			
	ACU	ADA	AFL-CIO	Chamber of Commerce
Workers' Rights				
Notice of Exposure to Toxic Materials	—	S	S	O
Minimum Penalties for OSHA Violations	O	—	S	O
Minimum Wage Increase	S	S	S	O
Restrict Davis-Bacon Act	O	O	O	S
Require Unpaid Family Leave	—	S	S	O
Increase Unemployment Benefits	O	S	S	O
Plant Closing Notification	—	S	S	O
Unlimited Polygraph Testing	—	O	O	S
Union Interests				
Strike Penalties	O	—	O	S
Ban on Double-Breasting in Construction	—	S	S	O
Limit Union Political Spending	O	O	O	S
Reduce Hatch Act Restrictions on Federal Employees' Political Activity	O	S	S	—
Impose Emergency Board in Eastern Airlines Strike	—	S	S	S
Rehire PATCO Strikers	O	—	S	O
Trade and Other Economic Issues				
Trade Law Reform	O	S	S	S
Import Restrictions	—	—	S	O
Disclosure of Foreign Ownership of Firms	—	S	S	—
Jobs Legislation	O	—	S	O
Economic Development Administration	O	S	S	O
Increase Economic Grants to Cities	O	O	O	—
Immigration Law—Foreign Farm Workers	—	O	O	—
International Issues				
South African Sanctions	O	S	S	O
National Endowment for Democracy Funding Cuts	—	—	O	O

TABLE 5 (Continued)
Comparison of Political Positions of Selected Interest Groups

Legislative Issues by Category	Interest Groups and Positions (O = Opposed Measure; S = Supported Measure)			
	ACU	ADA	AFL-CIO	Chamber of Commerce
Foreign Aid to Angola	S	O	—	—
Foreign Aid to Nicaragua	S	O	—	—
Foreign Aid to El Salvador	S	O	—	—
Tax Policy				
Increase Maximum Individual Tax Rate	O	S	S	O
Decrease Minimum Individual Tax Rate	O	S	S	O
Corporate Minimum Tax	—	S	S	O
Budget Policy				
Balanced Budget Amendment	S	O	O	S
Gramm-Rudman-Hollings Act	S	O	O	S
Presidential Line Item Veto	S	O	O	S
Social Security				
Benefit Cost of Living Adjustments	—	—	S	O
Energy Policy				
Natural Gas Deregulation	—	—	O	S
Social Issues				
Civil Rights Legislation				
1988 Civil Rights Restoration Act	O	S	S	O
1990 Civil Rights Restoration Act	O	S	S	O
Busing Restrictions	S	O	—	—
Pay Equity Study	O	S	S	O
Housing—Support New Construction	—	S	S	—
Education—Increase Federal Educational Spending	—	S	S	O
Education—Cut Department of Education Budget	—	O	O	S
Mass Transportation—AMTRAK Subsidies	—	—	S	O

TABLE 5 (Continued)
Comparison of Political Positions of Selected Interest Groups

Legislative Issues by Category	Interest Groups and Positions (O = Opposed Measure; S = Supported Measure)			
	ACU	ADA	AFL-CIO	Chamber of Commerce
Child Care—Increase Head Start Funding	—	S	S	O
Welfare—Workfare	S	O	O	—
Welfare—Food Stamp Program Enhancements	O	—	S	—
Medicare—Catastrophic Health Care Bill	—	S	S	—
Medicare—Funding Increase	O	S	S	—
Motor Voter Bill	O	S	—	—
Abortion	O	S	—	—
Environmental Issues				
Clean Air Act Amendments	—	S	—	O
Superfund	O	—	—	O
Superfund—Victims' Suits	—	S	—	O
Superfund—Medical Assistance	—	S	S	—
Other Governmental Issues				
Limit PAC Contributions	—	S	—	O
Public Funding of Senate Campaigns	S	—	—	S
Prayer in Schools	S	O	—	—
Defense Department				
Military Base Closings	S	—	—	S
Nuclear Test Bans	O	S	—	—
MX Missile	S	O	—	—
Strategic Defense Initiative	S	O	—	—
Chemical Weapons Production	S	O	—	—
Death Penalty	S	O	—	—
Interstate Gun Sales	S	O	—	—
AIDS Research Funding	O	S	—	—

Notes: (1) Abbreviations: ACU = American Conservative Union; ADA = Americans for Democratic Action; (2) — Indicates that no position was taken on the issue in question.

chemical weapons. Neither the AFL-CIO nor the Chamber chose votes in these areas during the years analyzed. The ADA and ACU thus appear to follow a more ideological approach to legislative action than do the AFL-CIO and the Chamber of Commerce.

Third, the general views of the Chamber seem to conflict with the interests of workers. It could be argued that the Chamber's support of business favors workers by creating job opportunities. But its opposition to giving workers notice of exposure to toxic substances, unpaid family and medical leave, and the establishment of minimum OSHA penalties, and its support of unlimited polygraph testing suggests that the Chamber's view is inconsistent with that of the average worker. Examination of issues not reported in Table 5 (because the Chamber alone rated votes that the other groups ignored) underscores this view. For example, the Chamber supported bills that would lessen a firm's burden of proof in adverse impact cases and limit remedies under the Americans with Disabilities Act.

Although the data should not be overinterpreted, the published positions of these interest groups suggest that workers' views may be more often supported by the AFL-CIO and the ADA than by the Chamber or the ACU. Competition across interest groups may ensure that a wide variety of opinions are presented to Congress, but it is unclear whether competing interest groups cancel out each other in the process. The extent to which interest groups adequately represent the views of workers is also unclear, so it is useful to compare the views of individuals and groups on selected political issues.

Interest Groups and the Representation of Individuals' Views

Apathetic political behavior by individuals is unimportant if interest groups adequately represent their interests. GSS data suggested that people are generally uninvolved in politics and political groups. The political data cited above indicated a wide range of issues that are emphasized by major interest groups. Overlap between interest groups' political emphases and individuals' preferences on specific issues may be inferred from other GSS data.

Interest Groups and Individuals' Political Views

In general, responses in the GSS show that people have a complex set of views. No clear ideological delineation seems to exist, as individuals hold some conservative and some liberal views. In some cases there are statistically significant differences in expressed views between employed persons and those not employed, but even there the pattern of differences defies an easy explanation.

It is clear that individuals hold views about most of the issues valued by American interest groups, but it is also clear that no single interest group seems to represent the positions of the average GSS respondent—employed or not employed. This should not be surprising, given the forces that lead to the formation of interest groups. From a theoretical perspective, if a prediction were made about the factors used by a legislator to make a decision in the absence of interest group lobbying efforts, that prediction would probably include some notion of the preferences of the median voter in the legislator's district. Given this, there would seem to be little valuable information that an interest group representing the "average voter" could provide to legislators. In turn, this suggests that interest groups will tend to organize around issues that are not "average," and individuals who perceive that their views differ from those of the average person are more likely than the average individual to join interest groups and support interest group activities.

While no interest group, including the AFL-CIO, can completely represent the average person (working or not working) across all issues, it should not be concluded that the average worker's interests would be protected in political arenas if the AFL-CIO were to substantially decrease its legislative efforts. Withdrawal of the labor movement from the political arena might cause other interest groups to "pick up the AFL-CIO's slack," but competing interest groups would clearly have less opposition to the pursuit of their agendas. Although it is unlikely that the AFL-CIO will cease its political activities in the near future, attempts to limit union political activities have increased dramatically in recent years (Delaney 1991). Events such as the *Beck* decision and President Bush's executive order regarding that decision, when combined with decreasing membership, could reduce the effectiveness of union political efforts. Thus, it is instructive to assess the alternatives that workers might use to ensure that their interests and concerns are expressed in political processes.

Ignoring (for now) the option of establishing a new interest group that would operate in a manner similar to the AFL-CIO, individuals would still have three options—individual action, joining an existing interest group, or allowing others to speak for them. Because the data presented earlier suggest that individuals are unlikely to pursue political action on their own or to join existing political groups, it is important to determine the extent to which existing interest groups speak for them generally. The examples in Table 5 suggest that most people are unlikely to be fully represented by either the ACU or the ADA because of the consistent ideological stances that these organizations take on "moral" issues. Although these ideological groups hold views on some issues that many people would accept, the groups' positions on certain issues are likely to alienate many people. ADA's liberal positions are generally consistent with the protection of workers' rights, but GSS data show that individuals are likely to disagree with certain ADA views (such as opposition to the death penalty). Thus, while the ADA takes the same stance as the AFL-CIO on many issues, it is unlikely on average that workers will join or actively support that organization. Further, the ideological nature of organizations like the ADA or ACU raises the possibility that they would subordinate the interests of workers (or average people) to the ideological objectives of the organization.

Examination of the positions taken by the Chamber of Commerce suggests that it does not generally represent the views of workers either. GSS data suggest that workers favor government spending on a variety of programs (such as education), and are not completely in favor of the continued government deregulation of industry. While we do not have specific information on individuals' positions regarding most workplace issues, it seems hard to imagine that employees generally oppose notification of exposure to toxic material, restrictions on their remedies under the Americans with Disabilities Act, and family leave provisions. Although the Chamber does not typically take a stance on "moral" issues, it does not seem to advocate positions that consistently reflect worker interests.

People have the option of joining organizations that have narrow objectives. For example, an individual who feels strongly that efforts against age discrimination should be strengthened could support the AARP, provided he or she is over the age of 50. Note that none of the organizations listed in Table 4 appear to have worker protection as a primary focus. Of course, if an individual deemed multiple work-related issues salient, he or she could join or otherwise support the efforts of multiple interest groups.

Ironically, the need to join more than one group, whether ideological in orientation or specific in objectives, might require individuals to join groups that have opposite interests in order to cover the range of their concerns. Although multiple memberships could serve the interests of those individuals, such behavior seems unlikely. Available evidence suggests that few individuals join organizations (other than groups affiliated with churches, work, or sports) and we suspect that few people belong to both the ADA and the National Right to Work Committee. Consequently, it seems likely that people would refuse to join any of the groups and hope that the combination of efforts of each group produced outcomes that served their interests generally. Of course, this "public goods" option does not truly provide representation in the political process because people who do not participate have little or no direct influence on the positions of groups attempting to influence legislators and laws.

On the other hand, workers might choose to join an occupational association or be represented by a trade association established by their firm or industry. Such organizations represent millions of workers in a variety of ways. As noted in the analysis, however, some of these associations are more responsive to employers and industries than to workers. Moreover, Knoke's analysis (1990, 199) indicated that such organizations are much less likely than unions to engage in political influence activities. Ultimately, however, this issue probably rests on a value judgment by workers about the ability of occupation- or industry-specific associations to adequately represent workers' needs.

Although the AFL-CIO is similar to other interest groups in that it does not represent the preferences of the average worker across all issues, it plays an important role in American politics. Workers may have more political positions in common with organized labor than with other interest groups for two reasons. First, the union movement represents workers both at work and in the political arena. This may allow organized labor to understand the interests of workers and to seek those interests in bargaining and political arenas. Second, data show that the AFL-CIO takes fewer ideological positions than the ADA or ACU. Few organizations that focus on a variety of workplace issues also provide a voice of opposition to the efforts of business and conservative groups. The view that the AFL-CIO is the political voice of working people is limited, however, by the extent to which it is perceived that organized labor is solely interested in advancing union workers' interests at the expense of other workers' interests. Skepticism about the union movement is likely to remain until labor educates the public about its bargaining and political efforts.

Conclusion

Can employees acting individually have a voice in the political process? Although the answer to this question is yes in theory, the average behavior of Americans suggests that the answer may be no in practice. As a result, this means that the role of groups in securing representation for Americans is paramount. For representation to occur, workers must be willing to join at least one group or to engage in intensive personal efforts to influence politicians and public policy. As joining a group provides strength in numbers—which may increase the likelihood of achieving favorable policy outcomes—and requires less time from individuals, we believe it is the most effective way for workers to secure representation. But the resulting representation depends strongly on the extent to which individuals and workers are willing to participate in group activities—behavior that is unusual, at least among GSS respondents.

Ironically, the movement away from group participation and toward individual rights may leave workers with *less* employee representation because, under a regime of guaranteed individual rights, people may become unwilling to accept the responsibilities that representation requires. Whether or not people desire group representation, it may provide the only means of securing the general political and work outcomes that they favor. The importance of representation is crucial for workers. For a variety of reasons, we believe that the labor movement provides workers with the greatest opportunity to achieve representation. Our belief is based on cross-national comparisons and a close examination of the approach of organized labor.

The patterns of individuals' participation in associations or organizations reported earlier have been corroborated by considerable research (see Knoke 1986). Moreover, available cross-national studies suggest that patterns of individuals' participation in the U.S.

are generally similar to patterns of participation in other western democracies (Finkel and Opp 1991; Olsen 1982). Indeed, the similarity of participation patterns raises some interesting questions with respect to the union movement's differential success in organizing and representing workers across nations (Freeman 1989). One explanation for the difference is the reliance of government on corporatist policies in many western democracies (see Addison and Siebert 1991; Kohler 1990). Corporatism is an approach to the ordering of a national economic system that emphasizes the importance of organized groups in mediating between individuals and the state. In rejecting both centrally planned economies and unrestricted economic competition, corporatism encourages organizations of employers and employees to act as "self-regulating bodies, providing the opportunity for a sort of ordered economic freedom" whose purpose is "to achieve the welfare of all" (Kohler 1991, 33). The legitimization of organized interest groups in countries such as Germany has led to more instances of cooperation between labor and management there than occurs in the U.S. (Knoke and Pappi 1991). This suggests that the underlying role of the state in other western democracies, which encourages the formation and operation of intermediary organizations, likely reduces the need for foreign workers to engage in politics.

In contrast to corporatism, the U.S. is characterized by a political system where individual rights are increasingly emphasized over group rights (Kohler 1990). Historically, there has been much less reliance on government to regulate working conditions in the U.S. than has been the case in Europe. Given this, the introduction of labor relations mechanisms such as works councils, employee involvement programs, or labor-management cooperation programs may not have the same effect in the U.S. as they do in other nations, where the programs reduce the need for political action on the part of individuals or local organizations.

Continuation of current trends toward employee representation forms such as employee involvement programs and away from organized labor will not lead to the long-term result of increased individual action in political arenas. We hold this view for three reasons. First, the GSS data presented earlier suggest that many Americans feel disenfranchised from the political process. This may be due in part to the fact that for an individual's voice to be heard, and for that voice to be reflected in policy decisions, the collective voice of opposing interest groups must be overcome. It is unclear whether a weakening of organized labor's political voice, given the continued political operation of business and conservative groups, will cause workers to perceive greater benefit to individual political action than they currently do. Second, while the costs of becoming informed on political issues (which is necessary for the effective practice of political action) will not change for most workers, costs will increase for persons who currently receive information from organized labor. Finally, there are reasons to believe that the political system itself benefits from the existence of interest groups. Without such groups, legislators would be forced to spend more time collecting, processing and summarizing information on the preferences of their constituencies across issues. Austen-Smith and Wright's (1992) examination of interest group lobbying activity suggests that legislators are better informed about policy consequences and constituency preferences when interest groups lobby them than when interest groups are not involved.

Each of these reasons points to the prediction that movement away from organized labor as workers' political representative will lead to the creation of another interest group to take the place of the AFL-CIO in political arenas. It is our belief, and history provides some supportive evidence, that business groups cannot dominate political discussion over work-related issues over the long run and, consequently, that a new organization would rise to provide worker representation. That organization may grow out of programs such as work teams at the local level; it may take the form of an entirely new organization; or alternatively, it may spring from an existing lobbying organization. Unless work teams and similar programs become mandated by law, however, it is unlikely that individuals in these programs can effectively coordinate across plants and firms because employers can freely dismantle them. If this view is correct, then a new organization established to represent workers in political arenas may operate only in those arenas and make few efforts to represent the economic interests of individuals at work. This would impose a serious cost on workers.

Workers seek representation to secure fair treatment at the workplace. In recent years, the decline of the union movement and the choice by the federal government to "leave business alone" have meant that the existence of fair treatment often depends on employers' voluntary decision to provide it. As a result, it is increasingly important for employees to be represented in the political process and it is increasingly likely that fairness at work will depend on legislative mandates. Ultimately, we believe that employee representation is best facilitated by encouraging workers to form groups as the basis of their participation, by encouraging democracy within those groups, and by empowering them to affect important decisions at work.

Acknowledgments

The authors are grateful to Peter Feuille, Paul Jarley, and Marick Masters for helpful comments on an earlier draft and to Steve Popejoy for research assistance.

References

AFL-CIO. 1991. "Priorities for Congress: Jobs, Safety." *AFL-CIO News* (February 4), pp. 1, 3.

Abramson, Paul R., and William Claggett. 1991. "Racial Differences in Self-Reported and Validated Turnout in the 1988 Presidential Election." *Journal of Politics* 53 (February), pp. 186-97.

Addison, John T., and W. Stanley Siebert. 1991. "The Social Charter of the European Community: Evolution and Controversies." *Industrial and Labor Relations Review* 44 (July), pp. 597-625.

Americans for Democratic Action. 1987. "A Look at the 1986 Voting Record." *ADA Today* 42 (January), pp. 1-7.

Austen-Smith, David, and John R. Wright. 1992. "Competitive Lobbying for a Legislator's Vote." *Social Choice and Welfare*. In press.

Close, Arthur C., Gregory L. Bologna, and Curtis W. McCormick, eds. 1991. *Washington Representatives*. 15th ed. Washington, DC: Columbia Books.

Delaney, John Thomas. 1991. "The Future of Unions as Political Organizations." *Journal of Labor Research* 12 (Fall), pp. 373-87.

Delaney, John Thomas, David Lewin, and Casey Ichniowski. 1989. *Human Resource Policies and Practices in American Firms*. Washington, DC: U.S. Department of Labor.

Delaney, John Thomas, Marick F. Masters, and Susan Schwochau. 1988. "Unionism and Voter Turnout." *Journal of Labor Research* 9 (Summer), pp. 221-36.

_____. 1990. "Union Membership and Voting for COPE-Endorsed Candidates." *Industrial and Labor Relations Review* 43 (July), pp. 621-35.

Downs, Anthony. 1957. *An Economic Theory of Democracy*. New York: Harper and Row.

Finkel, Steven E., and Karl-Dieter Opp. 1991. "Party Identification and Participation in Collective Political Action." *Journal of Politics* 53 (May), pp. 339-71.

Fiorito, Jack. 1987. "Political Instrumentality Perceptions and Desires for Union Representation." *Journal of Labor Research* 8 (Summer), pp. 271-89.

Folger, Robert, and Jerald Greenberg. 1985. "Procedural Justice: An Interpretive Analysis of Personnel Systems." In *Research in Personnel and Human Resources Management* (Vol. 3), eds. Kendrith M. Rowland and Gerald R. Ferris. Greenwich, CT: JAI Press, pp. 141-83.

Foundation for Public Affairs. 1988. *Public Interest Profiles, 1988-1989*. Washington, DC: Congressional Quarterly, Inc.

Freeman, Richard B. 1989. "On the Divergence in Unionism Among Developed Countries." NBER Working Paper 2817 (January).

304 EMPLOYEE REPRESENTATION

Greenberg, Jerald. 1990. "Looking Fair vs. Being Fair: Managing Impressions of Organizational Justice." In *Research in Organizational Behavior* (Vol. 12), eds. Barry Staw and L. L. Cummings. Greenwich, CT: JAI Press, pp. 111-57.

Heldman, Dan C., and Deborah L. Knight. 1980. *Unions and Lobbying: The Representation Function.* Arlington, VA: Foundation for the Advancement of the Public Trust.

Knoke, David. 1986. "Associations and Interest Groups." *Annual Review of Sociology* 12, pp. 1-21.

_____. 1990. *Organizing for Collective Action: The Political Economies of Associations.* New York: Aldine de Gruyter.

Knoke, David, and Franz Urban Pappi. 1991. "Organizational Action Sets in the U.S. and German Labor Policy Domains." *American Sociological Review* 56 (August), pp. 509-23.

Kochan, Thomas A., Harry C. Katz, and Robert B. McKersie. 1986. *The Transformation of American Industrial Relations.* New York: Basic Books.

Kohler, Thomas C. 1990. "Setting the Conditions for Self-Rule: Unions, Associations, Our First Amendment Discourse, and the Problem of *DeBartolo.*" *Wisconsin Law Review*, pp. 149-211.

_____. 1991. "Quadragesimo Anno." In *A Century of Catholic Social Thought*, eds. George Weigel and Robert Royal. Washington, DC: Ethics and Public Policy Center, pp. 27-43.

Lawler, Edward E., III. 1986. *High Involvement Management.* San Francisco: Jossey-Bass.

Lawler, John J. 1990. *Unionization and Deunionization.* Columbia, SC: University of South Carolina Press.

Masters, Marick F., and John Thomas Delaney. 1987a. "Union Legislative Records During President Reagan's First Term." *Journal of Labor Research* 8 (Winter), pp. 1-18.

_____. 1987b. "Union Political Activities: A Review of the Empirical Literature." *Industrial and Labor Relations Review* 40 (April), pp. 336-53.

National Taxpayers Union. 1991. *Congressional Spending Study: 101st Congress 2nd Session.* Washington, DC: National Taxpayers Union.

Olsen, Marvin E. 1982. *Participatory Pluralism: Political Participation and Influence in the United States and Sweden.* Chicago: Nelson-Hall.

Peters, Thomas J., and Robert H. Waterman, Jr. 1982. *In Search of Excellence.* New York: Harper and Row.

Rehmus, Charles M., Doris B. McLaughlin, and Frederick H. Nesbitt, eds. 1978. *Labor and American Politics,* rev. ed. Ann Arbor, MI: University of Michigan Press.

Sheppard, Blair H., Roy Lewicki, and John Minton. 1992. *Organizational Justice.* New York: Lexington Books.

U.S. Chamber of Commerce. 1991. *How They Voted.* Washington, DC: Chamber of Commerce.

Weidenbaum, Murray L. 1977. *Business, Government, and the Public.* Englewood Cliffs, NJ: Prentice-Hall.

CHAPTER 9

German Works Councils
and Firm Performance

JOHN T. ADDISON
University of South Carolina and Universität Münster

KORNELIUS KRAFT
Universität Fribourg

JOACHIM WAGNER
Universität Hannover

This paper investigates the impact on firm performance of the unique system of establishment-level codetermination in Germany, represented by that country's works council apparatus. To set the scene for our subsequent empirical discussion, we first describe the institution and its function. The relationship between works council and trade union is also commented upon. Having examined the manner in which the works council may be expected to impact performance, we then proceed with a review of the empirical evidence. This comprises a brief survey of the empirical literature followed by a presentation of new results. The focus of this new contribution is the measurement of council impact along the dimensions of productivity, profitability, physical capital formation, and earnings using 1990-91 establishment data for manufacturing industry in two German states (Niedersachsen and Baden-Württemberg). This material is supplemented by preliminary findings from a study of the employment adjustment process at establishment level currently being conducted by one of the authors. A concluding section draws together the threads of the empirical literature against the backdrop of recent moves by the European Commission to legislate greater worker involvement in their companies.

The Works Council Machinery

The German works council differs markedly from works councils in most other European nations in that it is an integral part of that country's codetermination system, with negotiating rights in addition to the more familiar advisory and consultative functions. Works councils in Germany thus perform many of the functions of shop stewards in Britain or union locals in the United States, albeit without the right to withdraw labor.

Works councils were first set up in 1920 under the Works Councils Law (Betriebsrätegesetz), which established codetermination rights in social and employment matters. (On earlier enabling legislation, see Lampert 1991.) Works councils, along with unions, were dissolved by the National Socialist regime—unions and employer organizations being merged into a unitary body, the German Working Front (Deutsche Arbeitsfront). After the war, several federal states (or Länder) passed legislation governing the operation of works councils, and federal legislation in 1952 established a uniform albeit somewhat less ambitious set of rights. That legislation was amended in 1972 under a new Works Constitution Act (Betriebsverfassungsgesetz), which prescribed in considerable detail the functions and responsibilities of works councils and which forms the basis of their current operation. (The Act was further modified in May 1976 and December 1988.)

Works councils are mandatory in all companies with five or more employees, once the employees or a trade union so petition. In firms with less than twenty employees a single Betriebsobmann is elected, who has more limited rights than a works council proper. The number of (exclusively) employee representatives increases with employment level up to thirty-one councillors in companies with nine thousand employees. Thereafter, two additional representatives may be elected for each three thousand increment in establishment employment level. (Company works councils, or Konzernbetriebsräte, may be set up in multiplant enterprises and group works councils, or Gesamtbetriebsräte, in groups of companies. No membership size limits apply in either case.) Blue-collar and white-collar employees are entitled to submit separate lists of candidates, although in practice the majority of workplaces have joint lists for both groups.

All employees aged 18 years and above are entitled to vote—young persons may be represented indirectly through a youth delegation (Jugendvertretung) which operates alongside the works council—including part-timers and those on fixed-term contracts. Any nomination must be supported by at least 5 percent of the work force or at least 50 employees and in all cases by at least two employees. In practice, the large majority of winning candidates, elected on the basis of proportional representation, are members of unions (see below).

The rights of the works council may be discussed along the dimensions of information, consultaɔn, and codetermination. Beginning with information, the employer has to provide the works council with comprehensive information (and in "good time") on matters connected with the fulfillment of its general duties and on matters relating to manpower planning and the introduction of new technology and working processes. (The employer's disclosure requirements in respect of the introduction of new technology were expanded in the 1988 amendments to the Works Constitution Act.)

In firms with more than one hundred employees an economic committee (Wirtschaftsausschuß) has to be set up, the members of which are selected by the works council. The economic committee has to be informed on a full range of economic and financial matters, including production level, sales, investment, profits, rationalization plans, plant closings, and changes in work organization. Proposed alterations, such as reductions in operation, closures, transfers, and the introduction of new working methods also have to be communicated to the works council in all firms with more than 20 employees.

Correspondingly, the employer is under a duty to consult with the works council on changes in the organization of work. Consultation covers the scaling down or closing of a plant or department, mergers of departments, significant changes in plant organization or equipment, and the introduction of new working methods or production techniques. In all such matters management must consult prior to taking any action. In undertakings employing more than 20 workers, works councils have the right to demand compensation for any proposed changes likely to entail substantial prejudice to employees such as "large-scale" redundancies, plant closings, and fundamental changes in work organization and/or technology. Where the parties cannot agree on a social plan (Sozialplan), an independent conciliation board may step in at the request of either side and formulate a compromise plan. (Newly established enterprises were freed from the obligation to conclude social plans for four years under the 1985 Employment Promotion Act [Beschäftigungsförderungsgesetz].) It is important to note that the labor courts, the final arbiter, have developed the notion of "social property rights" (sozialer Besitzstand), which would be damaged by substantial changes within the firm. The loss of these rights thus requires compensation. The social liability of property is indeed enshrined within the German Constitution. Not surprisingly, social plans predate their formalization and incorporation within the Works Constitution Act.

Note too that the works council must also be consulted on each and every dismissal. Without such consultation, the dismissal notice is null and void. The works council may object on the grounds that the employee could be either redeployed or retrained or (in cases of dismissal for firm-specific, that is, economic reasons) that the employer has not followed "social criteria" in his choice of those to be made redundant. Social criteria include length of service, age, health, family responsibilities, and the worker's financial situation. In practical terms, the power of the works council to object is less relevant than the legal terms defined by the labor courts. It has been argued that "because of the casuistic rulings of the courts and the high probability of employers being defeated, employers often prefer immediate severance pay to pursuing the case in court" (Soltwedel 1988, 192). In this sense, legislation designed to protect the job (the 1967 Kündigungsschutzgesetz), has become an instrument of severance pay. It is now often the case that German firms offer "voluntary" severance payments in order to avoid engaging the courts.

The works councils also have far reaching codetermination rights on so-called "social issues," as specified under sections 87 through 89 of the Works Constitution Act. Full codetermination rights apply in the following areas: the organization of working time; pay procedures; the scheduling of holidays and individual leave arrangements; the introduction and deployment of techniques to monitor employee performance; health and safety measures; social services specific to the establishment, company, or group; principles, methods, and changes of remuneration; and the fixing of bonus rates and other forms of performance-related pay. Wages and working conditions that are settled by collective agreements between unions and employers may *not* be the subject of agreements at works level (Betriebsvereinbarungen) *unless* the relevant collective agreement expressly authorizes such supplementary bargaining. But regional/industry-wide agreements have frequently provided for works agreements, most notably in connection with bonuses, wage guarantees, and job evaluation schemes. Indeed, the trend toward decentralization in indus ial relations has led to increasing use of such works agreements (see below) such that the distinction between formal codetermination rights and other areas of works council influence has become somewhat artificial.

The works council also has consent rights in matters concerning the engagement, grading, and transfer of personnel in firms employing more than 20 workers. For example, the works council can object to a recruitment if the individual in question endangers the "harmony" of the workplace (Betriebsfrieden). The power to object to recruitment is something of a theoretical curiosum, but is nonetheless indicative of the extent of the works council's sphere of influence in personnel matters.

Despite its collective bargaining role, in no case can the works council engage in industrial action, although works councillors may participate in exactly the same way as other employees in industrial action called by the union. Strike activity is specifically excluded under section 74(2) of the 1972 Act: "acts of industrial warfare between the works council and the employer shall be unlawful." Section 2(1) of that legislation moreover enjoins the employer and the works council to "work together in a spirit of mutual trust." Although there is no guarantee that relations between the firm and its works council will be cooperative, it is nevertheless considered logical to prescribe "mutual trust" under the law given the decision rights ceded to labor.

If labor-management relations are conducted at two separate levels, a question naturally arises as to the links between works councils and trade unions. Strictly speaking, wage councils are formally independent of unions. Under the 1972 Act unions do not even have the formal right to submit lists of candidates for election to the works council on their own behalf; rather, such lists are forwarded by unionized employees. (Changes to the Works Constitution Act in December 1988 gave all unions represented in the company the automatic right to nominate candidates, as well as reducing the threshold levels of employee support required for the nomination of candidates.) Nominations of candidates for election to the works council may be tabled by unionized and nonunionized workers alike; unlike the situation in Belgium, France, Italy, and Luxembourg, where nominations may be presented only by the unions. But in practice the preponderance of works councillors are union members and union sponsored, and the links between the two entities are close.

In the 1987 elections, for example, no less than 72 percent of works councillors were union members, well in excess of overall union density levels at that time (< 40 percent). As is well known, union density tends to increase much in line with establishment size, and this phenomena is also reflected in the union composition of works councils. In the case of blue-collar works councillors, for example, councillors having membership in one of the 16 affiliated unions of the German Trade Union Federation (Deutscher Gewerkschaftsbund) (DGB) are in a clear *minority* in firms with between 5 and 20 workers—DGB union members have 40 percent of the seats and nonunionized workers roughly 60 percent of the seats. The position is almost exactly reversed in firms employing between 51 and 150 workers, and in large firms with more than twelve thousand employees the proportion of nonunionized workers on councils falls to around 1 percent. A fairly similar pattern of representation holds for white-collar workers, jointly organized by the DGB and the German Salaried Employees Union (Deutsche Angestellten-Gewerkschaft), although nonunionized workers have a consistently higher percentage of seats: 70 percent in companies with between 5 and 20 workers, falling to 18 percent in large firms employing over twelve thousand workers. These averages do of course conceal marked differences by sector. Nonunionized wage councillors dominate in finance, the utilities, and hotels and catering, *inter al.* (Niedenhoff 1988).

In addition to their union affiliation, works councillors are often union officials and serve on trade union bargaining committees. The cooperation between the two is further facilitated by workers' education programs conducted by DGB affiliate unions. The Works Constitution Act also permits union representatives to attend works council meetings, under certain conditions, as well as the three-month meetings of general assemblies of the workers of the establishment. For all these reasons unions are by no means excluded from influencing the workplace despite their historical lack of workplace organization (Galenson 1991, 24).

This lack of workplace representation reflects the fact that employees' rights are largely regulated through *legislation*, enforced through the labor courts, with the result that the role played by unions in the protection of worker rights is altogether less pronounced than in other countries (Schregle 1978, 75). And, as we have seen, works councils, not shop stewards, are part of the formal apparatus of codetermination. *Vulgo*: collective bargaining at industry/regional level is a national union affair and works councils deal with local matters.

The ongoing decentralization of industrial relations in Germany, widely noted in the literature (e.g. Jacobi and Müller-Jentsch 1990), has to be understood in the context of this dual system. It does not mean decentralization in the U.S. sense of single-employer/union agreements (although these certainly exist in Germany, e.g. Volkswagen) but rather a (partial) transfer of traditional bargaining functions to management and works councils. This trend reflects the impact of technological change and recognition of the need for flexibility in the use of labor. Agreements on the protection of workers in the event of rationalization, on the "humanization" of work organization, the restructuring of wage payment systems, and reductions in working time have all delegated functions to negotiators at company level.

Management for its part has independently sought to pursue flexibility in the use of personnel via quality circles and in advancing its own group-work concepts. The former were initially opposed by works councillors and shop stewards; the latter were part of "humanization of work" proposals earlier put forward by the union movement.

If the popularity of works councils initially stimulated unions to increase their shop floor representation as a protective device, and hence limit works council influence, increased shop floor presence and enhanced powers of the works council in codetermination are today complementary activities, so that the links between union, works council, and shop steward may be very close. An obvious example is the Wolfsburg plant of Volkswagen, were IG Metall union-sponsored candidates dominate the works council (62 out of 69 seats), where union membership is high (95 percent), where there is a strong union shop floor presence (1,000 shop stewards for 62,000 employees), where the works council has adopted the IG Metall group work concept, where the works council engages shop stewards and workers in the design and implementation of the new work group organization, and where as a result there is said to be "unity within the works council and union" (Turner 1992, 225-232). Such arrangements are not the norm, and in any case should not be taken to imply that unionized works councils in plants with strong union representation are necessarily indicative of "cooperative" rather than "adversarial" industrial relations. One can speak of a diversified pattern of industrial relations at the establishment level which though it admits of a certain structure in large plants, apparently remains one dominated by informal practices and ad hoc regulation in small and medium-sized companies (Jacobi and Müller-Jentsch 1990, 152). This very diversity qualifies the conventional notion that the works council is the "extended arm" of the union movement.

Theoretical Conjectures

The Works Constitution Act provides an interesting study of how decision rights granted workers' representatives may affect firm performance. From the perspective of the simplest neoclassical model little benefit may be expected to accrue from mandated works councils. Thus, the rights extended under law to these bodies would be viewed as a constraint on management, while at the same time providing workers with additional bargaining leverage. Works councils will exercise these rights to affect the outcome of the decision-making process within the firm. Most obviously, they will demand additional pay, fringes and/or nonpecuniary benefits over and above the base wage fixed at industry/regional level. To repeat, this outcome may be achieved either through the use of explicit codetermination rights in supplementary pay determination or indirectly via rights granted the works council in other areas.

Continuing with this monopoly model, the works council would be viewed as a typical "insider" body. If this is the case, works councils may be depicted as concerned with sustaining (some critical level of) existing employment and not assisting in the employment of outsiders. Abstracting from wage considerations, the attempt to stabilize employment may be expected to yield reductions in the speed of adjustment to demand declines. Hiring decisions may also be delayed in order to avoid layoffs under subsequent adverse demand realizations. As a result, input adjustment will normally occur through variations in overtime work. The postponing of employment adjustment will raise costs and reduce profitability. Productivity might suffer as well because the optimal use of the capital stock is hindered. (German legislation on dismissals protection will operate in much the same manner to slow employment adjustment and reduce overall levels of employment. The argument here is simply that the works council exacerbates the problem.)

The simple monopoly model would also view with disfavor the participation rights granted works councils on the grounds that they cause important decisions to be delayed and the status quo to be perpetuated. Olson's (1982, 83) explanation of the delays in the adoption of new technologies in terms of "the slow decision making and crowded agendas and bargaining tables of distributional coalitions" is especially relevant here.

In sum, the monopoly model as applied to the institution of the works council would point to the distortion of factor prices and usage and to technical inefficiencies arising from constraints on the ability of management to manage. Costs will be higher and profits lower in such regimes.

Sharply differentiated from this monopoly view is Freeman and Medoff's (1979, 1984) application of the Hirschman (1970) exit-voice paradigm. The basic idea behind this collective voice/institutional response model is that by addressing job issues with the employer through the expression of "voice" the need for "exit" is reduced. Consultation between union and management should reduce quits, together with hiring and training costs, while encouraging investments in firm-specific human capital and hence increasing the value of the match. Firm profits and productivity should be enhanced.

Collective voice, it is argued, is superior to individual voice for a variety of reasons. Unorganized workers will be reluctant to express dissatisfaction over working conditions because of management retaliation, which is of course one reason why they quit (or even engage in "quiet sabotage"). In addition, unions can help overcome problems associated with the public goods nature of working conditions: such conditions affect the utility of all workers but without some form of collective decision making the incentive of the individual to express preferences will be too small and hence an inappropriate mix of conditions may be selected by management.

(Exit interviews for their part necessarily offer only limited information as to the preferences of the wider work force.) The effectiveness of individual voice is further undermined by the inability to establish readily enforceable agreements with management. In all these ways, then, unions assist in the formulation and execution of efficient contracts. Complementarities in worker effort inputs provide a further (public goods) justification for unionization by encouraging a joint determination of those inputs, and reducing the possibilities that an individual will shirk at the expense of his fellow workers.

Increased cooperation among workers and improved workplace morale point to improved productivity performance in union regimes. The presence of a union may also be expected to provide a vehicle for inducing management to alter methods of production and select more efficient practices. But note in all of this that much hinges on management's response to collective bargaining and that of the union to workplace reorganization. This is the "institutional response" component of the collective voice model: the industrial relations climate is central to actual outcomes. Relatedly, the effects of unions on other outcomes will also depend on a balance of forces. In particular, since it is not denied that unions are rent-seeking agencies, profits may fall because productivity gains may be dominated by cost increases. However, it is typically argued that wage gains will largely come at the expense of economic profits on an efficient rent extraction model (see below).

The institutional framework of industrial relations differs markedly between Germany and the United States. In Germany, as we have seen, the works council is responsible for negotiations between management and workers. Given its extensive information and consultation rights and collective bargaining powers stemming from codetermination rights, the works council would appear to be an exemplary collective voice institution in the Freeman-Medoff sense.

The skeptical neoclassical economist would nevertheless question why management is unable to introduce analogous but nonautonomous systems of this type, given the advantages attributed to some form of collective agency. It is a fact that internal organization differs between firms and will include the archetypal autocratic variant described by Freeman and Medoff. Yet modern management techniques recognize the value of team work and communications, so that it may strain credulity to argue that only by unionization is the organization made effective. German management has indeed made extensive use of team-work principles, quality circles, and other forms of employee involvement in recent years. The situation is complicated by the fact that the union "composition" of works council is not a datum, by the presence of quality circles alongside works councils in many companies, by varying levels of shop floor representation, and indeed by the nature of the framework of law which presumably reflects societal preferences and attitudes.

The traditional monopoly model points unambiguously to lower profits under unionism, and as a practical matter supporters of the collective voice model recognize that profits are lower in union regimes. Where the two part company is on the question of the consequences of this redistributive process. The traditional model points to distortionary effects in the form of lower overall investment and employment as firms react in predictable ways to the exogenous union wage premium. Protagonists of collective voice, on the other hand, argue that union wage premia are endogenous outcomes made possible by appropriation of the firm's monopoly returns. The view that unions might potentially efficiently redistribute economic rents might seem to imply few if any losses of economic efficiency. But appropriable quasi-rents need not be associated with monopoly power or supracompetitive returns. Instead, they may represent normal returns to long-lived investments, in which case a distinction needs to be drawn between short-run and long-run outcomes even under strongly efficient contracts. (If bargaining outcomes are noncooperative, investment activity will unambiguously be reduced.) If collective bargaining is characterized by repeated "games," cooperative bargaining outcomes are rendered more likely. A cooperative outcome is one which maximizes the joint value of the firm and the union, namely, the sum of the firm's market value plus the present value of union members' rents. This situation corresponds to a vertical contract curve: the firm and the union maximize the size of the pie and bargain over the distribution of the returns to labor and shareholders. Thus, output, price, and factor utilization will be the same as that determined under competition. At least this distortion-free outcome obtains in the short run. But if the union has a shorter time horizon than do shareholders, a union tax on the quasi-rents deriving from relation-specific physical (and intangible) capital will be distortionary vis-à-vis a parallel nonunion environment. (A democratic union may be expected to have a shorter time horizon both because of the seniority of workers who constitute the median voter and the inability of union members to sell or transfer their position in the firms to "outsiders.") Simply put, unions will give greater weight to current rents than to (potential) future rents, and as a result firms will decrease investment in long-lived, relation-specific physical capital *and* R & D that by its very nature has returns that are most easily appropriated.

It is well known that union rent-seeking will be distortionary in a noncooperative bargaining regime, but the results also hold for efficient bargaining *unless* it is possible to achieve incentive compatibility. Moreover, firms may still have an incentive to shift resources to lower-cost nonunion plants, *ceteris paribus*, even if the union tax is lump sum. It can thus be argued that unions will have both direct and indirect effects on physical and intangible capital formation. The direct effect follows from reduced investment in "vulnerable" capital. The indirect effect stems from lower profitability which is a potent source of investment funding (Hirsch 1991, 1992).

It is not immediately obvious how works councils might reduce these negative effects of unionization unless they are shown to be "forward-looking" entities or otherwise give weight to the preferences of relatively junior union members or yet-to-be union members. However, the widely acknowledged good labor relations environment may facilitate the development of "bargaining protocols" that are more neutral from the perspective of investment policy.

More narrowly, the Works Constitution Act contains specific clauses on technology. "Drastic" changes in technology have in effect to be approved by the works council, and social plans introduced to compensate those adversely impacted. Thus, the works council may influence the adoption of technology both directly by voicing opposition and indirectly by fixing compensation levels. It is interesting to contrast this role with Milgrom's argument (1988) that "it was wise or lucky that Western Governments established no agencies with authority to review and reject proposed innovations" (p. 45).

In any event, the Works Constitution Act also requires information disclosure and consultation on all questions of investment and rationalization. Changes to the legislation in 1988 require the employer to provide all the documentation relating to the proposed introduction of new technology when s/he informs the works council; and to extend consultation to all the possible implications for the work force of the proposed change and in sufficient time to enable the works council's suggestions and reservations to be taken fully into account. In short, although the adoption of new technology may not be blocked, its introduction might well be delayed.

On the other hand, consultation is not without merit. Technology adoption implies a learning process by both sides. In order to avoid long-term adjustment problems and extensive retraining of the work force, there is obvious utility in discussing the consequences of a new production technology with those directly involved. It does not therefore ineluctably follow that the influence of the works council in this regard is either detrimental to the interests of management or productivity retarding.

One can extend this line of reasoning. The representation of workers' interests through the mechanism of a works council can benefit industrial relations because of its influence on worker morale and in inculcating trust. The participation of workers in decision making may be said to legitimize the goals of management. Good industrial relations are assuredly good for productivity and other aspects of performance. There is of course the standard counterargument entered earlier to the effect that, if good industrial relations is in the interests of both sides, analogous institutional forms will spring up without the compulsion of legislation. It is at this point that supporters of the formal machinery need to note the factors that might be expected to impede this "natural" development (*and* address the incentive compatibility question). Presumably these factors will include the external economic environment in which firms operate (e.g. alternative systems of motivating workers may be cheaper when unemployment is high) and externalities that produce the result that participatory arrangements work best when they are also deployed by others (Levine and Tyson 1990). In short, an economy may have more than one equilibrium: a superior one with participation, and an inferior one in which it is absent. In addition, if the participation equilibrium once established is fragile and subject to erosion through "distortion" of competition, then a case may be made for legislation that maintains the equilibrium.

This brief review of theoretical considerations on the likely effects of works councils indicates the absence of any single-valued expectation as to their outcome. There is no single theory that defines the operation of a wage council, and we must look to the empirical evidence.

A Review of the Empirical Literature

Econometric work on the effects of worker representation on economic performance is limited. Early studies by Kotthoff (1981) and Kirsch, Scholl, and Paul (1984) confirm that there are important differences between works councils in terms of their attitudes toward and influence on management, and that the power of the works councils increases with union density. But such studies eschew analysis of the effects of either attitudes or power on the economic performance of firms.

We focus here on four studies with direct analytical content, each of which uses data on medium-sized firms in the metalworking industry. The first three studies examine the impact of unionization *and* works councils on profits, productivity, and innovation. The final study investigates the role of collective voice vs. individual voice in determining labor turnover. While doubt necessarily attaches to the representativeness of the results reported below, it is striking that no support is adduced for the notion that works councils *per se* have any beneficial impact on performance. It is also striking that in alighting on the German "model" as an exemplar of worker participation to which other systems should aspire and even harmonize, the European Commission has seen fit to ignore these studies. We shall return to this theme later.

All four studies considered here use the same data set. Typically, two years of data on the same firm are employed to increase the number of observations. The first study by FitzRoy and Kraft (1985) is notable for its attempt to estimate using simultaneous methods a four-equation system in which the endogenous variables are hourly wages, percent of work force unionized, profitability, and salaries. Each equation includes a dummy variable identifying the presence (or otherwise) of a works council. The system of equations is estimated over pooled data for 1977 and 1979 for a sample of 61/62 firms. The basic finding is that union density is positively and significantly associated with hourly wages, profitability, and salaries, while exactly opposite results are reported for works councils (which in addition appear to lead to increased shop floor representation in unions).

The authors' interpretation of these findings rests on a distinction between the nature of works councils and unions in the German system *and* between competent and less competent management. The positive effects of unions do not reflect collective voice because wage councils rather than unions are the instrument of voice. Rather, the role of unions is akin to an intervening variable. They are a response to management pressure as proxied by salaries, it being hypothesized that higher salaries reward managers who push workers harder. This pressure leads to a demand for unions by workers at the same time as it raises profitability (unionized workers only get partial compensation for their harder work). The negative effects of works councils, on the other hand, are supposed to reflect managerial competence or lack thereof. The existence of works council, as noted earlier, is associated with a marked reduction in profitability. Efficient managers, so the argument runs, can institute adequate systems of communication and decision making without the constraints imposed by autonomous works councils—and so avoid the reduction in profits and the threat to their salaries—by offering higher wages. (Unfortunately, the coefficient estimate for the presence of a works council in the wage equation though negative is not significantly so, which net outcome the authors attribute to the fact that works councils will also have a direct effect on wages because of their influence on bonuses, *inter al.*)

FitzRoy and Kraft (1987) sharpen the managerial pressure/managerial competence hypothesis in an altogether more transparent analysis of the effect of wage councils on total factor productivity, using the same sample of firms as in their earlier study. A novel feature of the exercise is the endogenization of works council status. (Works councils are observed in 80 percent of the firms.) Simultaneous equation estimates of total factor productivity and the probability of observing a works council are provided. Specifically, the authors first estimate the probability of observing a works council via an initial probit equation that includes all the variables hypothesized to influence total factor productivity as well as those determining works council status. The predicted value is then included in the productivity equation. The coefficient estimate for this variable provides an indication of the effect of works council presence on productivity in the absence of any feedback from productivity to works council status. In the next stage, estimated productivity is used as an instrument in a final probit regression to explain works council status. The coefficient estimate for productivity now measures the feedback from exogenous productivity (purged of any works council influence) on council existence. Workplace union density is a determinant of both productivity and works council status.

The authors report that works councils are associated with reduced productivity in the simultaneous system, offering support for the hypothesis that competent managers are able to avoid the formal paraphernalia of a works council with its constraints on internal organization. (Note that efficient communications and worker participation are hypothesized to be just as much a feature of the efficient management regime as higher pay and better working conditions.) Second, the instrumented productivity variable in the final probit equation modeling the determinants of works council presence is positive and significant at conventional levels. This provides support for the authors' management pressure hypothesis. That is, higher productivity purged of any influence of the works council increases the probability of observing a works council. Thus, so the argument runs, workers who are under strong pressure to sustain a higher than average level of productivity are likely to experience lower job satisfaction and elect a works council (and join a union).

In their final study, FitzRoy and Kraft (1990) focus on works council impact on innovation, defined as the proportion of sales consisting of new products introduced over a five-year interval. The sample now comprises 1979 data for 57 firms. Works councils are again endogenized but this time the dummy variable identifying the presence (or otherwise) of a works council is interacted with workplace union density. (The mean value of union density is only 10 percent in the one-fifth of firms without a works council but 45 percent in the remainder of the sample.) It is argued that not only is a more organized work force likely to elect a council but also that a works council will carry more weight in negotiations with management when density is high *and* more likely to take a hard line in conflict situations.

Innovation is modeled as a function of (a measure of) concentration, the nature of production (flow versus batch), capital intensity, the ratio of white-collar to blue-collar workers, total employment, market share exported, a proxy for average skill level, and share of capital held by top management. Workplace organization (the composite works council/union density variable) is explained by proxies for routinized work and mobility costs, incentive pay as a proportion of total pay, the proportion of blue-collar workers classified as unskilled, and all but two of the arguments used in the innovation equation (including capital intensity), *inter al.* The authors' simultaneous weighted least squares-Tobit regression estimates point to a strong negative effect of workplace organization on the innovation measure, with no reverse causality. They do not, however, offer a rent-seeking type of explanation for this result, simply arguing that formalized structures are inimical to the flexibility that is essential for innovation and modern technology. Presumably, in the light of their previous analyses, they would add the rider "formalized structures in low-trust environments." Interestingly, it is further argued that the insignificance of capital intensity in the Tobit is evidence against rent seeking, but in the absence of a separate equation for capital intensity in the same simultaneous system this interpretation remains somewhat speculative.

The final study considered here inquires into the black box of mechanisms through which unions/works councils are supposed to achieve the benefits that have so often been attributed to them. Again pooling two years of data for the same sample of 60 metal-manufacturing firms, Kraft (1986) regresses a dummy variable capturing high/low turnover among *unskilled* workers on an index of individual voice, presence of a works council, union density, blue-collar wages, a measure of training opportunities, firm size, and variables capturing production techniques and organization structure. The individual voice argument requires some elaboration. It is constructed on the basis of replies to questions on the decision possibilities open to blue-collar workers in the areas of investment and rationalization, coordination of work groups, and the determination of (individual) job design. Kraft's probit regressions suggest that turnover is sharply reduced, the greater the possibilities for exercising individual but *not* collective voice (that is, the coefficient estimate for the works council dummy is [positive and] insignificant). Unionization enters with a negative coefficient but one that is insignificant at conventional levels. The other variables are shown to have their hypothesized effect on turnover.

To allow for the possibility that voice is endogenous, Kraft estimates a simultaneous system of probit equations. (Additional variables included in the regression explaining voice are dummies for batch production and industry; and four variables earlier included in the turnover equation are dropped, the exclusion criterion being their lack of significance.) The changes in coefficient estimates vis-à-vis the single equation model are modest. Works council influence on turnover is again insignificant at conventional levels, as is union density. The role of individual voice is strengthened and better determined. Furthermore, no feedback effects from quits to voice are detected.

In sum, the results of this admittedly sparse extant literature show little evidence of any positive impact of works councils on firm performance. Much of the evidence actually points in an opposite direction. That said, the relation between union and works council remains somewhat vague, and furthermore the data do not enable a distinction to be drawn between "types" of works council. Here, as elsewhere, the role of unobservables casts a long shadow.

The generally negative impact observed for works councils is echoed in industry-level studies of union effects on productivity and innovation (e.g. Addison, Genosko, and Schnabel 1989; Schulenburg and Wagner 1991). But we would resist the temptation to regard these and other studies as providing a complementary test— on the grounds that unionization and presence of a works council are positively correlated—because of their (acknowledged) technical limitations, typically single issue focus, and the very nature of the dual system. Yet, taken in the round, these studies may call into question the idea that a given and widely admired system of industrial relations (e.g. Marshall 1992) necessarily produces the goods in terms of improved economic performance. This suggestion is perhaps only heretical to social engineers.

New Empirical Results

The literature review presented above has a basis in a single and rather dated data set. In this section, we provide new results on works council impact using information from a survey of 101 establishments in manufacturing industry located in the federal states of Niedersachsen and Baden-Württemberg. The survey is the first step of an ongoing research project to implement a comprehensive multiwave panel data base for German establishments. The data were collected during 1990-91 by Infratest, a leading German social and opinion research company, using a mixture of interviews and written questionnaires. A copy of the questionnaire and an outline of the research project are provided in Wagner (1990). For our econometric study we use subsamples of around 50 firms for which consistent data on profitability, productivity, investment, and wages are available. All firms in our sample, having more than five employees, are subject to the Works Constitution Act (section II), and in practice around 60 percent of firms report the presence of a works council. A full description of the endogenous and exogenous variables used, together with descriptive statistics, is provided in the appendix table.

Our approach in testing for works council impact along these dimensions of firm performance is chiefly via linear regression models (for the exception, see below). As a first step, all equations are fitted using ordinary least squares (OLS). But because heteroskedasticity of an unknown form is often present in samples of firm data, we report t-values corrected for heteroskedasticity using White's method. Furthermore, since the coefficient estimates obtained via OLS methods may be highly sensitive to a small number of extreme cases (both "true" outliers and coding errors), we also deploy least median of squares (LMS) combined with reweighted least squares (RLS) methods to detect such outliers and yield robust estimators (see Rousseeuw and Leroy 1987). This procedure is of course precluded in estimating the effects of works councils on the gap between negotiated and effective wages (wage drift) given that the dependent variable may include zero as well as positive values. A Tobit procedure is used to fit the wage drift equation.

We next present the results of our single equation estimates of the correlates of firm profitability, productivity, capital investment, and remuneration (including wage drift). At the outset we need to enter three caveats. First, and most obviously, our data set, though new, has the acute disadvantage of small sample size, leading us to treat works council status as exogenous. We fully recognize that works councils will not be randomly distributed across firms and industries. Factors such as firm size, profitability, the age and gender composition of the work force, and management "attitudes" to this form of worker involvement may all be expected to influence that status. But examination of this issue—by instrumenting works councils and thus presenting a fully simultaneous system of equations—is not technically feasible given the small sample of data at our disposal. Our estimates of works council impact may thus be subject to simultaneous equations bias as well as potential selectivity bias. Second, and relatedly, our data contain usable union density information for just 25 firms and even here the values are largely "guesstimates." Accordingly, our regressions omit the union density variable found in the studies reviewed earlier. Third, the influence of works councils is captured through a simple dummy variable indicating the presence or absence of the institution. As we have argued earlier, this construct admits of none of the potential subtlety of works council influence, but at least in this data set there is a considerable nonworks-council sector.

With these preliminaries behind us, first consider the correlates of firm profitability, namely, pretax profits as a percentage of fixed capital, shown in Table 1. The influence of market power is captured by five variables: an effect stemming from imperfect competition, as proxied by the respondent firm's subjective classification of the degree of *competitive pressure* it faces; a market structure variable describing the firm's *market share*; a *capital intensity* argument which purports to indicate barriers to entry; a customer relations dummy which assumes a value of unity where the respondent firm services primarily *big customers*, who may thereby enjoy oligopsonistic leverage; and finally, a measure of product differentiation represented by the firm's *advertising/sales ratio*.

Profitability is also expected to be a function of *capacity utilization* and *product innovation*. Capacity utilization is a dichotomous variable assigned the value of unity if it exceeds 90 percent. In the presence of fixed capital and quasi-fixed labor, capacity utilization is a measure of demand which will certainly impact profitability in the short run. Product innovation, which here simply identifies whether or not the firm introduced a new product during 1989, is of ambiguous directional influence since in the short run at least it may be expected to be a drain on profitability.

Finally, the inclusion of *firm size* may be justified on the grounds that the likelihood of observing a works council increases with the level of employment. In addition, of course, other studies have suggested strong effects of firm size on profitability (see Hirsch and Addison 1986).

TABLE 1

Profit Regression Results. Dependent Variable: Net Profit
Before Taxes/Fixed Capital
(absolute t-values in round brackets, t-values corrected for
heteroskedasticity in square brackets)

Estimation procedure/ Variable	OLS[a]	LMS/RLS[b]
Constant	110.38 (3.63)°° [4.31]°°	104.71 (4.43)°° [3.97]°°
Works council	−.57 (.03) [.03]	−1.47 (.10) [.11]
Firm size	−.08 (1.34) [1.83]	−0.06 (1.28) [1.34]
Capital intensity	−.16 (1.14) [2.13]°	−.13 (1.20) [1.83]
Advertising/sales ratio	−2.55 (.22) [.27]	−4.08 (.45) [.50]
Product innovation	−28.53 (1.57) [1.87]	−27.47 (1.90) [2.07]°
Market share	.07 (.29) [.30]	.05 (.25) [.28]
Big customers	−37.40 (2.13)° [2.93]°°	−31.69 (2.36)° [2.43]°
Capacity utilization	3.21 (.21) [.28]	−4.58 (.39) [.48]
Competitive pressure	.30 (.02) [.02]	.65 (.05) [.06]
R^2	.21	.26
$\bar{R}^2$	.04	.09
n	52	48

°, °° denote significance at the .05 and .01 levels, respectively

Notes: [a] OLS = ordinary least squares;
[b] LMS/RLS = least median of squares/reweighted least squares

The results provided in Table 1 indicate that the presence of a works council is negatively associated with profitability, but note that the coefficient estimate is insignificant. Most of the other variables are also insignificant. One interesting exception is the variable describing customer relations (big customers), which has a fairly strong negative effect on profitability. This result accords with our priors and points to the potentially important but hitherto neglected role of customer relations in firm performance.

Although the negative coefficient estimate for product innovation is readily explicable, the same cannot be said of that for capital intensity. The perverse sign of the latter coefficient may, however, reflect biases introduced by the appearance of total capital employed in both the denominator of the dependent variable and the numerator of the capital intensity measure.

Despite the use of rather interesting and rarely available exogenous variables, the explanatory power of our profits equation is meager. Given the absence of controls for managerial quality and the loose relation between accounting data and profits in an economics sense, these results are perhaps to be expected even if they are somewhat disappointing.

Our estimates of the correlates of total factor productivity are derived from an extended Cobb-Douglas production function and are presented in Table 2. (We are aware of the restrictive assumptions of this functional form but it makes little sense to use more flexible production functions, such as the translog specification, given the limited number of observations and five highly correlated factor input variables.) Apart from *fixed capital* and *employment* level a number of other arguments are used to explain productivity differences, the most important of which for the purpose of the present inquiry is of course the presence or otherwise of a works council. In addition, the specification includes two variables describing market structure—*competitive pressure* and *own market share*—plus a third to reflect international competition, namely, the *export to sales ratio*. These variables might influence the productivity measure either through price effects—recall that the dependent variable is value added, which will be affected by movements in product price—or through managerial slack in imperfectly competitive regimes.

We also add controls for *capacity utilization*, the percentage of the work force made up of *skilled labor*, and the existence of *profit sharing*. The latter (dummy) variable was included since a number of studies have suggested a positive line of causation running from

TABLE 2

Extended Cobb-Douglas Production Function Regression Results.
Dependent Variable: log (value added)

Estimation procedure/ Variable	OLS	LMS/RLS
Constant	3.68 (10.02)°° [13.51]°°	3.75 (12.28)°° [15.17]°°
log (employment)	.74 (7.14)°° [9.25]°°	.79 (9.23)°° [11.65]°°
log (fixed capital)	.27 (4.25)°° [4.69]°°	.23 (3.83)°° [5.24]°°
Works council	.03 (.13) [.14]	.35 (1.93) [1.92]
Exports to sales ratio	.01 (.38) [.46]	−.002 (.75) [.80]
Competitive pressure	−.08 (.57) [.62]	−.23 (1.81) [2.05]°
Market share	−.003 (1.26) [1.58]	−.002 (.96) [1.17]
Capacity utilization	.01 (.07) [.08]	−.13 (1.13) [1.24]
Profit sharing	−.10 (.56) [.66]	−.18 (1.19) [1.61]
Skilled labor	.002 (.67) [.70]	.001 (.44) [.47]
R^2	.92	.96
$\bar{R}^2$	.94	.95
n	53	49

Notes: See Table 1.

profit sharing to productivity (see, for example, the essays in Blinder 1990).

The results given in Table 2 confirm the importance of the production factors labor and capital and point to more or less constant returns to scale in conformity with other German estimates. Few of the control variables, however, are significant at conventional levels. But the positive coefficient estimate reported for the works council dummy only narrowly fails to achieve significance at conventional levels in our preferred specification, which result some may view as offering mild support for works councils. There is also some suggestion that competitive pressure exerts a negative influence on productivity which might reflect price effects.

Recent debate on the impact of unions has shifted toward a consideration of unionism's dynamic effects on long-run performance (Addison and Hirsch 1989). In particular, many theorists would today expect to gain clearer insights into union impact along the dimension of investment than by looking to differences in productivity, or even profitability (taken in isolation), between union and nonunion plants. This is no less true of works council impact, although there is disputation as to the relative strength of rent seeking versus the rigidities introduced by worker decision rights as causes of inferior investment performance where observed.

Our data set contains information on the level of investment. We deploy two measures: *gross investment* in relation to total capital stock and *net investment* likewise divided by total capital. We eschewed use of investment per employee on the grounds that such a measure would more reflect specific technological requirements than, say, worker decision rights. To the extent that our variables capture changes in investment behavior, they are perhaps better suited to time-series than cross-section analysis.

Apart from the familiar works council dummy, our exogenous variables include *capital utilization* and *hours of overtime per employee* to represent the state of demand and the *export to sales ratio* as an indicator of whether firms are more or less "up-to-date" and therefore more or less likely to display higher investment ratios. Other variables are *firm size* and *product innovation*, the inclusion of which do not require further elaboration.

The fitted regressions are given in Table 3. It can be seen that firms with a works council present have significantly lower gross investment ratios. This does not hold true for net investment behavior, from which it would appear to follow that depreciation charges must be lower in a works council regime. Because accounting conventions with respect to depreciation bear little relation to economic principles, gross investment is likely to be the

TABLE 3

Capital Investment Regression Results. Dependent Variables:
Capital Investment/Capital Stock; Net Capital Investment/Capital Stock.

Estimation procedure/ Variable	Gross investment		Net investment	
	OLS	LMS/RLS	OLS	LMS/RLS
Constant	104.92	52.70	65.77	14.97
	(4.93)°°	(5.62)°°	(3.31)°°	(1.57)
	[3.79]°°	[4.45]°°	[2.52]°	[1.47]
Works council	−33.15	−19.61	−10.90	1.12
	(1.62)	(2.36)°	(.57)	(.13)
	[2.45]°	[2.65]°°	[.95]	[.16]
Capacity utilization	−16.15	7.13	−25.78	−5.44
	(1.05)	(1.07)	(1.80)	(.82)
	[.94]	[1.05]	[1.55]	[.85]
Firm size	0.12	.02	.10	.01
	(1.95)	(.71)	(1.18)	(.35)
	[1.58]	[1.00]	[1.38]	[.49]
Exports to sales ratio	−.12	−.08	.06	.04
	(.34)	(.59)	(.19)	(.32)
	[.62]	[.77]	[.33]	[.34]
Hours of overtime per employee	−.11	−.17	−.05	−.07
	(.63)	(2.37)°	(.34)	(.92)
	[.87]	[2.93]°°	[.39]	[1.02]
Product innovation	−50.69	−.92	−52.61	−4.41
	(2.67)°°	(.11)	(2.98)°°	(.53)
	[2.07]°	[.11]	[2.22]°	[.50]
R^2	.24	.26	.22	.05
$\bar{R}^2$	.14	.16	.12	−.09
n	54	49	54	48

Notes: See Table 1.

more relevant figure. That said, a number of problems are raised by the findings reported in the table. First and foremost, innovative activity appears to have a *negative* impact on investment, which can hardly be the case. This result would seem to reflect the presence of outliers: the effect vanishes once we apply more robust estimation techniques. It is also apparent that both capacity utilization and overtime working have perverse signs, although the coefficient estimates are in most cases insignificant. Despite the strong showing of the works council dummy, the overall performance of the investment equations is rather weak and for this reason caution must be exercised in interpreting the result that works councils adversely impact investment behavior.

Finally, we investigate works council impact on remuneration. That influence is not automatic given that the locus of wage bargaining is typically external to the firm. But wage drift is a recognized phenomenon in Germany, and we noted earlier the possibility of supplementary works agreements. We use two measures of wages here: the log of total remuneration divided by the number of employees; and "average" wage drift as reported by the firm respondent, defined as the percentage difference between negotiated and effective wages. Since reported drift may include zero values, Tobit estimation procedures have to be used. Accordingly, it was not possible to estimate heteroskedastic consistent standard errors or employ robust estimation techniques in this case.

For each earnings equation, we include *market share* and *competitive pressure* to check for a rent-sharing effect. The addition of variables measuring the percentage of the work force that is *female*, *part-time*, *blue collar*, and *skilled* is self-explanatory and need not detain us further. *Firm size* is included as an additional regressor as is conventional in exercises of this type, while admitting that the source of its (typically) positive effect is a subject of continuing controversy in the labor economics literature.

The results provided in Table 4 indicate a significantly positive coefficient estimate for the works council dummy in the LMS/RLS regression. (It is somewhat less well determined in the OLS regression.) The suggestion would appear to be that worker representation through the vehicle of a works council raises remuneration. And yet our Tobit estimates suggest that wage drift is lower in works council regimes. The two sets of finding can only be reconciled if it is the case that the base wage is higher in firms with works councils. But base wages *per se* lie outside the control of the works council, and we are seeking to identify the role of the latter.

It may of course be the case that the imprecision of the average drift measure—this is not actually computed but is instead based on management estimates—may mask the true contribution of works councils to the upward drift of wages. Also, the principal effect of works councils may be upon nonwage labor costs, such as pensions, and hence escape identification in regressions of the type reported in Table 4. (We note parenthetically that our attempt to model the determinants of nonwage labor costs [betrieblich vereinbarte Personalnebenkosten] proved abortive.)

TABLE 4

Wage and Wage Drift Regression Results. Dependent Variables:
log (Wage Per Employee); Average Percentage Wage Drift.

Estimation procedure/	Wage		Wage Drift
Variable	OLS	LMS/RLS	Tobit
Constant	4.23	4.28	24.87
	(21.95)°°	(27.57)°°	(4.90)°°
	[20.78]°°	[23.97]°°	—
Works council	.20	.22	−5.97
	(1.80)	(2.49)°	(2.03)°
	[1.93]	[2.73]°°	—
Female	−.013	−.008	.04
	(4.63)°°	(3.48)°°	(.52)°°
	[3.92]°°	[3.88]°°	—
Blue collar	.0006	−.003	−.19
	(.23)	(1.39)	(2.81)°°
	[.23]	[1.30]	—
Part time	.005	−.005	.02
	(.84)	(1.14)	(.13)
	[.92]	[1.77]	—
Skilled labor	−.002	.001	.19
	(1.10)	(.61)	(3.59)°°
	[.94]	[.53]	—
Firm size	.0001	−.0002	−.003
	(.23)	(.82)	(.48)
	[.33]	[.82]	—
Market share	−.0007	.0001	−.03
	(.50)	(.12)	(.85)
	[.61]	[.15]	—
Competitive pressure	−.05	−.004	−4.68
	(.55)	(.06)	(1.91)
	[.67]	[.09]	—
R^2	.55	.65	
$\bar{R}^2$	.46	.58	
n	52	48	43

Notes: See Table 1.

In conclusion, the influence of works councils on remuneration is necessarily opaque. In addition to the ambiguity attaching to the interpretation of the works council coefficient in the wage equation, there is the point that, although the coefficient of determination is quite high, few individual variables are themselves significant. This result would suggest that the number of observations is too small in relation to the number of variables. As far as wage drift is concerned, the results are more consistent with a response to market forces than to bargaining power—note the opposingly signed coefficients on the blue-collar and skilled-labor variables.

Overall, our results are frankly inconclusive and underscore the need for further research with improved data. As noted above, inconclusive results such as these may well reflect the small number of observations; in effect too much is asked of the data.

We conclude this section with a brief summary of a different set of research findings having to do with the effect of works councils on the process of labor adjustment within the firm. In a study primarily intended to investigate the effect of the deregulatory 1985 Employment Promotion Act on employment development, Büchtemann and Kraft (1992) also examine the independent influence of works councils. The authors investigate the determinants of relative employment growth, 1985 to 1987, in a sample of 916 randomly selected firms from the service and manufacturing sectors. The most important exogenous variables in this connection are the (increased) possibilities of using fixed-term contracts under the Act and a dummy variable indicating the presence or otherwise of a works council. Additional arguments include firm size, age of the firm, short-time working, and labor force skill mix, *inter al.*

Since the likelihood of observing a works council is a function of firm size, the authors first instrument works council status to avoid simultaneous equations bias. The employment growth equation is then fitted for the sample of firms recording a positive change in employment using symmetrically censored least squares methods to correct for potential selectivity bias caused by the omission of firms with declining or stagnant employment.

It is reported that works council firms (constituting roughly half of the sample) have significantly slower employment growth than their counterparts without this body. The authors argue that this result is *not* produced by employment smoothing over the cycle. Had this been the case, the negative coefficient on the works council dummy would have been even greater for an employment growth equation estimated over the full sample (i.e. including negative employment growth firms), which result was not observed. Such secular effects are of course consistent with rent-seeking behavior and noncooperative bargaining.

Conclusions

The empirical material reported here consistently fails to provide statistically significant evidence of any positive works council impact on firm performance. Although the basic tenor of the earlier empirical literature is clearly favorable to the notion that consultation and participation are productive of efficiency, such benefits are viewed as occurring outside of the formal machinery of workplace governance embedded in works councils. Rather, consultation and participation are viewed as part of the efficient manager's bag of tricks. This conclusion follows more or less ineluctably from the empirical findings and the dummy variables approach used to separate out works council impact (in the absence of better data that would permit the researchers to evaluate works council "attitude," *inter al.*). It could nevertheless be true that works councils "work" for German workers while not necessarily retarding productivity, even if there is nothing about the institution *per se* that guarantees superior performance. Note that this latter interpretation still calls into question the "models" of social engineers, most notably the European Commission which appears bent on establishing set structures of worker involvement, often grounded in the German "experience." (For a detailed discussion of the participatory models selected by the Commission under such initiatives as the Fifth Company Law Directive, the European Company Statute, and the European Works Council, *inter al.*, see Addison and Siebert 1991, 1992.) There is evidently no such thing as a quick institutional fix.

Those of "collective voice" persuasion would not necessarily be surprised by the results uncovered here, doubtless noting the importance of the unobserved industrial relations climate to observed outcomes. Nevertheless, they might have expected to observe more positive readings of this exemplar of voice than we have been able to report. We would consider it unfortunate if such analysts were simply to focus on the issue of sample construction and write off these results on the grounds that like is not being compared with like. The apparently powerful role of *individual* voice in moderating quits should also be of concern to proponents of the collective voice model.

The formulation and testing of the management competence/ management pressure hypothesis represents a serious attempt to get to grips with endogenous unions and works councils even if implementation of a fully simultaneous system of equations is ruled out by data limitations. But there is an urgent need for larger data sets that incorporate a richer mix of industrial relations variables, including strikes, conflict management, codetermination at board level, presence of quality circles and team systems, and so on, in the absence of which discussion of works council impact will be cloaked in controversy. The frankly inconclusive results of our own empirical inquiry into works council impact which, though they do not cause us to abandon our conclusion to the effect that works councils are emphatically not a panacea, nevertheless strengthen the call for additional research. This call is especially urgent in the light of the ongoing decentralization of German industrial relations.

References

Addison, John T., and Barry T. Hirsch. 1989. "Union Effects on Productivity, Profits, and Growth: Has the Long Run Arrived?" *Journal of Labor Economics* 7 (January), pp. 72-105.
Addison, John T., Joachim Genosko, and Claus Schnabel. 1989. "Gewerkschaften, Produktivität, und Rent Seeking." Jahrbücher für Nationalökonomie und Statistik 206 (March), pp. 102-116.
Addison, John T., and W. Stanley Siebert. 1991. "The Social Charter of the European Community: Evolution and Controversies." *Industrial and Labor Relations Review* 44 (July), pp. 597-625.
_____. 1992. "The European Community Social Charter: Whatever Next?" *British Journal of Industrial Relations* 30 (December), pp. 495-513.
Blinder, Alan S., ed. 1990. *Paying for Productivity: A Look at the Evidence.* Washington, DC: The Brookings Institution.
Büchtemann, Christoph F., and Kornelius Kraft. 1992. "The Effects of the Employment Promotion Act and Works Councils on Employment Growth." Unpublished manuscript, University of Fribourg.
FitzRoy, Felix R., and Kornelius Kraft. 1985. "Unionization, Wages and Efficiency: Theories and Evidence from the U.S. and West Germany." *Kyklos* 38, pp. 537-554.
_____. 1987. "Efficiency and Internal Organization: Works Councils in West German Firms." *Economica* 54 (November), pp. 493-504.
_____. 1990. "Innovation, Rent Sharing and the Organization of Labour in the Federal Republic of Germany." *Small Business Economics* 2, pp. 95-103.
Freeman, Richard B., and James L. Medoff. 1979. "The Two Faces of Unionism." *Public Interest* 57 (Fall), pp. 69-93.
_____. 1984. *What Do Unions Do?* New York: Basic Books.
Galenson, Walter. 1991. *New Trends in Employment Practices: An International Survey.* New York: Greenwood Press.
Hirsch, Barry T. 1991. *Labor Unions and the Economic Performance of Firms.* Kalamazoo, MI: W.E. Upjohn Institute.
_____. 1992. "Firm Investment Behavior and Collective Bargaining Strategy." *Industrial Relations* 31 (Winter), pp. 95-121.
Hirsch, Barry T., and John T. Addison. 1986. *The Economic Analysis of Unions: New Approaches and Evidence.* London and Boston: Allen & Unwin.
Hirschman, Albert O. 1970. *Exit, Voice and Loyalty.* Cambridge, MA: Harvard University Press.
Jacobi, Otto, and Walther Müller-Jentsch. 1990. "West Germany: Continuity and Structural Change." In *European Industrial Relations: The Challenge of Flexibility,* eds. Guido Baglioni and Colin Crouch. London: Sage.

Kirsch, Werner, Wolfgang Scholl, and Günther Paul. 1984. *Mitbestimmung in der Unternehmenspraxis.* Munchen: Planungs-und Organisationswissenschaftliche Schriften.

Kotthoff, Hermann. 1981. *Betriebsräte und betriebliche Herrschaft. Eine Typologie von Partizipationsmustern im Industriebetrieb.* Frankfurt and New York: Campus Verlag.

Kraft, Kornelius. 1986. "Exit and Voice in the Labor Market: An Empirical Study of Quits." *Journal of Institutional and Theoretical Economics* 142 (December), pp. 695-715.

Lampert, Heinz. 1991. *Lehrbuch der Sozialpolitik.* Berlin: Springer-Verlag.

Levine, David I., and Laura D'Andrea Tyson. 1990. "Participation, Productivity, and the Firm's Environment." In *Paying for Productivity—A Look at the Evidence,* ed. Alan S. Blinder. Washington, DC: The Brookings Institution.

Marshall, Ray. 1992. "Work Organization, Unions, and Economic Performance." In *Unions and Economic Performance,* eds. Lawrence Mishel and Paula B. Voos. Armonk and London: M. E. Sharpe.

Milgrom, Paul R. 1988. "Employment Contracts, Influence Activities, and Efficient Organization Design." *Journal of Political Economy* 96 (February), pp. 42-60.

Niedenhoff, Horst-Udo. 1988. *Betriebsratwahlen: die Betriebsräte bis 1990.* Köln: Deutscher Instituts-Verlag.

Olson, Mancur. 1982. *The Rise and Decline of Nations: Economic Growth, Stagflation, and Social Rigidities.* New Haven: Yale University Press.

Rousseeuw, Peter J., and Annik M. Leroy. 1987. *Robust Regression and Outlier Detection.* New York: Wiley.

Schnabel, Claus. 1991. "Trade Unions and Productivity: The German Evidence." *British Journal of Industrial Relations* 29 (March), pp. 15-24.

Schregle, Johannes. 1978. "Co-determination in the Federal Republic of Germany: A Comparative View." *International Labour Review* 117 (January-February), pp. 81-98.

Schulenburg, Johann-Mattias Graf von der, and Joachim Wagner. 1991. "Advertising, Innovation and Market Structure: A Comparison between the United States of America and the Federal Republic of Germany." In *Innovation and Technical Change: An International Comparison,* eds. Zoltan J. Acs and David B. Andretsch. New York: Harvester Wheatsheaf.

Soltwedel, Rüdiger. 1988. "Employment Problems in West Germany—The Role of Institutions, Labor Law, and Government Intervention." *Carnegie-Rochester Conference Series on Public Policy* 28, pp. 153-220.

Turner, Lowell. 1992. "Industrial Relations and Reorganization of Work in West Germany: Lessons for the U.S." In *Unions and Economic Competitiveness,* eds. Lawrence Mishel and Paula B. Voos. Armonk and London: M. E. Sharpe.

Wagner, Joachim. 1990. "Das Firmenpanel-Projekt in Niedersachsen und Stand der Arbeiten im Herbst 1990." Vorträge im Fachbereich Wirtschaftswissenschaften, Band 8, Universität Hannover.

APPENDIX

Description of Variables and Means (Standard Deviations)

Table/Variable	Table 1 Col. 1	Table 1 Col. 2	Table 2 Col. 1	Table 2 Col. 2	Table 3 Cols. 1 and/or 3	Table 3 Col. 2	Table 3 Col. 4	Table 4 Col. 1	Table 4 Col. 2	Table 4 Col. 3
Profit rate (value-added less depreciation of less total remuneration of employees [= pretax profits] divided by total assets [= fixed capital], multiplied by 100)	53.28 (51.43)	47.75 (40.08)								
Firm size (number of employees at end 1989)	150.85 (164.53)	160.52 (167.60)			158.65 (170.30)	160.00 (171.83)	163.04 (172.33)	160.17 (172.93)	170.29 (176.23)	173.30 (178.37)
Advertising/sales ratio (advertising costs divided by sales, multiplied by 100)	.737 (.720)	.726 (.708)								
Market share (own market share [percent] of firm's most important product group)	39.39 (30.33)	37.25 (29.67)	38.49 (29.22)	39.16 (29.64)				40.10 (30.32)	38.54 (31.09)	36.72 (28.70)
Capital intensity (fixed capital divided by number of employees)	41.39 (58.97)	44.12 (60.61)								
log (value added)			8.89 (1.46)	8.90 (1.51)						
log (fixed capital)			7.53 (1.81)	7.57 (1.80)						
log (employment)			4.36 (1.28)	4.44 (1.29)						

APPENDIX (Continued)

Description of Variables and Means (Standard Deviations)

Table/Variable	Table 1		Table 2		Table 3			Table 4		
	Col. 1	Col. 2	Col. 1	Col. 2	Cols. 1 and/or 3	Col. 2	Col. 4	Col. 1	Col. 2	Col. 3
Exports to sales ratio (percentage of sales exported)			26.68 (25.49)	25.92 (25.07)	24.56 (25.44)	25.76 (25.32)	25.88 (25.57)			
Skilled labor (number of skilled workers, [Facharbeiter], divided by total number of employees)			33.91 (25.21)	32.90 (25.32)				32.30 (24.10)	31.05 (24.41)	34.01 (24.19)
Gross investment (investment in fixed capital divided by capital stock, multiplied by 100)					51.75 (58.57)	36.49 (23.26)				
Net investment (investment in fixed capital less depreciation divided by capital stock, multiplied by 100)					23.10 (54.04)		7.90 (20.23)			
Hours of overtime per employee (total number of hours of overtime in 1989 divided by total number of employees at end 1989)					56.85 (45.32)	54.89 (44.09)	55.87 (44.01)			
Female employees (percent female employment)								29.85 (21.50)	29.64 (21.51)	27.46 (20.00)
Blue collar (percent blue-collar employment)								63.17 (19.10)	64.16 (17.80)	62.37 (18.03)
Part-time (percent part-time employment)								6.64 (8.66)	7.19 (8.79)	6.05 (7.95)
log (wage per employee) (log of total remuneration divided by number of employees)								3.91 (.40)	3.97 (.32)	

APPENDIX *(Continued)*

Description of Variables and Means (Standard Deviations)

Table/Variable	Table 1		Table 2		Table 3			Table 4		
	Col. 1	Col. 2	Col. 1	Col. 2	Cols. 1 and/or 3	Col. 2	Col. 4	Col. 1	Col. 2	Col. 3
Average wage drift (percentage difference between contractual and effective wages)										12.49 (8.77)
Dummy variables										
Works council (1 if works council, 0 otherwise)	.596	.625	.62	.67	.57	.59	.60	.63	.65	.70
Product innovation (1 if firm introduced a new product in 1989, 0 otherwise)	.673	.708			.67	.71	.73			
Big customers (1 if firm has 1 or 2-10 big customers, 0 otherwise)	.596	.583								
Capacity utilization (1 if ≥ 90%, 0 otherwise)	.558	.562	.55	.53	.61	.63	.63			
Competitive pressure (1 if high competitive pressure, 0 otherwise)	.577	.562	.60	.59				.60	.58	.65
Profit sharing (1 if profit-sharing scheme in operation, 0 otherwise)			.17	.16						

CHAPTER 10

The Saturn Partnership: Co-Management and the Reinvention of the Local Union

SAUL RUBINSTEIN
MIT

MICHAEL BENNETT
UAW

THOMAS KOCHAN
MIT

Since its inception, the partnership arrangement between the Saturn Corporation and the United Auto Workers (UAW) has achieved international attention. The unique role the union played in the conception and design of Saturn and its present responsibilities in Saturn's operations management and governance breaks with many of the established legal doctrines, principles, and customs that have guided American labor-management relations since the New Deal collective bargaining system was first put in place. In implementing this partnership, Saturn management and the local union have gone well beyond past attempts by General Motors and the UAW to create more cooperative and productive relationships through participation in joint labor-management committees and teams. The institution of the partnership attempts to integrate labor into the organization's long range and strategic planning and day-to-day operational decision making. Unlike most labor-management efforts, Saturn's joint committees have responsibility for strategic-level decision making, and an even more radical departure from traditional organization has taken place at the shop floor and middle-management levels. Saturn's work force has been organized into self-directed work teams responsible to a middle-management organization half of whom are local UAW members. In this way the local union is in fact *co-managing* the business.

While much has been reported about the market response to Saturn, its technology, and the general principles used to design its initial labor-management system, few details have yet been provided on how its innovations in labor-management relations are evolving in practice. This paper describes the new role the local union plays in this partnership and reviews experience to date with this new organizational form. Special emphasis is given to the union's leadership, structure, and organization. Finally, we suggest an analytic framework for assessing the implications of this model of labor-management relations to the specific stakeholders involved and to the broader labor, management, and public policy communities.

This paper is only a preliminary portrait of the local union's role at Saturn. A more complete assessment of the Saturn partnership and the local union must be reserved for a later date after more experience has accumulated. We should also clarify our personal positions with respect to the partnership, the model of unionism described here, and the Saturn Corporation. Given our respective roles as the president of the local union (Michael Bennett) and researchers working closely with the union and management at Saturn (Saul Rubinstein and Thomas Kochan), we clearly believe in the principles on which the partnership is based.

We also see Saturn as an extremely important innovation in U.S. industrial relations and organizational governance that, if understood properly, could inform other efforts that we believe are needed to help transform traditional labor and management practices (Kochan, Katz, and McKersie 1986; Kochan and Useem 1992). Yet like any new experiment, implementing these principles is a trial-and-error process. Our action-research project is designed to help the parties learn from their experiences as they go along and then communicate these lessons to others interested in learning from Saturn.

This paper is part of a broader ongoing collaborative research program at Saturn involving several teams from MIT, Saturn management, and the UAW. While our focus in this paper is on the role of the local union, we are also studying other aspects of the organizational and governance system at Saturn (see LeFauve and Hax 1992). Future reports will examine in more detail aspects of the manufacturing and work organization, the role of information systems in supporting teams and problem solving, and Saturn's marketing and distribution system.

Background

Figure 1 presents a time line of some of the key events in Saturn's partnership history to date. Saturn is a separate wholly owned subsidiary corporation of General Motors. GM's expressed objective in creating Saturn was to build a small car in the U.S. aimed at what it refers to as "conquest sales" from Japanese automakers (i.e., sales that otherwise would have gone to a Japanese product).

In early 1982, General Motors concluded that it could not manufacture a small car competitively in the U.S. under the existing GM/UAW contract and so in 1983 approached the UAW International which led to the formation of a joint union-management committee charged with evaluating the key success factors of world-class manufacturing. This joint study team started with a clean sheet approach as it explored and evaluated practices throughout the world. Its findings were embodied in a set of basic organizing principles for Saturn (Figure 2).

Saturn's manufacturing operations are located in Spring Hill, Tennessee at a fully integrated 4.2 million square foot facility including foundry, engine and transmission plant, stamping, body fabrication, interior parts manufacturing, and assembly. Its engineering center is located in Troy, Michigan. Current investment is

FIGURE 1

Partnership Evolution and Development

1982:	GM Small Car Study
1983:	Joint GM/UAW "Committee of 99" Study World-Class Manufacturing
1985:	Memorandum of Agreement on Saturn Corporation
1986:	Joint Supplier Selection Begins First UAW Hiring
1987:	Approval of Initial $1.9 Billion Saturn Capitalization by GM Board of Directors
1988:	Addition of UAW Module Advisors as Partners
1989:	Addition of UAW Crew Coordinators and Staff Partners
1990:	First Car off the Line First Local Union General Election
1991:	Second Crew First Member-to-Member Survey Agreement Renewal Process Withdrawal of UAW International Representative From SAC
1992:	First Election of Team Leaders Work Unit Business Plan Development Initiation of Off-line Problem-Solving Process

estimated at $5 billion including product development costs as well as plant and equipment. Employment is currently over 7,000 with approximately 5,300 UAW members relocated from 136 GM locations in 34 states. Saturn is 100 percent union in a right-to-work state.

The original "Committee of 99," as the joint study team came to be called, envisioned a new form of organizational governance enabling management and the local union to jointly manage the business. Its intent was for the union to be a full partner in decision making through consensus at all levels of the organization with the right to block decisions and provide alternatives based on the needs of the people and the business. In 1985 a 28-page Memorandum of Agreement between the UAW International and the Saturn Corporation outlined the underlying principles of the partnership (Figure 2) and the team and committee structure (Figure 3).

FIGURE 2

Saturn's Organizing Principles

- Treat people as a fixed asset. Provide opportunities for them to maximize their contributions and value to the organization. Provide extensive training and skill development to all employees.
- The Saturn organization will be based on groups which will attempt to identify and work collaboratively toward common goals.
- Saturn will openly share all information including financial data.
- Decision making will be based on consensus through a series of formal joint labor-management committees, or Decision Rings. As a stakeholder in the operation of Saturn the UAW will participate in business decisions as a full partner including site selection and construction, process and product design, choice of technologies, supplier selection, make-buy decisions, retail dealer selection, pricing, business planning, training, business systems development, budgeting, quality systems, productivity improvement, job design, new product development, recruitment and hiring, maintenance, and engineering.
- Self-managed teams or Work Units will be the basic building blocks of the organization.
- Decision-making authority will be located at the level of the organization where the necessary knowledge resides, and where implementation takes place. Emphasis will be placed on the Work Unit.
- There will be a minimum of job classifications.
- Saturn will have a jointly developed and administered recruitment and selection process, and Work Units will hire their own team members. Seniority will not be the basis for selection, and the primary recruiting pool will consist of active and laid off GM/UAW employees.
- The technical and social work organization will be integrated.
- There will be fewer full-time elected UAW officials and fewer labor relations personnel responsible for contract administration.
- Saturn's reward system will be designed to encourage everyone's efforts toward the common goals of quality, cost, timing and value to the customer.[1]

FIGURE 3

Saturn Partnership Structure

- Work units are organized into teams of 6 to 15 members, electing their own leaders who remain working members of the unit. They are self-directed and empowered with the authority, responsibility, and resources necessary to meet their day-to-day assignments and goals including producing to budget, quality, housekeeping, safety and health, maintenance, material and inventory control, training, job assignments, repairs, scrap control, vacation approvals, absenteeism, supplies, recordkeeping, personnel selection and hiring, work planning, and work scheduling.

- Saturn has no supervisors in the traditional sense. Teams interrelated by geography, product, or technology are organized into modules. Modules have common Advisors.

- Modules are integrated into three Business Units: Body Systems (stamping, body fabrication, injection molding, and paint); Powertrain (lost foam casting, machining and assembly of engines and transmissions); and Vehicle Systems (vehicle interior, chassis, hardware, trim, exterior panels and assembly).

- Joint labor-management Decision Rings meet weekly:

    - At the corporate level the Strategic Action Council (SAC) concerns itself with company-wide long-range planning, and relations with dealers, suppliers, stockholders, and the community. Participating in the SAC for the union is the local president and, on occasion, a UAW national representative.

    - The Manufacturing Action Council (MAC) covers the Spring Hill manufacturing and assembly complex. On the MAC representing the local is the union president and the four vice presidents who also serve as the UAW bargaining committee.

    - Each Business Unit has a joint labor-management Decision Ring at the plant level. The local president appoints an elected executive board member who is joined by UAW Module Advisors and Crew Coordinators in representing the union.

    - Decision Rings are also organized at the module level. Module Advisors and the elected Work Unit Counselors (team leaders) participate in the module Decision Rings.

Key Features of the Saturn Partnership

As we will discuss below, the partnership organization and the structure of the local union have evolved significantly over time. At present we have identified four distinct dimensions or subprocesses of the Saturn partnership. Only two of these subprocesses appeared in the original design by GM and the UAW International: joint labor-management committees (Decision Rings) and on-line self-directed work teams (Work Units). Since 1985 two other subprocesses have been developed locally by the parties. These include off-line problem-solving teams (Problem Resolution Circles) and co-management through individual one-on-one (Partnering) between the union and management in both staff and line organizations. It is through this last dimension, co-management, that Saturn and the UAW have become unique in U.S. industrial relations with institutional arrangements that directly challenge long-held assumptions regarding the limits of labor's role in the management process.

Organizational Governance

To understand the joint governance arrangements at Saturn it is important to see not only the formal labor-management decision-ring committee structure described above and put in place by the 1985 memorandum, but also the individual one-on-one partnerships which have been developed over the past few years throughout the management organization. These individual partnerships were initiated by the local union leadership which recognized that they could not fulfill their managerial responsibilities simply through off-line decision rings meeting weekly. The development of one-on-one partnering provided union leaders with an opportunity to contribute to day-to-day management, making operating decisions and supporting the work units.

Figure 4 illustrates the four dimensions of Saturn's labor-management partnership. We propose this framework for analyzing these arrangements and comparing Saturn's joint governance system to other models of joint labor-management activity. We see the partnership providing opportunities for both off-line planning, decision making, and problem solving, as well as on-line control of day-to-day operations. Further, it is important to distinguish between the institutional arrangements involving the local union leadership and those organized around the work force involved in shop-floor production. While we have seen other U.S. joint labor-management governance arrangements include off-line labor-management committees and teams, as well as on-line self-directed work groups, we are aware of no other organization which has developed a process for *on-line co-management by the union*.

For example, union leaders have been partnered with nonrepresented Saturn employees through a joint selection process to carry out new roles as operations' middle management replacing the foremen, general foremen, and superintendents found in traditional

FIGURE 4

	Union (Institution)	Work Force
Off-line	Labor-Management Committees (Decision Rings)	Problem-Solving Teams (Problem Resolution Circles)
On-line	Partnering: Operating & Staff Middle Management	Self-Directed Work Teams (Work Units)

GM plants. At Saturn, self-directed work teams are organized into modules based on product, process, or geography. Each module has two advisors to provide guidance and resources. While both are jointly selected by the union and Saturn management, one is represented by the UAW, and the other is not.

The union views its selected members as supplementing the local leadership. Both partners approve payroll, overtime, and purchase orders. They also facilitate decision making with the elected team leaders. Module advisors have no authority to discharge, hire, or discipline workers, nor can they write grievances. Their focus is on organizing and managing resources. Module advisors also represent their work units at the business unit (plant-level) labor-management committee meetings. All nonrepresented module advisors now have union partners who share all of their responsibilities equally.

It should be noted, however, that this partnering arrangement in the production areas has not raised indirect staffing headcount when compared to traditional plants, since each pair of module advisors is responsible for supporting an average of 100 production employees. This high direct to indirect ratio of approximately 50:1 results from both the unique role of the module advisor and from the design of the work teams which are empowered to assume many of the responsibilities of traditional foreman. In most GM plants direct to indirect manning in production areas averages 25:1.[2] Even NUMMI with its team-based "lean production" system is operating at a direct to indirect ratio of 18:1.[3]

Further, in each business unit are middle managers known as crew coordinators, who are organized across each shift and are responsible for providing leadership and resources to the module advisors. Every nonrepresented crew coordinator has a union partner who shares decision-making and problem-solving responsibilities.

Represented module advisors were first put in place in 1988, and crew coordinators were added in 1989. From 1989 to 1990 functional partnering in the staff areas was extended to sales, service, and marketing; finance; industrial engineering; quality assurance; health and safety; training; organizational development; and corporate communications. Maintenance was added in 1991 and product and process development in 1992.

As of this writing, the partnering involves over 375 union members including 91 module advisors, 24 crew coordinators, 51 functional coordinators with site-wide responsibility, 53 functional coordinators at the business unit level, and 155 with module support responsibilities for quality, engineering, materials, etc. Elected union executive board members are partnered with business unit leaders (plant managers) or have partnership arrangements in staff or line positions. Jointly selected union members fill the balance of the partnerships. These union partners have had the opportunity to join directly in the managerial debates and decisions that shape Saturn's strategy. Thus, partnering goes beyond the formal labor-management committee structure. Essentially, what would be considered middle management in most organizations now contains a significant number of one-on-one partnerships between non-represented managers and their represented UAW counterparts. Saturn is the only organization we are aware of in the United States, in which union members are filling so many managerial operating and staff positions. We believe this example of labor's role in management represents the most far-reaching innovation in the Saturn governance system.

Given the importance of this unique feature, our future research will focus on more fully understanding how the partners jointly fulfill these new roles and responsibilities. Particular attention will be given to understanding how power, authority, functional responsibility, and decision making are shared and to understanding the effects of this arrangement on organizational performance and workplace democracy.

Does the Union Add Value?

A critical question that any outside observer of Saturn is likely to ask is whether the union actually adds value to the management of the organization through this partnership arrangement. And if so, how? These are extremely difficult questions to answer given the very nature of the partnership. That is, the essence of the partnership is that union and management representatives work together to achieve integrative (joint-gain) solutions to problems or decisions. In this type of co-management process, it is hard to estimate the independent effects or contributions made by one side of the partnership. Rather than attempt to make this type of assessment, we will illustrate, through a series of specific decisions and activities, the role that the union has played in various co-management tasks encountered to date. Then drawing on these and other examples from our research, we will offer a preliminary view on the ways union participation in Saturn's management and governance adds value.

Suppliers. The union was a full partner in supplier selection, helping to develop a sourcing process from 1986 to 1989. The original 1985 Memorandum of Agreement states:

> The mission of Saturn is to market vehicles developed and manufactured in the United States that are world leaders in quality, cost and consumer satisfaction through the integration of people, technology and business systems. Consistent with being quality and cost competitive, a goal of Saturn is to utilize American-made components in assembly of its vehicles.[4]

The union appointed representatives to each of more than 300 product development teams joining product engineers, manufacturing engineers, material managers, and financial/accounting management. These teams qualified suppliers based on a formula which evaluated quality, costs, delivery reliability, and labor relations. They reached consensus recommendations which were forwarded to the UAW International and Saturn management for review and approval.

Both management and the union reported a great deal of early struggle in supplier selection, yet over time common goals around quality and price were established. The international union maintained a strong preference for GM-allied suppliers employing UAW members. Non-allied UAW shops were seen as the next best choice followed by non-allied union shops. If GM-allied suppliers were not chosen, the international union would often put a "hold" on the decision. Partnerships were then established between Saturn and allied, as well as non-allied, suppliers to help them qualify. Help would include the development of a plan and demonstration of commitment to improve quality and productivity. For example, when the initial decision for a supplier of headlamps was going in the direction of a Japanese firm, the UAW International helped the GM Inland Fisher Guide division qualify as the supplier through an agreement to have them acquire the Japanese technology to produce the headlamps domestically. Thus, the UAW took on the role of upgrading the quality and operations of its member firms in order to help them qualify as suppliers while maintaining the integrity of Saturn's standards.

The result has been the development of a supplier network which provides 96 percent U.S. and over 98 percent North American content. Local Union 1853 continues to be active in new supplier selection and, in some cases, has acted to defend Saturn's decisions from GM and UAW International pressure to choose GM suppliers. This model of joint planning and decision making in sourcing could be a useful approach for other U.S. unions and management who are struggling to solve the problem of contracting out work or seeking high-quality domestic suppliers.

Marketing and public relations. The union also participates directly in the selection of retailers. Not surprisingly this is quite a change from the traditional GM management culture and has not occurred without some resistance. For example, when union representatives began their discussions with and selection of potential retailers, Saturn's marketing and sales officials resisted the UAW's involvement in the process. This resistance quickly subsided over time as union representatives demonstrated their ability to help convince potential retailers to invest in what was once seen as a risky undertaking. Both management and local UAW leadership now agree that it was the union, in discussing the partnership and Saturn's commitment to quality with potential retailers, that had the greatest impact in convincing them to individually invest the necessary $3 to $5 million. According to Saturn's President Richard "Skip" LeFauve, "In order for partnership and consensus decision-making process to have meaning, each party must put something at risk. The significance of UAW involvement in retailer selection is the commitment made to quality. They put themselves at risk, on the line for performance."

Today local union representatives are involved in the retail side of Saturn's business with marketing and sales representatives and retailers. The union was involved in the development of the new customer-focused sales approaches which included non-negotiable pricing, participated in the selection of the corporate advertising agency, and was an early supporter of the 1991 decision to replace rather than repair cars containing a defective coolant. Union representatives participate on both the Franchise Operating Team decision ring and the Customer Action Council. In this arena the UAW has experienced alliances with retailers, sometimes differing with executives who tend to give greater weight to the effects of a decision on the corporation's short-term bottom line.

Partnership planning. The local union leadership developed annual "Partnership Implementation Plans" in 1986, 1987, 1988, 1989, and 1990. These plans served to interpret and expand the initial 1985 Memorandum of Agreement and outlined detailed steps for the union's development, implementation, and administration of the partnership throughout Saturn. It is out of these plans that the partnering in middle management evolved.

Product development. The union had its most significant product development impact in Powertrain. UAW team members argued for building prototypes on the same fixtures that were to be used in production, a recommendation not originally supported by engineering. In implementing this recommendation the team found they could not perform the assembly on the intended fixtures and had to modify them. Thus Saturn was able to simultaneously debug both the product and the assembly process, convincing management of the benefit of early involvement of union members in product and process design.

In 1989 and 1990 Saturn engaged in a great deal of discussion about how to expand its product line. Saturn's marketing organization and retailers wanted a convertible and a station wagon. Both could not be introduced at the same time, and the convertible had structural problems which needed to be solved. The local union supported the position of introducing the station wagon first, arguing that while the convertible carried more product image for Saturn, the station wagon represented higher potential sales and therefore improved employment security. A consensus was reached to introduce the station wagon first.

Negotiations. During the 1991 agreement renewal negotiations, the local union surveyed the entire membership to determine their issues and needs. From this input the union developed its bargaining priorities and then worked with Saturn management in an attempt to find integrative solutions to the top ten issues identified. Three of these issues were economic (e.g., pensions), while the remaining seven were operational and specific to the partnership and the Saturn governance system (e.g., availability of technical and managerial experts to solve production and quality problems). Negotiations took over seven months and were conducted with no strike vote, no formal submission of demands or counter proposals, and no strike deadline. The membership ratified the agreement by 83 percent.

Training and development. Saturn and the UAW local are attempting to provide workers with skill sets normally not found in conventional manufacturing facilities. New Saturn members receive from 350 to 700 hours of training before they are allowed to build the car. The work force is trained in work team organization, problem solving, decision making, conflict resolution, and labor history. Further, they develop skills in areas traditionally reserved for management including budgeting, business planning and scheduling, cost analysis, manufacturing methods, ergonomics, industrial engineering, job design, accounting, recordkeeping, statistical process control, design of experiments and data analysis. Recognizing the need for a highly skilled work force, the union proposed linking the implementation of organization-wide training to the risk and reward compensation plan (discussed in greater detail below).

Operating plan and work schedules. In 1991 the union could not ignore the growing market demand and, in support of the retailers, reacted to the need to increase production. A joint task force was formed to explore a new staffing arrangement and eliminate bottlenecks, thus increasing throughput. This task force generated options that were presented to all work units. The plan they selected became the current operating plan which includes a 50-hour workweek until a third crew can be added and bottlenecks eliminated.

Business planning. In 1992 the union initiated a bottom-up planning process to identify problems that limited productivity, quality, and profitability. Over a six-week period work units identified 1,150 specific action items and presented these to Saturn's president and his top leadership team. One outgrowth of this process and related research was the realization that Saturn lacked an effective off-line problem-solving system for issues that involved multiple work groups or required joint action from the work units, middle management, and Saturn's engineering professionals. At the union's initiative a two-day meeting was held with the union leadership team and a cross section of Saturn executives representing engineering and operations. The participants discussed approaches to address the need for more extensive and effective problem-solving activity. This event also provided an opportunity for engineering management and union leaders to reaffirm their joint interest in solving quality problems. Local union representatives are now working together with Saturn engineering and operations management to implement an integrative off-line problem-solving process throughout the organization.

Performance appraisal. In 1992 the union took the initiative to implement an appraisal system for module advisors in order to better understand and improve performance in this newly created managerial position. The appraisals are based on input from work unit members and leaders, crew coordinators, and peer module advisors. As of this writing only the union module advisors have been appraised.

Measurement. In order to obtain more useful and accurate information on operations, the union has initiated a work team measurement system (i.e., information system tool kits) designed to help teams perform their various functions and produce the data they need to support their own problem-solving activities. This information system is an outgrowth of a Ph.D. student research project (Whipple 1993) and will provide teams with timely data on standard measures for quality, maintenance, costs, delays, attendance, and time spent on each of the 30 work unit functions.

These case vignettes, taken along with our broader research findings, suggest a number of ways in which union initiatives through the partnership have added value at Saturn. We will summarize these in our conclusions below.

Reinventing the Local Union

UAW Local Union 1853 has struggled to define its multiple roles in representing and defending the contractual interests of its members, participating in the management of the business, and jointly designing and administering the partnership arrangement. In the process of defining these multiple roles, Local 1853 is reinventing the local union. Local union leaders at Saturn define their role as being responsible for both the economic and social outcomes of Saturn (Bennett 1988). The economic outcomes must demonstrate Saturn's ability to meet the quality, productivity, market share, and long-term profitability levels set by its domestic and international competition. The social outcomes must meet the interests of the work force for stable employment with high wages, good working conditions, an effective voice on the job and in the enterprise, as well as meet the expectations the broader community holds for a modern corporation.

Local union leaders see these economic and social outcomes of Saturn as being highly interdependent. Saturn's model of worker representation is based on the premise that long-term employment security can not be negotiated independent of the economic performance of the firm nor solely through collective bargaining after all strategic decisions have been made by management. Rather, employment security can only be achieved over the long run by both contributing to the economic performance of the firm and participating directly in business planning and decision-making processes to ensure that worker interests are given appropriate consideration.

Traditionally the role of a local union was to represent and organize the membership while management managed the business. The local union at Saturn is attempting to break down this dichotomy.

It seeks to share responsibility for both the effective use of capital and for meeting the economic and social needs of the labor force. When both labor and management share these responsibilities, each comes to the task from differing perspectives and experiences. Instead of a division of responsibility based solely on constituency, both are responsible for managing people and capital.

Conflict and Its Resolution

The Saturn partnership has not eliminated conflict between the union and management. In fact, by involving more people in more decisions, more conflicts may be surfaced at Saturn than in comparable firms or union-management relationships. Yet the evolving partnership has provided new institutions and processes for conflict resolution. While a grievance procedure and the right to strike remain in place, most conflicts are resolved through ongoing problem solving or joint decision-making processes.

Throughout this paper are examples of conflicts that developed and were resolved through the partnership. For now we will note two common features we have observed about conflicts that arise at Saturn. First, they seldom can be described as clear-cut, bilateral, labor versus management conflicts. Instead, they often involve multiple groups with different interests and perspectives. For example, some of the conflicts discussed involve differences between local union leaders and their international union colleagues, some involve differences among managers and engineers located in Spring Hill versus those located in Troy, Michigan, and some involve debates between labor and management leaders at Saturn and GM executives. Second, few of these conflicts are resolved crisply through a single negotiated agreement or unilateral decision. Instead, they are subjected to a more extended set of discussions, often taking place in multiple forums until either a consensus emerges or a crisis forces a final decision.

It is difficult to assess whether this more continuous approach to problem solving and conflict resolution is more or less efficient or effective than traditional labor-management negotiations. Ultimately the effectiveness of decision making and conflict resolution at Saturn must be judged not only by comparing it against traditional forms of labor-management conflict resolution and problem solving, but also against traditional managerial decision making and internal conflict resolution. At Saturn these two activities are inseparable parts of the organization's governance system. What makes Saturn unique therefore is not the absence of conflict but the process by which the stakeholders work out their differences and search for common solutions. Clearly it does often take longer to reach a consensus than for one party to make a unilateral decision. But this approach is guided by a belief that once a decision is made, the shared commitment of the parties eases its implementation and reinforces the values and principles on which Saturn was built. These are viewed as long-run intangible, but nevertheless strategic, assets that have value of their own.

LeFauve believes this approach produces both better decisions and more effective implementation. The difference at Saturn compared to other joint activities in the GM system is the degree and quality of involvement. "The union is in the room, not talked to about the decision afterwards. The process is inclusion, not consultation."[5] The result, according to LeFauve, is more willingness to make decisions work, adjusting or rectifying if necessary. "Real value comes from shared ownership of the decision itself, which also produces better answers." Instead of spending time on symptoms and debating solutions, labor and management try to focus in on the root cause of problems, on prevention versus correction, often redefining issues.

An example LeFauve gives is the Saturn risk and reward package in which union and management redefined the problem, changing the basic concept from that which appeared in the original agreement.[6] During the 1991 negotiations the local union and management essentially separated the two issues, tying risk to training and reward to quality and productivity. The union proposed tying the risk portion (5 percent in 1992, 10 percent in 1993, 15 percent in 1994, and twenty percent in 1995) to a training goal of 5 percent of the annual work schedule or 92 hours. All Saturn employees, both union and management, share in the risk and reward. The reward portion of the compensation package is based on exceeding quality and productivity goals. As of this writing all Saturn members have earned over $2600 due to the reward formula, based on quality levels and production performance against schedule.

Other conflicts involve what Walton and McKersie (1965) describe as "mixed motive bargaining," a mixture of traditional distributive tactics along with integrative problem solving. One such conflict also occurred during the 1991 agreement renewal process over whether management was backing away from its commitment to quality in response to market pressures to increase production volume. The work units, wearing black arm bands that said "Stop Defects," initiated a plant-wide protest to highlight their perception of a lack of responsiveness to quality problems by engineering and management. The protest also resulted in a temporary production slowdown. For management it was a "transition from quality at any cost to quality at least cost. Management did not see this as erosion of commitment to quality. Yet the union was skeptical about management's commitment to quality. Arm bands were a signal we were not getting problems solved fast enough, particularly focused on engineering. There was an underlying frustration that management was not responding to problems. There was frustration that there were not enough problem-solving resources."[7]

These actions created considerable tension and conflict for Saturn management and engineering staff who saw this as a return to traditional bargaining tactics since it occurred during negotiations. For LeFauve, "There were two issues here, black arm bands and slow down. Yet we kept management support. It's still sensitive; reverting to old behaviors risks destroying the work and trust. I got criticized by management that it's all one way. The root cause was communications. Engineering saw very little value in communicating to the teams. We refocused on communicating the status of what was being done to solve the teams' problems. If management had not held the union in high regard, the partnership could have dissolved at that very dangerous point."[8] Management's response to the conflict helped to sustain the partnership, illustrating how they valued it.

Since this crisis, a joint off-line problem-solving process has been established including product and manufacturing, engineering, operations management, and union members. Further, Saturn has physically relocated an increasing number of engineers from Troy, Michigan to Spring Hill, Tennessee.

For the local union this episode demonstrated a willingness to stand up and protest what it saw as a gradual deterioration in the company's commitment to quality at a time when the market was beginning to intensify pressure on Saturn to increase the rate of production to meet strong customer demand. From their perspective it illustrates how the union can help sustain organizational innovation through periodic crises by serving as a countervailing force to management, who they perceived were responding to short-run pressures at the expense of long-term principles and values.

Another example illustrates the complexity of conflict resolution at Saturn which often involves multilateral negotiations between multiple stakeholders. In 1987 the union initiated a process for assessing the work units—the Team Growth and Development Process. Local union leaders were concerned that the corporation was not taking the steps necessary to fully develop the team concept on which Saturn was based. In response it initiated the development of training programs for the work unit team members, leaders, and module advisors. The union contends that some management participated and supported the process.

While some managers may have supported the unions' efforts, others expressed frustration that the conflict had not been worked out and that the local union, in taking the initiative, had acted on its own. They had agreed that something should be done, but not on what. This conflict has lingered over time and has, according to management, only now found partial resolution in the training component of the new reward system.

While union and management may disagree over the breadth of management support that existed for the Team Growth and Development Process, both concur that the question of managerial autonomy is an ongoing issue at Saturn, with each business unit—Body Systems, Powertrain, and Vehicle Systems—jealously guarding its independence. The union believes management is sometimes fragmented as evidenced in the varied practices across the three business units. To some extent this is understandable and may be appropriate given the different technologies, processes, and needs of these operations. Yet often this autonomy has made it difficult to achieve the level of coordination, consistency, and cross-unit cooperation needed to effectively manage the total operation. Each business unit has moved in a unique direction to a certain degree, somewhat resembling their parent organizations in GM (Fisher Body, GM Hydromatic, and GMAD). The local union, viewing itself as an organization with site-wide responsibility, often voices frustration at this independence.

Reacting to this perception of overdecentralization, the local union has attempted to provide its leadership with knowledge and experience covering the entire Saturn operation by rotating the union partners assigned to lead each business unit. Rotation has also expanded to the human resource development function which is responsible for training, recruitment, selection, assessment, compensation, benefits, and formal negotiations.

According to LeFauve, management "got *independent* business teams, when what we really wanted was *interdependent* business teams. We walk the line between providing independence and autonomy and having interdependence recognized and honored. In this management and the union balance one another, and the partnership brings to bear different needs for control. Yet it is interesting that it has been management who has promoted greater autonomy for the business teams, while the union has pushed for greater consistency of practices across the site. I would have expected the reverse."[9] This problem is exacerbated by turnover in leadership at the business unit level. As of this writing the average tenure of business team leaders (plant managers) is less than one year, providing less than an ideal environment for continuity and stability of leadership.

Another source of conflict at Saturn involves debate over just how broad and far union participation should extend into what has been traditional management domains. This issue arose first in the areas of product engineering, supplier selection, and marketing during the early organization building years at Saturn. As discussed above, similar issues arose more recently after production start-up over how to solve manufacturing problems that require cooperation among product engineers, manufacturing engineers, middle managers, and work units. The differences are not just between union and management, but occur *within* the union and management organizations themselves. In addition, traditional economic issues such as pensions, pay for performance, absenteeism, hours of work, and the selection and status of work unit module advisors have all been sources of considerable debate within Saturn.

Partnership Organization and Local Union Structure

The New Local Union: Servicing and Organizing

One of the distinctive features of this new local union is the combined focus on both servicing and organizing its membership. UAW Local 1853 has no grievance committee in the traditional sense, and only the president and vice presidents can write formal grievances. Yet it has developed new approaches to handling traditional services, such as conflict resolution and negotiations, by attempting to organize its members to allow for greater participation and input into the programs and policies of the union, the organization, and the partnership. These participatory processes are listed in Figure 5.

For example, through a series of off-site workshops and meetings during 1992, the leadership team, in response to increasing financial pressure on Saturn to break even, initiated steps to improve the union's management of the business. This included the development of a 1992 team-directed business plan, the implementation of an off-line problem-solving process, and the reorganization of union leadership roles in the business units. The latter involved rotating leadership and realigning responsibility for servicing members and operations management. The elected vice presidents are now more involved with member servicing, while the executive board and jointly selected members (crew coordinators, module advisors, functional coordinators) focus on co-management responsibilities.

FIGURE 5

Participatory Processes Used by the Local Union

Congress: Twice-a-month meetings attended by all local union executive board members, union module advisors, crew coordinators, and other key staff functional coordinators. The purpose of the Congress is to provide the local union with strategic direction and focus on specific issues.

Leadership Team: Approximately 50 top union leaders including elected officers, executive board members, and crew coordinators. It meets every week and conducts periodic workshops to discuss the partnership, union strategy, and business issues.

Work Unit Counselors: Bimonthly meetings are held between elected union officers and elected work unit counselors to discuss their roles and responsibilities as both production team leaders and elected union representatives.

Block Meetings: Weekly meetings between module advisors, work unit counselors, and crew coordinators to provide communications and discuss operating problems and issues in each module.

Rap Sessions: Monthly meetings held in each Business Team between the local union president and union members in an open question and answer forum.

Town Hall: Monthly local union meetings held twice during the normal work day to facilitate the participation by crews on both first and second shifts.

Member-to-Member Survey: This annual survey utilizes the team leaders to conduct formal 45-minute interviews with every individual union member (5300 in 1992) on the issues, concerns or needs they would like to see addressed by the union. The 1991 member-to-member survey served as the basis for the union's negotiating platform in the contract renewal process that year.

The member-to-member surveys provide significant opportunities for individual members to communicate their points of view on critical issues. This has occurred at strategic times such as contract renewal or when critical problems arise requiring leadership action. Moreover, because the member-to-member surveys involve personal interviews by UAW leaders of individual members, they allow members to raise issues that otherwise would not be uncovered in formal written questionnaire surveys, local union meetings, or traditional grievance procedures. They also reinforce the principle that part of the job of a team leader is to encourage this type of upward communications on an ongoing basis.

Also unique is the congress in which the leadership team meets with the module advisors to share information and discuss issues ranging from the partnership problems to corporate performance. During one such meeting in April 1992, the congress received the same detailed briefing on Saturn's financial performance and 1993 final budget which earlier that week had been given to Lloyd Reuss, then GM President. The top union leadership had participated in the budget generation at earlier stages.

These processes are designed to extend the principles of participation embedded in Saturn's organizational design to the management of the local union. Shifting to this type of leadership style has been described as one of the biggest changes required of local union leaders in organizations that promote teamwork and employee participation (Cutcher-Gershenfeld, McKersie, and Wever 1988).

The local union has experimented with a number of approaches to its internal structure as new problems surfaced. For the first few years the focus of the partnership was necessarily on designing and building the organization. However, in 1990 with the start of production, the priority shifted to building cars. Making the transition from organization building to automobile building challenged the union and required adjustments in the partnership arrangements. As discussed above, the union, recognizing that the SAC, MAC, and business unit Decision Rings were insufficient avenues for co-managing the business, initiated the one-on-one partnering.

Further, team leaders become union officials after their election. Therefore their responsibilities include team management as well as representing members' needs. This is not an easy assignment, as evidenced by recent data on team leader turnover. First elected in February 1992, by October of that year over 10 percent had resigned. Currently there are approximately 400 team leaders, however, after the third crew comes on line and holds elections in spring 1993, their number will exceed 600.

The Amalgamation of the Local

Local leadership has sought to expand the representation of the union to all employees of Saturn including contract workers. To date, two additional UAW units have been added to the original local union. The first of those units includes approximately 120 members incorporating the employees of the Morrison Milco Food Service, a contractor who runs Saturn's four on-site cafeterias. The second unit includes 240 employees of the Premier Corporation which provides services to Saturn for paint booth cleaning, janitorial services, on-site groundskeeping, and auto driveaway for vehicle transportation loading. A third unit that includes approximately 600 direct material truck drivers of the Ryder Corporation has already been certified and is in the process of being added to the amalgamated local.

Politics of Partnership

Historically the sustainability of efforts at labor participation in managerial decision making have been put at risk by internal political challenges to the union leadership. Indeed, the need to be responsive to the membership is one of the democratic checks that help assure that union participation does not devolve into simple cooptation and lack of responsiveness to rank-and-file concerns. True to this tradition, there is an active internal political process within the local union at Saturn, and there are some significant debates between the Saturn local and the UAW International.

For example, as of this writing, a member of the local union's leadership team is planning to challenge the current union president in this year's election. Among the issues that have surfaced is whether or not the crew coordinators and work unit module advisors should be elected (in a fashion consistent with the UAW tradition for shop committee representatives) or continue to be selected jointly by management and union representatives. The current leadership's position has been that electing module advisors and crew coordinators would politicize the partnership, diminishing the ability of individuals in these positions to equally balance the needs of people with the needs of the business. Popularity, not skills, knowledge, and ability, would become the dominant qualification. They fear that politicizing the process would lead to a return of the old grievance committeemen structure, an increase in adversarialism, and movement away from consensus decision making and joint problem solving. Management would then be excluded from the selection process and would likely require a more traditional nonrepresented supervisor as a counterpart. A referendum on the question of electing crew coordinators and module advisors took place in early 1993, with 71 percent of the membership voting to continue the current process of joint selection. This vote appears to reaffirm the commitment of the rank and file to the principles underlying the Saturn partnership.

This specific issue is symbolic of a broader debate over the extent to which the new roles of co-management are being effectively balanced with the more traditional servicing roles of local union leaders. Political challenges such as these are a normal part of the democratic process. The real question therefore is whether the partnership is institutionalized sufficiently to withstand these internal political contests or the possible turnover of elected officials.

Conflicts between local and international union interests have also arisen at Saturn. Some of these involve the degree of autonomy that the local should be afforded to depart from conventional UAW practices. But some also involve differences in philosophy and strategy as illustrated by debate in 1992 between local and international leaders over the effects of strikes in UAW-organized plants that supply components to Saturn (*Wall Street Journal* 1992). While differences between local and national leaders are not unique to Saturn, the degree of autonomy the local at Saturn requires is probably greater than that of other locals that are more closely tied to pattern bargaining or national contract negotiations in the GM and UAW structure (Katz and Sabel 1985; Katz 1992). Yet the local depends on the support of the international leadership in dealing with top GM management and in continuing to support the departures from UAW traditional practices. Thus the potential for local-national conflicts may be higher than in more traditional local-national relationships.

Assessing Performance of the Partnership

What criteria should be used to assess this new model of unionism? While there are no well-established measures for this purpose, clearly to be sustained over the long run this model must meet the expectations of its multiple stakeholders. We will review some of these below.

Rank and File

Ultimately the membership must decide on the viability of this model of unionism. In effect members must choose whether they want their elected representatives involved in the decision-making process prior to decisions being made unilaterally by management, or whether they are more comfortable with the traditional arm's-length relationship. In addition to these process considerations, any local union entering into this type of partnership arrangement must develop a long-range strategy that meets the substantive needs of its membership for jobs, employment security, good wages, and working conditions.

From the standpoint of the rank and file, Saturn will eventually provide over 7,500 UAW jobs in Spring Hill, Tennessee, and Troy, Michigan, including the new amalgamated local units. In addition it has already created an additional 3,500 UAW jobs in existing GM-allied division component plants, 350 UAW jobs in non-allied suppliers, and 250 union non-UAW jobs in suppliers.

While it is premature to judge the reaction of local UAW members to the new model, one early indicator is the 1991 contract ratification rate of 83 percent. Further, the 1992 member-to-member survey reported strong support for the local as well as the partnership arrangement. However, the survey also reflected that some members wanted to see more elected union officials involved in servicing as well as business decision making. Thus, both the survey and the recent referendum on the method of leadership selection indicate that a portion of the membership does have ongoing questions about the form of representation within the partnership.

General Motors and Saturn

GM will judge Saturn's success by the market's reception to its quality and by the ability of the organization to achieve continuous improvements in productivity, costs, profitability, market share, and the time it takes to bring new products to market. While the performance metrics listed above are some of those traditionally used by firms to evaluate *managerial* performance, in the case of Saturn, *both management and the local union* are being held accountable for performance.

While it is too early to make strong statements about Saturn's performance on these measures to date, Saturn has achieved higher ratings from consumers than any other domestic car line in initial vehicle quality, satisfaction after one year of ownership, and service.[10] Saturn has achieved world-class product quality, yet profitability and return on investment are more difficult to assess since they depend on factors such as product pricing and amortization of product development costs. Moreover, only after Saturn brings on its third crew and reaches full production capacity will it be able to meet its targets for productivity, costs, schedule, and profitability. While there are various views on how to calculate these numbers, everyone agrees that it is critical to make significant progress toward these financial performance targets in 1993. Thus a great deal of attention is being given to problem-solving efforts focused on these objectives.

For Saturn to demonstrate its full potential to meet even these traditional criteria, GM's commitment needs to be sustained over the long run, both in times of success and under the harsh realities of a company undergoing massive restructuring. This commitment is likely to be put to the test as GM restructures its operations in response to pressures from the corporation's shareholders and the board of directors to return the corporation to profitability. Whether or how Saturn is affected by these pressures remains to be seen.

Organizational Learning and Diffusion of Innovations

If GM or others simply judge Saturn or its local union on traditional financial or product success criteria, the opportunity to learn from the organizational innovations at Saturn will be lost, and the full value of Saturn will not be realized. Saturn can be seen as a learning laboratory (Senge 1990; Nonaka 1991) for both GM and the UAW International to test, learn, and transfer innovations to other settings. Both the local union and Saturn management question whether the Saturn model is being viewed this way and whether processes are in place to make this happen.

There is evidence that a few GM divisions are attempting to duplicate some of Saturn's systems and principles. Over 400 technical and process innovations have already been transferred to GM. For example, Saturn's retailing experience has impacted new marketing approaches, particularly within the Oldsmobile organization. However, the transfer of organizational innovations from Saturn to other parts of GM and/or the UAW has been slow in coming, particularly those around team concepts and the partnership arrangement for joint governance. Yet, Saturn has marketed its products and image as "A Different Kind of Car—A Different Kind of Company," and GM has gained enormous public relations benefits from this approach and from its quality performance to date. How much of this can be attributed to the role of the UAW and the partnership design is impossible to determine, but clearly they are an integral part of Saturn. Thus, the partnership itself may have real market value.

The UAW International Union and the Saturn Local

From the perspective of the international union, Saturn has provided jobs to members either out of work or transferring from plants that were downsizing. It has further increased UAW membership by organizing the amalgamated units and by providing work for GM and allied UAW plants. However, beyond increasing membership, what is the international union's interest in Saturn? Is Saturn seen as an example for other facilities or just an interesting experiment? Does the Saturn approach, with its focus on the competitiveness of the company, challenge the international's broader perspective of labor's interests throughout the auto industry? Rather than serving as a model for the local union of the future, does Saturn really represent the reinvention of "company unionism"?

The international's degree of involvement in Saturn has varied over time. At the early stages of development, the international union and GM led the effort by creating the joint study team and by developing the organizing principles articulated in the 1985 Memorandum of Agreement which provided enabling language. Absent this response by the UAW to GM's request to explore new contractual arrangements for small-car production, Saturn would never have been created. The enabling language and guiding principles allowed the parties, both union and management, to move beyond the boundaries of traditional agreements and organizational arrangements. In recent years full-time international staff representation has been withdrawn, and it appears that Saturn is seen more as one plant among many rather than as the UAW's model for the future.

Questions arise regarding the appropriate relationship between the local and the international union. What support, resources, and guidance from the international continue to be needed? How are the policies and practices of this local to be coordinated with that of other local unions? To be effective, how much independence does a local union such as this require in its negotiations and institutional arrangements, and how much can it be expected to adhere to broader national policies and concerns for solidarity?

As was demonstrated in strikes at selected plants in 1992 over issues of outsourcing, international leaders clearly have the ability to exert pressure on GM through strategic strike action. In this way they can play a unique role influencing policies such as sourcing, contracting out, and employment/income guarantees. Through their ability to coordinate action they can also provide some protection against whipsawing. However, the international can also go further and promote, through education and leadership development, the diffusion of "best practice" work organization models. Further, it is the international which has the greatest opportunity to pursue coordination with other international labor movements on issues of mutual concern.

On the other hand, local unions such as UAW 1853 have found new sources of power in their relations with management through acquisition of essential skills and information, the development of managerial competency among local leaders, and their ability to organize and mobilize human resources. This power can then be exercised, not through strike threats or other traditional tactics, but by challenging the positions taken by management that are believed to be against the long-term interests of the membership and perhaps of other stakeholders as well. This power has been increasingly valued as critical to the successful operation of fragile, "lean," high-performance work organizations. The very nature of these joint governance systems, based on the problem-solving and decision-making competency of the local work force, may require that they be created locally.

Local institutional arrangements and the flexibility to adjust rapidly to changing competitive environments may be critical to the survival of contemporary manufacturing organizations. It may no longer be possible to take wages out of competition in international markets. Therefore, unions must both respond directly to the interests of their members and generate power locally to protect those interests. However, the international union is critical to the local's success in achieving these objectives through fulfilling its coordinating, educational, policy-making and leadership roles. Thus in the long run, the performance of the local union will be dependent on local and international leaders working together to find the right mix of local autonomy, international leadership support, and mutual organizational learning.

Union-Management Relations and National Labor Policy

The labor-management partnership at Saturn is especially relevant to those concerned about the future of American industrial relations and worker representation, since it provides an approach for filling the void in worker representation that has resulted from the steady decline of traditional unions in the United States. Thus it adds another chapter to the research on alternative forms of worker representation, team-based work organization, employee involvement, and joint union-management participative structures (Piore and Sabel 1984; Kochan, Katz, and McKersie 1986; Rubinstein 1987; Heckscher 1988; Hoerr 1991; Locke 1992; Jacoby and Verma 1992; Bluestone and Bluestone 1992).

It is interesting, however, that some of the most innovative aspects of this model may be inconsistent with doctrines embedded in current labor law. For example, the use of a joint study team such as the "Committee of 99" serves as one way of avoiding the adversarial conflicts that often accompany the question of union representation in new facilities. The UAW was recognized as the bargaining agent before the Spring Hill facility was constructed. By bringing the union in as a partner in the design process, a potentially difficult issue was taken off the table in a way that promoted innovation in the new organization and reinforced efforts to sustain worker and union participation in innovative efforts underway in existing GM plants. The National Right-to-Work Committee pursued an unsuccessful legal challenge to this arrangement, arguing that it was inconsistent with voting procedures contained in the current labor law.

Similarly, the co-management role the union plays at Saturn appears on its face to be inconsistent with the sharp separation of labor and management roles assumed to exist under the current law. In the 1980 *NLRB v. Yeshiva University* case,[11] the U.S. Supreme Court determined that employees performing managerial work were not covered under the National Labor Relations Act. While the Yeshiva case related to academic faculties, Saturn represents an example of blue-collar industrial relations where large numbers of union members are performing work traditionally the responsibility of managerial employees. In this way it challenges the current statute and serves as another example of the need to update and transform current labor law so it encourages and facilitates rather than constrains innovation in American industrial relations.[12]

Conclusions

We believe the local union, through the partnership arrangements, adds significant value to the Saturn organization. First, because union leaders bring substantive expertise and an independent perspective to a problem, they add value by increasing the quality of decisions made in the various joint committees and forums from shop-floor teams to the Strategic Action Council. In a number of meetings we have observed union leaders speaking up directly to confront problems that were difficult for managers to voice openly with their superiors. Moreover, the presence of union leaders ensures that human resource dimensions of strategic and operational issues are considered in making decisions. Indeed, there is some concern by engineering that these issues may get too much weight relative to other technical or financial criteria. This is a question that the parties are now attempting to address by focusing their improvement efforts around specific production, cost, quality, schedule, as well as social objectives.

Second, as suggested in the quotes from Skip LeFauve noted above, once decided, the commitment of the union leaders helps to get a decision implemented quickly and effectively. The middle-management partnering, 1992 operating plan, team leader business plan, off-line problem-solving process, and module advisor performance appraisal process, are all illustrations of the union's implementation ability.

Third, whereas UAW members and leaders have severed their ties to the GM seniority and transfer system and therefore see their long-term security tied solely to Saturn's future, most managers and engineering professionals retain their links to GM. As evidenced by the turnover in business team leaders cited above, to some extent it is the union that provides continuity as well as site-wide and long-term perspective. Some managers may have conflicting loyalties between the interests of Saturn and their long-term careers which they see tied to their functional or technical discipline at GM.

Finally, the institution of individual partnerships between UAW and nonrepresented Saturn employees throughout the line and staff organizations has created a unique system of co-management. While future research will explore in detail the workings and results of this system, we believe these combinations of union and management leadership bring important and varied expertise, experience, and perspectives together on both the social and technical problems of production.

In summary, we see the union adding value by improving both the substantive and process dimensions of decision making. These views should be taken as only preliminary assessments, however, as more research is needed to fully understand the nature and long-run effects of the union's role in Saturn's management and governance process.

Further, we believe Saturn provides a new form of labor relations that embodies innovations that are currently believed to be "best practices" in high-performance manufacturing, while establishing a process that gives workers a strong voice in enterprise decisions allowing the parties to adopt new ideas more easily than does the traditional collective bargaining system. Yet we do not present this as the only new approach for worker representation which will fit all circumstances or remedy all the shortcomings of traditional U.S. industrial relations. One issue, for example, that the Saturn model does not address is how to provide equivalent voice and representation to the white-collar, middle-management, professional and technical workers who lie outside the UAW's jurisdiction or beyond the coverage of existing labor law. Indeed, some of these employees have expressed the view that their interests are not given sufficient weight in decision making at Saturn. Empowering these workers may require further institutional innovation through experimentation with some American equivalent of European-style works councils.

Thus, we see the partnership between Saturn and UAW Local 1853 as a promising example of one new form of worker representation that, along with other models, should be not only sanctioned but actively encouraged and promoted by policymakers as well as business and labor leaders. Only through additional experiments like this one, that test departures from longstanding practices and traditions, are we likely to develop the organizational forms, governance arrangements, and labor-management relations principles that are suited to the current and future needs of the American work force, economy, and society.

Acknowledgments

Funds for this research were provided by the MIT Leaders for Manufacturing Program and the MIT International Motor Vehicle Research Program. We wish to thank Skip LeFauve, president of Saturn, Bob Boruff, Saturn's vice president of manufacturing, and Ben Whipple of MIT for their comments on earlier drafts. However, the views expressed here should only be attributed to the authors.

Endnotes

[1] *Memorandum of Agreement*, Saturn Corporation, 1985.

[2] Interviews with G.M. human resource management from the Saginaw and Inland Fisher Guide Divisions, December, 1992.

[3] Interview with Wellford "Buzz" Wilms, UCLA, December 11, 1992.

[4] *Memorandum of Agreement*, op cit.

[5] Interview with Skip LeFauve, President, Saturn Corporation, July 14, 1992.

[6] Interview with Skip LeFauve, President, Saturn Corporation, December 17, 1992.

[7] Ibid.

[8] Ibid.

[9] Ibid.

[10] J.D. Power 1992 Customer Satisfaction Index. Saturn ranked highest among all domestic car lines and third overall behind Lexus and Infiniti.

[11] *NLRB v. Yeshiva University*, 444 US 672, 1980.

[12] *U.S. Labor Law and the Future of Labor-Management Cooperation*, U.S. Department of Labor, Bureau of Labor-Management Cooperative Programs, 1986.

References

Bennett, Michael. 1988. "New Roles for Unions in a Team Environment." Manuscript. Work in America Productivity Forum.
Bluestone, Barry, and Irving Bluestone. 1992. *Negotiating the Future*. New York: Basic Books.

Cutcher-Gershenfeld, Joel, Robert B. McKersie, and Kirsten Wever. 1988. "The Changing Role of Union Leaders." Washington, DC: U.S. Department of Labor, Bureau of Labor Management Relations and Cooperative Programs, 127.

Heckscher, Charles. 1988. *The New Unionism: Employee Involvement in the Changing Corporation.* New York: Basic Books.

Hoerr, John. 1991. "What Should Unions Do?" *Harvard Business Review.* Cambridge, MA: Harvard University 69, no. 3.

Jacoby, Sanford M., and Anil Verma. 1992. "Enterprise Unions in the United States," *Industrial Relations* 31, no. 1.

Kochan, Thomas A., Harry C. Katz, and Robert B. McKersie. 1986. *The Transformation of American Industrial Relations.* New York: Basic Books.

Kochan, Thomas A., and Michael Useem, eds. 1992. *Transforming Organizations.* New York: Oxford Press.

Katz, Harry C. 1992. "The Decentralization of Collective Bargaining: A Comparative Review and Analysis." Manuscript. Cornell University.

Katz, Harry C., and Charles F. Sabel. 1985. "Industrial Relations and Industrial Adjustment in the Car Industry." *Industrial Relations* 24, no. 3.

LeFauve, Richard G., and Arnoldo C. Hax. 1992. "Managerial and Technological Innovations at Saturn Corporation." *MIT Management* (spring).

Locke, Richard M. 1992. "The Demise of the National Union in Italy: Lessons for Comparative Industrial Relations Theory." *Industrial and Labor Relations Review* 45, no. 2.

Nonaka, Ikujiro. 1991. "The Knowledge-Creating Company." *Harvard Business Review* (Nov.-Dec.).

Piore, Michael J., and Charles F. Sabel. 1984. *The Second Industrial Divide.* New York: Basic Books.

Rubinstein, Sidney P., ed. 1987. *Participative Systems at Work.* New York: Human Sciences Press.

Senge, Peter M. 1990. *The Fifth Discipline.* New York: Doubleday.

Wall Street Journal, August 31-September 4, 1992.

Walton, Richard E., and Robert B. McKersie. 1965. *A Behavioral Theory of Labor Negotiations: An Analysis of a Social Interaction System.* Ithaca, NY: ILR Press.

Whipple, Benjamin. 1993. "Organizing for Team-Based Manufacturing: Information, Technology, and Organizational Learning." Ph.D. diss., MIT Sloan School of Management.

Chapter 11

Employee Representation in Historical Perspective

Daniel Nelson
University of Akron

Two developments largely defined the practice of industrial relations in the United States between the turn of the century and World War II. The rise of institutionalized personnel work, reflecting the expansion of corporate bureaucracy and concern over employee behavior, enhanced the role of the manager at the expense of the low-level supervisor and the worker (Jacoby 1985; Chandler 1977). On the other hand, the growth of the labor movement, especially in the late 1910s and the mid-1930s, created a regime of shared and regulated decision making at the bottom of the corporate hierarchy that compromised the authority of top managers. These developments and the tension between them also explain the rise and fall of the company union and the creation of a little-known legacy of employer-initiated worker organizations in the United States.

There was no company union movement per se, only a series of fitful, uncoordinated, and controversial efforts that often obscured as much as they revealed. The majority of company unions appeared between 1917 and 1920, and 1933 and 1936 and were superficial, transitory responses to government-sanctioned collective bargaining; they were at best contributions to the evolution of union-avoidance policies and provide little insight into the purpose or operations of the more durable and significant company unions which are the focus of this essay. The histories of this minority were diverse but not unrelated. Above all, their creators shared a commitment to extending managerial influence and enlisting rank-and-file employees in the operation of the enterprise. Their activities provide one gauge of the possibilities and limitations of employer leadership in human resources management.

Origins

The company union was a twentieth century phenomenon, a reaction to anxiety over the dehumanizing potential of the large organization, the exploitation of women in the labor force, and the perception of the trade union as a form of social pathology. Since every employer interpreted these problems differently, there was no coordinated response and many did nothing. Still, between 1900 and 1917 a small number of executives concluded that an appropriate antidote required some form of organization. By the time government became a promoter of employee representation during World War I, they had created most of the forms and procedures that would be used until the 1930s.

The first important company union was the Filene Cooperative Association (FCA), an organization of employees of the Boston department store. Business, humanitarian, and paternalistic considerations guided the Filene brothers. Like many of their contemporaries, they were especially concerned about the public perception of their employment of young women in sales positions. They reacted by introducing one of the nation's most extensive employee welfare plans. It included medical and insurance plans, a library and bank, social and athletic activities, and the FCA, created in 1898. A welfare manager "engaged and discharged the employees of the store, was educational director, acted as intermediary between the Firm and the people. . . ." (Sketch 1915, 24-25). This arrangement, particularly the role of the welfare manager, was daring and innovative; the first welfare secretaries had only appeared in the previous decade and very few of them had such extensive powers.

But the Filenes soon deviated from the emerging pattern among progressive employers. Rather than increase the powers of the welfare secretary and create a modern personnel department, they enlarged the authority of the FCA. The turning point was the creation of an elected council in 1905. Henceforth, the welfare manager served as the executive secretary of the FCA, accountable to the council. She continued to act as personnel manager but also represented the employees in discussions with the management. During the following decade, the FCA became increasingly involved in labor relations activities, including wage and grievance settlements (LaDame 1930, 119, 134-38). "Its purpose," noted an early history, was "to enable all of the employees of the corporation to have a sufficient voice in the store government . . . to make it just, considerate and effective" (Sketch 1915, 8). The meager evidence that survives suggests that Filene employees took their "voice in store government" seriously.

A second, pioneering institution of that period illuminated other possible functions of the company union. C. W. Post's National Trades and Worker Association, created in 1910, was an outgrowth of a virulent open-shop campaign in Battle Creek, Michigan. Post, a cereal manufacturer and promoter, embraced the open shop as a tactic for encouraging local industrial development. His NTWA was supposed to be a benign alternative to the AFL, a union that foreswore "strikes, boycotts, picketing" and other forms of "coercion" and relied instead on mediation and appeals to public opinion to achieve its goals. (McLaughlin 1973, 336). Announced with great fanfare in 1910, the NTWA was stillborn. Few employers or workers were attracted to the idea of an alternative union and Post burdened the organization with an expensive, derelict resort. The NTWA was nevertheless an early expression of what would be a persistent dimension of the company union impulse, the desire for a "good" union. Employers such as Post conceded that blue-collar workers had grievances and legitimate claims on the firm—a concession that most open-shop employers did not make—but scorned the disruptive tactics of conventional unions. Unlike the Filene executives, Post and his allies viewed the company union narrowly, as a representation and bargaining entity of modest scope and a bulwark against outside organizers.

The other company unions of the prewar years fell somewhere between the Filene and the Post approaches. Though not as ambitious or powerful as the FCA, they were more than substitutes for independent unions. Most were extensions of prior welfare programs. H. F. J. Porter, a personnel consultant who introduced company unions in several firms, wrote that his goal was "to elicit cooperation from the employees, not to engage in collective bargaining, settle grievances, or forestall trade unions" (Nelson 1982, 340). But translating this goal into an effective mechanism was a formidable task. Most managers retained the trappings of trade unionism (elected representatives, regular meetings with management, procedures for resolving disputes) and assumed that cooperation would grow out of improved communications.

One prewar company union overshadowed the others because of its size and visibility. The Colorado Fuel & Iron Company, with approximately 12,000 employees, introduced a Representation Plan in the aftermath of a violent miners' strike that culminated in April 1914, with the infamous Ludlow Massacre. The plan was the creation of John D. Rockefeller, Jr., the company's major stockholder, and W. L. Mackenzie King, Rockefeller's industrial advisor. Appalled at the violence, Rockefeller was determined to prevent a recurrence of the conflict. Though union recognition was the immediate issue, the underlying cause of the dispute was the capricious and often ruthless behavior of low-level supervisors and the intense hostility of the company's mine managers to the United Mine Workers. Under these conditions, CF & I's welfare program had failed to win the employees' loyalty or to deflect the pressures that had culminated in the strike. Rockefeller had little confidence in unions and, given the antiunion climate of the Colorado mining industry, little hope of promoting a more accommodating approach to them. What was he to do? Clearly a new approach was desirable, one that would affect the day-to-day relations between the miners and their superiors.

Rockefeller relied on King for specific proposals. King spent more than a month in Colorado, interviewing company managers, inspecting the camps, and studying the relations between the company, its supervisors, and the miners. The experience was illuminating. As H. M. Gitelman writes:

> When King came to Colorado, his employee representation scheme was mainly a device aimed at excluding the union from CF & I. By the time he left, it was an absolutely vital ingredient in the reformation of the company's management and its labor policy. In this new guise, employee representation was a tool for the modernization of corporate labor relations (Gitelman 1988, 145).

Under King and Clarence Hicks, who oversaw the actual operation of the plan, CF & I miners (and later steelworkers) obtained many of the benefits they might have achieved with a union contract. They won improvements in working conditions, extensions of the company's welfare programs, protection against arbitrary disciplinary actions, and a significant voice in personnel policy. Their elected representatives did not participate in wage decisions, a fact that preoccupied outside critics (Selekman and Van Kleeck 1924; Selekman 1924). With that exception the workers had good reason for satisfaction with their enhanced status. Most of them remained immune to the appeals of outside organizers, even during the peak years of union growth in the late 1910s.

What about the larger goal of improving CF & I management? In retrospect it is clear that King and Hicks bungled this part of their assignment. In their haste to introduce the plan they stripped the supervisors of their most cherished powers, the right to hire and fire at will, and gave the plan representatives equal responsibility for personnel policy. This move eliminated an important source of grievances but it also disrupted the mines' operations and demoralized the supervisors. Many foremen quit or tried to sabotage the plan. For five years the supervisors bitterly opposed the company union. If King and Hicks had studied the Filenes' operation, they would have realized that a company union was most likely to succeed as an extension of an aggressive program of personnel management, presided over by a staff with substantial powers. King and Hicks had omitted these all-important preliminary steps.

The CF & I plan gradually overcame these problems. By the early 1920s' the foremen and superintendents had reconciled themselves to the new order. They had "gained a new conception" of the value of "harmonious" relations with workers. The plan had "vitalized" the managers' awareness of the "practical aspects of an employe's life. . . . They are conscious of the interests of the men. . . . In turn the representatives of the men know and respect the officials" (Selekman and Van Kleeck 1924, 194-95).

By the eve of American entry into World War I, the company union was a reasonably well known response to the challenges of impersonal labor relations and unrest in industry. Although there were still only a handful of successful company unions, the experiences of the pioneers had clarified the benefits and costs of this novel effort to incorporate the production worker into the operation of the firm. In the following years of war and big business growth, a much larger group of executives would weigh the merits of similar initiatives.

The Company Union, 1917-1922

The industrial boom that accompanied American involvement in World War I resulted in spiraling inflation, social dislocation, and industrial unrest. Labor turnover, strikes, and union activity in turn encouraged employers to devote more attention to labor problems than at any time since the 1880s and, in many cases, to embrace personnel management, which had emerged from the earlier welfare movement. The growth of company unionism was a notable feature of wartime personnel work, as government forced many firms to introduce collective bargaining and other employers sought to preempt outside organizers. Yet most of these organizations were no more permanent than the AFL unions that appeared during wartime. Virtually all of the government-imposed company unions and many of the others that were obvious responses to union campaigns had disappeared by the early 1920s. The more significant employer initiatives occurred where the threat was more diffuse.

Several wartime company unions had direct ties to prewar activity and illustrated the value of those experiences. The best known of these organizations was the representation plan that Rockefeller proposed and Clarence Hicks installed and supervised at Standard Oil of New Jersey. In response to strikes at several refineries, Rockefeller brought in Hicks to survey the Jersey Standard facilities and propose improvements. By that time Hicks realized that company unionism was most effective as part of a comprehensive personnel program. In 1918 he won approval for an elaborate program of personnel management with offices and a full-time staff at every plant, an extensive benefit program, and company unions based on the CF & I plan. At Jersey Standard, industrial relations specialists assumed many of the foremen's former powers and became a buffer between the supervisors and the company unions. The foremen accepted the changes; the strikes ended; and a cooperative spirit seemed to animate the operation of the labor-management committees (Gibb and Knowlton 1956, 571-77; Wall and Gibb 1974, 131-32; Hicks 1941, 52-59). Whatever the employees' opinions, their behavior suggested that the Hicks program had a substantial effect. The results were so impressive that managers of other oil companies adopted similar plans (Larson and Porter 1959, 95-96, 209; Giddens 1955, 333-48). As a Jersey Standard executive and a consultant to other refiners, Hicks became the best known proponent of company unionism in the 1920s.

A second plan with close ties to prewar activity emphasized the diversity of the company union impulse. Morris E. Leeds, the Quaker president of Leeds & Northrup, a Philadelphia maker of industrial instruments, believed that personal relationships were essential to business success and resisted any form of bureaucratic personnel organization. Yet as the company prospered and the labor force grew to more than 1000, he became fearful of losing the "right spirit" and reluctantly concluded that some action was necessary (Nelson 1970). In 1918 he visited the Filenes and shortly afterward asked his employees to form an organization similar to the FCA "so that the old L & N spirit may be preserved and strengthened" (Nelson 1982, 349). They created the Leeds & Northrup Cooperative Association with an elected council. The council resolved grievances and administered the company's profit-sharing plan. At the urging of the Filenes, Leeds introduced a complementary personnel department in 1919. By the end of the war boom, the Leeds & Northrup program was virtually a clone of the Filenes' plan.

Leeds soon discovered that an organization alone did not guarantee success. Leeds & Northrup supervisors had become increasingly hostile to the cooperative association in 1919. When business declined in 1920, they demanded that it be curtailed. Leeds reluctantly agreed to disband the personnel department, cut wages, and lay off the least valuable employees. These actions were a near-fatal blow to the cooperative association. Many employees concluded that it was no more legitimate or influential than the transitory company unions of the war years. For more than a year the future of the cooperative association remained in doubt. Finally, Leeds concluded that he would have to give the council greater power and independence. He persuaded council members that they would be taken seriously and in 1922 introduced an innovative benefit, an unemployment insurance fund administered by the council. The cooperative association survived and became a fixture of the Leeds & Northrup management system (Nelson 1982, 350, 352).

The history of company unionism at Goodyear Tire and Rubber and American Telephone and Telegraph was probably more representative of the experiences of the large firms that accounted for most of the personnel innovations of the late 1910s and 1920s. Neither firm had direct contact with prewar company union activity. Neither faced serious challenges from outside unions. Yet both confronted problems that could be alleviated by the introduction of company unions. Goodyear had to deal with the strains of rapid expansion, escalating turnover, and labor shortages, while AT & T faced threats of increased government regulation. Both companies had extensive personnel programs with large staffs before they adopted company union plans.

Under Paul W. Litchfield, its chief production executive, Goodyear had adopted a sophisticated personnel program, featuring a wide array of benefit plans and a powerful labor department. Of particular relevance was a "flying squadron" of elite employees who did emergency work in the factory. Litchfield was delighted to discover that squadron members "perform their tasks with a spirit and breadth of vision." In 1919 he decided to build on this base and invited veteran employees to study the feasibility of a company union. With his assistance they created the Industrial Assembly (IA), a "congressional"-style company union, featuring an elected house of representatives and a senate. The house and senate were to legislate policies for the factory, subject to Litchfield's "veto." However, the form of the industrial assembly obscured its most important function. Like the flying squadron it was to encourage workers to perform their duties with "spirit and breadth of vision." During the tumultuous postwar years it performed many useful services. For example, in 1919 when Goodyear machinists joined an unsuccessful city-wide machinists' strike, IA leaders interviewed strikers who wanted their jobs back. They recommended all but a few "agitators" and "bolsheviki." In 1920-21, when business collapsed and layoffs decimated the labor force, the IA protected the seniority rights of veteran employees and coordinated private relief measures (Nelson 1988, 57-59, 70-71).

The AT & T plans, also introduced in 1919, had a more mundane origin. They were an extension of the company's benefit and personnel plans, which had been greatly expanded in 1913-15 despite the absence of "a clearly defined managerial philosophy (Gillespie 1991, 17). The war posed enormous challenges for AT & T management. Government controls, together with labor shortages and employee unrest in some of the operating subsidiaries, encouraged the company to view its employee policies more systematically. Company unions were part of its response. Elected representatives from the major divisions of each Bell company met with executives to discuss grievances, administer benefit programs, and consider business problems. The plans helped AT & T cope with the turmoil of the war period and became an important part of the company's concerted and successful longer-term effort to portray itself as a model corporate citizen—the "clearly defined" philosophy that emerged in the 1920s (Schacht 1975, 12-21; 1985; Greenwald 1980, 185-232).

At the end of the decade the divergent tendencies symbolized by the FCA and Post's NTWA were no less obvious than they had been in 1914. The attraction of the "good" union was evident in the trade union surrogates that appeared during the years of labor militancy and AFL growth and in the retention, in virtually all company unions, of employee elections, labor-management meetings, and other features of independent organizations and adversarial collective bargaining agreements. The legacy of the FCA was also apparent in notable company unions such as the Cooperative Association and Industrial Assembly which looked and behaved less and less like trade unions. Whether they would be able to do as much for the employees was still impossible to judge, given their comparative youth. That they would do more for the firm was an article of faith and the key to the continuing popularity of the company union in the following decade as trade unionism declined.

The Heyday of the Company Union, 1922-1929

The company union reached its highest development in the 1920s. By that time most of the government mandated plans had disappeared as had most of the AFL locals formed between 1915-20. Though some employers continued to organize company unions as substitutes for independent unions, notably in meat-packing plants and railroad repair shops after major strikes in 1921 and 1922, their numbers declined (Brody 1964, 99-102, 171-73). By the 1920s most antiunion employers recognized that the company union was a cumbersome and ineffectual way to circumvent outside organization. It was costly, difficult to manage, and dependent on rank-and-file leaders who could, and did, advance the interests of their constituents over the interests of the executives and stockholders. Most employers correctly concluded that it was easier to discharge militants and intimidate union-prone employees. The company unions that survived served another purpose. They were, and were perceived to be, a way to involve low-skill and low-wage employees in the management of the firm. A logical extension of the personnel innovations that had taken root in the 1910s, they were the most ambitious and controversial effort to penetrate the customary barrier between managers and production workers. (See NICB 1922, 5, 55, 66-67, 70, 71, 74, 104.)

A handful of small companies played notable roles in this process. The Filene store, Leeds & Northrup, Dennison Manufacturing, and a few others achieved extraordinary visibility because of their ability to combine growth and profitability with radical social experimentation. They became the *avant garde* of the business community, the embodiment of the contemporary ideology of social responsibility. Leeds's relationship with the cooperative association was illustrative. After the crisis of 1920-22, he "sought to compensate for his belated commitment to welfare work by deluging the council with proposals for new benefit programs such as pensions, group life insurance, and company-sponsored educational activities" (Nelson 1982, 354). Grievances had ceased to be important; they were handled by a minor council committee. The real work of the council was implementing and administering the various benefit plans and insuring that the employees approached their tasks in the "right spirit."

Large corporations, however, were the principal proponents of employee representation in the 1920s. Size and diversity greatly complicated internal communications while mass production technologies required increased coordination among departments and individuals. Large corporations also had the largest groups of college-educated executives, steeped in the doctrines of scientific management and personnel work which equated efficiency and social harmony. At AT & T and other utilities, regulation provided another compelling reason for policies that suggested broad-minded and enlightened management.

The experiences of the Goodyear Industrial Assembly in the 1920s illustrated the role of the company union in its heyday. By 1922 the industrial assembly had proven its value to the company and an important segment of the labor force, the high seniority workers. During the recession, Goodyear had had no strikes or overt labor problems; the veteran employees, on the other hand, had kept their jobs and benefits at a time when many of their neighbors and friends had lost both. The experience created a permanent bond between the assembly and this group. For more than a decade the IA would be a "union" of veteran employees (Nelson 1988, 103-104).

Assembly leaders negotiated their loyalty, demanding tangible recognition of the value of their cooperation and leadership (see

Zahavi 1988). They insisted on access to Goodyear managers, prompt resolution of grievances, and periodic wage increases. In 1922 they successfully pressured the company for a raise and a committee system to deal with shop floor grievances. In late 1925, when Litchfield tried to curtail the time that IA representatives devoted to grievances, they reacted even more vigorously. In February 1926 they suspended all assembly business, staging the only known company union strike of the 1920s. They won major concessions. Several months later a group of assembly militants unsuccessfully tried to form an independent, outside union. Their failure removed some of the most outspoken assembly figures but it did not weaken the resolve of the others to defend their interests (Nelson 1988, 106-109).

Goodyear managers encouraged this assertiveness, recognizing that it was a sign of the health of the IA. In the mid-1920s, the company embarked on a campaign of price cutting to increase its market share, a high-risk strategy that depended on increased manufacturing productivity. Technological change, relentless cost cutting, and faster machine times might have created a hostile and uncooperative labor force. The IA, however, served as a safety valve for unrest, a mechanism for alleviating the worst problems associated with the efficiency drive and a way to insure that production employees shared the benefits as well as the burdens of change. The surviving evidence indicates that it successfully performed that role.

The record of company unionism at other big businesses is less revealing, but it suggests a similar pattern. At Jersey Standard and other companies linked to the Rockefeller interests, at International Harvester, U.S. Rubber, and AT & T, and even at Swift, which had introduced employee representation as a union avoidance tactic, company unionism developed a corps of rank-and-file leaders who (if rarely as militant as the industrial assembly activists) became familiar with the problems of their industries and their constituents, attacked the worst shop floor problems and inequities, facilitated the extension of benefit programs, and enlisted the employees in production management to an unprecedented degree (see Ozanne 1967; Brody 1964; Schacht 1975). Critics often complained that company unions rarely were encouraged or even permitted to consider wage issues. Although the Goodyear experience illustrated the value of permitting wage discussions, most executives resisted.

From their perspective, the company union was an extreme expression of the move toward centralized personnel management. It required large expenditures of money and time and was justified only by reductions in production costs. To invite demands for wage increases or other initiatives associated with trade unions suggested confusion about the fundamental purpose of the company union.

Company Unionism in Decline

During the 1930s the company union attracted more interest and controversy than ever before. The severe economic downturn of the early 1930s, the decline in industrial production in particular, curtailed new initiatives and forced existing company unions to confront unaccustomed problems of retrenchment and decline. The economic recovery of 1933-37 and the federal government's recovery policy seemingly provided a new stimulus to company unionism. The number of large corporations with company unions increased by 40 percent between 1933 and 1934 after the Roosevelt program went into effect. Not since the World War I years had executives devoted so much attention to their employees.

In fact, the apparent change in corporate policy suggested by the growing number of organizations was illusory. The recovery of the mid-1930s was too tepid to encourage a revival of the expansive visions of the mid-1920s and federal policy encouraged company unionism only because it also encouraged trade unionism. The majority of company unions that appeared between 1933 and 1935 were similar to the company unions of 1917-19, weak substitutes for trade unions. Employers introduced them to avoid or to counter the efforts of AFL organizations (Jacoby 1985, 223-28). A high percentage of the new organizations were inconsequential and did not outlast the recovery program. Only a small minority remained viable in 1937 when the Supreme Court upheld the Wagner Act ban on employer-assisted employee organizations. The experience of the 1930s showed again that government policy was the surest stimulus to company unionism but that the results were likely to be pale replicas of the organizations that flourished in the 1920s. A more sensitive history of company union developments in the 1930s reveals a pattern of continuous decline.

The last chapter in the story of the Goodyear Industrial Assembly emphasizes the disparity between the company unions of the 1920s and those of the 1930s. Until 1933 the IA had operated only in the company's massive Akron, Ohio, complex where it performed a role in the early 1930s similar to the one it had played in 1920-21. However, economic recovery and particularly the National Industrial Recovery Act were highly disruptive. The reemployment of thousands of laid-off workers, together with the company's public acknowledgement of its employees' right to bargain collectively, spurred the growth of an AFL union among the newly rehired workers who had few ties to the IA. At first the AFL group considered itself a faction within the IA and plotted to take over the assembly council. But on orders of AFL leaders, who feared a repetition of their World War I era experiences, it became independent and antagonistic to both the company and the IA. For the next two and a half years the groups competed for the loyalty of Goodyear workers.

In other communities where Goodyear had plants, notably Los Angeles and Gadsden, Alabama, industrial assemblies appeared in 1933 in response to the National Industrial Recovery Act and performed a different function. Like most new company unions, the Los Angeles and Gadsden councils were designed to preempt the creation of independent unions. Goodyear managers viewed them as instruments of an aggressive antiunion policy and sustained them only as long as they contributed to the success of that policy. Los Angeles workers soon became disillusioned and inactive, though the majority did not join a United Rubber Workers local until the late 1930s because of fear of retribution. In Gadsden the assembly was so hostile to outside organizers that it became an embarrassment to the company. Together with employees from other antiunion firms, assembly leaders waged a violent war against AFL and CIO organizers and union members. Beatings and carefully orchestrated riots in 1936 and 1937, when the URW attempted to organize the plant, made Gadsden a synonym for violence and lawlessness. After the Supreme Court upheld the Wagner Act and its ban on company-supported organizations, a management-inspired "independent" union, the Etowah Rubber Workers Association, led by the same individuals, sustained the reign of terror into the 1940s (Nelson 1988, 234-45, 257-62, 316-17).

In the meantime the Akron assembly had encountered growing difficulties. As the company's policies became more overtly antiunion and the AFL organization became more assertive, the assembly was increasingly isolated. In February 1936 when the AFL union struck the Goodyear plants, the assembly ceased to operate.

Its loyal core, consisting of about 40 percent of the employees, formed a "nonstriker" organization that opposed the strike. After the strikers won a largely symbolic victory, the nonstrikers splintered into several antiunion organizations that lasted through the decade. In 1936 and 1937 a small terroristic group, with the implicit assistance of the management, waged a campaign of intimidation against union members.

Company unionism at Goodyear thus declined as it evolved. The decisive factor was the company's failure to sustain its personnel program in the face of economic upheaval and unprecedented worker militancy. The formation of transparently antiunion assemblies in Los Angeles and Gadsden signaled the end of an era. The most notable feature of this process, however, was not the company's shift from company unionism to union avoidance, which paralleled the approach of many corporations, but the cohesiveness of the employees most closely associated with the IA.

The Goodyear experiences provide a useful guide to the fate of the company union in the 1930s. Disregarding the large number of ephemeral antiunion organizations that appeared in 1933 and 1934, company unions fell into one of three categories. First were the survivors of the earlier era that continued to command the support of workers until 1937 and afterward. They were largely unaffected by the growth of the labor movement and only modestly affected by the Wagner Act. Second were a larger group that succumbed to the combined forces of depression, a growing labor movement, and government restrictions on company involvement in union affairs, but really to the employer's judgment that company unionism had become too costly. Finally, a small but highly visible group of company unions, virtually all of which dated from 1933-34, served as antiunion auxiliaries—like the Gadsden IA—for resolutely antiunion employers. Their history is more a chapter in the story of employer enmity toward the NLRB and the labor movement than an addendum to the history of the company union.

Company unions that evolved into independent organizations had a strong base of rank-and-file support. Like the IA in the Akron plant, they had roots in the 1920s and a record of achievement before the depression. Most of them did not face the severe economic problems that confronted the IA in the early 1930s or the challenge of an aggressive AFL union after 1933. They also benefited from more consistent personnel policies. At Leeds &

Northrup, for example, cooperative association members benefited from the unemployment insurance fund and the company's efforts to encourage the "right spirit." A dissident group emerged in the council in 1934, but it attracted little support and soon disappeared. Thereafter, the cooperative association operated without notable incident until 1937 when the Wagner Act forced it to suspend its economic functions. It continued to administer the company's social and educational programs while a separate, unaffiliated union of Leeds & Northrup employees bargained with the management (Nelson 1982, 355-56).

A similar process, though on a vastly larger scale, occurred at AT & T. Although the company laid off many workers in the early 1930s, it sustained its personnel and welfare programs. There was no outside union challenge. After 1937 AT & T managers encouraged departmental units to reorganize as independent unions and in many cases assisted this transformation. What executives probably did not anticipate was the rapid consolidation of these units into the National Federation of Telephone Workers, an organization that paralleled the size and structure of the company. In the 1940s the NFTW gradually evolved into the Communications Workers of America, a CIO union (Schacht 1975, 30-33).

The history of the DuPont company unions is also consistent with this pattern. Some of the DuPont organizations dated from the 1920s; others appeared only in 1933. In either case they were extensions of the company's ambitious personnel program. They faced little outside union competition between 1933 and 1937 and, as independent unions after 1937, only sporadic and usually ineffective challenges. DuPont executives were stongly antiunion and less wary of public opinion than their AT & T counterparts, which helps explain the failure of the DuPont organizations to consolidate as well as the meager efforts of the AFL and CIO. In the 1950s the company changed its policy and henceforth discouraged any organization in its plants with marked effect (Rezler 1963; Rumm 1992, 191-93).

A much larger group of corporations abandoned company unionism in the 1930s on grounds that it had become too costly, or that employees were unlikely to identify with the management under any circumstances. Some of the organizations at these firms collapsed; others became conventional labor unions. The most famous instance of the conversion of a company union into an adversarial union was the metamorphosis of the U.S. Steel employee representation plan in 1936 and early 1937 (Bernstein 1970, 455-57). In most other large corporations, such as Jersey Standard, company unions either affiliated with the AFL or CIO or disbanded and were superseded by AFL or CIO organizations that assumed their functions. Most revealing was the case of U.S. Rubber which had a well-developed personnel program and a longstanding commitment to company unionism. The architect of this activity was Cyrus Ching who had emerged as one of the leading personnel managers in the 1920s. By the 1930s the company's factory councils were well-established in many of its plants. They faced few challenges after 1933. The company was not provocative and the workers apparently believed that they had little to gain by affiliating with the AFL or CIO. In terms of union avoidance, Ching and U.S. Rubber may have had the best record of any large manufacturing company. But Ching was dissatisfied and by 1937 had concluded that trade unionism was inevitable. To avoid disruptive campaigns in the company's tire plants, he invited the United Rubber Workers to take over the factory councils. By 1940, all of the tire plants had CIO locals. Relations between the company and its unions were stable and placid (Nelson 1989).

The third category consisted of company unions that were analogues of the Gadsden assembly. These were usually products of the NRA period and reflections of the intensity of antiunion sentiment among small and medium-sized manufacturers. The employer controlled them and made only the most superficial efforts to enlist the support of the employees. A notable example was the Kohler Workers Association, a militant antiunion group that helped the Kohler Company defeat the AFL and CIO in the longest strike of the 1930s and kept outside organizations at bay through the 1940s. As grievances accumulated, however, KWA members became dissatisfied. In 1952 the KWA switched allegiance to the United Auto Workers. Two years later the management precipitated a strike that lasted for the rest of that decade (Uphoff 1966). The Thompson Products Workers Association, another company union of this type, had a similar history. As a company union and then an independent, company-supported operation, the TPWA helped defeat two UAW organizing efforts in the early 1940s, thwarted the NLRB, and sustained the company's antiunion policy (Jacoby 1985).

The fate of the company union was thus a measure of the intensity of the industrial upheaval of the 1930s. It reflected the growing role of government in industrial relations and the revival of the labor movement, particularly in manufacturing. But it had other, less well known implications as well. At its peak, company unionism had reflected the growth of an expansive conception of the firm that blurred customary distinctions between managers and non-managers. The turmoil of the 1930s obscured that feature of company unionism and made it impossible to sustain in many settings. By the end of the decade only a handful of independent organizations, such as the Leeds & Northrup Cooperative Association, retained a link to the earlier era and its conception of employee organization. The others that survived, the Kohler and Thompson Products unions, for example, reflected a more conservative perspective, based on a desire to limit worker influence in the interest of industrial peace and cost containment. This approach had been explicit or implicit in the C. W. Post plan, in the early Rockefeller Plan, in the meat packers' councils, and in other antiunion representation plans. After 1935, in the form of antiunion organizations, but also in expanded industrial relations departments and welfare plans designed to contain outside unions, it overshadowed and obscured the competing tradition. Another quarter of a century would pass before new efforts to enlist low-skill, low-wage employees in the management of industry emerged.

Conclusions

This review of the early history of the company union in the U.S. suggests several conclusions that may be helpful in evaluating more recent efforts to create or extend employee representation.

First, the company union of the first third of the century was many different things. It reflected a variety of motives, served varying ends, and operated in diverse and often contradictory ways. The statistics of company unionism are, as a result, largely meaningless. This essay has emphasized the most enduring and significant organizations, those designed to extend the managerial hierarchy to the shop floor and enlist employees in the operation of the firm. This was a controversial approach that violated prevailing conceptions of the responsibilities of managers and nonmanagers and relied on a strategy that most employers equated with outside adversarial unions. The evidence suggests that these organizations achieved most of their creators' objectives.

Second, the experiences of these organizations show that it was possible to enlist low-level employees in the study and resolution of production problems. The most successful company unions were those that immersed employees in what they knew best—the day-to-day affairs of the plant or store. Where this was done, employee representatives made valuable contributions to improvements in operations. Though no one attempted to measure this contribution, contemporary assessments—by managers and workers—were uniformly positive.

Third, in return for their cooperation, workers received a number of benefits, including better working conditions, guarantees against arbitrary policy changes, access to executives, and a sense of participation in the operation of the firm. These were modest achievements compared to the gains of successful trade union groups, such as construction workers and railroad operating employees, but they were substantial advances for workers in unorganized industries. Company union leaders who became AFL and CIO members in the 1930s and 1940s typically emphasized the continuity of their experiences. However, comparisons of the material achievements of company and trade unions obscure a more significant point. Company unions were particularly successful in winning benefits previously associated with white-collar jobs, including health and life insurance, pensions, paid vacations, and less often, nonfinancial benefits such as employment security, and clean and attractive workplaces. One reason for this emphasis was the presence of white-collar employees in many company unions. More important was the employer's association of these concessions (unlike wage increases) with increased loyalty to the firm and higher productivity. In later years AFL and CIO leaders would acknowledge the value of fringe benefits as wage equivalents. But company unions did more than anticipate the course of collective bargaining. They also reduced the gap between white- and blue-collar employees, introducing production workers to some of the prerequisites of middle class life.

Fourth, a successful company union made substantial demands on the time and resources of the management. As the contacts between managers and workers multiplied, the possibilities for misunderstanding also grew. The obvious antidote to this potential problem was continuous contact and consultation. Most employers found this prospect daunting and concluded, probably correctly, that a neglected company union was worse than no company union. Yet the record of the 1920s indicated that an elaborate organization and large budget were not the keys to success. More important were a conception of productivity that emphasized human activity and a commitment to continuous, small-scale improvements. Comparatively few employers of that era gave more than lip service to this approach. Those who did found that it paid important organizational and financial dividends.

By the late 1920s, William M. Leiserson, the labor economist and AFL ally, had concluded that company unions were a permanent and positive feature of postwar industry as worthy of scholarly research as the labor movement (William M. Leiserson to Morris L. Cooke, November 13, 1928, Leiserson Papers, Box 9). He was wrong about their permanence, of course, but his emphasis was not misplaced. Company unions like the FCA, the Leeds & Northrup Cooperative Association, and the Goodyear Industrial Assembly were formidable organizations that served the interests of employers and employees. In the absence of the New Deal they and not the transitory company unions of 1933-35 or the Kohler and Thompson Products organizations would have dominated discussions of employer-initiated representation plans in the 1930s. Would they also have been models for other employers? Company unionism had grown in tandem with personnel management which in turn had emerged with the rise of large impersonal business organizations and labor market disruptions such as the World War I industrial boom. The reemergence of labor turmoil in the 1930s, even without the stimulus of federal legislation, might have encouraged a new generation of employers to extend their personnel programs to include company unionism. In any event the survival of the notable company unions of the early twentieth century would have underlined the continuity between the actions of innovative employers of that era and the more recent developments discussed in this volume.

References

A Thumbnail Sketch of the Filene Cooperative Association. 1915. Boston.
Bernstein, Irving. 1970. *Turbulent Years*. Boston: Houghton Mifflin Co.
Brody, David. 1964. *The Butcher Workmen: A Study of Unionization*. Cambridge, MA: Harvard University Press.
Chandler, Alfred D. 1977. *The Visible Hand: The Managerial Revolution in American Business*. Cambridge, MA: Harvard University Press.

Gibb, George Sweet and Evelyn Knowlton. 1956. *The Resurgent Years, 1911-1927*. New York: Harper.

Giddens, Paul H. 1955. *Standard Oil Company (Indiana): Oil Pioneer of the Middle West*. New York: Harper.

Gillespie, Richard. 1991. *Manufacturing Knowledge: A History of the Hawthorne Experiments*. Cambridge, MA: Cambridge University Press.

Gitelman, Howard M. 1988. *Legacy of the Ludlow Massacre: A Chapter in American Industrial Relations*. Philadelphia: University of Pennsylvania Press.

Greenwald, Maurine Weiner. 1980. *Women, War and Work: The Impact of World War I on Women Workers in the United States*. Westport: Greenwood Press.

Hicks, Clarence H. 1941. *My Life in Industrial Relations*. New York: Harper.

Jacoby, Sanford M. 1985. *Employing Bureaucracy: Managers, Unions, and the Transformation of Work in American Industry, 1900-1945*. New York: Columbia University Press.

_____. 1989. "Reckoning with Company Unions: The Case of Thompson Products, 1934-1964." *Industrial & Labor Relations Review* 43 (October), pp. 19-40.

LaDame, Mary. 1930. *The Filene Store*. New York: Russell Sage Foundation.

Larson, Henrietta M., and Kenneth Wiggins Porter. 1959. *History of Humble Oil & Refining Co*. New York: Harper.

McLaughlin, Doris B. 1973. "The Second Battle of Battle Creek: The Open Shop Movement in the Early Twentieth Century." *Labor History* 14 (Summer), pp. 323-39.

National Industrial Conference Board. 1922. *Experience with Works Councils in the United States*. New York.

Nelson, Daniel. 1970. " 'A Newly Appreciated Art': The Development of Personnel Work at Leeds & Northrup." *Business History Review* 44 (Winter), pp. 520-35.

_____. 1982. "The Company Union Movement, 1900-1937: A Reexamination." *Business History Review* 56 (Autumn), pp. 335-57.

_____. 1988. *American Rubber Workers and Organized Labor, 1900-1941*. Princeton: Princeton University Press.

_____. 1989. "Managers and Nonunion Workers in the Rubber Industry: Union Avoidance Strategies in the 1930s." *Industrial & Labor Relations Review* 43 (October), pp. 41-52.

Ozanne, Robert. 1967. *A Century of Labor Management Relations at McCormick and International Harvester*. Madison, WI: University of Wisconsin Press.

Rezler, Julius. 1963. "Labor Organization at DuPont: A Study of Independent Local Unionism." *Labor History* 16 (Winter), pp. 5-36.

Rumm, John C. 1992. "Scientific Management and Industrial Engineering at DuPont." In *A Mental Revolution: Scientific Management since Taylor*, ed. David Nelson. Columbus: Ohio State University Press.

Schacht, John N. 1975. "Toward Industrial Unionism: Bell Telephone Workers and Company Unions." *Labor History* 16 (Winter), pp. 5-36.

_____. 1985. *The Making of Telephone Unionism, 1920-1947*. New Brunswick: Rutgers University Press.

Selekman, Ben M. 1924. *Employe's Representation in Steel Works*. New York: Russell Sage Foundation.

Selekman, Ben M., and Mary Van Kleeck. 1924. *Employe's Representation in Coal Mines*. New York: Russell Sage Foundation.

Uphoff, Walter H. 1966. *Kohler on Strike: Thirty Years of Conflict*. Boston: Beacon.

Wall, Bennett H., and George S. Gibb. 1974. *Teagle of Standard Oil*. New Orleans: Tulane University Press.

Zahavi, Gerald. 1988. *Workers, Managers, and Welfare Capitalism: The Shoeworkers and Tanners of Endicott Johnson, 1890-1950*. Urbana: University of Illinois Press.